Curriculum Change
in the Nineteenth
and Twentieth Centuries

Curriculum Change
in the Nineteenth
and Twentieth Centuries

Peter Gordon and Denis Lawton

HODDER AND STOUGHTON
LONDON SYDNEY AUCKLAND TORONTO

British Library Cataloguing in Publication Data

Gordon, Peter, b. 1927
  Curriculum change in the nineteenth and twentieth
  centuries.
  1. Curriculum planning – Great Britain – History
  I. Title II. Lawton, Denis
  375'.001'0941   LB1564.G7

  ISBN 0–340–21374–4
  ISBN 0–340–21375–2   Pbk

First published 1978

Printed in Great Britain for
Hodder and Stoughton Educational,
a division of Hodder and Stoughton Ltd,
Mill Road, Dunton Green, Sevenoaks, Kent
by Fletcher & Son Ltd, Norwich

Contents

Illustrations

Acknowledgments

We should like to thank the following for their kindness in granting us permission to use in this book extracts from their family papers: the Duke of Devonshire, the Marquess of Salisbury, the Earl of Harrowby, the Earl Spencer, Lord Cottesloe and Commander the Hon. J. T. Fremantle, Lord Hambleden, Lord Medway and Mr D. L. Arkwright of Kinsham Court, Presteigne. We are also grateful to the National Trust for allowing us to consult the Hughenden Papers, and to the University of London, the Chief Executive of Morpeth District Council and the Governors of Chester College for making available documents in their possession.

Much of the unpublished material is located in county and local record offices and a full list of these appears in the Bibliography. The ready assistance of the staffs of the offices made the search for relevant material an enjoyable experience. The cooperation of many publishers in permitting us to quote from a large number of books and magazines is also acknowledged.

We would like to record our grateful thanks to the staff of the University of London Institute of Education Library for their help in locating numerous references.

We are indebted to a number of individuals and institutions for the illustrations: Mr J. D. Buchanan, Headmaster of Oakham School, Rutland, Captain M. F. Buller, Mr A. E. B. Owen, the Trustees of the Haslingfield United Charities, Cambridgeshire, the Devon Record Office, Durham Record Office, Greater London Record Office, Greater London Council Photograph Library, Humberside Record Office, the Public Record Office, the Department of Education and Science, and the Proprietors of *Punch*. Miss D. M. Jepson, Chief Librarian, and Mr Mark Staunton, Senior Assistant Librarian, both of the Department of Education and Science Library, provided generous help in tracing official documents. Our colleagues, Richard Aldrich and Ian Michael of the University of London Institute of Education, kindly gave us the benefit of their wide knowledge in the field of the history of education.

Finally, we would like to express our thanks to our wives, Tessa Gordon and Joan Lawton, for their help and advice during the writing and preparation of the book for publication; and to David and Pauline Gordon for lightening the load in the later stages.

Introduction

The history of the curriculum is too vast a subject for one volume. In recognizing this fact our intention has not been to present a detailed chronological account of all the curriculum changes which have taken place, but to limit ourselves mainly to the nineteenth and twentieth centuries and to what we consider to be the most significant trends. Even in this more modest approach we have had to be satisfied with deliberately incomplete accounts: for example, in Chapter 3, on the manner in which various subjects were incorporated into the curriculum and altered their character after that, we have restricted ourselves to a mere six examples, which we have chosen to illustrate different kinds of development.

Our main aim therefore is to discuss and illustrate some of the processes of curriculum change, and in particular to try to detect some important pressures in society which have reacted on the curriculum. On the other hand we would not wish to suggest that curriculum change is determined by social events: there have often been individuals working in a counter-cyclical direction who have had a lasting influence, and we have tried to assess their significance also.

In Chapter 1 we look at some of the major 'landmarks' of an official kind— Education Acts, Reports of Committees, the work of Commissions and Councils of various kinds and also Codes and Circulars. We do not take the view that legislation and official directives are the only reasons for change in the curriculum, nor even the most important reason, but we have tried to provide a useful chronological narrative as a background for the thematic approach adopted in later chapters. This chapter also includes a brief account of one of the most important official bodies since 1964—the Schools Council.

Chapter 2 is concerned with the social, economic and political background to changes in educational theory and changes in the curriculum. In Chapter 3 we look more specifically at 'subjects' and how they have changed and been changed by the structure of the curriculum as a whole. In Chapter 4 we examine the relation between curriculum and teaching methods, dividing this task into elementary/primary and secondary. We are conscious of the artificiality of isolating 'method' from 'theories' and the content of other chapters, and we have tried to overcome this by extensive cross-referencing.

In our opinion examinations and testing have been very powerful influences on the structure of the curriculum in this country as well as being a reasonably clear reflection of some aspects of educational thought and practice. In Chapter 5 we have given a good deal of space to the interrelationship of curriculum change and examinations.

Finally, in Chapter 6 we examine the part played by influential groups of people or pressure groups. Throughout the book one of the dominant ideas is that curriculum change is the result of complex patterns of interaction between influential individuals and general processes of social, political and economic change. In some ways Chapter 6 sums up the whole of the book: some individuals have been extremely influential, some groups of individuals operating deliberately to produce change have sometimes succeeded, but all of this has to be seen in the context of a society undergoing fundamental changes of technology and ideology.

The major changes in society which have had important influences on the curriculum seem to us to be of three kinds: first, technological changes, especially those associated with what is popularly referred to as the industrial revolution; second, changes in knowledge, particularly—but not exclusively—the development of science as a dominant form of knowledge, challenging the pre-eminence of classical humanism as the basis for post-primary education, and also challenging religion as the basis of moral education; and finally, ideological changes, especially the move from an elitist view of society to a more democratic one. Each of these three overlaps with the other two and interacts with them, but it may be useful at this stage to consider each one separately, although in later chapters no attempt is made to isolate the factors in this somewhat artificial way.

Technological changes have been important at a number of levels. First of all they have brought about changes in the structure of society: by the beginning of the nineteenth century our society had ceased to be a largely rural, agricultural society with a semi-feudal system of ranks. As England became more industrialized, power and influence tended—very gradually—to pass out of the hands of the landed nobility and gentry into the hands of those who derived their wealth from industrial and commercial profits rather than agricultural rents. By 1900 this transition was by no means complete, and the conflict may be seen expressed in some attitudes towards education and the content of curricula both elementary and secondary.

In an agricultural society the kind of technology in use did not require 'schooling', and, as we shall see, even at the end of the nineteenth century many agricultural landlords objected to the idea of elementary education. But, as industry developed, different kinds of manpower were needed: factory hands who could read simple instructions, or perform elementary calculations, many more clerks in factories and commercial houses, as well as increased recruitment to the minor professions. In all these areas the schools lagged behind the 'needs of society'; for example, it is often said that at the end of the nineteenth century there was such a shortage of clerks in the City of London that large numbers of foreign clerks had to be employed.

A slightly less obvious way in which the curriculum failed to match changes in society concerned the upper classes and the public school curriculum. In a semi-feudal landed society the ruling class did not need much technological training; the appropriate kind of education for aristocrats and gentlemen mainly provided a badge of rank. The classics-based curriculum served this purpose admirably. The fact that the knowledge acquired in schools was no longer useful in any practical way was regarded as a virtue: high-status knowledge denoted membership of an exclusive social group—it was a sign of power but not an instrument of power. But in an industrial society the ruling classes really needed to acquire different kinds of knowledge. Science and technology should have become a major part of the public school curriculum in order to give the ruling classes some kind of justification for their continued power and influence. But only a few decision-makers saw this, one of them being Robert Lowe who argued that masters should know more about the new knowledge than their men.

The new knowledge that should have been incorporated into the curriculum included science, technology and mathematics, but as Raymond Williams (1961) has pointed out other post-Renaissance changes in world view had also been neglected. Some grammar schools and public schools were confined by their statutes to a purely classical curriculum but, even after the 1840 Act was passed, which allowed curricular changes to be made, progress was extremely slow. The process by which nineteenth-century public schools were used to socialize the sons of successful industrialists and to make them acceptable to the old landed classes has often been regarded as one of the educational success stories of the century. But there is another side to the story: the public school classics-based curriculum transformed many of the potential technologists and industrial leaders into 'gentlemen' who looked with disdain on the practical knowledge of science and engineering, and it may not be too far-fetched to link this attitude to some of the contemporary economic problems in the United Kingdom.

Finally we come to the ideological changes which took place in the course of the nineteenth century. These changes are connected with very complex and subtle modifications of attitudes to power and authority, and education is only one aspect of the processes of emancipation and participation. To some extent it is useful to look at changes in political control and see whether these are reflected in any way in educational changes. It is too naïve to see a direct connection between, for example, the parliamentary reform of 1832 and the first education grant of 1833. Closer connections are sometimes claimed between the Reform Act of 1867, which gave the vote to large numbers of working-class men, and the Education Act of 1870. But the relation is a very complicated one, the motives of those who advocated some kind of educational 'reform' were mixed, and the thinking behind educational changes was often confused. To see educational reforms and curriculum changes as a benevolent willingness to educate the new electorate is to ignore at least two factors: first, the enduring idea that the purpose of elementary education was to 'gentle the masses' rather than to equip them for power; second, the continuance throughout the nineteenth century and into the twentieth of the division of schools and curricula into those for 'leaders' and those for 'followers'. But even here the story is not a simple one: it is possible to trace the idea of divisive schools and curricula from the three kinds of schools advocated in the Taunton Report (1868) to Spens (1938), Norwood (1943) to the postwar tripartite system and streaming in comprehensive schools. This is only true in a limited way and we should not ignore subtle changes in the justifications used: in the first half of the nineteenth century the argument for separation was almost entirely in terms of social class and 'breeding'; later in the century differences in education and curricula were justified in terms of efficiency often determined by examinations; this gradually developed into the 'meritocratic' justification of I.Q. + effort = merit, i.e. that there were genetic differences of ability which, if supported by the right kind of training, would be the most efficient way of selection for superior jobs. More recently this meritocratic view of curriculum differentiation has been challenged on two grounds: first, 'tests' are neither as fair nor as efficient as they appeared to be in the 1930s (especially for working-class children); second, the justice of separating children according to supposed or real genetic differences is called into question: if certain knowledge and experiences are worthwhile, then in a democratic society they should be open to all. But not all educationists have accepted these arguments, and this implicit conflict sometimes expresses itself in the form of disputes about the curriculum as well as about general educational organization.

The following chapters attempt to trace some of the complexities in more detail and to show how the development of aspects of the curriculum still has relevance for educational problems today.

In writing this book we have used a wide range of sources to illustrate the changing nature of the curriculum during the last two hundred years. From official sources, the most detailed information is contained in the various royal commissions and select committees of the House of Commons concerned with education from the early nineteenth century. These are complemented by the reports of Consultative Committees and later the Central Advisory Councils, the series ending with the Plowden Report on Primary Schools. For an analysis of the curriculum of individual schools and the views of inspectors, the annual reports of the Committee of Council on Education from 1839 are of great value; subsequent developments are contained in the annual reports of the Board of Education and its successors the Ministry of Education and the Department of Education and Science. We have also looked at official circulars, instructions to inspectors and the Codes, as well as the policy files of the Department which are now deposited at the Public Record Office.

Special attention has been paid to the activities of the Schools Council in promoting innovation in a number of curricular areas. A steady stream of bulletins and pamphlets, issued since the Council's establishment in 1964, has provided useful material.

As a supplement to official publications we have explored the rich primary sources of borough, county and national record offices (full details are given in the Bibliography). They include school minute and log books, agendas and minutes of school board and local education authority committees, diaries, letters giving details of school life and accounts of teaching methods and organization.

The connection between politics and curriculum has always been a strong one. For this reason, we have undertaken a scrutiny of the private papers of leading politicians whose views and official positions affected the development of the curriculum and in some cases determined its direction.

Contemporary attitudes on a range of issues in our field have been gathered from pamphlets, biographies, journals, magazines and newspapers, method tutors and chronicles of individual institutions. Finally, we have referred to a small but valuable number of journals concerned with the history of education which contain some admirable articles on aspects of curriculum.

I

The Official Background

Legislation, Reports and Committees
Influencing the Curriculum

Legislation or the reports of government committees cannot usually be regarded as the cause of curriculum change, and frequently the recommendations of the committees of inquiry and royal commissions are ignored, but they do nevertheless provide us with a set of landmarks. We are including what we consider to be the major landmarks for two reasons: first, it may be useful to read the succeeding chapters, which are rarely completely chronological in approach, against a background of significant historical events; second, the landmarks are useful indicators of current social thinking and sometimes educational thinking.

We have usually attempted to make each entry self-explanatory but if technical terms (such as 'Code') are used without explanation, the Glossary (Appendix 2) should provide the necessary information.

References are occasionally made in the following pages to *the* school curriculum. This is a useful way of making generalizations, but all generalizations may be dangerous. To use a phrase like 'the school curriculum' is misleading for at least two reasons: no two schools ever have exactly the same curriculum even in the most centralized educational system; in England there is not a single curriculum tradition but at least two. Throughout the nineteenth century the elementary school curriculum was a deliberately inferior and limited kind of education designed for the lower orders. At the other extreme the public school curriculum was education for leadership—the kind of knowledge and character training suitable for an élite. The grammar school curriculum after 1902 had a good deal in common with the public school tradition, but some would prefer to regard this as a third tradition, rather than a modification of the public school curriculum.

We have confined ourselves to the nineteenth and twentieth centuries, and to begin roughly at 1800 is not an entirely arbitrary choice: by this time industrial development had reached a stage which made educational changes appear necessary to many decision-makers. The most obvious need was for a better educated labour force, but changes in the grammar and public school curricula were also being demanded by some.

1802   Health and Morals of Apprentices Act

This was the first of a series of Acts, often collectively referred to as 'The Factory Acts'. In many of these Acts education is referred to, but little is involved that would justify the use of the word curriculum.

In the 1802 Act, for example, the elder Sir Robert Peel attempted to prevent competing mill owners from gaining unfair advantages over enlightened employers by lowering standards of work conditions for child labour. Thus the state became involved in protecting pauper children employed as 'apprentices' not only by limiting hours of work (to 12 a day) and prescribing minimum standards of cleanliness and ventilation, but also specifying that apprentices should receive some kind of instruction in the three Rs and an hour's religious teaching on Sunday. This might be considered to be a primitive version of the basic minimum curriculum. The Act was very limited in scope and generally ineffective, but it was important as an example of government intervention by legislation, and later Factory Acts were more ambitious and effective.

1805   Lord Eldon's Judgment

By the end of the eighteenth century the financial position of most of the endowed grammar schools was unsatisfactory. The statutes governing the curriculum of the schools provided for the teaching of Greek and Latin only. As a result, many potential pupils were attending other schools where writing and arithmetic and modern languages were offered.

In an attempt to remedy this situation, the governors of the Leeds Grammar School put forward a scheme to Chancery in 1797 to extend the curriculum to include mathematics and modern languages. In 1805 Lord Eldon ruled that the school was only 'for teaching grammatically the learned languages'. This proved to be a setback to those schools wishing to provide a wider choice of subjects. A. F. Leach, the educational historian, wrote: 'This decision carried dismay to all interested in the advancement of education and nearly killed half the schools in this country.' (*Victoria County History: York* i, 1907, p. 459.) Some advances were possible, however, for those schools able to afford a private Act of Parliament which allowed the introduction of subjects not mentioned in the foundation deeds.*

1816–18   Select Committee on the education of the lower orders

Henry Brougham, later Lord Brougham, in May 1816 moved for a Select Committee of the Commons to inquire into the state of education among the poor of the Metropolis, and which was later extended to the whole country. Brougham's request was granted, and he himself became chairman of the Committee.

*For more details of this important case, see R. S. Thompson 'The Leeds Grammar School Case of 1805' in *Journal of Educational Administration and History*, Vol. 3, no. 1, December 1970, pp. 1–6.

In the First Report, issued in 1816, the Committee

> found reasons to conclude that a very large number of poor children are wholly without
> the means of Instruction although their parents appear to be generally very desirous of
> obtaining that advantage for them . . . they feel persuaded that the greatest advantages
> would result to this country from Parliament taking proper measures, in concurrence
> with the prevailing disposition in the country for supplying the deficiency of the means
> of instruction which exists at present and for extending this blessing to the poor of all
> descriptions.

By 1818, further recommendations were made for widening access to elementary schools. 'In places where only one school can be supported, it is manifest that any regulations which exclude Dissenters, deprive the Poor of that body of all means of education.'

The differences between the problems of education in urban and rural districts were recognized: 'In humbly suggesting what is fit to be done for promoting universal education, Your Committee do not hesitate to state, that two different plans are advisable adapted to the opposite circumstances of the Town and Country Districts.'

More radical changes were contemplated. Brougham's biographer claims that he

> was also suggesting the policy of government schools 'filling in the gaps' which was at
> last to be adopted in the great Forster Education Act of 1870. The Committee,
> Brougham said, had issued a circular letter, containing queries, addressed to all the
> clergy of England and Wales respecting their parishes. 7,000 had already reported, and
> study of the returns would indicate where need lay.
>
> (C. F. New, *The Life of Henry Brougham to 1830*, 1961, pp. 213–14)

To implement such an ambitious plan, considerable sums of money would have to be raised. Unfortunately, Brougham's zeal outran his discretion in this matter: in 1818, he turned to the idea of redistribution of educational charities as a means of financing the project. An inquiry was made into the management of, for instance, Westminster and Charterhouse, and was later widened to include Oxford and Cambridge. The education of the poor came to be linked with the subversion of the public schools and the universities and as a result Brougham's efforts were not translated into action.

1833 First government grant for education

In 1833 the Radical MP John Roebuck asked the House to consider 'the means of establishing a system of National Education' on the grounds that it would promote political tranquillity and public virtue. The scheme proposed was a complex and ambitious one and involved so much state control (including teaching method and curriculum) that it was unacceptable to the Commons. However, there was sufficient support voiced for the idea of giving some financial help towards the education of the poor and eighteen days later Lord Althorp, the Chancellor of the Exchequer, included in the Report of the Committee of Supply a sum of up to £20,000 for education. The money was made available to the two religious societies (the National Society and the British and Foreign School Society) to be spent on school building, and the Treasury laid down the rules governing the payment of grant. This was the first successful attempt at state intervention in elementary education in Great Britain, although at this stage great care was taken to deny any intention of state control and no mention was made of the curriculum.

From the beginning there were very mixed motives for giving support to elementary education: for some, 'popular education' was part of the age of reform and a natural consequence of the 1832 Reform of Parliament; but even Radicals like Roebuck argued for education in terms of public order, and some writers have linked elementary education with Peel's new police force (1829) and the Poor Law Amendment Act (1834) as part of the Victorians' obsession with law and order obtained for the lowest possible price. The Factory Acts passed between 1802 and 1874 provided for part-time education in the three Rs, but without laying down any educational standards.

1834   Report of the Parliamentary Committee on the state of education

In June 1834 Roebuck again raised the question of a committee to inquire into a system of national education. This was rejected, but a committee was set up to see what effect the government grant was having. The committee sat for two months and the evidence of the witnesses was issued as a report.

The conflict which soon become apparent was that, while many witnesses objected to state interference in the work of the two religious bodies (the National Society and the British and Foreign School Society), there was also a feeling that Parliament needed to supervise and control the spending of public money. Other problems which were raised included that of schools which had to cater for both Church of England and Nonconformist children, and also the inadequacy of teacher training. Both these problems were potentially issues concerning the curriculum.

1838   Select Committee on education of the poorer classes

This Committee's terms of reference were 'to consider the best means of providing useful Education for the Children of the Poorer Classes in large Towns throughout England and Wales'. Its membership included William Gladstone, T. D. Acland, Lord Ashley and Sir Robert Peel. While exonerating the religious societies who made some educational provision, the Committee's Report found that 'in the Metropolis and the great Towns of England and Wales, there exists a great want of Education among the Children of the Working Classes'; but as many children in manufacturing districts were employed in factories, it was considered adequate to provide for a proportion of not less than about one-eighth of the population. Government assistance on a limited scale was to remain confined to the National and British and Foreign School Societies.

The importance of this Committee lay in the fact that it took evidence on the *nature* of the curriculum offered in schools as well as dealing with the general *provision* of education. Two important motions—one calling for the establishment of a Board or Office of Education under parliamentary control and the second calling for the collection of statistics and for inspection of schools—were defeated. These points were achieved shortly afterwards in 1840.

1839 The Committee of the Privy Council on education

In 1833 the Whig government had established a grant of £20,000 for the building of schools. Six years later, a Committee of the Privy Council was set up to superintend its allocation. The 1838 Select Committee on Education had exposed the need for educating the poor, and action was called for, though not through the agency of the two Societies. The new Committee, consisting of the Lord President, the Lord Privy Seal, the Home Secretary and the Chancellor of the Exchequer, were to superintend the application of any sums voted by Parliament for the purpose of promoting public education.

This was the first indication of the responsibility of the state for a policy in education but, as Frank Smith remarked, 'the Whigs were now committed to an educational policy, with the Church hostile to every proposal they might make'. (*A History of English Elementary Education 1760–1902*, 1931, p. 171.) This hostility was to persist throughout the century, especially where attempts to introduce 'secular' schools were made: it can also be seen in the opposition to the 1870 Elementary Education Act.

The Council's Secretary, Dr J. P. Kay-Shuttleworth, was responsible for the issuing of a Minute in 1839 which made the award of grants conditional upon inspection. The reports of inspectors were published annually from that year: these were important in spreading information on current practices as well as providing a forum for the discussion of aspects of the curriculum by the inspectorate.

1840–56 From council committee to education department

A further Minute of 1840 included recommendations for different types of school buildings according to the educational instruction being given: for instance, whether the monitorial system was to be used or the more enlightened methods advocated by Stow and Wilderspin (pp. 132–3). 'The building plans of the Committee of Council brought into being a new profession, namely that of the school architect. Thus an architect, H. E. Kendall, produced an album of designs for schools and school houses in 1847, which included a number of plans and sketches of schools which he had built in accordance with the official requirements.' (S. J. Curtis, *History of Education in Great Britain*, 7th ed., 1967, p. 245.)

The Council introduced in 1846 the pupil-teacher system to replace the outmoded monitorial system of Bell and Lancaster, and training colleges were established. By the time of Kay-Shuttleworth's retirement in 1849, much had been achieved in promoting elementary education. In 1856, the title of the Committee was changed to the Education Department of the Committee of Council with the

Lord President as head and a Vice-President in the House of Commons with direct responsibility for the expenditure and administration of the Department.

1840   The Grammar Schools Act

The purpose of this Act 'for improving the Condition and extending the Benefits of Grammar Schools' was to clarify the ambiguous situation left by the Eldon Judgment. The preamble to the Act begins:

> Whereas there are in England and Wales many endowed schools both of Royal and Private Foundation, for the Education of Boys and Youth wholly or principally in Grammar; the term 'grammar' has been construed by Courts of Equity as having reference only to the dead languages, that is to say, Greek and Latin: and whereas such Education, at the Period when such Schools, or the greater Part, were founded, was supposed, not only to be sufficient to qualify Boys or Youth for Admission to the Universities, with a view to the learned Professions, but also necessary for preparing them for the Superior Trades and Mercantile Business: And whereas from the Change of the Times and other Causes such Education without Instruction in other Branches of Literature and Science, is now of less Value to those who are entitled to avail themselves of such charitable Foundations, whereby such Schools have, in many Instances, ceased to afford a substantial Fulfilment of the Intentions of the Founders, and the System of Education in such Grammar Schools ought therefore to be extended and rendered more generally beneficial, in order to afford such Fulfilment . . .

This Act allowed schools to dispense with the teaching of Latin and Greek as they were now no longer bound by the terms of the original statutes. Many schools took advantage of the provision of the Act and introduced elementary mathematics, English language and literature, modern languages and modern history and geography for the first time.

1846   Minutes of Committee of Council on Education on Pupil-Teachers

The training of teachers up to 1846 took place within special colleges. Dissatisfied with the products of the system, Kay-Shuttleworth devised a scheme for apprenticing pupils to head teachers. These pupil-teachers were chosen from elementary schools at thirteen years of age and served a five-year apprenticeship. If they were successful in the annual examination, they might qualify to enter a training college.

All pupil-teachers pursued studies in English grammar, composition, history, geography, arithmetic, religious knowledge, vocal music, school method and organization. Boys, in addition, took mechanics, surveying, algebra and mensuration; girls took sewing. Extra grants were given to masters where their apprentices were instructed in gardening, a mechanical art, knitting, cookery or laundry work. Assistance was offered to managers if they intended to add to their schools field gardens, workshops of trades and wash-houses—an early instance of state grants for specific curriculum activities.

Despite the pressures which this training put upon pupil-teachers, the numbers who became certificated were impressive, a tenfold increase between 1850 and 1860. 'They [the certificated] rapidly formed a social class of some importance.

Their status and the obligations that their employment imposed on the managers forced upon the public a new idea of education.' (Mary Sturt, *The Education of the People*, 1967, p. 197.)

1853   The Science and Art Department

One of the results of the 1851 Great Exhibition was the recognition of a need for better organized scientific and technical instruction for the industrial classes. The Science and Art Department was formed two years later to carry out this programme.

Grants were given to schools whose pupils were successful in examinations devised by the Department in a range of subjects, including mechanical and machine drawing, naval architecture, physics, chemistry, zoology and botany. These graded syllabuses provided teachers with useful curriculum guides. The Department's financial encouragement in the promotion of science and art subjects was an important factor in their development in elementary and secondary schools for the rest of the century.

To increase the number of art and science teachers, the Department offered grants for teachers taking qualifying examinations in these subjects. Unfortunately, these were book-based rather than practically oriented and this was reflected in the subsequent teaching. Nevertheless, Henry Cole, the first Secretary of the Department, provided a basis for later expansion though without uniting the scientific and technological elements in any systematic way.

It is significant that until 1856 the Science and Art Department was under the control of the Board of Trade, and very little contact was maintained with the Education Department. This was later to cause problems of curriculum planning.

1861   The Newcastle Commission

This Commission was appointed in 1858 under the chairmanship of the Duke of Newcastle

> to inquire into the present state of Popular Education in England, and to consider and report what Measures, if any, are required for the extension of sound and cheap elementary instruction to all classes of the people.

The Report issued in 1861 drew attention to a number of unsatisfactory features of the existing system of elementary education. The supply of schools was inadequate. Of the pupils in such schools, not more than a quarter were receiving a good education; undue emphasis was being placed on the instruction of older scholars at the expense of the younger.

Teachers also tended to neglect the more elementary subjects. Thus, in good schools, senior classes offered a sound education while reading, writing and arithmetic were less well taught in the lower forms. The Commission was anxious, therefore, to raise the standard of the basic subjects 'to a larger body of inferior schools and inferior scholars'. The Commissioners noted that of the pupils in elementary schools, only a half were under any sort of inspection.

> There is only one way of securing this [desired] result, which is to institute a searching examination by competent authority of every child in every school to which grants are to be paid, with the view of ascertaining whether these indispensable elements of knowledge [i.e., reading, writing, arithmetic] are thoroughly acquired, and to make the prospects and position of the teacher dependent, to a considerable extent, on the results of this examination. (Report, vol. I, p. 157)

This solution to providing 'cheap and sound education' was quickly taken up in the Revised Code of 1862.

The Newcastle Report is often quoted as a classic example of a nineteenth-century official document recommending an elementary curriculum which was not only limited but deliberately inferior.

1862   The Revised Code

Robert Lowe, Vice-President of the Committee of the Privy Council on Education, was responsible for introducing the Revised Code which had been drafted by the secretary, R. R. W. Lingen. The Code set out the conditions on which grants were to be paid and stated specifically the contents of the elementary school curriculum.

So far, grants had been made to teachers according to their qualifications; from 1862, grants were paid to managers, largely based on an annual examination of all children in the three Rs (together with plain needlework for girls). The pupils were in six stages or standards, the first to be taken by children of six years of age. This was the beginning of the system of 'payment by results' which was to prevail until the end of the century.

Although the Code did not exclude the teaching of other subjects, it nevertheless led to excessive concentration on the three Rs and to complaints by inspectors of mechanical teaching. Teachers, for their part, protested at the prescription of detailed syllabuses which restricted what could be taught. This narrowness was before long recognized by the Committee of Council; in 1867 extra grants were offered to schools if they included at least one 'specific' subject (i.e. different from ordinary reading-book lessons), such as history, geography and grammar, in addition to the three Rs.

The Revised Code represented an advance in state control of education at the expense of the Church. Religious instruction now took its place as a non-examined subject. The Code also attempted to grade the syllabus according to age of the pupil; previously, there had been no consensus on what was considered appropriate for pupils at the various stages.

1864   The Clarendon Commission

Mounting criticism of the public schools in the early 1860s led to the appointment in 1861 of a Royal Commission to inquire into the endowments, administration, finances, methods, subjects and teaching at nine of the older foundations.

The Commission, headed by the Earl of Clarendon, favoured a more liberal approach to the education of the élite. 'A young man is not well educated who cannot reason or observe or express himself easily and correctly . . . if all his information is shut up within one narrow circle.' Their Report denounced the exclusiveness of classics in the curriculum while agreeing that it should continue to hold the principal place. Mathematics and divinity were also to be taught to every boy, with modern languages and natural science for some part of the time, while drawing and music should form a lesser part. It was contemplated that scholars would be able to drop classics in order to devote more time to modern languages, mathematics and natural science, but specialization was in fact limited. Ancient history and geography were to be taught in connection with classical teaching, both separately and in combination with each other. This model was based closely on the German *Gymnasium* which was much admired at the time.

One of the difficulties facing the schools in introducing new subjects was that the universities could not give a lead in teaching methods in non-classical subjects and this slowed down their introduction into the schools. However, modern studies were encouraged by the Public Schools Act of 1868 which re-cast the governing bodies and the ancient statutes of the institutions.

1868   The Taunton Commission

To complete the inquiry into the state of education after the Newcastle Commission had examined elementary schools and the Clarendon Commission the leading public schools, the Taunton Commission was in 1864 given the task of investigating some 800 endowed grammar schools.

Unlike elementary education, there was no central policy-making body for secondary schools and therefore no influence over the curriculum. The Commissioners conceived their task to be the redeployment of the often misused endowments to create a system of efficient schools corresponding to three grades of society, each with its own curriculum. The first grade would prepare pupils for the university and would necessarily be classical schools, but elements of political economy, modern languages, mathematics and natural sciences should find a place in the timetable. Schools of the second grade were for boys preparing for professions, business and the army, giving an education up to sixteen years of age. Latin was recommended with a modern language, mathematics and science; 'the minds of the learners should be perpetually brought back to concrete examples instead of being perpetually exercised in abstractions'. Third-grade schools were considered to be the most urgent need, catering for future artisans leaving school at fourteen. No precise syllabus was recommended, but the curriculum could include rudiments of inorganic chemistry, drawing and practical geometry as well as basic subjects.

No links between the three grades were contemplated, but the beginnings of the 'scholarship ladder' are seen in the awarding of exhibitions and scholarships to needy scholars.

Although originally outside the Commission's terms of reference, the education of girls was also considered. The Report drew attention to large differences which existed between curricula in boys' and girls' schools.

One recommendation would have provided a central authority for secondary education, with provincial authorities responsible for curricula. Inspection of schools was also contemplated. The Commission also considered the relationship between school work and examinations and recommended an independent Examinations Council. Some progress was made in remodelling the schemes of instruction in individual schools through the efforts of the Endowed Schools Commission which was set up in 1869 to implement the Endowed Schools Act which incorporated many of the Taunton Report's recommendations, especially those concerning redistribution of endowments, but some of the most important recommendations were omitted.

1870   The Elementary Education Act

The intention of this Act was to provide efficient elementary schools in England and Wales wherever they were needed. W. E. Forster, the Liberal Vice-President responsible for the Act, avoided the issue of a state system of education. Where there was a deficiency of accommodation in voluntary schools, a school board, elected by the borough or parish, could build its own schools. This was the beginning of the dual system which still exists today.

Much controversy centred on the provision of religious instruction in the board schools. A compromise solution, which pleased neither church nor secular interests, was that a 'conscience clause', giving religious liberty to parents, was made obligatory on all public elementary schools receiving a grant. A further clause stated that no religious catechism or formulary distinctive of any particular denomination should be taught in board schools. Clerical inspectors were no longer appointed. A number of the new school boards, such as London, were quick to make a survey of curricular needs in their districts and to make recommendations to schools.

1871   The Elementary Code

Some widening of the curriculum followed the Forster Education Act, 1870. The 1871 Code increased the list of 'specific' subjects to include, for example, the natural sciences, political economy and languages. These had to be taught 'according to a graduated scheme of which the Inspector can report that it is well adapted to the capacity of the children and is sufficiently distinct from the ordinary reading-book lessons to justify its description as a specific subject of instruction'.

'Specifics' were limited to pupils examined in Standards IV, V and VI and not more than two subjects could be taken at the same time. Drawing and music were excluded from the list.

Drill also appeared in the syllabus although this was limited to two hours a week and twenty weeks in the year.

Infant teaching was recognized as an important feature of elementary education and special grants were awarded where a separate specially furnished room was provided for instruction.

1872–5   The Devonshire Commission

Science teaching, in universities and schools and other institutions, was exhaustively examined in a series of Reports by this Royal Commission, headed by the seventh Duke of Devonshire. The Sixth Report, which was concerned with teaching in public and endowed schools, showed that science was still being neglected. It recommended that not less than six hours a week on the average should be devoted to natural science and a sixth of the total marks of school examinations. In the Third Report, the Commissioners categorically stated that 'no one should receive a degree who has not proved himself to be well grounded in science as well as in Languages and Mathematics'. An adequate number of professorships needed to be established to make this possible. In this way, a supply of well-qualified science teachers could be trained for schools.

The Revised Code had prevented the development of science in the elementary schools. To counter this, it was recommended that the inspectorate should have some scientifically qualified men and that certificated teachers should train as science teachers.

1875   The Elementary Code

Besides the elementary or obligatory subjects—the three Rs—and specific subjects, a third category was now introduced, namely 'class' subjects. These consisted of grammar, geography, history and plain needlework which, unlike the other two categories, were to be based not on the proficiency of individual pupils, but on that of the class as a whole. No more than two subjects could be taken at a time but they had to be taught throughout the school above Standard I.

In the specific subjects, the importance of practical work in science was stressed. Some relaxation in the obligatory subjects was allowed—for example, pupils could reproduce a story read to them instead of being examined in dictation.

Practical cookery lessons were permitted, and two years later all girls taking a specific subject were required to make domestic economy their first choice.

English literature, first introduced in 1876 as a specific subject, quickly became the most popular subject in this category.

1882   The Elementary Code

Three important advances were made by the 1882 Code:

1. A new Standard VII was introduced—a recognition of the fact that pupils were now staying on longer at school.
2. The introduction of a new subject, elementary science, which extended from Standards I to VII. Specific subjects now included electricity, chemistry and agriculture.
3. Greater recognition of the importance of practical training for girls, especially cookery, by means of special grants.

A new method of paying grants to schools was devised. Inspectors classified schools as fair, good or excellent and a merit grant was awarded for outstanding work. Critics of the code claimed that the new system led to 'overpressure' of pupils by teachers.

The Code, the work of A. J. Mundella, the Vice-President, was accompanied by the establishment of a 'Code Committee' consisting of Education Department officials, the political heads and inspectors. The Code Committee became a considerable influence on the curriculum, and determined the contents of the Code from year to year.

1882–4   The Samuelson Commission

The terms of reference of the Royal Commission on Technical Instruction were 'to inquire into the instruction of the industrial classes of certain foreign countries in technical and other subjects for the purpose of comparison with that of the corresponding classes in this country, and into the influence of such instruction on manufacturing and other industries at home and abroad'. Concern had been expressed at the growth of European industry and the effects of competition; the Commission included visits to factories as well as technical education institutions in their visits abroad.

The Second Report in 1884 made recommendations of far-reaching importance. In elementary schools, drawing was to be incorporated with writing as a single subject throughout the standards, and object lessons for teaching elementary science should include geography. Proficiency in the use of tools for working in wood and iron should be paid for as a specific, although the work was to be done, as far as possible, out of school hours. Links between elementary schools and the Science and Art Department should be forged, especially at the higher levels of work.

Until secondary schools were improved, technical instruction would not flourish. Bernhard Samuelson, the chairman of the Commission, favoured the establishment of such work in suitable schools or departments where natural science, drawing and mathematics would replace Latin and Greek; local authorities should be able to apply ancient endowments to support this work. In addition, local authorities ought to be empowered to establish and maintain secondary and technical schools and colleges. It would be necessary to coordinate the different grades of technical schools, though the responsible body was not stated.

1886–8   The Cross Commission

In 1886 Sir Richard Cross (the Home Secretary in the first Salisbury government) was asked to chair a Royal Commission 'to inquire into the working of the Elementary Education Acts, England and Wales'. This was the first review of elementary education since the 1870 Act, and the work of the Commission was of considerable importance; however, it sat during a period of hectic political activity (the Irish question, industrial unrest, three elections in 1885–6, the

Liberal Unionists eventually holding the balance of power) and this was reflected in the division among the members, resulting in two Reports, a majority report supporting voluntary schools and a minority report giving the radical and Nonconformist objections to allowing church schools a share of the rates and other matters.

There was, however, agreement on a number of issues, especially those concerning the curriculum. It was considered essential to include the following in elementary schools: the three Rs, needlework for girls and linear drawing for boys, singing, English, English history, geography 'especially of the British Empire', and common objects in the lower standards, leading to an understanding of elementary science in the higher standards. The Commission reiterated the case made out by the Samuelson Commission for both manual and technical instruction for boys.

Flexibility in the interpretation of the Code was recommended while retaining the seven standards. For example, the Commission recognized 'that, as the time of the girls gets taken up by needlework, the time they can give to arithmetic is less than that which can be given by boys . . . this disadvantage will be best compensated . . . by modifying the arithmetical requirements of the Code in the case of girls'. Some choice of rules of arithmetic ought to be allowed, in order to meet the industrial requirements of different districts. The Commission considered that the restriction of history to the fifth and higher standards had greatly discouraged its development. Research by training colleges into the possibility of a safe and scientific system of physical training was suggested. Because of the lobbying of Welsh Nationalists, the Commission agreed to include Welsh in the list of specific subjects as well as bilingual reading-books in Wales.

The new 'higher elementary' or 'higher grade' schools in the 1880s, made possible by grants from the Science and Art Department, offered a curriculum similar to the endowed grammar schools; the distinction between elementary and secondary education was becoming blurred. The Commission observed that the meaning and limits of the term 'elementary' had not been set out in any Act, Code or Court of Law and called for a definition by Parliament.

1889 Technical Instruction Act

The lack of science and technical education became a serious problem in the second half of the nineteenth century. At the 1851 Great Exhibition Great Britain was superior in nearly all branches, but at the Paris Exhibition of 1867 it only excelled in 10 per cent. Lyon Playfair, one of the judges in Paris, suggested that England's decline was due to the fact that her competitors had developed good systems of industrial education for masters and managers. A parliamentary committee confirmed this view, but nothing was done until 1881 when a Royal Commission was appointed under Samuelson. Reports were published in 1882 and 1884 and five years later the Technical Instruction Act was passed. The Act allowed county and county borough councils, established by the Local Government Act in 1888, to levy a penny rate for technical education, and abolished the restriction that limited the work of the Science and Art Department to the 'industrial classes'. However, despite this Act, technical instruction was generally regarded as having a low status compared with a 'liberal education'.

1890–5   The decline of payment by results

This was a period of remarkable educational activity, including the end of the worst aspects of payment by results. The system had been considered by the Cross Commission and was one of the issues which divided the minority and majority reports. The minority condemned payment by results outright but the majority merely wanted it 'modified and relaxed'. This was achieved by the 1890 Code.

In 1892 the Salisbury government was defeated and in Gladstone's fourth Liberal administration the Vice-President of the Council for Education was A. H. D. Acland, who was not only one of the ablest men in the government but the most radical reformer.

A number of important changes were introduced in successive Codes from 1890 to 1895: following on the recommendations of the Cross Commission, alternative schemes of work for use in small schools in English, geography, elementary science and history were introduced. Manual instruction was recognized and drawing was made compulsory for boys. Commercial subjects, especially bookkeeping and shorthand, quickly established themselves. Domestic subjects for girls, science and mathematics were allocated increasing amounts of time: this was matched with a decline in the emphasis on English subjects in the curriculum.

Circular 322 for Inspectors on *The Instruction of Infants* (1893) contained a list of varied occupations suitable for infants' schools which embodied Froebelian principles and marked the official acceptance of modern teaching.

'Having for thirty three years deprived the teachers of almost every vestige of freedom the Department suddenly reversed its policy and gave them in generous measure the boon which it had long withheld.' So E. G. A. Holmes wrote later on the Code of 1895 which abolished the annual examination of pupils in the higher standards. This was replaced by 'surprise visits' and allowed the teacher to evolve his own curriculum.

The lack of continuity in the curriculum between the infants' and later stages of education was recognized with the introduction of object lessons and 'one suitable occupation' for the three lower standards.

1895   The Bryce Report

A. H. D. Acland's reforming zeal was not confined to elementary schools, and in 1894 he persuaded Gladstone to appoint a Royal Commission on secondary education. The Bryce Commission was asked 'to consider what are the best methods of establishing a well-organized system of secondary education in England'. There was a vast range of schools within this category and reform was urgent despite the reforms introduced after the Taunton Report.

In essentials, the Commission called for a central authority which would include the educational aspects of the Charity Commission, the Science and Art

Department and the Education Department under one Minister. As a counter-balance to this, local authorities would become responsible for the supply and maintenance of secondary schools. The new department would thus supervise rather than control education. Four years later, in 1899, the Education Act created a central authority for both elementary and secondary branches of education.

As the Commission was largely concerned with questions of organization and administration, little attention was paid to the curriculum. Indeed, it was not considered 'desirable to lay down definite model curricula for schools of the various types'. Three elements were identified as the basis for a well-balanced curriculum: the literary, scientific and technical. Experience alone would show which forms and proportions were likely to be best, but the Report encouraged authorities to attempt experimental schemes of work.

Two other outcomes of the Report are of interest. Co-education was advocated for secondary schools on the grounds of efficiency; and a generous provision of scholarships was made for elementary pupils to provide a bridge between the two types of schools.

1899   The Board of Education Act

A good deal of the curricular changes suggested by committees and councils during the twentieth century were made possible by the 1899 Board of Education Act: the Board of Education came into being in 1900, and the Education Act two years later gave an additional impetus to the work entrusted to the Board.

An interesting innovation of the 1899 Act was the provision under section 4 for a Consultative Committee to be formed. The Committee was to consist of 'not less than two-thirds of persons qualified to represent the views of universities and other bodies interested in education'. It was envisaged that the committee would have two functions: to form regulations for a register of teachers, and to advise the Board of Education 'on any matter referred to the committee by the Board'. As a result of this latter task, a number of important reports, such as Hadow and Spens, followed.

1900   The Elementary Code

A new and simple method of payment, the 'block grant', replaced the elaborate and piecemeal system of grants for subjects, discipline and organization (except for some practical subjects).

The previous division of the subjects—obligatory, class and specific—was also replaced by a list of subjects which elementary schools were expected 'as a rule' to teach. This constituted for the first time a comprehensive official statement of what should be taught in the elementary school. It consisted of English, arithmetic, geography, history, singing, physical exercises, drawing for boys and needlework for girls. Where practicable, subjects such as science, French and algebra might be taught.

Infants' schools were to teach elements of reading, writing and arithmetic, varied occupations, common things, easy physical exercises and simple needle-work for girls and drawing for boys.

No specific syllabuses were laid down, and, with the ending of payment by results, by 1900 almost all elementary schools were subject to general inspection only. The elementary curriculum was finally freed from the requirement of examinations.

1901   Elementary schools and the Cockerton Judgment

In 1899 Cockerton, the Auditor of the Local Government Board, questioned whether rates were being spent illegally by the London School Board in educat-ing children in elementary schools on lines not provided for in the Elementary Code. The judgment was made against the London School Board by the Court of the Queen's Bench in 1901 and upheld by the Court of Appeal.

This judgment had two important results: it accelerated the demand for more secondary schools which were provided for in the following year by the Balfour Act, and it sharpened the curricular distinction between secondary and elemen-tary education.

1902   Education Act

This Act, known as the Balfour Act but largely the work of Morant, put into operation some of the recommendations of the Bryce Report on administrative structure. These were made easier by the creation of county and county borough councils in 1888 and the Board of Education Act of 1899.

By the 1902 Act local education authorities (LEAS) were created and were permitted (but not compelled) to establish and be responsible for secondary schools. Managers were to be appointed who would carry out the directions of the LEAS, including matters of the secular curriculum, but LEAS were to be guided by the Board of Education which was also the arbiter in cases of dispute. Details of the secondary curriculum were not specified until the publication of the 1904 Regulations.

1902   Board of Education Regulations. The Day School Code

The Elementary Code system still continued to operate after the 1902 Act, and curricular requirements were laid down in some detail:

Course of Instruction Article 15
(i) The Course of instruction for older scholars (i.e. 7+) is as follows (to be taken as a rule in all schools):

English, by which is to be understood reading, recitation, writing, composition, and grammar insofar as it bears upon the correct use of language

Arithmetic

Drawing (for boys)

Needlework (for girls)

Lessons, including object lessons on geography, history and common things

Singing, which should as a rule be by rote

Physical training

N.B. It is not necessary that all these subjects should be taught in every class. One or more may be omitted in any school which can satisfy the inspector and the Board that there is good reason in its case for the omission.

For the purposes of Section 1 (1)(*a*) of the Technical Instruction Act 1889, reading, writing and arithmetic are obligatory or standard subjects.

(ii) One or more of the following to be taken when the circumstances of the school, in the opinion of the Inspector, make it desirable:

Algebra
Euclid
Mensuration
Mechanics
Chemistry
Physics
Elementary physics and chemistry
Animal physiology
Hygiene
Botany
Principles of agriculture
Horticulture
Navigation
Latin
French
Welsh (in Wales)
German
Book-keeping
Shorthand
Domestic economy or domestic science
Drawing (for boys)
Needlework (for girls)

(iii) For girls: cookery, laundry work, dairy work, household management

   For boys: cottage gardening, manual instruction, cookery (for boys in seaport towns)

Article 16. Any subject other than those mentioned in Article 15, may, if sanctioned by the Board, be included in the Course of Instruction, provided that a graduated scheme for teaching it be submitted to and approved by the Inspector.

Article 17. Instruction may be given in religious subjects but no grant is made in respect of any such instruction.

1904   The Elementary Code

Eaglesham (1967) has described those sections of the 1902 Act dealing with elementary education and the 1904 Regulations as part of Morant's policy for 'a standstill in elementary education' (p. 51) and 'training in followership' (p. 53). But others have seen the 1904 Code as a more enlightened document—at least in some parts:

The purpose of the Public Elementary School is to form and strengthen the character and to develop the intelligence of the children entrusted to it, and to make the best use of the school years available, in assisting both girls and boys, according to their different needs, to fit themselves, practically as well as intellectually, for the work of life.

With this purpose in view it will be the aim of the School to train the children carefully in habits of observation and clear reasoning, so that they may gain an intelligent acquaintance with some of the facts and laws of nature; to arouse in them a living interest in the ideals and achievements of mankind, and to bring them to some familiarity with the literature and history of their own country; to give them some power over language as an instrument of thought and expression, and, while making them conscious of the limitations of their knowledge, to develop in them such a taste for good reading and thoughtful study as will enable them to increase that knowledge in after years by their own efforts.

The School must at the same time encourage to the utmost the children's natural activities of hand and eye by suitable forms of practical work and manual instruction; and afford them every opportunity for the healthy development of their bodies, not only by training them in appropriate physical exercises and encouraging them in organized games, but also by instructing them in the working of some of the simpler laws of health.

It will be an important though subsidiary object of the School to discover individual children who show promise of exceptional capacity, and to develop their special gifts (so far as this can be done without sacrificing the interests of the majority of the children), so that they may be qualified to pass at the proper age into Secondary Schools, and be able to derive the maximum of benefit from the education there offered them.

(Introduction to the Elementary Code, 1904)

In spite of the high-flown phrases it is difficult to see this other than as a blueprint for an inferior curriculum for the majority; a 'ladder' was provided only for the exceptional minority. The 1904 Code has to be seen as another example of the tendency towards a deliberately created curriculum gap between elementary and secondary pupils.

1904   Regulations for Secondary Schools

These regulations, like the 1902 Act from which they derive, were partly the work of Morant, who wanted to steer the secondary schools away from a curriculum which was, in his view, much too scientific and technical; some of Morant's critics have suggested that his desire for secondary education to be quite different from the 'illegal' higher grade elementary curriculum resulted in secondary schools becoming mere imitations of the 'academic', classics-dominated public schools. The regulations recommended that instruction should be 'general'. It was recommended that specialization in science or literature should only begin after a good deal of general ground had been covered. Another important recommendation was that the course of instruction should be complete by the age of sixteen or seventeen. The regulations made detailed recommendations as to what the curriculum must contain and the time that should be spent on each part.

The Course should provide for instruction in the English Language and Literature, at least one language other than English, geography, history, mathematics, science and drawing, with due provision for manual work and physical exercises, and, in a girls' school for Housewifery. Not less than 4½ hours per week must be allotted to English, geography and history; not less than 3½ hours to the language where only one is taken or less than 6 hours where two are taken; and not less than 7½ hours to science and mathematics, of which at least 3 must be for science. The instruction in science must be both theoretical and practical. When two languages oher than English are taken, and Latin is not one of them, the Board will require to be satisfied that the omission of Latin is for the advantage of the school.

The detailed time prescriptions were officially only in force until 1907 but probably continued to influence timetables for some years after that.

1905 Board of Education Blue Book: Handbook of Suggestions for the Consideration of Teachers and others concerned with the Work of Public Elementary Schools

This publication is usually thought to mark an important stage in the liberalization of the elementary school. Centralized control of the curriculum in the form of regulations was replaced by a *Handbook* of 'suggestions'.

A chapter is devoted to each of the following: English, arithmetic, observation lessons and nature study, geography, history, drawing, singing, physical training, needlework and housecraft, handicraft and gardening. The Appendices also include 'specimen schemes' for most of the above, but the fact that these were 'suggestions' was stressed.

> The only uniformity of practice that the Board of Education desire to see in the teaching of Public Elementary Schools is that each teacher shall think for himself, and work out for himself such methods of teaching as may use his powers to the best advantage and be best suited to the particular needs and conditions of the school. (p. 6)

The *Handbook* was frequently revised and reissued. (See p. 27 for comparison between 1905 and 1927 versions.)

1907 Supplementary Regulations for Secondary Schools

Detailed control of the curriculum in terms of hours per subject was relaxed, but the academic tradition was continued by, for example, the insistence on Latin.

The regulations also included rules for charging fees and the provision of free places. Normally 25 per cent of the annual entry was reserved for scholars who passed approved tests. Thus the scholarship ladder was established, but since only a small minority of elementary pupils were admitted this tended to widen the curriculum gap between elementary and secondary schools.

1911 Report of the Consultative Committee of the Board of Education on Examinations in Secondary Schools

The Chairman of this Consultative Committee was A. H. D. Acland. The 1902 Education Act encouraged the expansion of secondary education, and one of the byproducts of this expansion was the increase in numbers of pupils taking a wide variety of examinations especially at age fourteen or fifteen. By 1909 there was clearly a need for some national guidelines to be laid down, and the Board of

Education referred the problem of examinations to the Consultative Committee. The terms of reference of the Consultative Committee were:

> To consider when and in what circumstances examinations are desirable in secondary schools (*a*) for boys and (*b*) for girls. The committees are desired to consider this question under the following heads:
>   (i) Examination at entrance to school
>   (ii) Examination during school life
>   (iii) Examination at leaving school

The Committee came down on the side of examinations in school and firmly supported a system of *public* examinations for school-leavers at age sixteen which they suggested should be called the Examination for the Secondary School Certificate.

The Board of Education incorporated the major recommendations into Circular 996 in 1917.

1913   Board of Education. Memorandum on Curriculum of Secondary Schools. Circular 826

This circular was an attempt by the Board to clarify policy about general education and specialization in secondary schools. The Board's Report for 1912–13 had already indicated that it was not completely opposed to some kinds of specialization which did not encroach upon the work of technical schools.

The memorandum on Curriculum of Secondary Schools pointed out that schools had a twofold function: providing a general education for those who would go on to further professional training or university degrees, and for those who would leave at sixteen and whose formal education would at that age be completed. One of the problems for secondary schools was to work out a way of providing common courses for these two groups of pupils. The Board was also concerned with the lack of specific preparation for the world of work for the second group of pupils.

It was stated that some kinds of vocational courses would be acceptable to the Board, e.g. in commercial, agricultural and domestic subjects. In those schools wishing to provide commercial courses, for instance, it was recommended that specialized work should not begin before the age of fifteen and should not usually occupy more than 20 per cent of school time.

1917   Board of Education. Circular 996. Examination of Secondary Schools

The 1911 Report of the Consultative Committee had recommended that the number of external examinations should be reduced and coordinated so that a reasonable uniformity in standards was attained. This recommendation had to be accepted by the university examining boards and prolonged negotiations took place from 1914 to 1916. By 1917 the examining bodies had accepted the Board's suggestions and a Circular was issued.

The effect of these negotiations and the Circular was to produce what came to be known as the School Certificate. The First School Examinations for pupils of about sixteen were *general* and required that at least five subjects be offered, one from each of three groups, i.e. English subjects, foreign languages, science and mathematics. The Second School Examinations were *specialized* in one of three groups: classics, modern studies or science and mathematics.

The Board established the Secondary School Examinations Council (SSEC) as an advisory body to coordinate the standards and methods of examinations.

1918 Education Act (the Fisher Act)

This Act contains very little about the curriculum as such but proposed raising the school-leaving age to fifteen and recommended the provision of compulsory part-time education for young people up to the age of eighteen. Both proposals disappeared in the economic slump of the 1920s, but other reforms were retained including the abolition of 'half-time' education, and restrictions on children working, as well as provision of advanced and practical courses.

1922 Board of Education. Circular 1294 on the Curricula of Secondary Schools in England

Between 1915 and 1919 four committees were appointed to look into the principal subjects of the secondary curriculum: natural science, modern languages, classics and English. Reports on science and languages appeared in 1918, on classics and English in 1921. The recommendations of all four reports were considered and coordinated in Circular 1294. The main conclusion of this circular was that the curriculum was congested and the timetable overcrowded. It was felt that the time demanded by each of the four subjects was so great that it was impossible for a secondary curriculum to be 'general' in the sense of dealing with all the traditional subjects. (Circular 1294 was quoted in the Spens Report 1938, p. 188, to support the idea of an increase in specialization.)

1923 Board of Education Report of the Consultative Committee on Differentiation of the Curriculum for Boys and Girls in Secondary Schools

This is a very interesting report because it not only examines the question of the supposed differences in ability of boys and girls, but also surveys the history of the curriculum and changing ideas about boys' and girls' education. The traditional curriculum was criticized for its narrowness:

> . . . we feel that, alike for boys and for girls, there has been a stunting of aesthetic taste and capacity owing to the concentration of attention upon the studies of the dry intellect. Education is not only a preparation for the doing of work; it is also a preparation for the spending of leisure, which, if it is less in amount, is perhaps no less in importance than work. Nothing can conduce more to that right spending of leisure, which means so much for true happiness, than an eliciting and training of the gift of aesthetic appreciation. (p. xiv)

The possibility that some girls' school curricula might have been superior to what was provided for boys did not escape the Committee members: 'In some respects the absence from girls' schools of old-established tradition has been a distinct advantage to girls' education' (p. 44).

Other criticisms of the curriculum for boys and girls at the time included the suggestions that it was too academic (p. 58), over-burdened (p. 60), too rigid (pp. 61–3), and that the curriculum for girls was modelled too much on boys' (pp. 63–4), was too competitive for girls (p. 64), and was not sufficiently developed aesthetically (p. 67).

1926 Report of the Consultative Committee of the Board of Education on the Education of the Adolescent (the Hadow Report)

The 1920s and 1930s may be seen as a time of conflict between those who, in the Morant tradition, wanted to see elementary and secondary education kept as distinct as possible from each other, and those who wished to replace the two parallel systems by a single 'primary and secondary for all' system. The Hadow Report represents a half-way stage in the process.

The committee included R. H. Tawney, editor of the Labour Party's document *Secondary Education for All* (1922). Its terms of reference (February 1924) were:

> (i) To consider and report upon the organization, objective and curriculum of courses of study suitable for children who will remain in full-time attendance at schools, other than Secondary Schools, up to the age of 15, regard being had on the one hand to the requirements of a good general education and the desirability of providing a reasonable variety of curriculum, so far as is practicable, for children of varying tastes and abilities, and on the other hand the probable occupations of the pupils in commerce, industry and agriculture. (ii) Incidentally thereto, to advise as to the arrangements which should be made (*a*) for testing the attainments of the pupils at the end of their course; (*b*) for facilitating in suitable cases the transfer of individual pupils to Secondary Schools at an age above the normal age of admission.

The Committee was set up in 1924, ten days after the formation in December 1923 of the first Labour government, one of whose slogans had been 'secondary education for all'.

Its main recommendations were:

1. Separation of primary and secondary education at about eleven. 'There is a tide which begins to rise in the veins of youth at the age of eleven or twelve.'
2. All children to have secondary education of some suitable kind. Allocation to be made by examinations.
3. Two types of secondary school—grammar and modern—for two different types of child: 'all go forward, though along different paths'.
4. The modern school curriculum would be similar to that of the grammar school but more practical and shorter (three to four years). Modern schools should *not* become inferior secondary schools.
5. School-leaving age to be raised to fifteen.

Despite its 'left-wing' origins, the Report puts forward an essentially traditional view of education in the form of different kinds of curricula for different kinds of people. In this sense the Hadow Report is in a direct line of succession from Taunton to Spens, Norwood and the post-1944 tripartite system.

1927 Handbook of Suggestions for Teachers

The *Handbook*, originally published in 1905, was rewritten and reissued from time to time, and these revised versions provide us with some indications of changes in official policy and general educational theory. R. J. W. Selleck in *English Primary Education and the Progressives 1914–39* (1972) makes a comparison between 1905 and 1927:

> In the period between the wars the Board's official guide to educational practice, the *Suggestions*, became steadily more sympathetic to progressive theory. The 1927 edition, for example, was full of advice which the progressives would have found satisfactory . . .
>
> His [the teacher's] starting point must be no rigid syllabus or subject, but the children as they really are: he must work always with the grain of their minds, try never to cut across it . . .
>
> Self-education should be the key-note of the older children's curriculum, just as free expression is of the youngest children's; but in neither case is it expected that the teacher will abdicate . . . (pp. 123–4)

1931 Report of the Consultative Committee on the Primary School

This Report marks an important stage in the development of primary education and could be regarded as the transition from the elementary tradition of schools 'for the children of the labouring poor' to a new and in some respects 'progressive' view of the type of schooling that was appropriate for all children up to the age of eleven. Its terms of reference were: 'To inquire into and report as to the courses of study suitable for children (other than children in Infants' Departments) up to the age of 11 in Elementary Schools, with special reference to the needs of children in rural areas'.

The main recommendations supported the view of the 1926 Hadow Report on the Adolescent that all children should normally progress from the primary school to some form of secondary school at the age of 11: 'the curriculum is to be thought of in terms of activity and experience rather than of knowledge to be acquired and facts to be stored' (p. 93).

This sentence is, however, often quoted out of context: there was no support in the report for extreme versions of the child-centred approach. 'We are . . . definitely of opinion that it would be unnecessary and pedantic to attempt to throw the whole of the teaching of the primary school into the project form' (p. 104). 'It is . . . essential that provision should be made for an adequate amount of "drill" in reading, writing and arithmetic' (p. 140).

Physical education, dance, drama, language training (including 'oral expression and communication'), 'aesthetic subjects' such as handwork, drawing and music, literature, science, mathematics, history and geography were all specifically mentioned as desirable elements of the primary curriculum, but not necessarily to be taught as separate subjects taught in distinct lessons.

1935   Regulations for Secondary Schools

One of the firmly held beliefs about the curricula of English secondary schools is that they have always been free from central control. But the regulations as late as 1935 were quite specific:

> Except with the previous permission of the Board, adequate provision must be made for instruction in the English Language and Literature, at least one language other than English, geography, history, mathematics, science, drawing, singing, manual instruction in the case of boys, domestic subjects in the case of girls, physical exercises, and for organized games.

1938   Report of the Consultative Committee of the Board of Education on Secondary Education with special reference to Grammar Schools and Technical High Schools (the Spens Report)

This is a very important report in the history of the curriculum for at least two reasons. It contains a good historical sketch of the development of the traditional secondary curriculum in England and Wales, and a chapter on the principles of the curriculum; and its espousal of the doctrine that there should be different kinds of curriculum for different types of pupil had very far-reaching and unfortunate effects on curriculum as well as school organization. Its terms of reference were:

> To consider and report upon the organization and interrelation of schools, other than those administered under the Elementary Code, which provide education for pupils beyond the age of 11 +; regard being had in particular to the framework and content of the education of pupils who do not remain at school beyond the age of about 16.

On the basis of very doubtful psychological evidence the Report suggested:

> It is becoming more and more evident that a single liberal or general education for all is impracticable, and that varying forms both of general and quasi-vocational education have to be evolved in order to meet the needs of boys and girls differing widely in intellectual and emotional capacity. (p. 2)

It also expressed the opinion that secondary schools attempted to teach too much:

> ... that there is a strong tendency to adjust the pupil to the curriculum rather than the curriculum to the needs and abilities of the pupil, and in particular that the needs of the less academic pupil receive inadequate attention; that there is a grave tendency to over-work and over-strain adolescent pupils, especially girls. (p. 145)

The Report's main recommendations were:

1. There should be three kinds of secondary school: grammar, modern and technical schools.
2. Parity of esteem should be ensured between all three kinds of school.
3. Transfer should be possible.
4. Multilateral schools were not recommended.

5. Curriculum: despite the critical historical survey of the traditional curriculum, no major changes were suggested for grammar schools; modern schools would have a less academic curriculum—for the more practical child—and technical schools would concentrate more on science and technical subjects. But to facilitate transfer all types of schools should have similar curricula for the eleven to thirteen age group.

The Report also included an interesting appendix by the Secretary (Dr R. F. Young) on the Development of the Conception of General Liberal Education (Appendix II), as well as a memorandum by Professor I. L. Kandel on Secondary Curriculum (Appendix III) which is often in conflict with the Committee's recommendations. Appendix IV by Professor Cyril Burt attacked faculty psychology and provided a psychological rationale for the tripartite system.

1943   Board of Education White Paper on Educational Reconstruction (July 1943)

The White Paper (based to some extent on the Green Book of June 1941) was a more discursive version of the ideals contained in the famous Education Act of 1944. (It was originally intended to bring out the White Paper and the Bill together, but the Bill became too complicated and was delayed.) The White Paper also preceded the publication of the Norwood Report, so very little reference is made to curriculum:

> The curriculum of secondary schools, and especially that of the grammar schools, will be the subject of a report by the Norwood Committee. Public opinion will, undoubtedly, look for a new approach to the choice and treatment of school subjects after the war. In particular, consideration must be given to a closer relation of education in the countryside to the needs of agricultural and rural life and, more generally, to creating a better understanding between the people of the town and of the country. A new direction in the teaching of history and geography and modern languages will be needed to arouse and quicken in the pupils a livelier interest in the meaning and responsibilities of citizenship of this country, the Empire and of the world abroad. Education in the future must be a process of gradually widening horizons, from the family to the local community, from the community to the nation, and from the nation to the world. (p. 11)

Paragraphs 36–42 are concerned with religious education which was the only subject to be officially required on the timetable.

1943   Curriculum and Examinations in Secondary Schools: Report of the Committee of the Secondary School Examinations Council (the Norwood Report)

Much of the thinking of the Spens Report is seen reflected and developed in this Report. In some respects the Report may be seen as a justification of the tripartite system which developed after 1944—especially the idea of different kinds of curriculum for different types of pupil. The Committee's terms of reference

(1941) were 'To consider suggested changes in the Secondary School curriculum and the question of School Examinations in relation thereto'.

Types of curriculum

In a wise economy of secondary education pupils of a particular type of mind would receive the training best suited for them and that training would lead them to an occupation where their capacities would be suitably used; that a future occupation is already present to their minds while they are still at school has been suggested, though admittedly the degree to which it is present varies. Thus, to the three main types sketched above there would correspond three main types of curriculum, which we may again attempt to indicate.

First, there would be a curriculum of which the most characteristic feature is that it treats the various fields of knowledge as suitable for coherent and systematic study for their own sake apart from immediate considerations of occupation, though at a later stage grasp of the matter and experience of the methods belonging to those fields may determine the area of choice of employment and may contribute to success in the employment chosen.

The second type of curriculum would be closely, though not wholly, directed to the special data and skills associated with a particular kind of occupation; its outlook and its methods would always be bounded by a near horizon clearly envisaged. It would thus be closely related to industry, trades and commerce in all their diversity.

In the third type of curriculum a balanced training of mind and body and a cor-related approach to humanities, Natural Science and the arts would provide an equipment varied enough to enable pupils to take up the work of life: its purpose would not be to prepare for a particular job or profession and its treatment would make a direct appeal to interests, which it would awaken by practical touch with affairs.

Of the first it may be said that it may or may not look forward to University work; if it does, that is because the Universities are traditionally concerned with the pursuit of knowledge as such. Of the second we would say that it may or may not look forward to the Universities but that it should increasingly be directed to advanced studies in so far as the Universities extend their orbit in response to the demands of the technical branches of industry. (p. 4)

The Norwood Report was received critically by some educationists:

In this field, there recently appeared a Report, namely that of the Norwood Committee on *Curriculum and Examinations* in Secondary Schools, which covers somewhat the same ground as the present book. Without being suspect of *parti pris* or of lack of charity, one may express the view that this Report is not a very satisfactory piece of work. It has been received by teachers without enthusiasm. It fails either to give a lead or to examine in a philosophic way the bases of the curriculum and the principles which should guide the curriculum designer. We must, therefore, still go on considering in what ways we can make the content of our education more relevant to the needs of the present age.

(*The Content of Education*. Interim Report of the Council for Curriculum Reform, 1945, p. 7)

The Spens Committee, in 1938, may have had to rely on overconfident psychological evidence; the Norwood Report of 1943 was concerned not with evidence but with assertion. It has less of a basis in discriminating analysis and concern for data than any other modern report on education; it was produced by a narrow committee and, it has been said, the circumstances in which it was published were 'a perfect example of that departmental procedure which to the uninitiated seems like official chicanery'. The report contained 'obscurities and inconsistencies, perhaps not quite unintentional'.

(J. Lawson and H. Silver, *A Social History of Education in England*, 1973, p. 422)

Despite criticisms of the Report the 1944 Act was generally interpreted along Norwood tripartite lines; the Ministry of Education pamphlet *The Nation's Schools*

(1945) was withdrawn after protests about its tripartite recommendations, but *The New Secondary Education* (1947) made much the same kind of assumptions.

The Report also recommended the replacement of the School Certificate *group* examination by a subject examination (later put into effect as GCE O Level); there should also be a school-leaving examination for eighteen-year-olds (to replace the Higher Certificate) acceptable as university entrance and professional

THE BUTLER'S DREAM

"It came out of my head."

I   A cartoon of R. A. Butler, then President of the Board of Education, during the passage of the 1944 Education Bill in the House of Commons. In its final shape, the Act made no mention of curriculum.

Punch

qualification (GCE A Level); and eventually examinations should be run by the schools themselves, based on curricula devised by teachers.

1944 Education Act

This is a very important statute which completely changed the administrative structure of education, but the word curriculum is never used.

The three stages of the system

The statutory system of public education shall be organized in three progressive stages to be known as primary education, secondary education, and further education; and it shall be the duty of the local education authority for every area, so far as their powers extend, to contribute towards the spiritual, moral, mental, and physical development of the community by securing that efficient education throughout those stages shall be available to meet the needs of the population of their area. (Section 7)

The only subject mentioned as a requirement in the Act was religious education or religious instruction (the two words seem to be used interchangeably):

Religious Education in County and Voluntary Schools

Subject to the provisions of this section, the school day in every county school and in every voluntary school shall begin with collective worship on the part of all pupils in attendance at the school, and the arrangements made therefor shall provide for a single act of worship attended by all such pupils unless, in the opinion of the local education authority or, in the case of a voluntary school, of the managers or governors thereof, the school premises are such as to make it impracticable to assemble them for that purpose. (Section 25 (i))

Despite the lack of specific curricular requirements, the responsibility for ensuring 'efficient' education was placed firmly on the parents:

It shall be the duty of the parent of every child of compulsory school age to cause him to receive efficient full-time education suitable to his age, ability, and aptitude, either by regular attendance at school or otherwise. (Section 36)

1956 Ministry of Education White Paper. Technical Education

The aim of the Paper was to stimulate scientific and technical education at all levels. Surprisingly little attention was devoted to the problem of the technical curriculum, but a plea was made for scientific and technical subjects to be included in a programme of liberal education:

11. In a sense, all technical progress rests upon the common foundation of language, and more attention will have to be given to the teaching of good plain English, the use of which saves time and money and avoids trouble. Without it bridges are hard to build over the gulfs that separate experts in different specialized subjects not only from the general public but from one another. Moreover a place must always be found in technical studies for liberal education. The time available often limits what can be done in the way of introducing into the curriculum subjects such as history, literature and the arts, but in any event a wide treatment of scientific and technical subjects is essential if students who are to occupy responsible positions in industry are to emerge from their education with a broad outlook. We cannot afford either to fall behind in technical accomplishments or to neglect spiritual and human values. (p. 5)

1959   Ministry of Education. Primary Education: suggestions for the consideration of teachers and others concerned with the work of Primary Schools

After 1944 elementary schools ceased to exist, so the *Handbook of Suggestions* for teachers and others engaged in the work of public elementary schools became obsolete. In any case the last revision had been in 1937 and some changes were called for.

Part 3 of the *Handbook* is devoted to 'The Fields of Learning', with one chapter (Chapter VIII) on the curriculum in general and Chapters IX–XVII on separate 'fields'.

(ii)   Education in school is much more than is stated in the curriculum
It is most important to emphasize that the curriculum, stated merely in terms of subjects or activities, omits what schools would regard as fundamental in the education they offer. From the nursery school upwards, education in school is concerned primarily with the development of children as persons. The achievement of each child in this or that school activity is important, and it is especially important that he should be doing his best in each; but the ultimate criterion of the quality of his education is the quality and balance of the personality which results—the child's competence and confidence in using and enjoying the knowledge and skills he has acquired, and above all, the nature of his attitudes and his behaviour towards those with whom he works and plays. (p. 115)

(iii)   Interpretation of the following chapters
The chapters that follow deal with learning under the headings that have become familiar in the schools. These headings are not intended as items for a timetable, but are chosen as a convenient way of considering what might be studied in the primary school. They merge and overlap. Many different schools interpret and cover the various fields in ways best suited to their own circumstances and staffing.

The content of any particular chapter should not be taken as a syllabus or scheme of work in any subject, and still less as a compendium of methods. Each chapter is intended to suggest the study, activity or procedures which might be considered by teachers as offering something of value to the children. No chapter makes any claims to completeness or to novelty. Much that teachers are already doing with success could not be included here, and there is nothing here that in some way has not been practised with success in some schools. But, as has been said repeatedly, good education cannot be merely imitative or carried out by rote, and the best suggestions are helpful only if they are adapted and used with discretion. (p. 116)

The fields considered worthy of a chapter were as follows: religion (IX), physical education (X), language (XI), mathematics (XII), art and craft, and needlework (XIII), handwriting (XIV), music (XV), history (XVI), geography and natural history (XVII).

1959   Ministry of Education: 15 to 18, Report of the Central Advisory Council for Education (England) (the Crowther Report)

The Council's terms of reference were:

To consider, in relation to the changing social and industrial needs of our society, and the needs of its individual citizens, the education of boys and girls between 15 and 18, and in particular to consider the balance at various levels of general and specialized studies between these ages and to examine the interrelationship of the various stages of education. (p. xxvii)

This report is about the education of English boys and girls aged from 15 to 18. Most of them are not being educated. (p. 3)

One of the recommendations in the Report was that the school-leaving age should be raised to sixteen between 1966 and 1968. The Council also recommended compulsory part-time education in county colleges up to eighteen.

The curricula of secondary schools were also discussed—especially the sixth-form curriculum. The problem of over-specialization within the sixth form was discussed but specialization was accepted as necessary and desirable.

There is a danger in a further division of society, and in our opinion the community ought to insist that no man or woman should in future complete his or her education in such ignorance both of the dialect and of the philosophy of science as has been customary for so many in this country. To this proposition there is the natural corollary that greater efforts should also be made to see that the scientists and technicians should be exposed to the radiation of humane letters. (para. 77)

A theoretical view of curriculum design was also attempted:

There seem to us, then, to be four main strands out of which the curriculum of the county colleges should be woven. There is, first, the task of helping young workers, many of them of limited intelligence, to find their way successfully about the adult world—to spend their money sensibly, to understand the many ways in which the welfare state touches their lives and can assist them, to see how its services are paid for, and to play their part as useful citizens. Secondly, there is the more difficult job of helping them to define, in a form which makes sense to them, a standard of moral values by which they can live after they have left the sheltered world of school and find themselves in novel situations where they desperately need guidance. There is, thirdly, the easier, and infinitely rewarding, task of helping them to carry over into their working life the pursuits and activities, physical and aesthetic, which they practised at school and too often abandon. Finally, there is, as we have seen, a strictly educational task in the narrower sense. (para. 274)

1960   Ministry of Education. The General Certificate of Education and Sixth Form Studies. Third Report of the Secondary School Examinations Council

By the late 1950s (*see also* Crowther Report), one of the complaints about sixth-form curricula was that the A level examination structure encouraged a cramming attitude to knowledge.

Put very briefly, the predicament of the sixth forms seems to us to mean this: the pressure to show results in terms of examination achievements for purposes such as university admission has become so intense that the curriculum is in danger of becoming seriously overloaded, and specialization carried to a point at which general education is in jeopardy. (p. 2)

The schools have a further problem. A substantial proportion of their sixth formers, and one which is not likely to grow less in the next few years, leave without the intention of going on to university. The schools feel the need for a school leaving examination suitable to be taken by these pupils at the end of two years in the sixth form. A number of them find that the present Advanced level is not entirely suitable for this purpose; and some of them question whether any examination which adequately stretches the powers of the potential university honours student can also be suitable for the non-university sixth-form leaver. (p. 3)

1960 Ministry of Education. Secondary School Examinations other than GCE. Report of a Committee Appointed by the SSEC (the Beloe Report)

One symptom of the failure of the policy of parity of prestige (i.e. that secondary schools were different but equal) was the insistence by many parents and employers that secondary modern pupils should take examinations. This Report analysed the arguments about examinations and the curriculum, especially for those pupils who might be described as 'non-grammar-school pupils'. The Committee's terms of reference were:

To review current arrangements for the examination of secondary school pupils other than by the General Certificate of Education examination, to consider what developments are desirable, and to advise the Council whether, and if so, what, examinations should be encouraged or introduced, and at what ages and levels. (p. 1)

The recommendations included:

Any new pattern of examinations, if they are to play a constructive role, and their potential dangers minimized, should conform to certain criteria, namely those numbered (i) to (vi) below.

(i) The examinations should be appropriate for pupils at the end of the fifth year of a secondary school course, when they will normally be aged about 16 . . .

(ii) Assuming that up to 20 per cent of the total 16-year-old age group may be expected to attempt GCE O level in four or more subjects, we think the examinations we propose might be taken in four or more subjects by candidates in the next 20 per cent below these, and should be so designed that a substantial majority of pupils within this group would obtain passes in this range of subjects. We think that up to a further 20 per cent of the age-group might attempt individual subjects. There should be both pass and credit standards.

(iii) They should be on a subject and not a group basis.

(iv) They should be specially designed to suit the needs and interests of pupils in the ability range concerned and should not simply provide a replica of GCE examinations at a lower level.

(v) They should be largely in the hands of teachers serving the schools which will use them . . .

(vi) The Examining Bodies should act under the general guidance of the central consultative body . . . (pp. 47–8)

The idea of a new examination was accepted and became the Certificate of Secondary Education (CSE) administered by fourteen Regional Boards. A new kind of tripartite system seemed to be envisaged in this Report: GCE, CSE and non-examinable pupils, with three different kinds of curriculum.

1963   Report of the Committee on Higher Education appointed by the Prime Minister (the Robbins Report)

There is little in this Report which has a direct bearing on school curricula, but it should be noted as of some relevance because it had been alleged in the 1950s and early 1960s that the universities were having a distorting effect on the teaching of sixth formers and hence the curriculum for secondary schools as a whole. The key to the problem was thought to be the fact that higher education (and universities in particular) had not expanded as fast as the demand for places from sixth formers. Thus there was a bottleneck at 18+ which increased the competitive tendency of sixth formers to over-specialize on two or three subjects to the neglect of their general education.

The main recommendations of the Report included an ambitious target for the expansion of higher education in the 1970s. There were also some recommendations about the content of first-degree courses:

First-degree courses: England and Wales

13. The syllabuses of first-degree courses should be regularly reviewed to avoid overloading. (para. 255)

14. A higher proportion of students should receive a broader education for their first degrees. (para. 262)

15. There should be more courses involving the study of more than one main subject. (para. 264)

16. Arrangements should wherever possible allow a student to postpone his choice of special subject until the end of the first year or to change his course of study then, if necessary with an extension of grant. (para. 271)

17. Students who do not live up to their early promise should be transferred, after their first or second year, to less exacting courses. (para. 272)

(p. 278)

1963   Ministry of Education. Half Our Future. A Report of the Central Advisory Council (England) (the Newsom Report)

The Crowther Report of 1959 had given some indications of inadequacies in secondary schools, especially for those pupils who were not in grammar schools. In 1961 the CAC was given the following brief:

To consider the education between the ages of 13 and 16 of pupils of average or less than average ability who are or will be following full-time courses either at schools or in establishments of further education. The term education shall be understood to include extra-curricular activities.

In many respects the Report shows some aspects of the state of educational thinking in 1963. Even the Foreword by the Minister, Sir Edward Boyle, contained a sentence which provoked a good deal of discussion:

. . . all children should have an equal opportunity of *acquiring intelligence* and of developing their talents and abilities to the full. [authors' italics]

A good deal of the Report is concerned with the curriculum, in terms both of general principles and of specific changes in content and methods:

> All boys and girls need to develop, as well as skills, capacities for thought, judgment, enjoyment, curiosity. They need to develop a sense of responsibility for their work and towards other people, and to begin to arrive at some code of moral and social behaviour which is self-imposed. It is important that they should have some understanding of the physical world and of the human society in which they are growing up. (p. 27)

> There are, in any case, some objectives which can and ought deliberately to be pursued through every part of the curriculum. Very high in this list we should place improvement in powers of speech: not simply improvement in the quality and clearness of enunciation, although that is needed, but a general extension of vocabulary, and, with it, a surer command over the structures of spoken English and the expression of ideas. That means seizing the opportunity of every lesson, in engineering or housecraft or science as well as in English, to provide material for discussion—genuine discussion, not mere testing by teacher's question and pupil's answer. (p. 29)

The Report not only reinforced the Crowther Report recommendation for raising the school-leaving age to sixteen but also suggested that the school day should be longer.

It was also felt that the curriculum should provide a link with the adult world of work and responsibilities—and some critics accused the Report of being over-conformist.

In general the Report tried to steer a middle way between the traditional elementary school insistence on the three Rs and the less tangible objectives of 'progressive education' and went some way towards the idea of a common curriculum for all pupils:

> What should be taught? We have already made clear the importance we attach to literacy, numeracy and that part of religious upbringing which falls to the schools. Physical education, too, is something which all growing boys and girls need. The next three chapters are devoted to the various subjects of the curriculum as a whole. Each chapter deals with a broad field of knowledge in each of which boys and girls ought to be getting some experience all the time they are at school. If this report were about all the pupils in secondary schools instead of only half we should still hold that up to the age of sixteen nobody should go without some practical work, some experience in mathematics and science and some in the humanities. And it ought to be a sizeable share of each, not a concession to idealistic theory which sensible folk need not take too seriously. Up to this point we are rigorists. We would like to prescribe this for all pupils in all secondary schools as an obligation.
>
> But beyond this point we become permissive. We would neither draw up a fixed table of information, subject by subject, which all pupils should master, nor even prescribe beyond the minimum essentials set out in the preceding paragraph a set list of subjects which all should study. A universal fixed curriculum ought to be ruled out if only because of the wide range both of capacity and of tastes among the pupils with whom we are concerned. (p. 124)

1964 DES Report of Working Party on Schools' Curricula and Examinations (the Lockwood Report)

Since 1917 the Board of Education and later the Ministry of Education had taken advice on examinations in schools from the Secondary School Examinations Council (SSEC). But during the late 1950s and early 1960s it was felt that examinations and curricula should be considered together. In 1962 the Minister of Education set up a Curriculum Study Group within the Ministry which brought together HMIs and other educationists to give advice. For a variety of reasons, including fears from the teaching profession that a centralized curriculum plan would be imposed on them, the Curriculum Study Group was not retained on a permanent basis. Instead a Working Party was set up with Sir John Lockwood as chairman to consider the need for some kind of cooperative machinery on school curricula and examinations. The Lockwood Working Party reported to the Minister in March 1964 and recommended the establishment of a Schools Council for the Curriculum and Examinations.

The Schools Council began to operate in October 1964 under the chairmanship of Sir John Maud. This Council took over the advisory function of the SSEC and also the role of the Curriculum Study Group, but an important difference was that it was recommended that the membership of the Governing Council and the major committees should contain a majority of teachers. It is financed jointly by the DES and the LEAS. Since 1964 the Schools Council has not only given advice on curriculum and examinations but has also financed a great deal of research.

A summary of the work of the Schools Council will be found at the end of this chapter.

1967   Report of the Central Advisory Council for Education (England). Children and their Primary Schools (the Plowden Report)

By the 1960s an inquiry into primary education was overdue—the last official report had been that of the Hadow Committee on Infant and Nursery Schools in 1933. The CAC's terms of reference (1963) were 'To consider primary education in all its aspects, and the transition to secondary education'.

Perhaps its most dramatic recommendations were the doctrine of 'positive discrimination' and the idea of Education Priority Areas (EPAs). These had considerable implications for the curriculum, but the Report also included a good deal of direct discussion about the primary curriculum. It also recommended that the structure of primary education should be changed to First Schools (five to eight) followed by Middle Schools (eight to twelve). Thus the transfer to secondary school would be delayed for a year; in addition more continuity between all stages was strongly recommended.

In general the Committee adopted a 'progressive' viewpoint on primary education and curriculum. Part 5 of the Report is on 'The Children in the Schools: Curriculum and Internal Organization'.

> Rigid division of the curriculum into subjects tends to interrupt children's trains of thought and of interest and to hinder them from realizing the common elements in problem solving. These are among the many reasons why some work, at least, should cut across subject divisions at all stages in the primary school. (p. 197)

Flexibility in the curriculum
The extent to which subject matter ought to be classified and the headings under which the classification is made will vary with the age of the children, with the demands made

by the structure of the subject matter which is being studied, and with the circumstances of the school. Any practice which predetermines the pattern and imposes it
upon all is to be condemned. Some teachers find it helpful in maintaining a balance in
individual and class work to think in terms of broad areas of the curriculum such as
language, science and mathematics, environmental study and the expressive arts. No
pattern can be perfect since many subjects fall into one category or another according
to the aspect which is being studied. For young children, the broadest of divisions is
suitable. For children from 9 to 12, more subject divisions can be expected, though
experience in secondary schools has shown that teaching of rigidly defined subjects,
often by specialist teachers, is far from suitable for the oldest children who will be in the
middle schools. This is one of our reasons for suggesting a change in the age of transfer
to secondary education. (p. 198)

The idea of flexibility has found expression in a number of practices, all of them
designed to make good use of the interest and curiosity of children, to minimize the
notion of subject matter being rigidly compartmental, and to allow the teacher to
adopt a consultative, guiding, stimulating role rather than a purely didactic one. The
oldest of these methods is the 'project'. Some topic, such as 'transport', is chosen, ideally
by the children, but frequently by the teacher. (pp. 198–9)

The Committee also suggested that it was important to have accurate information about levels of national attainment, especially in mathematics and reading,
which could be obtained by recurring surveys conducted by the DES and NFER.
Secondary schools should also inform primary schools of pupils' progress.

From a curriculum point of view probably the most interesting recommendation was that concerning EPAs: in 1968 the DES and SSRC gave a large grant
for three years' 'action-research' in this area. One of the results of this research
has been to focus discussion on 'community schools' and the kind of curriculum
suitable for them.

1968 Inquiry into the Flow of Candidates in Science and Technology into Higher Education: Council for Scientific Policy (the Dainton Report)

The Dainton Committee was set up in 1965 to look into the 'swing from science'
in schools—especially in sixth forms.

The relative decline in the study of science and technology is, in our view, potentially
harmful both to individuals and to society. Man lives in a physical world which from
curiosity as much as necessity he seeks to understand and control. The search for
understanding of the physical world is the pursuit of science; engineering and technology make the parts of society increasingly interdependent, for example through
developments in communication and transport. As our dependence on science and
technology increases so also does everyday life become more complex; they bring new
benefits, for example in medicine and agriculture, but also generate new and powerful
concepts which are difficult to grasp without some basic scientific education. Those
who have no scientific understanding are cut off from a great human activity; and may
well feel excluded from intercourse with those who have such understanding. The study
of these subjects should form part of everyone's educational experience. Scientific
interests in young children are a natural expression of their curiosity about the world;
and they have a right to the opportunity to nurture such interest. Whatever the
subsequent careers of boys and girls now in schools may eventually be, they should for
their own sake know and appreciate something of the aims, techniques and achievements of
science and technology. (pp. 1–2)

The main recommendations of the Committee included the following points on curriculum:

> 1. There should be a broad span of studies in the sixth form of schools, and irreversible decisions for or against science, engineering and technology should be postponed as late as possible . . . (para. 174)
>
> 2. Normally, all pupils should study mathematics until they leave school; the teaching of mathematics should show the effects of associating mathematical thinking with other studies, such as experimental or engineering sciences, or with economics . . . (para. 179)
>
> 3. Breadth, humanity and up-to-dateness must be infused into the science curriculum and its teaching . . . (para. 181)
>
> 4. Schools and Local Education Authorities should take steps to ensure that within the next five years the majority of pupils in secondary education should come into early contact with good science teaching . . . (para. 182)

1968   Committee on Manpower Resources for Science and Technology. Report of the Working Group on Manpower for Scientific Growth. The Flow into Employment of Scientists, Engineers and Technologists (the Swann Report)

In the main this Report reinforced the curricular recommendations of the Dainton Report. It did also, however, emphasize the need for the social implications of science to be reflected in curricula:

> 158. Education must also instil into graduate scientists and technologists the idea that they should be prepared to use their ability in a variety of employment, where they are most needed. This willingness must spring from an appreciation of their roles in society. That the typical British education for scientists and technologists does so little to generate these qualities is, in our view, largely a consequence of its specialized nature. From the age of 15 or thereabouts these students receive little formal education outside their specialities, and it is hardly surprising that they may emerge with little knowledge of, or interest in, the problems of the society of which they are to become responsible members. They may see little place for themselves except in the specialities in which they have been trained. Are they to be blamed for preferring the academic world here or abroad (even without a permanent post) to industry or school teaching in this country? (pp. 75–6)

1972   Teacher Education and Training. Report by a Committee of Inquiry appointed by the Secretary of State for Education and Science (the James Report)

During the late 1960s there had been much discussion and some criticism of teacher training. In 1970 Area Training Organizations were asked by Edward Short, the Labour Secretary of State for Education and Science, to review their training work, but before these reports were completed the new Conservative Secretary of State, Margaret Thatcher, set up a Committee of Inquiry under the chairmanship of Lord James of Rusholme, 'to enquire into the present arrangements for the education, training and probation of teachers in England and Wales . . .'. The recommendations of the Committee included the following:

1. The education and training of teachers should be seen as falling into three consecutive stages or 'cycles': the first, personal education, the second pre-service training and induction, the third, in-service education and training.

2. The highest priority should be given to the expansion of the third cycle, i.e. of opportunities for the continued education and training of teachers.

3. The pre-service higher education and training of all teachers for the schools should extend over at least four years.

4. The initial training of teachers in the second cycle should last at least two years (one in a professional institution and one in a school), should be the same for all intending teachers in its organization and length, however much it might vary in content and style, and should lead to the same terminal award: a new professional degree of B.A.(Education).

5. Successful completion of the first year of the second cycle should lead to recognition as 'licensed teacher' and successful completion of the second year to recognition as 'registered teacher' and the award of the B.A.(Ed.).

6. Serving teachers in the schools and F.E. colleges should be directly involved in professional training and a high priority should be given to the improvement in staffing ratios which such an involvement, together with the substantial release of teachers for third cycle work, would inevitably require.

7. A new two-year qualification, the Diploma in Higher Education (Dip.H.E.), together with new three-year degrees based on and developed from it, should be introduced into the first cycle, initially in the colleges of education and the polytechnic departments of education . . . (p. 107)

1972 Education: A Framework for Expansion. DES White Paper

This White Paper (published as the government response to the James Report on Teacher Education and Training) covered all sectors of education from nursery schools to polytechnics and universities, but once again almost no mention is made of curricula in any of these institutions.

A few comments which might be interpreted as indicating some kinds of view of curriculum may be discovered; for example, on the under-fives:

19. The value of nursery education in promoting the social development of young children has long been acknowledged. In addition we now know that, given sympathetic and skilled supervision, children may also make great educational progress before the age of five. They are capable of developing further in the use of language, in thought and in practical skills than was previously supposed. Progress of this kind gives any child a sound basis for his subsequent education. (p. 5)

The White Paper was to have important effects on the curricula of colleges of education, however. One of the major recommendations was that colleges of education should generally not remain as 'monotechnic institutions'—i.e. teachers should be educated side-by-side with non-teachers. This policy, combined with the fact that fewer teachers would be required, forced many colleges to adopt a unit or modular structure for their B.Ed. courses (so that some units could be common courses for B.A./B.Sc./Dip.H.E. programmes). This has brought about very important changes in the curricula and methods of assessment in many colleges. The White Paper also encouraged colleges to drift away from University validation to the Council for National Academic Awards (CNAA).

1975   A Language for Life. Report of the Committee of Inquiry appointed by the Secretary of State for Education and Science (the Bullock Report)

The Committee's first term of reference was to consider in relation to schools 'all aspects of teaching the use of English, including reading, writing and speech'. It interpreted its brief as *language in education*, beginning with the influence of the home in pre-school years and ranging from the growth of language and reading ability in the early stages to the teaching of English in secondary schools. The Report was based upon the principle that reading, writing, talking and listening should be treated as a unity, and that there should be continuity across the years. Reading, which is often discussed as if it were a separable activity, is seen in the Report as part of a child's general language development and not as a discrete skill to be considered in isolation from it. A main argument of the Report is that there is no one method that holds the key to the process of learning to read, and that there is no substitute for a thorough understanding of all the factors at work.

Chapter 12 of the Report is concerned with 'Language across the Curriculum'. The Committee believed that a stimulating classroom environment, although very important, would not of itself develop children's ability to use language as an instrument of learning. The teacher has a vital part to play and his role should be one of planned intervention. The Report made suggestions about the form this might take and considered in detail the operation of small group work and its relation to large group situations. An important aim in English and other subjects is to increase the complexity of the child's thinking, so that he does not rest on the mere expression of opinion but uses language in an exploratory way. A child's accent should be accepted and attempts should not be made to suppress it. The aim should be to provide pupils with awareness and flexibility. Children should be helped to as wide as possible a range of language uses so that they can speak appropriately in different situations and use standard forms when they are needed. Language work should take place within a purposeful context, through which the pupil is led to a greater control over his writing and growing know-ledge of how to vary its effects.

Throughout the Report the point was made that all teachers, whatever their subject or the age-range they teach, should be involved in developing the lan-guage ability of their pupils. In the primary school the individual teacher is in a position to devise a language policy across the various aspects of the curriculum, but there remains the need for a general school policy to give expression to the aim and ensure consistency throughout the years of primary schooling. In the secondary school all subject teachers need to be aware of the linguistic process by which their pupils acquire information and understanding, and the implications for the teacher's own use of language. They also need an explicit understanding of the reading demands of their own subjects, and ways in which the pupil can be helped to meet them. The chapter devoted to elaborating these ideas proposed that to bring about this understanding every secondary school should develop a policy for language across the curriculum, the responsibility for which should be embodied in the organizational structure of the school.

1975 Sex Discrimination Act

On 29 December 1975 the Sex Discrimination Act came into operation. From that time it became possible for parents of girls (and boys) to use the machinery of the Equal Opportunities Commission to challenge any kind of sex discrimination in schools, colleges and universities. It became possible, for example, for a girl's parents to bring to the attention of the Commission any decision made by teachers or administrative staff which prevented the girl from studying any aspect of the school curriculum, such as science or woodwork.

One probable result of this legislation is that schools, and possibly the profession as a whole, will find it necessary to draw up a rationale of the curriculum or a code of practice, defining some subjects as essential for all and others as optional. Without some kind of consensus on what must be included in any curriculum it is difficult to see how an individual could be regarded as being deprived of an essential benefit.

In other respects the discussion of boys' and girls' curricula is likely to develop some of the issues raised by the 1923 Report of the Consultative Committee on Differentiation of the Curricula for Boys and Girls in Secondary School.

The Schools Council for the Curriculum and Examinations

Since 1964 the Schools Council has not only been responsible for the work previously carried out by the SSEC and the Ministry's Curriculum Study Group, but has also become the most important source of finance for curriculum development and research in England and Wales.

The following report on the work of the Schools Council is not meant to be a full description or history of the Council; it is merely a commentary on selected publications which seem to us to have made some kind of contribution to current thinking about curriculum or which represented an important point of view when they were published. (A complete and up-to-date list of publications and curriculum projects may be obtained from the Schools Council Information Centre, 160 Great Portland Street, London W.1.)

In 1963 Sir Edward Boyle, the Minister of Education, chaired a meeting to discuss the need for some kind of cooperative organization to guide the development of curricula and examinations in schools. As a result, a Working Party under Sir John Lockwood was set up to make recommendations. The Lockwood Report suggested the title, 'The Schools Council for the Curriculum and Examinations'; the Report also recommended that this Council should take over the functions of the SSEC in September 1964. These recommendations were accepted.

From the beginning the Schools Council has emphasized that its role is not to determine schools' curricula, but to make available a wide choice of materials and suggestions. A list of priorities was soon established where it was felt that guidance or a wider range of choices was needed:

1. The primary school curriculum
2. The curriculum for the early leaver
3. The sixth form
4. The English programme
5. Examinations for the 16 + age group

We shall consider each of these in turn.

1. The Primary Curriculum

The Council took as its guiding light the Plowden Report (1967) including the recommended new structure of first and middle schools. Thus most projects and reports are labelled either '5–13' if they cover both age-ranges or '8–13' if they are middle-year projects. The projects which have made some impact on curriculum re-thinking include: Science 5–13, Social Studies 8–13, and a general report on *The Middle Years of Schooling*.

2. The 'Early Leaver'

Much of this work followed on from some of the recommendations of the Newsom Report (1963). The major recommendation of this Report was that the school-leaving age should be raised to 16. One of the best documents produced by the Schools Council dealt with this issue: Working Paper No. 2, 'Raising the School Leaving Age: a Cooperative Programme of Research and Development' (1965).

The Pupils

33. . . . More of the same will not bring success. It is not the 'extra year' that makes the difference; the opportunities of a five-year course are totally different from those of a four-year course. They require new assumptions, attitudes and understandings, and a new approach to the development of a five-year course which will be truly secondary in character. (p. 8)

48. What is at issue is, therefore, the bringing of the best traditional view of what constitutes a liberal education within the grasp of ordinary people. When every man is King how does he become enough of a philosopher to wield power wisely? When every man is aware, as all are today at least in some degree, of the complexity of the world in which we live, how can every man be helped to gain some kind of access to a complex cultural inheritance? How can all be brought to have some kind of hold on their personal lives, and on their place in, and contribution to, the various communities—family, neighbourhood, club, occupational, national and international—in which they play a part? And what are the limits to what the schools can hope to achieve? (p. 11)

53. The view of the curriculum put forward in this paper is therefore holistic. It is suggested that it should possess organic unity, and that the organizing principle most likely to provide a sound basis for development is the study of Man, and of human society, needs and purposes. (p. 12)

A number of publications and curriculum development projects concerned with aspects of the education of 'the young school leaver' followed on from this basic Report.

In 1967 appeared Working Paper No. 11, 'Society and the Young School Leaver: A Humanities Programme in Preparation for the Raising of the School-Leaving Age'. This Working Paper arose directly out of the recommendations contained in Working Paper No. 2, but the attempt to translate these ideals into practical terms was not generally regarded as a success. Some educationists, such as John White, did not see the new 'humanities' as 'the bringing of the best . . . within the grasp of ordinary people' (Working Paper No. 2) but as fobbing off pupils with low-status knowledge.

The Council also commissioned a survey of the attitudes of teachers, pupils and parents towards ROSLA. The report—*Inquiry 1*—gives some very important information which has sometimes been interpreted in a negatively 'child-centred' way (e.g. suggesting that because pupils do not see the point of some subjects this is a valid argument for omitting them from the curriculum).

Nevertheless within the 'early leaver' programme a number of important projects were financed: Geography for the Young School Leaver; Integrated Studies; Mathematics for the Majority; Integrated Science; Project Technology; Moral Education; and Religious Education. The Council also gave support to a local project based on a group of fifteen Teachers' Centres—the North-West Regional Curriculum Development Project. Teachers have cooperated to bring out handbooks of curriculum objectives for ten subjects or curriculum areas. This objectives approach to the curriculum is highly controversial, but the method of teacher involvement is of very great interest.

Much of the discussion of these curriculum innovations is summarized in a report of a conference held in 1969 which was published as Schools Council Working Paper No. 33, 'Choosing a Curriculum for the Young School Leaver'.

3. The Sixth Form

The key publication in this area was Schools Council Working Paper No. 5 (1966), 'Sixth-Form Curriculum and Examinations'. Two major problems were involved: first, the 'new sixth forms' which would include large proportions of students for whom A levels would be unsuitable; second, the excessive specialization common to sixth forms which was in urgent need of reform. In 1967 a progress report was published showing the agreement reached between schools' representatives and universities: Schools Council Working Paper No. 16, 'Some Further Proposals for Sixth-Form Work' (1967). The agreement included the desirability of a broader sixth-form curriculum with specialization coming as late as possible. In 1968 a joint statement of two working parties was presented to the Schools Council and the Standing Conference on University Entrance— 'Proposals for the Curriculum and Examinations in the Sixth Form'—but this was not accepted. After further discussions three more Working Papers were published: Working Paper No. 45, '16–19 Growth and Response, 1: Curricular Bases' (1972); Working Paper No. 46, 'Growth and Response, 2: Examination Structures' (1973); Working Paper No. 47, 'Preparation for Degree Courses'. These proposals for a broader sixth-form curriculum generated much controversy but in July 1974 the Schools Council decided that the proposal for a five-subject, two-tier ('Normal and Further') examination structure had attracted enough support to warrant the initiation of studies of possible types of syllabuses and assessment techniques but without operational trials.

The Council, in 1970, had also recommended that the problem of the 'new sixth former' should be met by the development of an extended CSE examination—the Certificate of Extended Education (CEE).

4. English

The programme for research associated with the teaching of English in primary and secondary schools was outlined in Schools Council Working Paper No. 3, 'A Programme for Research and Development in English Teaching'. Some of this work anticipated the findings of the Bullock Report, especially the 'Developmental Study of Difference in Writing Abilities among Eleven to Eighteen Year Olds', and 'Oracy'. Other projects included 'Language in Use', 'English for Immigrant Children' and 'Teaching English to West Indian Children'.

5. GCE, CSE (and a common examination at 16+)

The Beloe Report (1960) had recommended a new examination for pupils for whom GCE was unsuitable (i.e. the 40 per cent below the top 20 per cent in the ability range). In 1965 the first Certificate of Secondary Education (CSE) examination was conducted by nine of the fourteen regional boards set up in 1963–4. In 1965, 66,000 candidates were examined; by 1974 this figure had increased to 516,000 (Modes 1, 2 and 3). A CSE Grade 1 was established as equivalent to a GCE O level pass.

By 1970 the Schools Council recommended that there should be a single examination at 16+: feasibility studies in a range of subjects and boards were mounted, and a special unit—the Central Examinations Research and Development Unit (CERDU)—was set up to monitor developments. The results of the feasibility studies were published in 1975 and were sufficiently positive to justify going ahead with a project for a common system of examining. This should be of considerable assistance to schools operating a common curriculum up to sixteen.

After ten years' existence the Schools Council would appear to have had a mixture of success and failure: a vast number of Working Papers, Examinations Bulletins and other publications have been produced, but the quality has been uneven.

A final verdict on the Schools Council must await the degree of success with which the Council tackles the task of involving a much higher percentage of teachers in its work, and also in establishing some kind of common basis of discussion on curriculum throughout the teaching profession which will avoid the need for legislative control.

Social and Educational Theories Influencing the Curriculum

Introduction

An early draft of this chapter had as its main purpose an examination of the views of educational theorists on curriculum and how these views affected what happened in schools. In retrospect this intention seems naïve: we very soon discovered that it was extremely difficult to find many direct links between theory and practice in the curriculum field. Decisions affecting the curriculum have usually been made by politicians, administrators and teachers in a pragmatic way. This is not to say that there is no connection between the prevailing social and educational ideas at any particular time and changes which take place in the curriculum, only that the relationship is a very complex one. For example, one of the most influential politician–administrators in the nineteenth century was Robert Lowe, often classified as a Utilitarian, but Sylvester in his book *Robert Lowe and Education* (1974) makes this point:

> Lowe published no substantial volume of educational theory. His educational views arose in the heat of the day: in debate, in pamphlets or in newspaper articles upon some current issue. They were grounded in the political and social realities of his time. They were closely related to Lowe's general views on the nature of society, politics and economics. To understand them they must be seen in this wider context. (p. 14)

The intention of this chapter is now to see the curriculum changes outlined briefly in Chapter 1 against a background of political and social reality of which educational theory is only one aspect. The inter-connection between educational theory and other kinds of social thinking has been hinted at by other writers on educational theory. For example, T. W. Moore in *Educational Theory: An Introduction* (1974) has suggested that general theories of education must include at least three elements: assumptions about the nature of *man* and particularly of children; assumptions about educational ends or *aims*, often interpreted as an idea of what kind of person should be regarded as educated; and assumptions about *knowledge* and the relative value of different kinds of knowledge. Clearly these kinds of assumption do not arise in a social vacuum, but will be either a reflection of current social thinking or a reaction against it. We are not concerned in this book with educational theory in general, only with those aspects of educational theory which have some kind of influence on school curricula. However, we must sometimes look at the prevailing educational theories and see what relationship these have with other kinds of ideology or theory which are current at that particular time.

In Chapter 1 we started our chronological account of curriculum change at the beginning of the nineteenth century. Lawson and Silver (1973) suggest (p. 226) that by 1780 education had become one of the main areas of conflict in the changing society. The conflict was not simply a struggle between educational traditionalists and a new wave of progressives. Those who wanted changes in education were not agreed on the nature and extent of these changes, and wanted change for a wide range of motives. Similarly those resisting educational changes did so for a variety of reasons.

Although we realize that it is somewhat artificial to force historical events into a mould set by dates of educational importance, it is nevertheless useful for our limited purpose to tell the curriculum story from the end of the eighteenth century in five stages which we label as follows:

1. 1800–33: the conflicting groups and issues emerge
2. 1833–70: the triumph of Utilitarianism: an inferior curriculum for the lower orders
3. 1870–1902: the elementary curriculum—growth and decline
4. 1902–44: from elementary curriculum to primary and secondary curricula
5. 1944–77: towards a comprehensive curriculum

Our suggestion is that for each of these stages the educational and curriculum changes should be seen as arising out of a conflict between changing sets of ideas or ideologies: political, economic, social and educational.

There are obvious difficulties in this attempt. We have deliberately defined our ideologies rather widely, and one problem is that even at any one time the character of, say, political radicalism is not clear-cut. At any one period there are conflicting views within an ideology. There is, moreover, never a simple tale to tell of victory and defeat between the ideologies: much more common is a partial advance, a temporary retreat and a re-grouping. But out of all the conflict at an ideological level we suggest that the educational and curricular changes are to some extent a reflection of these wider social and political ideas.

We introduce educational theorists at points where we feel their influence to be important rather than in chronological order.

1.   1800–33: the conflicting groups and issues emerge

We begin our account by outlining some of the background to the first government grant for education in 1833, which we regard as an event of major educational significance.

Political radicalism

The Industrial Revolution had produced a whole catalogue of social problems such as poverty, over-crowding in towns, as well as a lack of any apparent responsibility for dealing with such problems. In addition the French Revolution of 1789 had stimulated the already existing pressure for parliamentary reform. The group referred to as political radicals were concerned with both social and political reform, and they saw education as an extremely important part of any reform programme. One of their basic beliefs about human nature was that human beings could be improved—perhaps to the point of perfectibility—by means of education. Such writers as Tom Paine, Mary Wollstonecraft, William Godwin, Erasmus Darwin and Joseph Priestley were influenced by the views of the English philosopher Locke as well as the continental thinkers who had influenced the French Revolution such as Helvetius. In dealing with the beginning of the nineteenth century it is sometimes difficult to make satisfactory distinctions between the political radicals who are the predecessors of working-class radicalism and socialism, and the middle-class radicals whom we will consider below under the general heading of philosophical radicals and Utilitarians; all were proposing changes in education and some were anxious to improve the curriculum.

Philosophical radicals and Utilitarianism

One of the major social changes which had taken place in English society by the beginning of the nineteenth century was that industrialization had largely broken down feudal ties which had associated the privileges of a socially superior aristocracy and gentry with certain duties and responsibilities towards their subordinates. The market attitude to workers by which they were regarded as so many hands rather than human beings meant that the only link between master and servant was the cash nexus. This change was greatly regretted by many conservative thinkers, but by the beginning of the nineteenth century, two related kinds of justification for the new order were available—the *laissez-faire* economics of Adam Smith, and the Utilitarian philosophy of Jeremy Bentham, James Mill and John Stuart Mill. *Laissez-faire* economics was predominantly concerned with efficiency, whereas Utilitarian philosophy was concerned with happiness (though in practice it often seemed to amount to the same thing). Both views justified the new industrial social order by the argument that society was better without government interference and legislation. One of the very few exceptions was education, which most Utilitarians and *laissez-faire* economists regarded as a justifiable subject for state intervention on grounds of human investment or for the greatest happiness of the greatest number. Thus the Utilitarians at the beginning of the nineteenth century supported monitorial schools for the poor, the reform of secondary education and a non-denominational university in London. The Utilitarians, for reasons of order and stability, advocated different kinds of education and different kinds of curricula for the different levels in society. Sound and cheap instruction in obedience for the lower orders; a curriculum for leadership for the middle classes. For all levels the curriculum should consist of 'useful knowledge'.

The most important theorists on education in the Utilitarian camp were James Mill (1773–1836) and Jeremy Bentham (1748–1832). James Mill's views on education as a means of developing powers of reason were of very great impor-

'usefulness'

tance and influence. Bentham also emphasized human rationality as the key factor in education. His book *Chrestomathia* (1815) was a collection of papers on useful learning based on the felicific calculus, or the greatest happiness of the greatest number. The most systematic version of Utilitarian educational theory was, however, James Mill's essay 'On Education' published in the *Encyclopaedia Britannica* (1818).

James Mill attempted to explain man's mental behaviour in the light of the psychological theories of his day. One of his basic assumptions was that man is essentially selfish and will only become social as a result of careful training. This was connected with another assumption, namely that at birth the child's mind is a blank—or *tabula rasa*—which develops as a product of what is fed into it. This process begins with simple sensory impressions followed by more complex learning which takes place by the process of association.

For the Utilitarians the main aim of education was to increase the sum of human happiness and to diminish pain. This view has sometimes been unfairly criticized as too naïve, but it should be stressed that they saw happiness not necessarily as immediate satisfaction but as long-term benefit to humanity as a whole. Thus an important means of increasing man's happiness was to develop his rationality by means of education. The qualities necessary for happiness to be fostered by education were sagacity, temperance, justice and generosity.

James Mill saw the need for an explicit theory of knowledge to illuminate educational practice, and his theory of knowledge is closely connected with the assumptions he made about the nature of the human mind. Following these assumptions the curriculum and teaching methods were advocated. According to Mill the origin of all knowledge is sense experience. The principle of association is the means by which knowledge is built up, extended and diversified; language is a key factor in the process of knowledge acquisition by association.

Another Utilitarian assumption was that knowledge could be divided into useful knowledge and the kind of less important knowledge which could be ignored in education. James Mill, for example, was particularly opposed to the idea that knowledge has a value in itself—it must always have some social use.

These views of knowledge and the purpose of education led to the idea of a relevant curriculum. Jeremy Bentham was perhaps more explicit on this than James Mill. Bentham advocated science and technology as more relevant to the needs of society than the traditional classical curriculum. James Mill, however, in his own practical attempts at curriculum planning—notably the curriculum laid down for his eldest son John Stuart Mill—was more orthodox, starting with Greek at the age of three.

Despite their almost entirely theoretical quality—attempts to establish a Benthamite school foundered on practical problems—Utilitarian ideas on curriculum were influential throughout the nineteenth and twentieth centuries, and the criterion of 'usefulness' is often applied to education today.

Social and political conservatism

We do not confine 'conservative' to the Tory or Conservative Party but use 'conservative' to cover the wide variety of groups of people who believe that society is about as good as it can be and that changes are likely to make conditions worse rather than better. Our definition of 'conservative' would also include those who believe, with the Duke of Cambridge, that the right time for change is when it can no longer be resisted. At the beginning of the nineteenth century it would include the Tory Party, a large section of the Whig Party and also the Church of England evangelical movement. This group tended to accept, albeit reluctantly, the changes that had taken place in society as a result of the Industrial Revolution, but wanted to use education to preserve traditional Christian values and the traditional English way of life as much as possible. According to Lawson and Silver (1973) this group (which developed within the Church of England in the late eighteenth century) aimed 'not to adapt people to new conditions, but consciously to warn against social and moral dangers, in order to reinforce traditional religious codes of behaviour. It was a movement at once to redeem an apathetic church, to educate an illiterate populace and to protect the social order' (p. 231).

In some ways this movement had started earlier in the eighteenth century with the work of John Wesley himself (1703–91). Wesley's assumptions about the nature of men and children were very clear. Man is naturally depraved and wicked. Original sin may be wiped away by baptism but after that there is still a constant struggle between the temptations of the Devil, the world and the flesh, and the will to resist evil which is only developed by overcoming the child's natural tendency to succumb. Wesley's views on the aims of education followed from his views on human nature. The purpose of a school was to convert or redeem souls.

The kind of knowledge appropriate to this kind of education followed logically. Put in its simplest form, knowledge was divided into the godly and the ungodly. More specifically, drama and secular music were ungodly, and there was a certain general suspicion of learning as being worldly. The only really safe knowledge was studying the Bible, and some extremists wanted education to contain nothing more. The Classics were more than doubtful, having been written by heathens. The curriculum of Kingswood School, founded by Wesley, consisted of reading, writing, arithmetic, English, French, Latin, Greek, Hebrew, history, geography, chronology, rhetoric, logic, ethics, geometry, algebra, physics and music. This was, of course, a middle-class curriculum. Together with nearly all eighteenth-century evangelical educationists, Wesley felt that it was God's will to provide a less ambitious curriculum for the lower orders. Wesley and his later followers saw education as a means of disciplining the masses; the curriculum therefore should be clearly defined and basic. Evangelical education reformers such as Hannah More were at great pains to point out that education for the lower orders should not be too good:

> My plan for instructing the poor is very limited and strict. They learn of weekdays such coarse work as may fit them for servants. I allow for no writing. My object has not been

in teaching dogmas and opinions, but to form the lower class to habits of industry and virtue. (Hannah More, *Annals*, 1859 ed., pp. 6–9)

The Evangelicals formed societies (for example, the Society for the Suppression of Vice) which prosecuted books such as those of Tom Paine. According to Lawson and Silver (p. 232) two million copies of Hannah More's tracts were sold in 1795. This group was generally opposed to government involvement in education, believing that education should remain in the hands of the Church of England, and that state interference would mean a secular curriculum. The curriculum, in their view, should concentrate on reading of religious tracts and the Bible; writing was not necessary.

Other conservative influences included those who were opposed to education for the lower orders for a variety of other reasons. Some felt that education of the masses would encourage them to develop ideas above their station; some objected to education for the poor being paid for by ratepayers and taxpayers; and many members of the middle classes objected to paying for education for lower-class children who would compete with their own children for jobs in society. Thus education for the poor should either be resisted or kept in the hands of the churches and paid for by voluntary subscriptions.

The 1833 grant was a defeat for these groups but not a total victory for many of the reformers who wanted a *state* system of education, not just help towards its running costs.

Educational theories

The education radicals of the eighteenth century were involved in the attack on what A. A. Evans has described as the traditional view of education which had four main propositions: that children are by nature evil; that the function of education is to prepare the child for adult life; that educational knowledge is the knowledge needed by an educated adult; that the main value of learning is its moral and intellectual training—intrinsic interests being totally unimportant. (W. A. C. Stewart, *Progressives and Radicals in English Education 1790–1970*, 1972, p. 21.)

The educational theorist whose views attacking the classical Christian tradition were most lasting was Rousseau (1712–78). In many respects his ideas—or some of them—have dominated progressive education ever since. Rousseau's assumptions about the nature of man (and especially the nature of children) were that man is naturally good but may be, and usually is, corrupted by his social institutions. Children should be seen not as miniature adults but as individuals passing through stages which were important in their own right, not merely as preparation for adult life.

On the question of the aims of education Rousseau demanded that education should not teach children to fit into society but to be free from its shackles. In a good society which followed the 'general will' an adult would obey, but this would be obedience to his own rational self as expressed in the laws. In the ideal society, adults would thus be both social and free, but one task of education was to avoid premature, irrational obedience by children.

As for educational knowledge, Rousseau felt that knowledge of nature, not of books, was what young children needed. He also had a good deal to say about how children should learn, again providing slogans for child-centred educationists ever since:

A man must know many things which seem useless to a child, but need the child learn, or indeed can he learn, all that the man must know? Try to teach the child what is of use to a child and you will find that it takes all his time. Why urge him to the studies of an age he may never reach, to the neglect of those studies which meet his present needs? (*Emile*, 1911 edn., p. 175)

In England Rousseau's ideas, even when accepted enthusiastically, were treated in a pragmatic way. All the recorded examples of pure Rousseau experiments were failures—for example, Thomas Day and Richard Lovell Edgeworth both tried to bring up children to demonstrate Rousseau's principles, but both failed. Nevertheless many of Rousseau's ideas have persisted in progressive education literature up to and beyond the Plowden Report. But in the early nineteenth century Rousseau was ignored in all the official reports and documents, and the educational radicals played little part in the changes which took place up to 1833; their influence was to be of a long-term nature.

It is most important to emphasize that the followers of Rousseau in England, like Rousseau himself, were not concerned with mass or popular education, nor with education as an element of more general social reform. The British educational radicals were middle-class intellectuals carrying out experiments on small groups of middle-class children, often their own. They had unorthodox views on human nature and how children should be brought up, but it would have seemed totally unrealistic to them to suppose that similar treatment, and a similar curriculum, could be made available for all children. Thinking of that kind developed in a very different way later, stimulated by Robert Owen and others.

Summary 1800–33

The major issue up to this time, and beyond, was the controversy about the provision of popular or mass education. On this the supporters of educational reform were not united, and they were, of course, faced by strong opposition. By 1833 none of the issues had been resolved but some critical decisions had been made. Little progress had been made on curriculum change, but government intervention was assured even though the grant was made by political subterfuge rather than straightforward Act of Parliament (see Chapter 1). The fact that Lord Althorp's manoeuvring succeeded where Brougham's and Roebuck's radicalism failed is itself not without significance. For many in both Houses of Parliament educational reform was still associated with revolution. But when the major breakthrough of government intervention had been made the real question of the curriculum emerged.

2.   1833–70: the triumph of Utilitarianism: an inferior curriculum for the lower orders

As we saw in Chapter 1, the year 1833 was a major landmark in government intervention in education. This was a partial victory for the Utilitarians and others who favoured state intervention. Some saw this first government grant as the end of the story of state intervention—as a way of helping the voluntary bodies to provide schools; a second group saw the grant as a first step towards more, but limited, government intervention; and others saw the grant as a step towards a real system of national elementary education for all. The thirty years after 1833 saw the continuance of this debate which was largely an argument about the quality and range of curriculum content. A second major controversy in this period was the question of the secondary school and its curriculum.

From Radicalism to Socialism

The ideas of Robert Owen (1771–1858) were of importance, direct or indirect, throughout the nineteenth century.

In 1813 Owen published *New View of Society* which was in many respects not very different from the ideas of Utilitarians such as James Mill and Francis Place. At this time Owen was mainly concerned with poverty, and he felt that it was possible to combine efficient industry with humane treatment of workers. Since a large proportion of the workforce consisted of children, it was necessary for him to develop a policy for educating children, and the treatment of children at New Lanark became a model for the rest of the country.

Owen's basic assumption about human nature was that 'man's character is formed *for* him, and not *by* him'. This kind of environmentalism was based on the views of Priestley and James Mill, but he combined with it a care for humanity and social justice which many of the Utilitarians lacked.

As for the aims of education, Owen was equally clear. An educated person should have a rational understanding of the physical and social world. Thus much of what was traditionally regarded as educational knowledge was useless: religious stories and the Classics were mere superstitions. For Owen the curriculum should consist of science, history and geography taught by interesting methods, as well as music and other subjects which would enrich leisure time.

Owen's educational theories might be thought by some to be less fully worked out than those of James Mill, for example. But he had the advantage over most theorists of putting his theories into practice, especially in New Lanark school from 1816 to 1824. His views on education were, of course, part of a much bigger plan for reforming society which he later called socialism: the idea that competition should be replaced by cooperation, exploitation by social harmony and the elimination of the excesses of the division of labour.

He was by no means the only 'socialist' writer of importance. Brian Simon's *Studies in the History of Education 1780–1870* contains accounts of many other influential early socialist thinkers, such as Richard Carlile who, in his *Address to*

Men of Science (1821), appealed for a science-based popular curriculum, and William Thompson (1785–1833) who recommended that the working class needed to understand how their society worked as well as the scientific nature of the universe.

By 1833, however, such writing had not influenced the curriculum either of secondary schools or of the embryo elementary schools, but many of the ideas became part of the mid-century debate and may have had a long-term influence on working-class radicalism and education. 'Socialist' views on education generally advocated a national system of elementary education with a reformed curriculum: it was certainly not achieved by 1870, but much of what happened in this period may be seen as a reaction—usually hostile—to Owenite ideas.

After the 1832 Parliamentary Reform Act had clearly excluded the working classes from the franchise there was a sharpening of the distinction between middle-class and working-class radicalism. Working-class radicalism moved in the direction of Owenite socialism, Chartism and trade unionism, all three of which included educational reform as important aspects of their programmes.

The growing Owenite Cooperative Movement in the 1830s stressed the importance of classes for adult workers and schools for children, with an emphasis on useful knowledge such as mathematics, science and politics. Free libraries and news rooms were also aspects of the educational programme of several cooperative societies. Owenite socialism tended to collapse in the mid-1830s but many of the cooperative society activities continued and certainly the ideal of working-class education was by then well based.

The Chartist movement, apart from advocating parliamentary reform, was also developing its own programme of 'self-culture'. For example, *Chartism: A New Organization of the People* (1841), published by William Lovett and John Collins, advocated a national system of schools and adult education. Chartists and other working-class radicals were extremely dissatisfied with the provision of education for the majority of the population and wanted much more government intervention and in the long run free compulsory education for all children. In the meantime they organized their own classes and libraries. Chartism also began to decline in the 1840s and by 1850 was a spent political and social force, but the ideals had been established, and became part of the 'labour movement' tradition.

Trade union interest in education began with the Owenite unions of the 1830s, but intensified with the growth of the 'new model' trade unions of the 1850s. For example, Robert Applegarth of the Amalgamated Society of Carpenters and Joiners combined with other trade unionists to campaign for a national system of education, and they were strong supporters of the National Education League (1868). Individual unions also ran classes for their own members, both of a technical kind and for more general education. The Trades Union Congress, which was founded in 1868, immediately concerned itself with education and the demand for a national system of free and compulsory schooling.

None of these movements by 1870 had made any direct impact on either the primary or secondary curriculum of the time. The nearest they came to influencing government policy was in their support of the views of the Utilitarians who demanded a national system of education. This came about in 1870 with Forster's

Education Act—a great disappointment to the radicals who wanted much stronger intervention and an immediate, free, compulsory system of elementary education.

From Utilitarianism to Liberalism

The Utilitarians generally had supported the 1833 grant as a necessary government intervention into mass education. They had also supported the monitorial system and the kind of curriculum which would encourage the lower classes to function efficiently in their allotted place in society. They stressed the idea of efficiency in education and it was regarded as important in an industrial society for the government to intervene. Throughout this period Utilitarianism was certainly the dominant social theory; the real question now became how this theory would be interpreted and put into practice. Between 1833 and 1870 the two most important figures in this debate were Dr J. P. Kay and Robert Lowe. Both of them would be classified as Utilitarians but their policy was noticeably different on crucial questions. Kay was the more humane figure and his major insight was that the curriculum was nothing without good teachers; Lowe was a forerunner of the worst kind of twentieth-century curriculum planner—who believes that if the curriculum is carefully packaged then teachers are unimportant.

Dr J. P. Kay (later Sir James Kay-Shuttleworth) was the first Secretary of the Privy Council Committee for Education from 1839 to 1849. Before this he had been a doctor working in the Manchester slums and an Assistant Poor Law Commissioner. These experiences had convinced him of the need for working-class education, partly for humanitarian reasons and partly as a means of avoiding revolution. He had a particular dislike of working-class movements such as Chartism which he saw as 'an armed political monster' indoctrinating the young with revolutionary ideas. He saw state intervention as a means of counteracting such movements and controlling the curriculum: 'If they [the working classes] are to have knowledge, surely it is the part of a wise and virtuous government to do all in its power to secure them useful knowledge and to guard them against pernicious opinions'. (Letter from Kay to Lord John Russell in 1839, quoted by B. Simon, 1960, p. 338.) It would be wrong, however, to classify Kay as one who simply wanted to use education to keep the working classes in their place. He also had a genuine desire to improve their standards, although he saw this in the conventional Utilitarian framework of his time. We saw in Chapter 1 how Kay was largely responsible for replacing the monitorial method of teaching by the more enlightened pupil-teacher scheme. Training colleges for teachers offered them a curriculum which combined personal education with the skills necessary to transmit knowledge to their pupils. Kay was also personally interested in teaching method as well as the content of the curriculum and he was to some extent influenced by the views of Pestalozzi (see below).

Between the years 1849 when Kay-Shuttleworth resigned as Secretary and 1859 when Robert Lowe became Vice-President the debate about popular education continued. The major concern was the quality and content of mass education as well as the familiar religious question. These debates resulted in the Newcastle Committee being set up in 1858.

Robert Lowe was a much more tough-minded advocate of Utilitarianism than Kay and his name is most often associated with the restricted curriculum of the Revised Code and payment by results. For this reason he has generally been criticized as an arch-reactionary in education. We suggest, however, that it is quite unhistorical to treat Lowe as a 'monster', and that he should rather be regarded as simply an efficient, clear-minded advocate of the dominant philosophy of his time, Utilitarianism. Lowe did not despise the working class any more than did most members of his own upper-middle class and, as Sylvester (1974) shows, he was a meritocrat rather than a reactionary advocate of patronage; evidence of this is provided, for example, by his support for the Civil Service reforms of 1869–73. He believed that the best and wisest men should rule, and that these qualities correlated very highly with ownership of property: on this he was a typical Victorian liberal. His desire for economy in government expenditure generally, and educational expenditure in particular, was merely an orthodox Utilitarian view shared by Gladstone and most Liberal politicians of his time. On the question of the 1862 Revised Code Lowe behaved predictably: the 1833 grant had been £20,000 but by 1861 it had risen to over £800,000; the Newcastle Report supported some of the criticisms about inefficiency in the way this money was used; inspectors appeared to be too lenient. The Revised Code of 1862 was a straightforward application of Utilitarian philosophy and Adam Smith's economics to achieve value for money.

A more just criticism of Lowe is that he underestimated (or chose to ignore) the effects the Revised Code would have on teacher training. It might be argued that given the teaching force available at the time, concentration on a basic curriculum in schools was a reasonable expedient; but to reduce the quality of the teacher training programme and its curriculum was far more damaging. A criticism of Utilitarian philosophy is that it is mechanistic; Lowe's application of the philosophy to education is certainly open to this criticism: 'The colleges, as the Principal of St Mark's College, Chelsea put it, should educate men not machines and provide a class of free agents not "the caste of elementary schoolmasters" '. (Sylvester, op. cit., p. 76.) His policy tended to reduce curriculum planning to a mechanical formula and teachers to drill sergeants. As a result the curriculum was impoverished, and learning in elementary schools became 'mechanical'.

When it came to the secondary curriculum, however, Lowe was much more enlightened, and is regarded by Sylvester as a curriculum reformer and 'the father of curriculum theory':

> We must invent for ourselves a sort of new science—a science of weights and measures; of ponderation, if I may coin a word—in which we shall put into the scales all the different objects of human knowledge, and decide upon their relative importance. All knowledge is valuable, and there is nothing that is not worthwhile to know; but it is a question of relative importance—not decrying this branch of knowledge and praising and puffing that—but of taking as far as possible the whole sense of human knowledge, and deciding what should have priority, which should be taught first and to which our attention should be most urgently directed.
>
> (Lowe, *Primary and Classical Education*, 1867, p. 13)

Sylvester suggests that Lowe put forward four basic principles to guide his 'ponderation'. First, 'As we live in a universe of things and not of words, the knowledge of things is more important to us than the knowledge of words'. This would justify science rather than ancient languages, for example, and also have important implications for teaching method. Second, 'It was more important to know what is true than false'. Again a criticism of classical studies in secondary schools which might be replaced by the history of England. Third, Lowe suggested that utility should be one of the main criteria for selecting curriculum content, 'As we cannot teach people everything, it is more important that we should teach them practical things than speculative things' (ibid., p. 14). Fourth, 'The present is more important to us than the past' (ibid., p. 23). He felt that pupils should be taught where Australia was rather than the geography of ancient Greece.

Some of these ideas are, of course, very similar to Herbert Spencer's essay, 'What Knowledge is of Most Worth?', which was first published as an article in the *Westminster Review* in 1859. Lowe, however, is often not given credit for applying Utilitarian philosophy to the curriculum in this way. In other respects Lowe's policies show a regrettable lack of knowledge of educational theory. He had, for example, an exaggerated faith in the power of examinations to discriminate and select. Despite his own personal involvement in education and great interest in it, he lacked the insights of Kay-Shuttleworth and HMIs such as Matthew Arnold into the real purpose of education and the true relationship between teacher and pupils. It is difficult completely to refute the charge that he seemed to desire not only a different kind of education for the masses but also an inferior curriculum.

Conservatism: from complete opposition to containment

Conservatism was to some extent still identified with the Church of England which resisted most educational innovation during this period; but there were other, more general, social and political ideologies resisting change. During this period religious conservatism was beginning to be less important than social and economic conservatism associated with the growing class of industrialists employing labour.

The Church of England in 1839 resisted the powers of the new Privy Council Committee for Education, especially the influence that inspectors would have over the curriculum; they resisted Kay's new plans for training teachers and all attempts to have a national, secular system of elementary education. They gradually lost their influence, however, and even the 1862 Revised Code was a hidden victory for secular education inasmuch as it brought about a switch of emphasis from the study of Scripture to more basic work on the three Rs.

This period also saw a hardening of the class structure and the beginning of bitter class conflict, all of which was reflected in educational reform and the resistance to it.

> Some such startling defeat of the Chartists was inevitable, even if the leadership had been wiser. The enemy, the capitalist class, which the Chartists were attacking, was

enormously stronger than they believed. It was nothing like the feeble landowners who had surrounded George IV. So far from being in decay, it had during this period, and the immediately subsequent years, begun to use fully its economic powers of expansion for the first time and had provided itself with legal instruments which enabled its progress to astonish the world.

(G. D. H. Cole and R. Postgate, *The Common People*, 1961, p. 291)

This kind of class conflict was revealed in education partly by conservative reluctance to agree to working-class education, or, if they agreed to it, to make sure that it was of an inferior kind to instil obedience. In secondary education it resulted in those aspects of the Taunton Report (1868) (q.v.) which recommended that there should be three different kinds of school with three different kinds of curricula for three social classes. Within education itself conservatism predominated in the form of an exaggerated respect for traditional curricula and traditional methods of teaching. Lawson and Silver (1973) (p. 301) quote the case of Wellington School which was originally intended to be a prototype of a modern school with an emphasis on science, but soon developed a traditional public school curriculum.

Nevertheless Conservatism itself was changing. For example, until the 1867 Parliamentary Reform Act many Conservatives resisted popular education, but after that date the argument about educating the working classes so that they would make reasonable electoral choices began to prevail. It seems very difficult to distinguish some Conservative views on education from the attitude of those Utilitarians who saw mass education as a means of preserving the status quo in society and wanted an inferior kind of schooling for the lower orders, to tame rather than educate them. The 1870 Forster Act was certainly seen in this way by some Conservatives and some radicals.

Educational theories

It is difficult to see any direct link between educational theory and curriculum change during this period, but we have already commented on the fact that both Robert Owen and Kay-Shuttleworth were to some extent influenced by the writings of educational theorists, Johann Heinrich Pestalozzi (1746–1827) in particular.

As a young man, before the French Revolution, Pestalozzi was a member of a group calling themselves 'the patriots' who demanded radical political and social reform. During this period of his life he read Rousseau's *Emile* (1762) and, although he described it as 'a highly impractical dream-book', he was influenced by it—particularly by the idea of stages of child development and Rousseau's view of 'natural education'. After the Revolution Pestalozzi's views tended to become more 'conservative' and he saw education as a means of avoiding social conflict.

Like Rousseau, Pestalozzi believed that the child was born good but was in danger of being corrupted or damaged by an imperfect society. As well as accepting the validity of 'innate goodness' Pestalozzi developed Rousseau's idea of the child's world being significantly different from that of the adult. Pestalozzi also felt that the teacher should pay attention not only to the general stages of development, but also to the unique qualities of each individual child. Intellectual, moral and physical development took place without education—the teacher's job was to harmonize with nature to assist these three innate processes.

Reacting against what he saw as the unnatural cruelty and harshness of contemporary schools, Pestalozzi, who believed in a completely benevolent Nature, felt that a teacher should care for each pupil and protect him from the evils of society just as Nature looks after plants. This view of education led directly to Pestalozzi's method, which 'aims at finding and grasping essential elements, i.e. the unalterable points of departure and links of all instruction and all education. It aims at uncovering, not discovering, the elements.'

For Pestalozzi, educational knowledge could be divided into three categories: training for the head, the heart and the hand—intellectual, moral and physical education. This knowledge should not be imposed from outside, but should be drawn out of the developing child: intellectual knowledge was acquired as a result of awareness of the world through the senses, not from books. The most important kind of knowledge was, for Pestalozzi, moral education which never developed as a result of instruction but from a gradual awareness of self and others. Pestalozzi was much ahead of his time in advocating physical activities such as gymnastics and exercise, with a view to assisting the work of nature to improve the health of the pupils.

He had little to say about the content of the curriculum, except that moral education deserved much higher priority; he was, however, very concerned with method. His contribution to curriculum planning was concerned with the need to plan for each stage of development. In some respects he could be said to have anticipated Piaget in this respect. Essentially the method was to observe the child carefully and to construct a teaching programme around the immediate objects of his curiosity. To this extent Pestalozzi may be seen as an early advocate of curricula being based on the interests and activities of the individual child. Owen, Kay and others influenced by Pestalozzi did not go that far, but his ideas encouraged them in their view that education could be more humane without being less efficient.

Conclusion 1833–70

The two major issues during this period were mass education and secondary education. The question of mass education was resolved temporarily in 1870 by the compromise solution of the dual system of education. This fell short of a completely secular national system of compulsory free education desired by the Chartists and other radicals, but it went beyond what many people had thought desirable at the beginning of this period in 1833. The result was described by H. G. Wells: 'Not an Act for a common universal education, it was an Act to educate the lower classes for employment on lower class lines, and with specially trained, inferior teachers.' (*Experiment in Autobiography*, 1934, p. 93.) In the secondary sphere, educational theory was much less important than the developing nineteenth-century class structure. The Taunton Report recommendation about three kinds of school with three different kinds of curriculum suitable for the three social classes lasted well into the twentieth century.

3. 1870–1902: the elementary curriculum— growth and decline

It is a common mistake to regard the history of education as steady uninterrupted progress from the earliest beginnings to the present system. We suggest that education in the nineteenth century suffered many setbacks and that the period from the Forster Act to the Balfour Act is an excellent example of one particularly unfortunate wrong turning. The 1902 Act was a victory for those who wished to contain mass education as an inferior kind of schooling with very limited links or access points to the real education of a secondary kind which they wanted preserved for their own children. We suggest, therefore, that 1902 was a partial victory for those who wanted educational and curricular segregation. On the way to this point, however, a number of interesting skirmishes were fought and limited advances made.

Opposition to payment by results

For those who wanted popular education of a worthwhile kind, opposition to the 1862 Revised Code and the system of payment by results became a rallying point. Some of the members of the Social Democratic Federation protested bitterly about the quality of working-class education produced by the drilling methods resulting from the Revised Code. Simon (1965) gives a long list of the early socialists who were involved in this struggle. They were, of course, in the company of Liberals and Utilitarians such as Matthew Arnold and Kay-Shuttleworth, and opposition to the Revised Code—especially payment by results—continued throughout this period. Simon (1965) gives an excellent description of the interesting evidence given by Thomas Smyth, who described himself as 'a representative of the working class', at the Cross Commission in 1887. Smyth showed himself to have an excellent grasp of the current educational problems and argued for a form of state education far superior to the current form of elementary instruction. He wanted a curriculum which would allow children to pass from elementary schools into secondary schools and then on to university. Smyth wanted reforms which would avoid over-worked teachers and large classes, but he was particularly scathing about the uneducational methods of cramming facts caused by the payment by results system. He wanted a much wider curriculum including science and mechanics and he also advocated a common school for all the social classes rather than the separation which existed at that time.

Free education–secular education

We should not, however, exaggerate the influence of working-class spokesmen for education during the nineteenth century. They were never more than a small minority, even if sometimes a vocal minority, on any of the school boards, including the radical London School Board. But in the last quarter of the nineteenth century the 1867 Parliamentary Reform Bill began to have the effect of making the two major political parties compete with each other for working-class voters by supporting policies which they had often previously regarded as obnoxious. Some educational issues came into this category, including the demand made by certain sections of the working class—especially the trade unions—for free education. Many reformers were very disappointed by the fact that the 1870 Act did not sweep away fees for elementary education, which had been one of the main demands of the working-class education movement as far back as the 1851 Chartist Convention. In 1885 the TUC unanimously passed a resolution demanding free elementary education and kept up a lively campaign for the next few years. By 1890 the Gladstonian Liberals came out with the policy of free elementary education, and the Tory administration under Lord Salisbury, which had been completely opposed to free education, saw the need to gain working-class support, and passed the Free Education Act in 1891.

Free education had been opposed and continued to be opposed by the Church of England and some other supporters of voluntary schools. Their opposition was based on two considerations: first that school fees added to their revenue and made them slightly more independent of government interference; second, they had objections to free education because they felt that it would inevitably lead to secular education. Fears were raised that Christian taxpayers would find themselves paying for the teaching of agnosticism and atheism. On the other hand, the secular implications of free education were regarded as an important reform by working-class and other advocates of the abolition of fees. In particular, many in the Owenite tradition saw the secularization of the curriculum as an opportunity to sweep away the superstition inherent in the religious aspects of the curriculum, and to replace it by a scientific understanding of the universe and an increased awareness of the political and economic aspects of society.

Control of school boards: control of curriculum

Another important educational issue at this time which had implications for the curriculum was the attempt to abolish the half-time system. For example, Edwin Chadwick made a speech at the Social Science Congress of 1880 in favour of half-time schooling on the grounds that it was personally and economically beneficial for children to be employed in the factories. Others also argued that the combination of school and work was essentially educative, and the best kind of policy for working-class children. However, opposition was increasing, and in 1895 the Annual Conference of the Independent Labour Party demanded that the minimum age of child labour should be raised from eleven to twelve years.

Many of those demanding full-time schooling also felt that the only way to

Science

improve education, including achieving a reformed secular curriculum, would be to capture control of the school boards. In 1888 the SDF (Social Democratic Federation), the Fabian Society and the Metropolitan Radical Federation combined with the London Secular Federation to form a Central Democratic Committee to fight the London School Board elections. They failed to capture the Board but became a strong influence on it. For example, Simon quotes the case of H. W. Hobart who had frequently been an SDF candidate for the London School Board but sought an outlet for his educational ideas in a series of articles in *Justice* in 1894. Hobart was an advocate of a good deal of curriculum reform, including history textbooks with fewer references to war, geography which was not confined to the British Empire, and a wider curriculum which would not inculcate submission and obedience in working-class children. The payment by results system was an obvious target, but criticisms of the curriculum and teaching methods were much wider. This group of reformers also objected to the harsh methods of punishment being used in elementary schools and the generally inhumane treatment of children.

It may be difficult now to realize the extent to which organized religion, especially the Church of England, was regarded as one of the great enemies of genuine education for the working classes. This view was shared by a wide range of social critics: from those like Hobart and Annie Besant who were anti-imperialist and anti-establishment in their attitudes, to the more extreme views of Engels who saw religious education as a simple plot by the capitalist class to keep the children of the workers in captivity and compliance.

We should also remember, of course, that Darwin's *Origin of Species* had been published as recently as 1859 and that the controversy about science and religion was still raging in Victorian society. The growing demand for science in the curriculum was strongly urged by T. H. Huxley and others giving evidence to the Devonshire Commission. However, it has to be seen against a background of vocal religious opposition to science which was regarded as a great moral danger. Another fear, expressed by Robert Lowe in particular, was the danger that working-class pupils would know more about this new knowledge than their social superiors from secondary and public schools.

There were many pressures to enlarge and improve the curriculum of elementary schools; on the other hand, there was still considerable feeling that elementary education should not be too good. The Cross Report (1888) produced a compromise. Morant, who was entrusted with the task of translating these recommendations into practice, managed to do this in such a way that elementary education and secondary education were kept firmly apart. The 1902 Act and the regulations which followed it (see Chapter 1) ensured not only that the elementary curriculum would be different from the secondary curriculum but that it would be inferior. Simon (1965) also suggests that the fear that working-class and reformist groups might take over the school boards was sufficiently great to lead to their abolition: the county councils were much 'safer' politically.

The development of the teaching profession

The National Union of Elementary School Teachers held its first conference in 1870. One of the major lines of policy of the Union was complete opposition to payment by results; they persistently demanded its abolition and a return to the method of inspection of 1846. At first they had very little influence on educational policy, but by 1902 they were beginning to be a force to be reckoned with and were sponsoring MPs. They were mainly concerned with the organization and structure of education rather than the curriculum as such, but the restricted curriculum imposed by the Revised Code was a major target for attack. As time went on they looked for support from educational theory as well as their political strength as a means of supporting their arguments.

Educational theories

It is again difficult to see direct connections between the writings of educational theorists and specific changes in the curriculum between 1870 and 1902. But the reformers often had the views of educational theorists on their side in the debate. For example, for some of the socialists and working-class educational reformers William Morris (1834–96) had become an inspiration, and although his ideas were too utopian to be translated into immediate practice, some of his views (such as the importance of art education) had a long-term significance in the history of the curriculum.

However, the general educational theory at this time took two main forms. First, there was a search for theoretical backing for reformist ideas in education, such as more humane treatment of children and more enlightened methods and curricula. A second source of importance for educational theory was that the National Union of Elementary Teachers and more importantly training colleges were seeking a scientific basis for a teaching method which would enable them to establish themselves as a genuine profession with professional expertise. For the first of these the views of Froebel were particularly important; for the second the writing of Herbart. In 1897 Adams produced his influential book, *Herbartian Psychology Applied to Education*, which became particularly popular in training colleges.

Johann Friedrich Herbart (1776–1834). Herbart accepted the idea that society was imperfect and that one of the purposes of education was to improve society by improving individuals. He did not, however, accept Rousseau's idea of natural goodness nor the view of a soul endowed with the faculties which would gradually unfold unaided. Herbart's view of the child was based on the idea of a mind which was subject to presentations and impressions. He was thus in partial agreement with the psychological views of the Utilitarians; he advocated that teachers needed to exercise care in how they stimulated pupils' imagination— discipline and order were essential. Herbart's view of the purpose of education was Platonic: the formation of a moral character with a will to goodness.

For Herbart there were many real worlds and the purpose of education was to expose the mind to a variety of worlds in the form of different kinds of knowledge.

Knowledge was seen as being of two main kinds: knowledge of nature, and knowledge of humanity. Each of these two main categories could be subdivided: science, mathematics, geography on the one hand; history, religion and literature on the other.

His view of knowledge was much more clearly connected with curriculum than was the case with many other theorists. He felt that the curriculum should be wide and balanced, catering for the many-sided development of the individual; the curriculum should also be integrated in the sense of being carefully planned as a whole. Herbart was also quite clear that this curriculum could not succeed without a well-motivated pupil, so he stressed the need for attention and interest (although, unlike some child-centred theorists, his view was that interest could follow from learning as well as precede it).

Herbart's influence on the curriculum in England has often been underestimated. During the last quarter of the nineteenth century there was felt to be a need for manuals of practice for students in training colleges as well as for elementary school teachers. The Herbartian 'Method' was frequently taken as a model for this kind of crude curriculum planning, so that model lessons (and real lessons) were arranged according to the five stages of 'preparation, presentation, association, systematization and application'. Herbart's method has been criticized, and over-simplifications of it even more, but it was an important and influential attempt to apply psychology to a philosophical view of curriculum knowledge.

Friedrich Froebel (1782–1852). The dominant influences on Froebel's educational ideas were German idealist philosophy and his personal reflections on Christian theology. It might be said that these two influences were never completely reconciled in what emerged as his own philosophy of education.

Froebel was, like Rousseau, an example of an educational theorist whose views were dominated by the idea of innate goodness: 'My teachers are the children themselves, with their purity and innocence, their unconsciousness, and their irresistible claims, and I follow them like a faithful, trustful scholar'. (Letter to his cousin quoted by P. Woodham-Smith in *Friedrich Froebel and English Education*, 1952, E. Lawrence ed., p. 23.) Froebel's view of the child was that not only was he pure and innocent but also an expression of divinity; even to suggest that the child was morally neutral was blasphemous. The purpose of education was, for Froebel, a harmonious development of the child; harmony within the individual, with others and with God. Unlike Rousseau, however, Froebel did not see the development of the individual as being in conflict with the need to adjust to other people in society; Froebel felt that this was essentially part of the same harmonious development.

Froebel's view of knowledge was an almost mystical belief in unity. Children acquired knowledge of themselves and others by doing things—by activity and play. The child was not like a lump of wax to be moulded by a curriculum into the teacher's view of knowledge, but was much more like a plant which should be allowed space and opportunity to grow as in a well-planned garden. No detailed curriculum could be planned for this growth, only general principles.

Despite these inadequacies of educational theory, Froebel's influence on educational practice has been considerable. In 1854 a private kindergarten was opened in Bloomsbury by a disciple of Froebel; in 1874 the Froebel Society was formed by Maria Grey and others, and three years later Maria Grey Training College came into operation. Kindergartens were often simply middle-class alternatives to elementary schools, presenting a more attractive régime than the hated three Rs and payment by results. Gradually the kindergarten type of method began to be introduced into the lower standards of elementary schools, however, and eventually much of the Froebelian child-centred ideology was reflected in the official reports such as the Hadow Reports and the 1927 and 1937 *Handbooks of Suggestions*. The influence of Froebel was partly beneficial in that children were regarded as individual human beings, rather than as potential workers in a factory. But from a curriculum point of view Froebel has been partly responsible for exaggerated child-centred views and interest-based curricula. The metaphor of the kindergarten is probably one of the most misleading in education.

4.   1902–44: from elementary curriculum to primary and secondary curricula

1902 was a year of triumph for Robert Morant. He had succeeded in keeping elementary and secondary schools separate, and he had ensured that the ambitious work taken on by higher grade elementary schools should be pruned. Once again it was firmly laid down that elementary education should not be too good—an upper age of fifteen was to be rigidly enforced and anything resembling a secondary curriculum was barred.

It would be quite wrong, however, to attribute this policy to the idiosyncratic behaviour of one man or even of a small conspiratorial group; it was the result of a tradition pursued throughout the nineteenth century and accepted by the majority of the Liberal and Tory parties. But in addition to the tradition of keeping the working class in their place, Simon (1965) argues that the growth of imperialism was also a cause of the 1902 decision. England did not follow the pattern of continental countries, especially Germany, in developing scientific and technical education, partly because the great depression of the 1870s and 1880s had intensified the tendency for British capital to be invested abroad, especially in the Empire, rather than in our own home-based industries. England became the world financial centre for banking, insurance and commerce and the manpower need was predominantly for clerks rather than technologists. Thus it was not only politically expedient but economically necessary to develop grammar schools rather than elementary and secondary education of a scientific and technical kind. In the long run, however, this decision may have been very damaging to the British economy.

For whatever reason, it is certainly the case that Britain failed to develop an adequate scientific and technical curriculum; a related issue was that the 'ladder of opportunity' became the official policy for education rather than the 'broad highway', which had been advocated by the early radicals and socialists. Another important aspect of curriculum history between 1902 and 1944 was the lack of any strong opposition to this policy even with the rise of the Labour Party.

The Labour Party and education

There are at least two versions of this story which may be represented by two books: Parkinson (1970) and Barker (1972). Parkinson suggests that the Labour Party policy was a conscious attempt to implement the socialist ideals of equality of opportunity and the right to self-development; Barker argues that the Labour Party has rarely pursued socialist policies in education, and usually carried on where the Liberal Party or even the Tory Party left off.

Before the Labour Party was established in 1906 two very different views were developing within the Labour movement. In 1897 the TUC demanded secondary education for all, condemning the segregation of elementary and secondary schools and the élitist basis of the grammar school curriculum; on the other hand, the Fabian Society under Sidney Webb's influence was pursuing a policy very much in the Utilitarian tradition, justifying selection on grounds of economic and social efficiency. Webb's book *London Education* (1904) described in detail the kind of 'capacity catching' machinery of scholarships which would ensure efficient leadership for society at home and in the Empire. Webb was explicitly opposed to the idea of a common school with a common curriculum, and accepted the Morant policy of differentiation between elementary and secondary curricula. So similar were Webb's views and Conservative proposals that in January 1901 Sir John Gorst, Conservative Education Minister in the House of Commons, had distributed proof copies of the Fabian manifesto, *The Educational Muddle and the Way Out*, in support of his own policy of clearly separating elementary and secondary schools but providing a narrow scholarship ladder between them. In the House of Commons the two Members sponsored by the Labour Representative Committee (Hardie and Bell) opposed the Education Bill in 1902, and most of the Labour movement was on their side; nevertheless an influential body of opinion had established a non-socialist tradition which the Labour Party was to inherit and retain.

The Labour movement generally saw the 1902 Act as another piece of class legislation, very much in keeping with the anti-union policies of the Tory government after the Taff Vale Judgment of 1901. Unions wanted to fight back inside Parliament and increasing numbers affiliated to the Labour Representation Committee which was able to get twenty-nine MPs elected in the 1906 anti-Tory landslide. This was also the real beginning of a Labour Party which all told now had fifty-three MPs. But in 1906 it was impossible to generalize about the views —educational and otherwise—of the Labour MPs. Barker recounts that W. T. Stead after the 1906 election wrote to all Labour and Lib–Lab MPs asking what books had most influenced them: socialist writers were virtually unread (Marx being mentioned only twice, the same score as Plato). In their social and educational views the Labour movement similarly covered a very wide range: 'Elitism and egalitarianism with Webb at one end, Thorne and Hobson at the other, and the ILP somewhere in the middle, provided the limits within which Labourism was set rather than the framework on which it was built.' (Barker, 1972, p. 18)

Very soon this lack of clear policy was associated with specific issues: in 1907 the proposal to establish a formal scholarship link from elementary to grammar school was welcomed uneasily—it was a poor substitute for real education for all pupils. This feeling continued after the First World War when Ramsay MacDonald and F. W. Goldstone (a Labour MP sponsored by the NUT) joined in protesting against a secondary school system which merely skimmed off the cream from elementary schools. Others such as Snowden, however, seemed to support the system which had brought them up the hard way; Snowden even objected to the end of the half-time system of education in 1918.

R. H. Tawney (1880–1962) has often been regarded as the great educationist of the early Labour Party, but even he failed to avoid all confusion on the controversy over equality and élitism. His *Secondary Education for All* (1922) appeared to provide a clear view of equality, but within it were the seeds of the policy of different kinds of schools for different kinds of children. These differences were later to be emphasized by the Hadow Report (1926) and the Spens Report (1938) as the basis for the postwar tripartite system of three kinds of school with three different curricula. Barker complains that Tawney simply accepted the educational system of the time. Similarly C. P. Trevelyan, the first Labour President of the Board of Education, behaved in a way little different from many Liberals and Conservatives, including his Tory predecessor Lord Eustace Percy. There was almost a bipartisan educational policy during the first two Labour governments.

By 1930 there was a minor shift from this position with the publication by the National Association of Labour Teachers of a pamphlet, *Education: a Policy*, which advocated common schools with common curricula; but the Labour Party in Parliament could not undertake such a seemingly utopian programme. The idea was revived, however, in 1935 by the LCC Elementary Education and Higher Education Committee, which wanted to introduce multi-bias or multi-lateral schools, but were prevented by the separate regulations for elementary and secondary schools. In 1938 the New Fabian Research Bureau recommended that there should be a common curriculum for the first two years of all post-primary schools to facilitate transfer. The Labour Party was now stuck in a position of trying to advocate secondary education for all with parity of esteem between the schools, and at the same time to advocate that more elementary pupils should have access to the high-prestige grammar schools. This conflict between the egalitarians and the 'capacity-catchers' within the party continued into discussions of the 1944 Act and beyond it.

Changes in Liberal and Conservative views on education

By the beginning of the twentieth century there was a general decline in acceptance of *laissez-faire* economics and social philosophy. More typical of the new Liberalism was Lord Rosebery: 'In the rookeries and slums which still survive, an imperial race cannot be reared.' (Quoted by Simon, op. cit., 1965, p. 169.) Efficiency was still held in high regard, but the recommended means of obtaining it had changed, and state interference was accepted as desirable and necessary. The philosophical justification for this can be traced to the neo-Hegelianism of T. H. Green and others in Oxford from about the 1860s: Asquith and Milner were among Green's many influential students. State interference was, however, only acceptable if the right kind of leaders were in control. The implication of this for education was that at all costs education should remain élitist with a secondary curriculum quite different from that of the masses.

Changes of a somewhat similar kind had also taken place within Conservative thinking, but Tory democracy in the view of Disraeli and Balfour would only work so long as the masses elected suitable leaders from the élite. However, this élite needed to be an intellectual élite, not simply an aristocracy of birth. Although Balfour was himself an aristocrat he realized that he was by no means a typical member of his class. Balfour and other Conservatives had accepted Utilitarian arguments about competition at least in this limited form.

Both parties agreed that the working class needed to be educated, and that elementary schools should be more efficient. But they were still suspicious of schemes which were extravagant in terms of finance or quality. Despite talk of Liberal and Tory democracy real education was for the few: an inferior—more limited—curriculum was appropriate for the many. They were on the road to a meritocratic view of education and the curriculum, but that was a long way from the egalitarian view of common schools and common curricula.

Control of curricula

Between 1902 and 1944 two decisions were taken on curriculum which have had important consequences. Since 1926 the elementary curriculum has ceased to be prescribed; the 1944 Act similarly removed all curricular requirements from secondary schools with the exception of religious instruction. These two decisions need to be seen in their political and educational setting.

There are at least three possible interpretations of each of these decisions. The first, represented in most conventional histories of education, portrays the two decisions as the central government 'freeing' teachers to decide for themselves, and this is backed up by the wording of documents like the *Handbook of Suggestions for Teachers*. A second view, put forward by J. P. White (1975), is that in 1926 the Conservative President of the Board of Education, Lord Eustace Percy, fearing the possibility that a Labour government might wish to exert a strong influence on the curriculum, decided to reduce the amount of central control in a way which would be difficult to reverse. White suggests that there could have been similar thinking behind the lack of curricular prescription in the Butler Education Act of 1944. A third interpretation would be that the two decisions were acts of British compromise—or hypocrisy—which appear to leave the curriculum in the hands of the teachers, but in reality retain so many constraints that teachers are no more free in England than in most continental countries; however, indirect control is less efficient so that the lowest permissible standards are not defined and sometimes become very low indeed. We shall have to return to the question of curriculum control in the next section, 1944–76.

Educational theories

So far our discussion of educational theorists has been confined to those who wrote mainly from a philosophical standpoint. In this period we must also look at the work of psychologists and sociologists.

The period 1902 to 1944, and especially the years following 1914, has been described by Selleck (1972) as the period of the 'New Education' dominated by the so-called progressives in education. Selleck emphasizes that this group had no common creed except opposition to the drilling and regimentation in elementary schools which were still suffering from the after-effects of payment-by-results. Unfortunately, one of the false conclusions of some of this group was that a belief in greater individual freedom of children and a greater emphasis on enjoying school work also involved hostility to the idea of any kind of planned curriculum: teachers as well as children should be free from the restrictions of a syllabus or programme. The group bracketed together by Selleck included a number of very different figures. One influence was Edmond Holmes, whose book, *What Is and What Might Be* (1911), contrasted his experiences as a school inspector with the vision of a better kind of education that he found in one enlightened school. Another was Homer Lane (1876–1925), an American advocate of extreme permissiveness in education who practised what he preached in England at the 'Little Commonwealth' from 1912 to 1918. Another overseas influence was Maria Montessori (1870–1952) who combined a belief in more enlightened treatment of children (including the handicapped) with methods based on individual use of structured apparatus—significantly, she was later to repudiate much of the efforts of her so-called followers. A. S. Neill (1883–1973), a well-known British progressive, based his educational theory and practice on a mixture of the views of Homer Lane and an over-simplified reading of Freud. He too advocated an extreme version of child-centred education without a formal curriculum. T. Percy Nunn (1870–1944) was a much more respected educational figure and based his book, *Education: Its Data and First Principles* (1920), on the biology and psychology that he had studied as a professional scientist, together with anti-Hegelian philosophical ideas which valued individual freedom. As well as providing a textbook for the progressives, Nunn also had direct influence on reformers such as Tawney and played a part himself in the work of the Consultative Committee (q.v.).

Many of the progressives derived their philosophical backing, such as it was, from John Dewey who also had to dissociate himself from the American progressive movement because he thought they were distorting his views. Dewey's philosophy was much too complex for use as a popular slogan. Dewey theorized about education for the 'common man' in democratic America, whom he saw essentially as a practical man with something remaining of the frontier spirit. Dewey saw man as an active, problem-solving animal who wanted to master his environment and cooperate with his fellows. A child should therefore be naturally receptive to education if it coincided with his own environment. He believed that children developed according to a natural pattern and that education should follow this pattern of development; but what he was advocating was quite different from allowing children to do whatever they wanted to do at any particular moment. For Dewey the purpose of education was to provide the child with whatever was necessary for 'growth', but he was very critical of naïve views of unguided 'growth'. He also saw the acquisition of knowledge largely as a social process, and in this respect also he differed from the extreme progressives who concentrated on the child as an individual.

Dewey was, however, opposed to the traditional view that schools should hand on to pupils a fixed body of knowledge organized in subjects. He regarded knowledge as a means of personal development, but it should be experienced rather than taught and learned. Passing on various subdivisions of the cultural heritage was less important to Dewey than developing the ability to deal with present problems. There was a need for a curriculum, but it could not be planned according to traditional subject-matter. Dewey approved of subjects like geography or topics which related rather than isolated or compartmentalized. He rejected a subject-based curriculum in favour of 'inquiry'. It was the teacher's task to plan a course of learning situations for children, but the principles for making these decisions were never clear. It is easy to see that his ideas have been oversimplified and distorted rather than followed by the progressives. His influence both in the USA and in Great Britain has nevertheless been considerable.

The educational progressives also sought support for their view in some of the psychological writing of the time. Perhaps the dominant figure at this time was William McDougall (1871–1938), whose book, *An Introduction to Social Psychology* (1908), was widely read for many years. McDougall stressed the importance of instinct in human behaviour and, even after the word 'instinct' was dropped by later psychologists such as Cyril Burt and Godfrey Thompson, they retained the idea that heredity was of supreme importance in human behaviour. This stress on individually inherited personality gave some support to the progressives in their desire to treat children individually, but it also led psychologists to search for means of finding those who were gifted by heredity—hence the importance attached to tests of intelligence as a means of selecting the able from the average and the less able. This kind of research was also stimulated by the current social philosophy, which, as we have seen, tended to view secondary education in terms of a select few rather than as a programme for the majority. Psychology was also seen by many educationists as a means of making education scientific, and for them intelligence tests were the concrete manifestation of scientific research. We saw in Chapter 1 how the claims of psychologists to be able to select and categorize children at the age of eleven into three types distorted the findings of the Hadow, Spens and Norwood Reports. Selleck (1972) reminds us that Burt, for example, assured the Hadow Committee that future scholarship winners could be predicted with some success at the age of six (p. 139). But we should also remember that psychologists did not create the desire for selection; they merely responded to it. The basic decision was an administrative–political one.

Selleck suggests that the educational progressives were not theorists but missionaries. They were likely to make use of those parts of educational philosophy and psychology which they found supportive and to ignore the rest. Certainly they oversimplified complex philosophical views such as those of Dewey, and ignored some aspects of psychology and misinterpreted others such as Freud. Nevertheless progressivism became an almost official doctrine in the training colleges and in the official government reports. Selleck suggests that, in the 1931 Report on Primary Education and the 1933 Report on Infant and Nursery Schools, the Consultative Committee followed the advice of the progressives in trying to dissolve the formal curriculum of the primary school, to relax its discipline, to reduce competition and to increase the time given to art, drama and music (p. 143).

Before the end of the period 1902 to 1944 we also have to look at the work of early social investigators and sociologists who indirectly had an effect on curriculum. In 1926, for example, Lindsay published a book called *Social Progress and Educational Waste* which stressed the unfairness of a system which allowed so few working-class children real educational opportunity at the secondary level. Gray and Moshinsky (1938) examined the degree of inequality of opportunity existing in the selection system for grammar schools. They used the results of IQ tests to demonstrate the degree of inequality of opportunity related to social class. Such work served to point out that children of the same level of intelligence had access to quite different kinds of curriculum and paved the way for the sociological studies of the postwar period.

5.   1944–77: towards a comprehensive curriculum

From the curriculum point of view the 1944 Education Act was both a significant landmark and a missed opportunity. It was significant as an expression in legislation of the ideal of secondary education for all and equality in education. It was a missed opportunity in the sense that the legislation ignored the problem of curriculum as a question of equality of access to knowledge as distinct from the mere legal right of access to some kind of educational institution. Since 1944 the educational scene has been dominated by conflict and confusion over the meaning and content of secondary education. Other curricular issues in primary schools, for example, have not been ignored, but the central problem has been the 11–16 age group, and this is reflected in much of the work of the Schools Council. Another interesting feature of the postwar period was the emergence of the economics of education as part of the background to decision-making. After the war there was a good deal of discussion about education as investment, and this line of argument was strongly represented in Reports such as Crowther, Robbins and Dainton. Secondary schools have, however, generally been reluctant to make major changes to the traditional curriculum, and have responded to arguments about economic efficiency and social justice by minor repairs rather than complete rebuilding.

The Labour Party

> Labour has never passed any major piece of educational legislation, but has worked
> within the blueprints provided by other governments.

> (D. Marsden, *Fabian Tract 411*, 1971, p. 3)

In the 1940s and early 1950s the Labour Party continued in a state of confusion
over the curricular implications of secondary education for all. Having been
ceded this major prize by the Butler Act, Labour politicians seemed unable to
take advantage of it. The confusion was typified by the general attitude towards
the tripartite system and the particular case of the Ministry of Education pamphlet, *The Nation's Schools* (1945). This pamphlet, which had been drafted before the
Labour government took office, recommended that secondary schools should be
organized on a tripartite basis. Despite some protests within the party that the
1942 Labour Party Conference had supported multilateral schools, Ellen
Wilkinson, the Minister of Education, accepted the main proposals of the pamphlet (even after it was withdrawn). Her successor, George Tomlinson, continued
this policy, which probably represented the views of the party as a whole. There
were some dissenting voices, especially from ex-teachers like W. G. Cove who at
the 1946 Conference demanded that all pupils should have access to a common
curriculum. But the party in general remained confused about the meaning of
secondary education for all, and was slow to recognize the internal political
contradictions of the tripartite system. Pedley (1969, p. 37) suggests that the
Labour Ministers of Education were no match for Ministry officials who strongly
favoured retaining the grammar schools and secondary modern schools with
quite different curricula.

The majority of the party were still talking about equality when they were
really advocating meritocracy. Michael Young's book (1958) was a devastating
attack on the meritocratic position, but it did not convert the party. The confusion continued even when comprehensive schools were established: in London,
for example, the policy was to 'stream like mad' (R. Pedley, 1969, p. 98). No
central guidance was forthcoming about the secondary curriculum, and it was
left to a Conservative administration to set up a curriculum study group and the
Schools Council which followed. Even after the party as a whole had been
converted to the idea of comprehensive schools the naïve belief persisted that
regulations designed to change organizational structure would automatically
produce significant educational changes in schools. Circular 10 of 1965 which
requested LEAs to prepare comprehensive plans ignored the problems of
teachers' attitudes and the need for an appropriate curriculum.

In summary, it would not seem unfair to say that the Labour Party has shown
itself to be obsessed by structure and to have neglected the need to think out a
comprehensive curriculum from basic principles.

Conservative views

> As a Conservative, I am concerned that secondary education in Britain should be organized so that there is the maximum opportunity for ability to be recognized and fostered at the lowest economic cost.
>
> (Rhodes Boyson, 'Threat to Tradition', in Nicholas Smart (ed.), *Crisis in the Classroom*, 1968)

R. A. Butler has sometimes been regarded as a politician who was out of step with his own party on educational matters; but a careful reading of the 1943 White Paper, the 1944 Act and his own autobiography shows that he was a clear-minded exponent of segregation in education: one curriculum for those who show signs of excellence and leadership, a different kind of curriculum for the majority. Similar remarks might be made of other Conservative educationists such as Sir Edward Boyle whose support for comprehensive schools stopped short of an egalitarian common curriculum.

More commonly, however, the Conservative support for the ladder of opportunity rather than the broad highway has taken the form of opposition to comprehensive schools as well as new methods, new curricula and new forms of examination. Curriculum innovation has usually been seen as a threat to standards, or as an expensive gimmick.

By the late 1960s a Conservative counter-attack took shape in the very interesting form of the Black Papers. The first of these, *Fight for Education* (1969), although not a Conservative Party publication, was frankly political in its intention: a copy was sent to every MP, and the editors urged all readers to write to their own MPs as a means of exerting pressure. The first article in the collection was by a Conservative MP, Angus Maude, on 'The Egalitarian Threat'. Singled out for criticism were primary 'play' methods, comprehensive schools, expansion of higher education and departures from the traditional curriculum. The second Black Paper, *The Crisis in Education* (1969), contained an even longer introductory letter to MPs. In other respects the message was much the same as that of the first Black Paper. Despite its emotionalism and exaggerated arguments, a number of interesting points were made about modern curricula and methods which needed to be answered. An unfortunate aspect of the Black Papers was the confusion of issues: to be in favour of a common comprehensive curriculum did not necessarily mean approval of all modern methods and a lowering of standards, but that was the implication of the Papers. The third Black Paper was published in November 1970 after Mrs Thatcher had become Secretary of State for Education and had withdrawn Circular 10/65: this Paper was called *Goodbye Mr Short* and gave the impression of being on the winning side at last. The Black Papers are interesting social documents, representing a strong body of opinion inside the teaching profession as well as the general public.

Educational theories

As we have seen, by 1944 the views of the educational progressives had become almost part of the official doctrine of the Ministry of Education publications and the training colleges. This was particularly so in primary education, and probably reached a peak with the publication of the Plowden Report. The Black Papers represented part of the popular backlash against this orthodoxy, but there were many critics of 'progressivism' within the ranks of professional educationists. One important publication was *Perspectives on Plowden* (1969) edited by Professor R. S. Peters, who argued that the Report was not satisfactory from a theoretical point of view. Peters suggested that the very proper reaction against some aspects of the elementary tradition had resulted in a one-sided and misleading set of beliefs in the Plowden Report. He proceeded to criticize a number of the unexamined concepts and assumptions in the Report, including 'development'; he suggested that 'development' in an educational sense would include scientific, mathematical, moral, historical, inter-personal, aesthetic and religious forms of awareness. (This important view has also been expressed by P. H. Hirst, R. Dearden and J. White in various publications as a basis for curriculum planning.) There were also criticisms in *Perspectives on Plowden* about psychological and sociological inadequacies in the Plowden 'theory', and a plea was made by Lionel Elvin for teachers to have a positive role to play. Although the word 'curriculum' was not much used, the clear implication was that the Plowden Report lacked a clear view on curriculum content and the part to be played by teachers in its transmission.

A very different kind of psychological theory is represented by the views of the behaviouristic psychologists who have been particularly influential in the USA and not without significance in the UK. B. F. Skinner applied the behaviouristic psychological theory of stimulus-response learning to programmed instruction as well as a basis for general classroom learning; Ralph Tyler took the idea of objectives and from it built a theory of curriculum planning; Benjamin Bloom took this systematization one stage further and developed a taxonomy of educational objectives.

The essential behaviourist assumption about the nature of man is that he is a product of his environment. Stimulus-response learning theory, in an extreme form such as J. B. Watson's, assumes the *tabula rasa* mental state which we have already referred to in our discussion of the Utilitarian view of psychology. One criticism of the behaviourist point of view is that its concentration on method trivializes the process of education. Although behaviourists claim that they want to avoid theory, they are driven to some kind of social theory when they have to decide what behaviour they want to shape and what they want to eliminate. In Skinner's case his version of Utopia in his novel *Walden Two* is a smooth-running, efficient, cooperative society in which everyone is educated for success. In many respects the Skinnerian point of view rests in the same assumptions as the Utilitarianism of James Mill, namely that all individuals are basically selfish and self-seeking. The behaviourist view of education is 'education for society' and is opposed to the child-centred theories of Rousseau and Froebel. The result is not necessarily a system of education for mere conformity, however, since the individual can be taken into consideration in the planning process. A serious weakness of the behaviourist position is its lack of theory regarding the structure of knowledge and questions of worthwhileness. Bloom's *Taxonomy of Educational*

Objectives (1956) suggests a means of categorizing objectives to secure a range of levels, but it does not claim to be a means of stating objectives in terms of what kinds of knowledge we need for education. Generally this approach to the curriculum is an attempt to combine efficient planning with the democratic ideal of education for all. At its worst this degenerates into meaningless lists of behavioural objectives and an assembly-line view of processing pupils for society; but at its best—including much of Bloom's more recent work—it presents a view of education as a genuine opportunity for all pupils to acquire knowledge which has traditionally been regarded as available only to an élite minority. In England this view of behavioural objectives has been influential in some thinking about curriculum planning and in some of the curriculum development projects. For example, the Science 5–13 project uses an objectives approach to curriculum planning, and the North-Western Region Curriculum Development Project attempted to employ the objectives approach in encouraging teachers to re-think the purpose of their own teaching.

Other Americans not of the behaviourist school, for example Jerome Bruner, have also been influential but rarely at the level of national decision-making. Bruner's *Process of Education* (1960) and *Toward a Theory of Instruction* (1966) have emphasized structure in curriculum planning and the need for teachers to re-think their teaching in terms of the major generalizations rather than petty detail. The *Man a Course of Study* materials have been used on a small scale in the UK and this has also encouraged teachers to think seriously about curriculum planning, but this is a long way from the scene of national decision-making.

Sociology has also changed considerably since 1944. In the 1950s there was a good deal of important work in the tradition of the prewar social demographers, and Floud and Halsey, for example, were very influential in producing statistics to demonstrate the lack of equality of opportunity after the 1944 Act. These studies probably assisted the move away from the tripartite system towards comprehensive schools, and later studies such as that of Julienne Ford (1969) encouraged the further change towards unstreamed comprehensive schools. Another stage in curriculum history was reached when attention was directed at the curriculum of comprehensive schools rather than their structure and organization. M. F. D. Young (1971) suggested that the school curriculum should not be taken for granted but should be regarded as problematical; other sociologists have taken up the challenge and have looked very critically indeed at the content of curriculum. In some cases this has resulted in hopeless despair when some sociologists call into question the idea of knowledge itself as being a cultural artefact, and suggest that even rationality is merely a cultural habit or matter of taste. However, if these excesses can be avoided the new sociology has much to offer in encouraging teachers to look closely at the content of the curriculum.

Conclusion

In recent years a number of events have focused attention on to questions of primary and secondary curricula: in an atmosphere of economic cuts, politicians and others have been asking whether we are getting value for money in education; particular cases, such as the William Tyndale inquiry, publicized the lack of any outside control over a school's curriculum (or lack of curriculum); and it has been increasingly questioned whether the Schools Council's 'cafeteria' approach to curriculum—simply offering a range of alternatives from which to choose—has been sufficiently successful. There have been various suggestions, often linked to proposals for monitoring standards, for more central direction of the curriculum. In 1976 the House of Commons arts and education subcommittee inquired into priorities and decision-making at the DES and appeared not to be convinced by Schools Council representatives who claimed that it was a 'fundamental principle that schools should be allowed to decide their own curriculum' (*The Times Educational Supplement*, 2 April 1976). More than a year before this the DES had set up the Assessment of Performance Unit (APU) with the intention of 'monitoring the whole curriculum' (B. W. Kay, *Trends*, No. 2, 1975). The APU seems to have been given little publicity, but its influence is potentially very great: it seems likely that assessment will take place across the whole common curriculum in six areas: English language, mathematics, science, social and personal, aesthetic and physical development. It is, as yet, too soon to gauge the possible results of the APU. It is almost inevitable that a national system of testing will have some influence on curriculum. It might be simply a concealed pressure towards a common core curriculum, but monitoring might also have the effect of encouraging to teach for the tests, and thus limit the range and quality of the curriculum in an undesirable way.

3

Some Examples of Changing 'Subjects'

In a single volume it would be impossible to look at each subject in the curriculum and trace its origins and development. We have therefore confined ourselves to examining six 'subjects' to illustrate some of the different kinds of processes which have helped to put new subjects into the curriculum as well as other kinds of pressures which have sometimes changed the character of the subject once it has become established.

We have taken English and mathematics as subjects which usually, in some form, appear in the curriculum; we then take moral education, which made a fairly early appearance, but then faded out to some extent and has recently made new claims; home economics as a subject which has been dramatically transformed yet retains some of its original flavour; and finally social studies and science which, in our view, have very strong claims but have never been given the prominence they deserve.

English appeared in the elementary curriculum in the form of reading as the first basic requirement; in the public school curriculum English at first was subordinate to the classics and may not even have appeared on the timetable. The account of English in the curriculum is largely one of change: change in status, in content and in teaching style; and in the process of change the acquisition of a clearer set of aims. As we shall see, the story is by no means complete.

Mathematics illustrates admirably our thesis about the two traditions; the elementary curriculum from the beginning included arithmetic or 'ciphering', whereas the public school curriculum in the nineteenth century was more likely to include abstract mathematics such as geometry and algebra. To some extent our account of the development of this area of the curriculum is the gradual convergence of these two traditions, but the problem of what kind of mathematics is suitable for all pupils in primary and comprehensive schools is by no means solved, the argument sometimes being polarized into traditional versus modern mathematics.

Religious and Moral Education have also changed in a number of ways. In the nineteenth-century public school, moral education in the form of religious instruction and compulsory attendance at chapel was taken for granted. Similarly one of the origins of popular—or elementary—education was the desire to inculcate Christian values. For a long time elementary education was the scene of a dispute between those who felt that education was meaningless unless it included moral instruction of a denominational kind, and those who favoured a secular form of elementary education. The result was a series of compromises which have certainly confused the issue to the extent that in the 1944 Education Act every school was required to have a daily act of corporate worship; and officially religious education is the only required subject. The fact that this aspect of the 1944 Education Act was passed with so little dissension was probably an indication that most people—including Members of Parliament—thought of religious education as the only possible form of moral education. The section of this chapter dealing with moral education will show that this was not the case, and includes an account of those in the nineteenth and twentieth centuries who have advocated secular moral education of various kinds.

Home Economics today is a subject for which its supporters make very great claims. But it has its origins in the domestic subjects thought suitable for training the children of the poor to develop elementary skills of hygiene, cooking and 'plain needlework'. As the years passed, teachers of the subject—especially in secondary schools—have become more and more ambitious and rather less practical, so that home economics today might include quite advanced work of a scientific kind to deal with nutrition, as well as aspects of sociology, psychology and economics.

Social Studies of some kind has always been present—at least in the hidden curriculum—of both elementary and public schools. We have seen elsewhere in this book that one of the motives behind elementary education was to 'gentle the masses' and to instil the idea of respect for the property of their betters. This is what is referred to by Eaglesham and others as 'education for followership'; at the other extreme the public school curriculum was 'education for leadership' fostered by the prefect system, team games, etc. Social Studies teaching has gradually evolved in at least two ways: first, to develop from a narrow view of training for citizenship to a genuine understanding of society, and second, by treating the content of social studies as respectable academic subject-matter, especially in the form of economics, political science and sociology.

Science might also be used as an example of a subject which has never been given the attention it deserves. This was certainly the case with the nineteenth-century elementary school curriculum, and—for very different reasons—the public school curriculum. It is still an area of comparative neglect today. This chapter contains an explanation of the complex reasons for this continuing deficiency in the curriculum—an explanation which is partly one of administrative muddle, partly ideological and partly a problem of teacher supply.

There will inevitably be some overlap between these six accounts, and also between this chapter and other parts of this book. Each of the six sections is no more than a sketch, in the form of a short essay, of the development of one aspect of the curriculum.

English

There are at least two important, and interconnected, ways of looking at English in the curriculum: how it came to be accepted as part of the curriculum, and how the subject changed its identity not once but a number of times. In the case of English the problem of exactly what it is meant to be is more difficult than with other subjects and has not yet been completely resolved. An examination of the history of the curriculum may serve to throw some light on why some teachers of English today appear to have a confused view of the purpose of their own subject.

English, which is now generally accepted as an essential subject in all schools, is a comparatively new subject. Up to the fourteenth century, French was the language primarily used in schools and at Oxford and Cambridge. This situation began to change after 1362 when English became the language of the Law Courts and Parliament.

By the end of the fourteenth century a standard form of 'King's English' had emerged, but it was not taught in schools as a subject. Latin was still an international language, and an important means of communication for the profes-

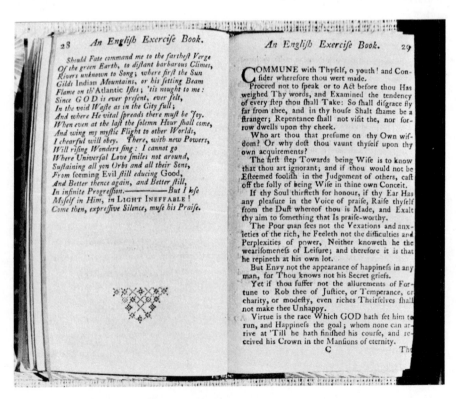

2   *An English Exercise Book* by A. Fisher 1770
The fourth paragraph begins 'The first step Towards being Wife is to
know that thou art ignorant'.

sions. The reasons for teaching Latin in schools were functional rather than humanistic throughout the Middle Ages. It was only after the Renaissance that Latin as the core of the curriculum could be justified in terms of a liberal education which would, by a study of literature, produce good citizens capable of sound judgment in all aspects of life. Clearly the language had to be learned very thoroughly before literature could be used in this 'liberal' way, hence the amount of time devoted to Latin grammar. Once the theory had been accepted that education should be based on classical literature, very little time was left for anything else.

After the Reformation, however, and especially after the Puritan revolution, there was some pressure on schools to teach English. The reading of the Bible in English was regarded as extremely important, but this was not thought to be a good enough reason for English to replace Latin. By the end of the seventeenth century the practical importance of Latin had gone, and there was by now a body of literature available in English, but Latin survived, bolstered up by a new theory put forward by Locke and others, that education was a matter of discipline: it was the process of learning not the content that mattered. Certain subjects were better than others because they needed application and concentration and developed certain faculties of the mind. Latin scored very highly according to this theory but English did not. There was also a strong element of social élitism in this view: according to Locke, 'Latin I look upon as absolutely necessary to a gentleman'.

Even by the end of the eighteenth century English had no more than a very minor part to play in the curriculum of grammar schools—often as a kind of introduction to Latin grammar and literature. In the famous dispute over Leeds Grammar School in 1805 Lord Eldon made the judgment that there could be no legal provision of 'modern subjects'.

English in popular education

At the beginning of the nineteenth century the curriculum thought suitable for the 'lower orders' was confined to reading, writing, ciphering and religion. English—of a very rudimentary kind—was therefore part of the basic curriculum of elementary schools. Some felt that the instruction given should be deliberately restricted (and many advocates of popular education even doubted the wisdom of teaching writing); others, like Dr James Kay, had a more enlightened view of what might be attained, especially if teachers of the right kind could be made available. This had the support of Matthew Arnold and other inspectors, and a curriculum for training colleges was devised which included literature for teachers' own personal development and also some which might form the subject-matter for elementary schools. But the English which began to develop was already distorted by the formalism and teaching methods of public school classics teaching. For example, the syllabus for training colleges included as suitable content for elementary schools: English language, grammar and literature, the classification and inflection of words, the analysis of simple sentences, syntactical parsing and paraphrasing—which was considered by the Newcastle Committee

Clarence House Academy,
Brighton. April 4th 1845.

My Dear Parents,

My Education I hope will shortly be very much improved, and I trust that when I leave this school, you will be pleased with the improvement I shall have made, in the different branches of my Education, under the tuition of Mr. Erredge. Give my respects to Aunt Charlotte, and my cousins.

I remain
Dear Parents
Your ever affectionate Son
Charles Harman.

Melancholy frequently occasions insanity.
Melancholy frequently occasions insanity.
Melancholy frequently occasions insanity.

3 Preparation for the Professions
An example of the work of Charles Sargant Harman, pupil at Clarence House Academy, Brighton, 1843–5.

to be a diet hardly conducive to forming a taste for reading among school teachers.

Despite this kind of evidence, the Newcastle Report's recommendations went in the opposite direction and resulted in the Revised Code of 1862 with a narrow and rigid curriculum governed by the 'payment by results' system. The Code did not require a child to be tested on a book previously studied (nor did it require composition).

Some relaxation of the Code came about in 1867 in the form of 'specific subjects' which could be taught to individual pupils in the upper standards: both grammar and English literature could be offered as specific subjects. The syllabus for English literature in 1876 was as follows:

> 1st Year—One hundred lines of poetry, got by heart, with knowledge of meaning and allusions. Writing a letter on a simple subject.
> 2nd Year—Two hundred lines of poetry, not before brought up, repeated; with knowledge of meaning and allusions. Writing a paraphrase of a passage of easy prose.
> 3rd Year—Three hundred lines of poetry, not before brought up, repeated; with knowledge of meaning and allusions. Writing a letter or statement, the heads of the topics to be given by the Inspector.

In 1882, however, English became a class subject and the syllabus was changed so that it became simply a study of grammar: once again the influence of public schools classics teaching. Frederick Temple, a former head of Rugby, when asked by the Secretary of the Education Department for his views replied:

> It is in every way more useful to a boy to know the nature and use of a 'relative pronoun' than to know the nature and use of 'specific gravity' or of 'latent heat'. All these are phenomena subject to scientific handling. But for human purposes the human phenomenon is far the most important, and its study the most cultivating and the most useful.
>
> (Temple to P. Cumin, 10 April 1882, Spencer MSS.)

In 1895 payment by results largely disappeared and with it there was a slight swing away from a rigid grammatical approach to English, but the basis of parsing and analysing still remained. Inspectors' reports on reading also complained of the mechanical teaching methods employed so that pupils rarely related reading to their real world. Part of the problem was that reading was often left to inexperienced pupil-teachers or even to monitors. By the beginning of the twentieth century English in elementary schools was still usually a dull and arid exercise.

By 1910 the writers of the Board of Education Circular 753, *The Teaching of English in Secondary Schools*, no longer found it necessary to justify the subject:

> The claim of English to a definite place in the curriculum of every Secondary School is admitted. It would only be wasting words to refute the view that knowledge of English . . . will be 'picked up' naturally, or that, though systematic instruction is necessary in such subjects as mathematics or foreign languages, the mother tongue may safely be left to the occasional direction and influence of home. . . .

This important circular defined English as 'training the mind to appreciate English literature', and as 'cultivating the power of using the English language in

1880   89

Jan 23rd Mrs Scott called to-day, and said that her husband had desired her to come and thank the teachers for their kindness and attention to their daughter.

Jan 28th Dr Jackson called this afternoon, and wished to see the Government Report which was shewn to him.

Jan 30th Scripture Examination held this morning.
Mrs Arnott thanked me to-day for the care and attention which had been paid to her child, and also wished me to convey her feelings of gratitude to Miss Thomson.

Feby 6th In questioning the children about their Library Books, I found one entitled "Sense and Sensibility" which I consider unfit for circulation among young children.
I shewed the book to a Manager, who advised me to see Mr Buck and to ask

4   Entry in a London girls' elementary school log book, requesting the withdrawal of the novel *Sense and Sensibility* from the library 1880.
Greater London Record Office

speech and writing'. It divided English into two main, but closely related, areas of literature and composition. It did not lay down a syllabus—merely 'suggestions and guidance'. Although the circular was designed specifically for secondary schools, the principles were regarded as applying to elementary schools as well. It reaffirmed the necessity for reading aloud, something which teachers had tended to neglect. Formal grammar lessons as such were to be dispensed with. The

90.

1880

him what steps should be taken to stop its circulation, both in this and other Schools.

Feb. 10th. Mr Buck called to-day and said:—

(a) The Library Book had better be sent to Mr Rodgers, with a letter of explanation

(b.) That Mrs Davis must send up 31 children from Infant Department.

(c.) That only a half-holiday should be given after the Government Examination.

In previous years a whole holiday has always been given.

Feb. 11th. Library Book "Sense and Sensibility" sent to the Rev. J. Rodgers.

Mr Mott called and promises to get the Union to pay school pence for Mrs Bray children till March 25th.

Mrs Matthews sent me a very handsome penknife to-day, with thanks for attention to her child.

circular recognized that in the past the formal teaching of grammar had been based on rules governing Latin grammar which were inapplicable to English.

Literature was seen as 'first-hand study of the works of great writers', the choice of suitable books being left to the teachers, bearing in mind the ability of pupils. Learning passages of poetry and prose by heart was strongly recommended, but pupils should be given some choice of what to learn. Abridged versions and histories of literature were not recommended, and books should be read for their literary value, not as aids to teaching history (or any other subject).

The other main area of English—composition—included spoken as well as written language, and it was in fact recommended that spoken composition should precede written. A nod of approval was given to interdisciplinary work: exercises in composition could often be naturally suggested by, and profitably based on, the work children were doing in other subjects. Quality, not fluency, was to be aimed at. Teachers were reminded that there should not be a dual standard in schools for composition and other written work.

Circular 753 remained the official view of the teaching of English until the publication of the Newbolt Report (*The Teaching of English in England*) in 1921.

Official thinking during the first two decades of the twentieth century had been overtaken by developments in a number of other fields. Edmond Holmes's influential writings stressed the need for self-realization and self-expression in children. Drama was seen as an important dimension of English, starting with Harriet Finlay-Johnson's book, *The Dramatic Method of Teaching*, published in 1911. Creative work, in poetry, plays and historical reconstructions was achieved by educationists of whom the most important was probably H. Caldwell Cook. Cook had developed his ideas at the Perse School, Cambridge. They were based on three principles: that learning came from action rather than reading and writing, that spontaneous effort and free interest by the pupil are essential and that the natural means of study in youth is play. The so-called 'Play Way' method made its influence felt in the publication of the Perse Playbook series containing suggestions for developing imagination in younger pupils—tales of desert islands, ghosts, animals and castles.

The Newbolt Report 1921

Some of these developments were reflected in the Newbolt Report, a major official inquiry into the state of the subject. One major difference between the Newbolt Report and the 1910 Circular was that the Report was officially concerned with all levels of English teaching: elementary, preparatory, secondary, teacher training colleges, as well as university and adult education. The Report marks a further advance in the centrality of English in schools. This is shown in a variety of ways, including the doctrine that 'every teacher is a teacher of English' and the recommendation that the study of classical and foreign languages in preparatory schools should be postponed in order to allow a better grounding in English. The Report acknowledged that the use of literature is 'a possession and a source of delight, a personal intimacy and the gaining of personal experience, an end in itself and, at the same time, an equipment for the understanding of life' (para. 13).

The Report as a whole is a fascinating mixture of high ideals combined with attitudes towards some pupils which would make the attainment of the ideals impossible. It seems difficult now to believe that an official document could contain such insensitive comments as:

66. Teachers of infants sometimes complain that when the children come to school, they can scarcely speak at all. They should regard this rather as an advantage . . .

English was accepted in the Report as the basis of a liberal education for all pupils, but the nineteenth-century idea of education involving the imposition of a superior culture on to the barbarian masses still dominated conventional educational thought. Even in those passages where the Report is trying to be most 'democratic' the choice of words is often unfortunate: as in discussing the place of dialect in English teaching. The Report approvingly quoted one witness who described her methods as 'guiding the child to that refinement of speech which, in a subtle manner, is an index to the mind, and helps to place it beyond the reach of vulgarity of thought and action' (para. 69).

The Report also emphasized the importance of English by recommending that for pupils up to the age of twelve, at least one period a day should be devoted to English. For older pupils, however, it was still necessary to fight against the tradition of teaching English in the same way as classics were taught in public schools, i.e. overemphasizing grammar and treating literature as a text to be mastered rather than appreciated.

By 1921 the advocates of teaching grammar were staging a successful rear-guard action. It looks as though the Committee may have been divided on this issue, but some certainly viewed with sympathy the fact that the reaction against grammar had proceeded too far. The views of witnesses from both sides were quoted (Dr P. B. Ballard spoke firmly against grammar), and the Committee eventually put forward a compromise standpoint identical to that of the 1910 Circular.

Three years later a much briefer document was addressed specifically to secondary school teachers—*Some Suggestions for the Teaching of English in Secondary Schools in England* (1924). The general message was essentially the same as that of the 1921 Report, but more detailed guidance was given without going as far as specifying syllabuses. In addition a few paragraphs of warning were devoted to various new trends such as 'self-expression' which was only to be used under the guidance of a skilled teacher and then only rarely. A distinction was attempted between what was teachable and what was not, the impression being given that teachers should concentrate on what they really could teach, namely accuracy and clarity of expression.

The Appendices to the *Suggestions* contain interesting discussions of English and mathematics, English and science, as well as lists of suggested prose texts for reading in class which might be regarded as telling us more about those responsible for writing the *Suggestions* than about the tastes of pupils in 1924.

First Year ($11\frac{1}{2}$–$12\frac{1}{2}$)

Bunyan, *The Pilgrim's Progress*
Cervantes, *Don Quixote* (selections)
Gatty, *Parables from Nature*
Hawthorne, *Tanglewood Tales*
Homer (prose translations of the *Iliad* and the *Odyssey*)
Kingsley, *Heroes*
Kingsley, *Madam How and Lady Why*

Lamb, *Adventures of Ulysses*
Livingstone, *Travels*
Lucien, *Trips to Wonderland*
Macdonald, *Phantasies*
Morris, *The Story of the Glittering Plain*
Marco Polo, *Travels*
Mungo Park, *Travels*
Nibelungenlied (prose translation)
Swift, *Gulliver's Travels*
Tales from the Northern Sagas
Thackeray, *The Rose and the Ring*
The Seven Champions of Christendom

By the 1930s, examinations in English, both at the 'scholarship', i.e. 11 +, and School Certificate levels, were tending to distort the curriculum. One historian of the subject has recently written:

> Reading through a book such as Dudley Bateman's *One Hundred and Seventy-Five English Scholarship Tests*, 1938, the whole business takes on the air of something strangely detached, an objective tester's nightmare, where a pupil's capacity to use or respond is supposedly to be estimated from the answers to such questions as 'Write complete sentences containing (i) a second personal pronoun (ii) a Weak Verb in the Subjunctive (iii) an Adverbial Clause of Concession (iv) a Proper Noun in the Possessive Case.'

> (D. Shayer, *The Teaching of English in Schools 1900-70*, 1972, p. 111)

As we have seen in the section on the Spens Report (1938), educational thinking at this time was also being influenced by psychological views of children's development and abilities—often oversimplified and grossly distorted versions of psychological theories. These views had some effect on the teaching of English.

> In general it seems important that the pupil's knowledge should be active knowledge. A boy may write better English if he has discovered the principles of English composition for himself than if he has merely learnt these principles from a teacher or textbook. This does not necessarily imply that the pupil is to make the discovery unaided. The skilful teacher should be able so to arrange situations that the need for the principle involved and eventually its basic character are gradually brought home to the child as a result of active work. The earlier psychologists, who maintained that there was no transfer without identity of materials, overlooked the fact that identity of method might be an even more important factor. If therefore transfer be aimed at, more stress should be laid upon method than on mere results. (p. 131)

Another theme which comes clearly through the Spens Report is the idea of English as citizenship training (as well as 'communication'). Apart from this there is little difference between Spens and Newbolt on the teaching of English. Similarly the Norwood Report (1943) adopted very much the same position.

By the end of the Second World War English was approaching a time of great difficulties: having been rescued from the narrow rigidity of the Elementary Code and the arid teaching methods of public school classics, English as a subject had yet to establish its own identity. To some extent this had been indicated by Spens's subdivision of aims: *communication*, which was itself very wide and also overlapped nearly every other subject on the timetable; *social value*, which was incredibly vaguely defined but potentially extremely wide in its coverage; and *literary appreciation*, which was still thought of in terms of a conventional range of accepted works. Added to this breadth of subject-matter and vagueness of objectives was the complete 'freedom' of syllabus construction given to teachers after the 1944 Education Act, and the growing assumption (resisted in 1910 but marginally referred to by Spens) that English might also be expected to contribute to the pupil's individual development by means of 'creative expression' rather than merely transmitting other people's ideas.

The difficulties of teaching English—or even being clear about what might be taught—as compared with any other subject may be seen from the Ministry of Education 1954 Pamphlet No. 26, *Language: Some Suggestions for Teachers of English and Others*. Before getting near to any practical help for teachers, Part I of the pamphlet contained twenty-two pages of a highly theoretical and abstract kind about the nature of language. This pamphlet is very interesting to read but it gave very little help to teachers of English; it only told them what a difficult and complex task they had. Teachers of English who read the pamphlet might have had their confidence shaken in standards of 'correctness' by being exposed to scientific linguistic views on language, thought and culture, but no new standards were provided to replace those which were discarded. In the preface M. M. Lewis's plea for a study of the problems of communication was quoted, but no real answers were provided:

> Teachers find themselves in a world dominated by communication and devoted to the production of more, and more complex, means of communication. Those who are sufficiently critical of themselves and of their tasks recognize that somehow they lack guidance in what society really demands of them and in the proper use of the instruments with which it so copiously surrounds them.

In the years that followed further doubt was cast on what English teachers were doing. The Newsom Report (1963) highlighted the difficulties of finding ways of reaching pupils defined as 'average and below average' and by implication 'non-academic'; the problem of relations between teachers and working-class pupils was singled out for graphic description, and teachers were urged to make English relevant and to include film and television as part of English. The problem of defining and limiting the scope of English was still apparent.

During the 1960s the London Association for the Teaching of English and later the National Association for the Teaching of English as well as *Use of English* (a journal for teachers of English) all showed a growing concern with what English should be and what methods should be used. Two kinds of English studies grew: 'social awareness' English, seen in such English textbooks as *Reflections*, by S. Clements, J. Dixon and L. Stratta; and 'self-expression' English, popularized by David Holbrook and others. This situation was discussed and to a certain extent clarified by the Anglo-American Conference on the teaching of English at Dartmouth, New Hampshire, in 1966. The issues discussed included such topics as 'What is English?', and 'Language Standards and Attitudes'; the conference seminar was summarized by John Dixon in a very important book, *Growth Through English* (1967).

In the map that emerges from the Dartmouth Seminar, one dimension is historical. Among the models or images of English that have been widely accepted in schools on both sides of the Atlantic, three were singled out. The first centred on *skills*: it fitted an era when *initial* literacy was the prime demand. The second stressed the *cultural heritage*, the need for a civilizing and socially unifying content. The third (and current) model focuses on *personal growth*: on the need to re-examine the learning processes and the meaning to the individual of what he is doing in English lessons. Looking back over the history of our subject, we see the limitations in the earlier models and thus the need to reinterpret our conception of 'skills' and 'heritage'. (pp. 1–2)

Dixon dismisses the skill and cultural heritage models and clearly pins his hopes on 'language and personal growth', which he describes as a process rather than a product.

The Plowden Report (1967) added little of value by way of advice to primary teachers. The whole Report is remarkable for its unquestioning acceptance of a vague and sentimental 'child-centred' ideology (see R. S. Peters's *Perspectives on Plowden*, 1969), and much of what is recommended on English is an oversimplified and distorted version of the views in *Growth Through English*.

A description of English teaching in the 1960s would not be complete without some reference to the 'backlash' against the new emphasis on the pupil as an individual. The *Black Papers* represented the views of many teachers and non-teachers who felt that standards were falling as a result of 'progressive education' and English teaching was often singled out for special abuse:

> According to some present-day psychologists, all teaching of young children must be child-centred: the teaching must grow from the child's interests and not be limited by any timetable divisions. Freedom of expression is all-important and the method of conveying it is relatively unimportant. So far so good, but at what point should the child learn that correctness and accuracy have their place? All may be well at the junior school stage, but the freedom of the look and say method of reading, of the outpouring of ideas without arrangement or plan has disastrous results at a later stage. For instance, when learning a foreign language, one incorrect letter may well alter the whole meaning of a sentence.
>
> Some of my friends in junior schools tell me that marking and correcting is a thing of the past as it may bring a sense of failure to a child.
>
> (C. M. Johnson, 'Freedom in Junior Schools' in B. Cox and A. E. Dyson (eds.), *Fight For Education: A Black Paper*, 1949, p. 49)

The conflict between individual growth and established standards had not been resolved at the time of the publication of *A Language for Life* (1975). This report, usually referred to as the Bullock Report, was the response of a committee originally set up by the DES to examine the teaching of reading in schools. However, the Committee interpreted its brief very widely, considered reading as part of language development and recommended that every school should have an organized policy for language across the curriculum as well as a systematic policy for the development of reading competence (see p. 42). Essentially the Bullock Report was an attempt to steer a way through the criticisms of those who feared that standards were falling as a result of progressive methods, and those at the opposite extreme whose belief in freedom and child-centred methods appeared to rule out any systematic teaching of English.

Mathematics

The development of mathematics in the curriculum is clearly a good example of the 'two traditions' in English education. In the public schools, the pursuit of abstract truths favoured the teaching of geometry and algebra, whereas the elementary schools, which laid stress on the practical arts, looked for competence in arithmetical processes.

Arithmetic was considered, from early times, to be a separate and lower branch of mathematics:

> The following couplet occurs in an arithmetic book published about 1550:
> Pupil (to Master):
> 'And I to your authoritie my witte do subdue,
> Whatsoever you say, I take it for true.'
> Broadly speaking, it may be said with justice that this couplet expresses the educational attitude of pupil to master in the arithmetic lesson as dominant for several centuries both in England and on the Continent. During the nineteenth century, the efforts of reformers to break away from this tradition of rule of thumb and to develop the subject by rational and truly educative methods began to be more or less successful, but only after about a half century of struggle.
>
> (London County Council, *Report of a Conference on the Teaching of Arithmetic in London Elementary Schools 1914*, reprinted 1923, p. 16)

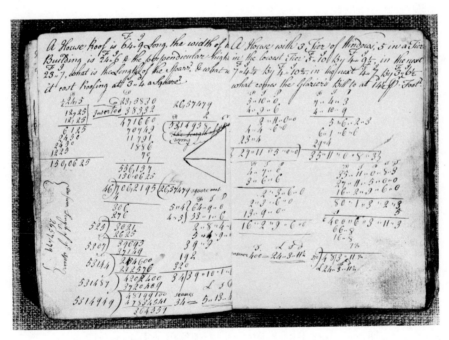

5   A village schoolboy's Arithmetic exercise book, East Yorkshire, 1786–7
    Note the practical nature of the problems set.

There were a number of reasons for the low status of arithmetic. Perhaps the main one was the excessive emphasis placed on the purely utilitarian value of the subject and its use for commercial purposes. This effectively isolated it from other branches of mathematics and it became the hall-mark of elementary education. It is not surprising to find, therefore, that the public schools tended to discourage the teaching of arithmetic. Methods of computation had remained unchanged since the Middle Ages: for example, the Treasury was still using the tally until 1826.

Well before 'payment by results' was introduced, textbooks were produced such as those of James Trotter, published in 1853 and containing 3,400 exercises, and J. W. Colenso, whose 1862 edition introduced trillions and quadrillions on the first page. The imposition of 'standards' from 1862 in elementary schools made for a more mechanical teaching approach in order to obtain good results.

P. B. Ballard, a mathematics inspector of the London County Council in the early part of the twentieth century, analysed the state of arithmetic under this system.

> The golden age of accuracy was the period of payment by results, the duel between the inspector and teacher reaching its most acute stage about 1890. It was then that the

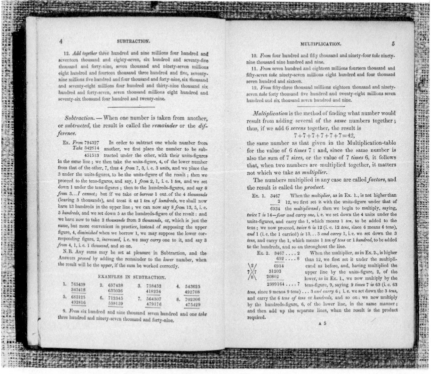

6   A popular Arithmetic textbook
The Rev. J. W. Colenso, Mathematics Master at Harrow and later Bishop of Natal, published his *Arithmetic designed for the use of schools* in 1843. It rapidly went through a number of editions.

teacher seems to have arrived at the highest stage of strategic skill. I have examined a large number of tests set by Her Majesty's Inspectors during the period in question and have arrived at the following generalizations.

The test for each standard consisted of four sums—three 'rule' sums and a problem. The rule sums for a given standard remained constant in type and fairly constant in difficulty from year to year. The problems were by no means complex and made less demand upon the intelligence of the examinees than the problems set at the Junior County School Examinations. The tests often involved very large numbers and called for considerable accuracy in computation. Standard IV seems to have borne the biggest burden of figures. The three 'rules' for this standard were reduction of money, weights and measures, and multiplication and division of money. Examples of the reduction tests:

1. Reduce 126,987 tons to ounces (The answer runs into thousands of millions)
2. Reduce 849,612 drams to cwt
3. Reduce one million square feet to square poles

Examples of tests in the other two rules:
1. £26.15.7¾ × 278   2. £416,073.12.7½ ÷ 381

A striking feature is the extremely narrow range of work prescribed for a given year: the three set 'rules' exemplified by numbers whose magnitude could be approximately predicted formed the staple of the work. And the cases where the class teacher ranged beyond these limits were very rare. In other words, he prepared his children during the whole year for an examination of narrow and easily predictable limits. And the time he devoted to it was vastly greater than the time now allowed for arithmetic. There were as a rule two lessons per day—one each session. Moreover, it was the almost universal custom to set the children three examples at twelve o'clock and to keep them in till they got the three right. In many instances this procedure was repeated at 4.30. In some schools this irregular work was continued all through the year: in others it was restricted to the three months preceding the annual examination. One head master is of opinion that 2½ hours per day was often devoted to arithmetic in those times. We may fairly state, therefore, that the nominal time allowed to arithmetic in those days was nearly twice the time now given, and that the extra time raised the proportion to 3 or 4 times as much. This estimate takes no account of homework, which was very much more pressed in those days than these, and which nearly always meant either spelling or 'sums'.

The so-called 'problem' was either neglected altogether or was practised during the last three months of the year. Two sums out of four would secure a pass: why then trouble about the problem? I know of one teacher of those days who conceived the idea that if two out of three rules were thoroughly taught, both the third rule and the problem could then be left to chance. She went one better than her colleagues in the policy of narrowing, and two better than the Education Department. And it paid, for she obtained the coveted hundred per cent for several years in succession.

(P. B. Ballard, *On the Alleged Decline in Arithmetic Accuracy in Elementary Schools. A Defence, a Criticism and a Few Digressions*, 19 November 1911, MS Report, EO/PS/2/1, Greater London R.O. (London Section))

However, even at the time this report was written, there were critics who argued that much of the arithmetic in schools was still artificial. In one of the two volumes on mathematics teaching in the Special Reports on Educational Subjects series published in 1912, illustrations were given by one writer from contemporary textbooks, together with a commentary:

(i) A fortress is supplied with 92,000 lb of bread and contains 1,400 men, who consume each 10 lb per week; how long will the provision last? (Answer. It depends on the climate.)

(ii) A wine merchant has 100 gallons of wine which are worth £81; find what quantity of water he must add to it so that it may be worth 12s. a gallon. (Answer. The effect on the value of wine of adding 35 per cent of water to it depends on the nature of the wine, and the question is insoluble.)

(iii) If seven boys catch four fish in six days, how long will it take a house of 21 boys to catch one fish at the same rate? (You can but wonder, and at the same time notice how much the literary value of the question would suffer if the words 'a house of' were omitted.)

(iv) A bath is filled by a pipe in 40 minutes. It is emptied by a waste pipe in an hour. In what time will the bath be full if both pipes be opened at once? (This question has its humour, but such questions might be allowed if it were not for the deplorable frequency with which householders are supposed to fill their bath with the waste pipe open.)

Boys have more common sense than Mathematics as a rule, and this kind of thing must surely give them an instinctive, if not a reasoned, contempt for the subject. Surely it is possible in a subject like Arithmetic, which has countless applications in practical affairs, to obtain a sufficient supply of sensible examples. If no such examples can be found in a particular section, is not this a sufficient reason for excluding it from the curriculum?

(Board of Education, Special Reports on Educational Subjects, Pt. 2, The Sadler Report. *The Teaching of Mathematics in the United Kingdom* No. 13, The Teaching of Arithmetic in Secondary Schools by G. W. Palmer 1912, pp. 15–16)

Little change was effected in teaching methods until the early 1960s, when a new approach to mathematics was introduced into primary schools. As late as 1959 it could be said that

a main reason for failure in arithmetic is that teachers are inclined to teach the subject as they themselves were taught as children, thus tending to perpetuate the use of unsound methods. The traditional outlook remains deeply entrenched in our schools and there still occurs teaching of a type which can only be justified in terms of outworn theories of mental training. Most, if not all, teachers were brought up and nurtured in the shadow of these theories. Each of us tends to base his teaching on them without realizing it. We are, indeed, as much prisoners of the contemporary system of education as were our colleagues of the 1850s and the first step towards detachment and freedom of thought is to realize this.

(W. Flemming 'The Teaching of Arithmetic', *Educational Review*, Vol. 11, No. 1, 1959, p. 188)

In the public schools, mathematics was hardly to be found at the beginning of the nineteenth century. At Harrow, instruction in this subject was given privately before 1819. It was made compulsory there in 1837 and Eton followed in 1851. The Eldon Judgment of 1805 inevitably raised the status of classics teaching, yet the future of mathematics was to be linked with classics.

Dr Arnold at Rugby introduced a system whereby boys were taught in three divisions—classical, mathematical and French. Mathematics was taught by the classics form masters who interpreted Euclid in the strictest fashion. Practical applications were ignored and geometry received purely abstract treatment. Algebra was similarly divorced from both geometry and arithmetic and tended to degenerate into a mechanical manipulation of symbols.

Although the Clarendon Commission on the Public Schools reported that 'mathematics at least have established a title of respect as an instrument of mental discipline' this was not reflected in their recommendations: arithmetic and mathematics should occupy three hours a week against classics, with history and divinity taking eleven hours. (Report, 1864, Vol. I, p. 34.)

The importance of mathematics was at last recognized by the Taunton

Commission in 1868. In proposing the three grades of schools, the Commission stated that the three leading subjects should be language, mathematics and natural science. The Commission made clear that the standard of teaching in geometry was poor, the only textbook used being that of Euclid.

It was at this time, during the late 1860s, that there was a growing demand for the recognition of science as an important element in any curriculum claiming to be liberal. The British Association for the Advancement of Science established a committee to consider possible improvements in the teaching of elementary geometry, and their first report, issued in 1873, stated that examination requirements were stultifying teaching methods. Equally important was the Anti-Euclid Association formed in 1870 which questioned the existing state of mathematics in schools.

A new aspect to the mathematical debate was the attention directed towards the need for more and better technical education, following the Royal Commission in the 1880s. A lead was given by the new technical institutions, established after the 1889 Act, in newer methods of mathematics teaching, which included trigonometry, analytical geometry and calculus. Reform of the school curriculum was to wait until the beginning of the twentieth century.

At a meeting of the British Association in Glasgow in September 1901 the teaching of mathematics was attacked by Professor John Perry as being out of date and largely irrelevant to the needs of many pupils. A committee under the chairmanship of Professor Forsyth was set up to report on possible improvements. The previous month, at Forsyth's instigation, twenty-three schoolmasters had addressed a letter to the Association on this topic. This letter appeared in *Nature* on 16 January 1902. 'It proposed a reform of the whole school curriculum in elementary mathematics, and not simply in geometry, and was clearly intended to be read by examiners as well as teachers. One result was the formation of the Teaching Committee of the Mathematical Assocation. . . . In rapid succession in 1902–3 the Oxford Local Delegacy, the Civil Service Commission, the bodies responsible for the Cambridge Previous Examination and the Oxford Responsions agreed to accept "any proof of the proposition, which appears to the examiners to form part of a systematic treatment of the subject instead of the standard Euclidean proof".' (Quoted in Department of Education and Science: *Teaching Mathematics in Secondary Schools:* Education Pamphlet No. 36, 1958, pp. 9–10.)

Although the struggle over the textbooks had been won, official reports between the wars still questioned the value to be placed upon mathematics in the curriculum. The most hard-hitting criticism is contained in the 1938 Spens Report on Secondary Education:

> We believe that school mathematics will be put on a sound footing only when teachers agree that it should be taught as art and music and physical science should be taught, because it is one of the main lines which the creative spirit of man has followed in its development. If it is taught in this way we believe that it will no longer be true to say that 'the study of mathematics is apt to commence in disappointment', and that it will no longer be necessary to give the number of hours to the subject that are now generally assumed to be necessary.

(Spens Report of the Consultative Committee on Secondary Education, 1938, p. 177)

A recent comment upon the final sentence in the paragraph quoted above is as follows:

> A justification for the criticism contained in the Spens Report is made clear in certain statistics published by the Organization for Economic Cooperation and Development in 1965. In these we see that pupils in the science streams of secondary schools in the United Kingdom spent considerably more time studying mathematics than did their counterparts in, say, the Federal Republic of Germany (22 per cent of total time against 12·8 per cent). Indeed no secondary school pupil in the OECD countries devoted more time to mathematics than did the British pupil in the 'Science stream'. Yet if we consider the British pupil who opted for an arts-based course, the position changes, for such a pupil devoted on average only 10 per cent of his total time in secondary school to mathematics, a smaller percentage than pupils in similar streams in Belgium, Denmark, and several other countries. The ratio of the time spent studying mathematics by pupils in the science streams, to that of the pupils in the arts streams, was, in fact, considerably higher in the United Kingdom than in any other OECD country.
>
> This distinction did not go unnoticed by the Dainton Committee when they reported in 1968 on *The Flow of Candidates in Science and Technology into Higher Education*. They argued, 'In our view normally all pupils should study mathematics until they leave school, and only in exceptional circumstances should it be held to be possible or desirable for a pupil to opt out. At present a high proportion of pupils with O level passes in the subject abandon it in the sixth form, and some pupils drop it even earlier. We believe that the overwhelming majority are capable of benefiting from continued study of the subject'.
>
> Although at first sight the recommendations of the Dainton and Spens Reports may seem opposed, this is not really the case. What both Committees asked educators to do was to reconsider the amount of time traditionally allocated to mathematics and to note changes in the objectives of mathematical education, and new methods of teaching the subject. They then asked if these observations did not call for radical changes in the way in which mathematical education in the school was organized.
>
> (H. B. Griffiths and A. G. Howson, *Mathematics, Society and Curricula*, 1974, pp. 21–2)

Two factors have been responsible for recent changes in the content and methods of mathematics teaching, the first psychological and the second the establishment of curriculum development projects.

New approaches in primary school mathematics have been largely the result and influence of the psychological findings of Jean Piaget who in his book *The Child's Conception of Number* (1941) analysed how children learnt mathematical concepts:

> Piaget set himself the task of finding out, as accurately as possible, how the principles of conservation and of reversibility, as applied to numbers and to spatial thinking, develop in the minds of young children. These two principles are fundamental to all mathematical (and logical) thinking. For example, in the field of numbers, conservation means that the number of objects in a group remains the same however the objects are arranged (in a heap, in a long line, etc.). Or if we are considering quantities, a quantity of lemonade remains the same if it is poured, for example, from a shallow dish into a tall, narrow glass. The understanding of reversibility involves a realization that reversing an action would result in a return to the original state of affairs.
>
> (Schools Council Curriculum Bulletin No. 1, *Mathematics in the Primary School*, 1965, p. 5)

Even before the launching of Sputnik I in 1957, the National Science Foundation in the USA had provided money for the planning and writing of new mathematical programmes. This had a world wide influence on attitudes towards the reform of school mathematics. In the United Kingdom this led to the formation of a number of groups to devise and organize new primary and secondary mathematics programmes. Examples of these are the School Mathematics Project (1961), the Nuffield Mathematics Project (1964) and the Schools Council Mathematics for the Majority Project (1967). Basically, their aims are similar and the following statement, which favours, the synthesizing nature of modern mathematics, would be applicable to each of the projects:

> To list the basic concepts around which a school course for the 1970s should pivot is to risk wrenching them from their context. Nevertheless, it may be helpful to mention a few of the ideas which most projects have tried to emphasize in their texts, and to relate them to each other. Thus, stress is laid on the appreciation of spatial relationships and the associated geometrical, algebraic, and arithmetical reasoning; the recognition of certain features or patterns common to apparently different situations, leading to the notion of structures and also to that of modelling; the variety of forms of mathematical relationships and in particular the functional relation; rates-of-change and their formalization in the calculus; mathematical modelling of all kinds of situations, with attention given to the distinctions between continuous and discrete situations; statistics; and the effect that the computer has, and will have, on the applications of mathematics and of the development of research in mathematics.
>
> Over and above all this is the fact that the ideas of mathematics and its language are becoming increasingly used in day-to-day communications between individuals and organizations, and the next 10 years will provide ever more startling manifestations of this fact. Thus, at the various levels, there should be practical work involving observation and measurement; experience of concepts of space, number and relation; careful development of symbols and their manipulation, and of computational skills using appropriate tools; and the formation of mathematical models of the physical world.

> (A Statement on the Present State of Change in Mathematics at Secondary Level: A Report prepared by the Joint Mathematical Council of the United Kingdom, 1970, p. 6)

While there is some agreement among mathematicians on the content of the mathematics curriculum, criticisms have been directed at some problems arising out of the projects. The Mathematics for the Majority Project has a view of the curriculum as something geared to a particular type of child, i.e. the early school leaver. By means of different real-life experiences such as buildings, advertising and fashion, mathematical experiences are built into the project. It has been argued that a project aimed at a particular group of pupils 'labels' the participants and makes subsequent transfer difficult. Another criticism of this approach is that by painlessly absorbing mathematical skills via projects, the pupils may never be able to identify mathematical techniques.

The School Mathematics Project has also been attacked but on a different ground, namely that the mathematical skills gained from working through the Project materials are inadequate to support, for example, the teaching of science. To counter this, the Project issued a definitive pamphlet, *Manipulative Skills in School Mathematics* (1974). This final quotation from an educationist concerning the SMP booklet indicates some of the worries which are being voiced about standards:

> A useful table has been laid out, enumerating 21 basic processes and the age by which it expects different classes of pupils to have gained a 'High degree of proficiency'. This

is useful as it shows specifically the way SMP is thinking and provides a programme with which others may agree or disagree.

I would guess that many scientists would not be happy to accept the low level of attainment that the mathematicians would expect to provide. For example, the average pupil (one likely to be graded at CSE) would only be expected to have mastered the first three of these by the age of 13. He would not be expected to be able to cope with the addition, subtraction, long multiplication and division of numbers with up to three significant figures nor to be able to handle simple use and application of units of length, area and volume.

By the age of 14 he would still not be expected to manipulate competently simple formulae involving $+$, $-$, $\times$ and $\div$ and use of brackets. And even by the age of 16 our average pupil would not be expected to have mastered the use of standard form with positive or negative indices. For the able pupil, too (one likely to get an O level pass) the SMP mathematicians will expect him to need rather less than most science teachers would want. For the able student at 13 would not, according to this (definitive) scheme be expected to cope with simple ratio calculations or any algebraic manipulation.

(B. Woolnough, 'All at sea over new mathematics', *The Times Educational Supplement*, 24 January 1975)

Religious and Moral Education

The history of the appearance of moral education in the school curriculum is reflected in two ways: the changing concept of childhood over time, and views on how mental, physical and moral capacities should be educated; and the challenging of the notion that social control and order can be best achieved by means of religious instruction.

In the public schools of the last century, religious and moral training took a different form from that of elementary schools:

> Religious training was centred in the school chapel, where school values were too often identified with Christian values, but were never less 'than a kind of dedication of adolescence to a belief in the honour of a gentleman, the duty of self-control and faith between friends'. But neither the honour of gentlemen nor their capacity for self-control were regarded as adequate safeguards for the proper behaviour of boys in their spare time. The restrictions placed upon the free occupation of leisure rather suggested that boys were neither gentlemen nor given to exercise restraint on their baser passions. Schoolmasters, obsessed with the conviction that idle hours were the source of all youthful corruption, punctuated the school day between work, chapel and compulsory games with frequent roll-calls to ensure that no boy was alone or too far away for too long. It was not the grosser temptations purveyed by bookmakers and inn-keepers that worried the largely bachelor staff; such crude manifestations of appetite were not included in the higher categories of sin. It was the hidden evil within the surge of adolescence itself that was most feared—sexual indulgence, to which alone the general term of 'immorality' was applied.

(E.B. Castle, *Moral Education in Christian Times*, 1958, p. 361)

Religious education was considered to be one of the basic elements in all schools during the nineteenth century. The Committee of the Privy Council on Education declared: 'Religion ought to be combined with the whole matter of instruction and to regulate the entire system of discipline.'

The 1870 Elementary Education Act brought to a head the controversies concerning the form religious instruction should take in the elementary school.

With the need to provide extra school places, school boards were established to 'fill the gaps'. The dual system of education made necessary some compromise formula which was acceptable to both Church and non-Church schools. This took the form of a provision in the Act, called the Cowper-Temple Clause (Section 14(2) of the Act), which stated that 'no religious catechism or religious formulary which is distinctive of any particular denomination shall be taught in Board Schools'.

During the course of the debate on the Act, Mr W. F. Cowper-Temple, the Chairman of the National Education Union, made reference to the teaching of moral education, which was to have a firm religious basis.

> The question was whether or not there should be moral training in the schools founded by the state. . . . It would be impossible to enact that children should not be instructed in the duty of obedience to the moral law, and in a sense of responsibility to their maker. . . . If there was to be moral training, it must be based upon the sanctions of the Divine law, not upon the dictates of self-interest.

> (Hansard, 3, cc, col. 289, 18 March 1870)

However, as a result of this enactment, children were not required, as a condition of admittance to a school, to attend a place of worship; and, if the school provided religious instruction, parents were allowed to withdraw their children from it. The school teacher was thus given a new authority in religious education. Disraeli had warned the government:

> You will not entrust the priest or the presbyter with the privilege of expounding the Holy Scriptures to the scholars; but for that purpose you are inventing and establishing a new sacerdotal class. The schoolmaster who will exercise these functions, and who will occupy this position, will be a member of a class which will, in the future, exercise an extraordinary influence upon the history of England and upon the conduct of Englishmen.

> (Quoted in W. H. G. Armytage, 'The 1870 Education Act', in *British Journal of Educational Studies*, Vol. 18, No. 2, June 1870)

Some of the larger boards, using London as a model, provided schemes which included reading the Bible with explanations and instruction in 'the principles of Morality and Religion'. Exceptionally, three boards—Burton on Trent (1878), Birmingham (1883) and Huddersfield (1889)—set special time apart for moral lessons. In all these cases, however, the lessons supplemented, not replaced, Bible studies. Here is the earliest example:

BURTON-UPON-TRENT

LESSONS ON PRINCIPLES OF MORALITY, VIRTUE AND GOOD BEHAVIOUR

> Once a week, in all departments, in the time devoted to religious instruction, a lesson on a subject that will come under the above heading shall be given. A few topics are named below, others may be added by the teacher, and they may be combined and arranged in any way found advisable. These lessons are not intended to take the place of the moral teaching which is given as occasion requires and as the Bible studies suggest, but are intended to supplement and to be in addition to such teaching. The

lessons should be illustrated as far as possible from the portions of Scripture given in the syllabus for repetition and study, but other illustrations, both secular and scriptural, should be used. In speaking of a virtue, the character and effect of the opposite vice should be commented upon. It is hoped that the lessons will be made as practical as possible and brought down to the level of the children's daily experience. The object of the lessons should be kept well in view, namely, the influencing for good of the present and future character and conduct of the pupils.

Scripture Syllabus and Moral Lessons.

The following topics are suggested in the syllabus as subjects of instruction: Love to God; love to man; a sacred regard for truth in word, act and suggestion; consideration for others; respect for and obedience to those in authority (parents, teachers, &c.); politeness; purity in thought, word and act; industry and diligence; thrift; frugality; sobriety; perseverance; honesty; patriotism; heroism; kindness to animals; pride; envy; bad company.

(H. Johnson, *Report of Moral Instruction in Elementary Schools in England and Wales*, 1908, pp. 10–11)

Much of the subsequent, if short-lived, success of the moral education campaign was due to the activities of F. J. Gould (1855–1938). He had worked as a schoolmaster for twenty-five years, sixteen of them under the London School Board. Two events in 1881 influenced his decision to become an agnostic and devote his time to the cause of moral education in schools: one was Bradlaugh's parliamentary struggle against disqualification for refusing to take the oath on the Bible; the other was a meeting Gould attended when he heard Frederic Harrison speak on 'The New Social System, Positive Philosophy and the Religion of Humanity'. Together with a group of friends who included Gustav Spiller and C. J. Pollard, Gould planned an Ethical Society in 1889: subsequently a Sunday School was opened in the East End which was attended by, among others, the children of Tom Mann and George Lansbury.

The Moral Instruction League, founded in 1897, sprang out of the Ethical Movement. At the first Annual Congress of the Union of Ethical Societies in the previous year, it was decided to call a Moral Instruction School Board Election Conference. A protest and a petition, with Gould's specimen lesson on 'Courage', were widely circulated: it asked for instruction in personal and civic duties rather than Bible lessons, to be given by specially trained Board teachers.

The aims of the League at its opening meeting were more bluntly stated: 'To substitute systematic non-theological moral instruction for the present religious teaching in all State schools, and to make character the chief aim of school life'.

Gould's work in Leicester was crucial in forwarding the movement. He was elected to the School Board in 1900, promising the electors that he would press for courses of moral lessons in the curriculum. In 1901, the Board agreed to the introduction of such courses. (F. J. Gould, *Moral Education: Chapter from the Story of Schools in England and Wales*, 1895–1925, 1929, pp. 5–6)

The Leicester model was widely followed. By the end of 1904, eleven LEAs had made provision in their schools for systematic moral instruction: by 1906 this had risen to thirty-four. The scheme of West Riding of Yorkshire closely followed the guidelines suggested by the Moral Instruction League:

COUNTY COUNCIL OF THE WEST RIDING OF YORKSHIRE

Education Department

Scheme of Training in Citizenship approved by the Education Committee, December 29th, 1904, as part of the Secular Instruction in all West Riding Public Elementary Schools.

Infants

1. CLEANLINESS
   - (*a*) Clean hands, faces, and clothes
   - (*b*) Clean habits, e.g. the proper use of the lavatory

2. TIDINESS
   - (*a*) In the home, school, and street
   - (*b*) Personal tidiness, care of clothing
   - (*c*) Care of furniture, books, toys, and other property

3. MANNERS
   - (*a*) Greetings at home, at school, and in the street
   - (*b*) Punctuality and promptness

4. KINDNESS
   - (*a*) To parents, elders, and teachers
   - (*b*) To each other in the home, school, and street
   - (*c*) To animals, e.g. dogs and cats

5. FAIRNESS
   - (*a*) Mine and thine
   - (*b*) Fairness towards others

6. TRUTHFULNESS
   Confidence in parents and teachers to be encouraged

7. COURAGE
   - (*a*) When alone
   - (*b*) Darkness, shadows, and strange noises

Standard VII

1. PATRIOTISM
   - (*a*) The vote: its nature and responsibilities
   - (*b*) The nation and its government
   - (*c*) Local government
   - (*d*) Society as an organism, its development through the family, tribe, and nation

2. PEACE AND WAR
   - (*a*) International relations
   - (*b*) Value of arbitration

3. JUSTICE
   - (*a*) The development of the idea of justice from the earliest times
   - (*b*) The development of the humane spirit in laws

4. OWNERSHIP
   (*a*) Individual and collective ownership
   (*b*) Responsibilities of ownership

5. THRIFT
   (*a*) Simplicity of living
   (*b*) The evils of debt and gambling

6. COOPERATION
   (*a*) Between citizens
   (*b*) Between nations; interchange of thought, arts, and material productions

7. THE WILL
   (*a*) The training of the will
   (*b*) The right to be done intelligently, unhesitatingly, thoroughly, cheerfully, and zealously

8. SELF-RESPECT
   Self-respect and self-restraint in thought, word, and action

9. IDEALS
   The value and beauty of an ideal for life

(G. Spiller, *Moral Education in Eighteen Countries*, 1909, pp. 152–3)

Gilbert Murray, the classical scholar, has left this rare account of one of Gould's lessons:

I was at the Board of Education during the War, and was deputed to attend an example of Moral Teaching by a Mr Gould, of whom I knew nothing beforehand. I went with a sigh, feeling sure that such a thing must be dull. I found a room with about forty children seated in rows, a group of adults standing behind them, and in front by the fireplace a quiet-looking elderly man in an arm-chair. It was summer and there was no fire in the grate.

The lesson was on Service, though we were not told so beforehand. We were only allowed to gather it afterwards. He began by saying that he was sitting by a warm fire reading a book; the children were asked to choose the book; among various suggestions he selected *Treasure Island*. Then he looked discontentedly at the empty grate, rang an imaginary bell and directed an imaginary servant to put on coal, which she did. The children by this time were amused, and were asked why she performed this service. Obviously, because she was paid.

Next came a story of a British Ambassador in Persia, living in an old Persian palace. He wished his drawing-room ceiling re-decorated, and agreed with a Persian artist to do it for a stated sum. The work took longer and the artist put more into it than had been expected, and the Ambassador began to be afraid that he would demand a higher fee. The Persian indignantly repudiated this; he admired the old ceiling so much that he wanted to make it perfect. What was he working for? Clearly not for pay. Various shots were made by the children till they agreed that it was the artist's love of his art.

Then came stories of some travellers in Siberia who arrived bitterly cold at an empty hut provided for their use, found a store of wood, made a fire, and fed and slept. Next morning they started off, but before starting, what had they to do? All kinds of guesses: of course they had to collect more wood and leave a store for the next party that came. Service for others. Then came more stories and more problems of casuistry and psychology. The grown-ups at the back caught the children's excitement, and made their own guesses till they were reproved and told they were to be seen and not heard.

The last story was that of the great Japanese Temple, built in thanksgiving after a pestilence, to which every class of people made their contribution; the land-owners gave their trees, the woodmen cut down the trees, the carpenters shaped them and built them, the poets made songs, the various artificers prepared their decorations. Only the women seemed to be left out. But they too wanted to serve. So they gave their hair to be twisted into ropes for binding the wooden pillars together; and there the temple stands, comprising the gifts of everyone in the community for the common good. We had laughed again and again during the lesson, and I think tears were in most eyes at the end.

(F. H. Hayward and E. M. White, *The Last Years of a Great Educationist*, 1939, pp. 63–4)

During the period when the new LEAS were being formed intensive lobbying culminated in an impressive memorial, signed by members of both Houses of Parliament, eminent professors and school board representatives, requesting the President of the Board of Education to introduce 'regulations enforcing definite daily instruction in personal and civic duties [which] may be included in the Code of Regulations for Day Schools'. Accordingly the Education Code of 1904 and those in the years following included an Introduction by Morant recommending teachers to follow the principles of moral education in their schools:

> They can endeavour, by example and influence, aided by the sense of discipline which should pervade the school, to implant in the children habits of industry, self-control, and courageous perseverance in the face of difficulties; they can teach them to reverence what is noble, to be ready for self-sacrifice, and to strive their utmost after purity and truth; they can foster a strong respect for duty, and that consideration and respect for others which must be the foundation of unselfishness and the true basis of all good manners; while the corporate life of the school, especially in the playground, should develop that instinct for fair-play and for loyalty to one another, which is the germ of a wider sense of honour in later life. In all these endeavours the school should enlist, as far as possible, the interest and cooperation of the parents and the home in a united effort to enable the children not merely to reach their full development as individuals, but also to become upright and useful members of the community in which they live, and worthy sons and daughters of the country to which they belong.

(Board of Education 1904 Code of Regulations for Public Elementary Schools)

This official recognition of the moral education movement alarmed religious authorities, coming soon after the 1902 Education Act where the Church had lost much ground. A letter appeared in *The Times* in January 1905, signed by both archbishops and eight bishops of the Church of England and the undenominational bodies stating that efficient moral training in state schools should be inspired by Christian motives and be based on Bible teaching.

Political events were also tending to threaten the moral education movement. The growing rivalry of European nations from the beginning of the twentieth century seemed likely to lead to war. It was widely held that patriotism and self-discipline were values to be inculcated, and the methods suggested by the Moral Instruction League did not appear to be the most effective way of carrying out this task.

This viewpoint is supported by a mass of contemporary writings of which the following is a typical example. A special 'Duty and Discipline' series of leaflets was published in 1910 with a preface headed 'To British Men and Women Who Love Their Country and Its Children'. This series was published, not for profit, but with a view to counteract the lack of adequate moral training and discipline, the effects of which are so apparent in these days amongst many British children, in rich as well as in poor homes.

   Where such conditions are not apparent, it is yet advisable to closely scrutinize present educational and social developments, lest relaxed discipline, false sentiment, or an immoderate pursuit of pleasure should tend to weaken the moral fibre of the children.

   The writers feel strongly that the present juvenile indiscipline is a serious social danger, and a peril to the permanent security of the Empire.

   Supporters of this view whose names appeared in the preface included representatives from the whole spectrum of political and social life: Baden-Powell, A. J. Balfour, General Booth, Louis Botha, John Burns, Churchill, Conan Doyle, Kipling, the two archbishops and Lord Rosebery. The majority of contributors were concerned with aspects of discipline. Among the titles of essays appeared the following: 'Lack of Discipline in the Training of Children—and the Remedy'; 'Things We Don't Want—Spoilt Children'; and 'The Value of a Certain "Hardness" in Education'.

   One of the essays in the series includes this passage:

   The backbone of steel has been removed from the national body, and one of putty has been placed in its stead, to the national detriment. . . . Take for instance, the views of the middle and lower classes upon the corporal punishment of their children. . . . Today the contemptible sentimentality of a certain degenerate section of the English people banishes the rod from the schoolroom and the nursery, and, in consequence floods the country with a band of undesirable hooligans on one hand and contemptibly softened individuals on the other. They will not realize that a boy who cannot take a well-deserved thrashing without crying out about it is not worth calling a boy at all. And yet the finest men have resulted from the old system.

   (Raymond Blathwayt, 'Sentimental England. Are we Becoming Degenerate Through Lack of Discipline?', in *Essays on Duty and Discipline*, 1910)

   The high point of the Moral Instruction League's success had come with the return of the Liberal government in 1905. Augustine Birrell, the Minister of Education, gave his blessing to moral instruction in the Commons in May 1906: 'I do not think for a moment that morality can only be taught on a theological basis.' But by 1909 the word 'non-theological' had been omitted from the original object, 'to introduce systematic non-theological Moral Instruction into all schools', and 'civic' was added in its place. Attempts in that year to persuade the Board of Education to put pressure on LEAs to adopt moral instruction in schools failed. Gustav Spiller, the historian of the League, pointed out another difficulty which occurred in the same year (1909). In changing its title from Moral *Instruction* League to Moral *Education* League, the challenge implied in the original title was weakened. At the same time, the problem of general moral education such as discipline and the ethicizing of school subjects received no closer attention.

   The League's strategy now changed: efforts were made to persuade training colleges to provide moral education courses for their students in the form of demonstration lessons and manuals of instruction, but with only moderate success.

The policy of substituting moral education for moral instruction proved to be the main reason for the decline in the League's influence. By 1916, the title had been changed once again, this time to the Civic and Moral Education League, with a growing involvement in training for citizenship. After the war, it became the Civic Education League before it ceased to exist.

The failure of the League has been ascribed to its narrowness of approach.

> Had the League's efforts, certainly from 1909 onwards, been directed not simply to-wards producing manuals and textbooks of moral teaching containing largely 'secular' material but towards encouraging a broader approach to moral teaching which incor-porated the best of the religious *and* secular teaching material, it might well have helped permanently to raise the whole standard of moral education in schools.

> (F. H. Hilliard, 'The Moral Instruction League 1897–1919', *Durham Research Review*, Vol. 3, No. 12, Sept. 1961, pp. 61–2)

The 1944 Education Act with its mandatory provision for non-doctrinal bib-lical teaching in schools raised again the question of the place of moral education. Research, such as that of Piaget in *The Moral Judgment of the Child* in 1932, had shown that there were three stages of moral maturity which a child passed through. Subsequent researchers in this field confirmed the view that 'straight' religious teaching was hardly likely to be effective. Without any specific guidance on whether the Act was intended to encourage practising Christians in their faith or to improve the moral tone of pupils, many teachers were reluctant to teach religious instruction in isolation from other areas of the curriculum.

Official reports, such as Newsom and Plowden, underlined the difficulties of separating religious and moral teaching, a view shared by many writers on religious education, especially Harold Loukes in *Teenage Religion* (1961) and Sir Richard Acland in *We Teach Them Wrong* (1964).

In the past few years, much more attention has been paid to research into moral education in Britain and the United States; perhaps the most distinguished American work has been carried out by Laurence Kohlberg. In England, the Farmington Trust Research Unit at Oxford has been involved since 1965 in studies which attempt to link psychology and sociology to moral education as well as to define the nature of moral education.

> Both as a research subject and as a practical undertaking, moral education must rely very largely upon the application of different disciplines: and the importance of good communications can hardly be over-emphasized. In this Unit we have tried to do our best in facing the implications of having workers trained in philosophy, psychology and sociology living and working in the same building and on the same project.

> (J. Wilson, N. Williams and B. Sugarman, *Introduction to Moral Education*, 1967, pp. 29-30)

Philip R. May at Durham University carried out a nationwide survey in 1967 on the attitudes of teachers to both moral and religious education. Over 60 per cent of respondents agreed that special periods should be set aside for moral education in maintained schools. May suggests some ways in which this work be undertaken. Courses could be mounted in elementary psychology concerning the

way individuals develop intellectually, emotionally and morally and how attitudes are formed and changed. Pupils should also be trained in educating the
emotions, training in judgment and practice in exercising responsibility and self-
control. (P. R. May, *Moral Education in Schools*, 1971, pp. 168–9.)

A large-scale project on moral education commissioned by the Schools Council
as part of the Raising of the School Leaving Age programme was started by Peter
McPhail at Oxford in 1967. It has now produced a set of teaching materials
called *Lifeline* which is designed to help children from thirteen to sixteen 'to adopt
a considerate style of life, that is to adopt patterns of behaviour which take other
people's needs, interests and feelings into account as well as their own'. The
project's two main research conclusions have governed the form the materials
took: first, that adolescents learn much of their behaviour by social experiment,
and second, that behaviour is contagious so that the principal moral influence on
adolescents is the treatment they receive. Moral education therefore is not
thought of as a separate school subject and an attempt is being made to introduce
a morality of communications at both interpersonal and organizational levels.
(Schools Council *Profile*, 1973, p. 22.)

The current debate on moral education in schools reflects the problems of a
changing society. For example, the multi-cultural nature of the school community and the lack of value consensus preclude a 'correct' set of responses to problem
situations. In the light of such changes, a redefinition of the working relationships
between religious and moral education is being sought.

Home Economics

The origins of the introduction of domestic subjects into schools can be traced
back directly to the concern expressed by social reformers in the 1840s about the
condition of the poor. Kay-Shuttleworth sought to ameliorate these conditions
through education.

His famous experiment at the Norwood school for pauper children in 1838
tested his thesis that attention to children's cleanliness, regular diet and outdoor
occupations would combat some of the worst problems of the urban poor. The
curriculum had a practical element; for the boys, workshops were built.

> The domestic training of the girls was equally varied and stimulating: it included the
> cleaning of the teachers' apartments, waiting on them at meals, plain cooking, instruc-
> tion in the wash-house and laundry, domestic hygiene, the care of infants, and the
> rudiments of sick-nursing.
>
> (F. Smith, *Life and Work of Sir James Kay-Shuttleworth*, 1923, p. 58)

Kay-Shuttleworth's chance to generalize this routine came in 1846 when the
Whig government promised to 'give special attention to the subject of
Education'. The Minutes of the Committee of Council (August and December
1846) provided for a generous provision of teacher-training and the establishment
of the pupil-teacher system. One of the stated aims of the Minutes was 'to render

the school popular among the poor, as a means of introducing their children to more honourable and profitable employments'. In a commentary on the Minutes, Kay-Shuttleworth stressed the need for domestic subjects:

> The domestic arrangements of the poor are often extremely defective, from the want of a knowledge of the commonest arts and maxims of household economy. A girl who works in a factory or a mine, or who is employed from an early hour in the morning until the evening in field labour, has little or no opportunity to acquire the habits and skill of a housewife. Even the rudest traditions of domestic thrift are liable to be lost, when public employment interferes so much with the proper training of the labourer's daughter at home. Commerce offers a larger variety of productions for the sustenance of the common people of this country, than of any other; but they are unacquainted with the use of any articles of food besides those which are of home production, with the exception of tea, coffee, and sugar. From these defects, a considerable portion of the earnings of the labourer is unskilfully wasted, his home is deprived of comfort which he might otherwise enjoy, and discontent often drives him to dissipation.
>
> To remedy these evils it has been proposed to make the school itself a means of instructing and training girls in the arts of domestic economy. It has been conceived, that a considerable portion of the oral lessons given in the girls' school, might be devoted to the subject of household management, and that if a wash-house and kitchen were connected with the school, they might, by proper arrangements, receive a practical training in cottage cookery, and in the care of the clothes of a labourer's family. For the encouragement of such plans their Lordships have proposed to grant assistance towards the erection of the requisite buildings, and gratuities to the mistress for success in the instruction of her scholars.
>
> (J. P. Kay-Shuttleworth, *Four Periods of Public Education*, 1862, pp. 492–3)

This work could only be carried on successfully in the women's training colleges, but progress was slow. The Rev. F. C. Cook HMI, later to become HM Inspector of Female Training Schools, in a memorandum to the Secretary of the Education Department, outlined the contents of a suitable curriculum and some of the problems to be overcome in providing it:

> A large proportion of those who tried for certificates could not spell common words, parse an easy sentence, or work a sum correctly in compound multiplication. To teach such persons to wash, bake, and to manage a household, was quite unreasonable. When the pupil teachers are admitted, this difficulty will at once be overcome. They will have time to learn whatever the school managers may find it expedient to teach, and will be in every way benefited by the alternation of industrial occupations and economical instruction with their usual studies. On the other hand, none of the institutions which I have visited have made proper arrangements for this purpose. The kitchens and other offices are not in any way adapted for the industrial training of students. But alterations have already been proposed and, as I understand, are now in course of adoption at Whitelands, Salisbury, and other places; and it may be hoped that this deficiency will be generally supplied.
>
> I do not feel myself qualified, at present, to express an opinion as to the best mode of encouraging managers and students to devote more time and attention to this subject.
>
> The proficiency of the students can scarcely be made a subject of oral or written examination. The most intelligent girls will produce the best papers, and even those who shrink from industrial and domestic occupations will find it easy to impose upon the most experienced Inspector. At the same time there can be no doubt that a system may be devised, and carried out, which will be satisfactory to their Lordships and to the managers of the institutions.
>
> Bearing in mind that our schoolmistresses are to be the educators of the mothers of the peasantry, of our domestic servants, and, to no small extent, of the wives and sisters of the small shopkeepers and tenant farmers, I am most anxious that their training

should be of a thoroughly practical character, and it will be a subject of most serious consideration in the inspection of each establishment.

(Minutes of the Committee of Council on Education, 1850–1, Vol. I, Memorandum 13 July 1850, 1851, pp. 79–80)

Cook was in regular communication with Angela Burdett (later Baroness Burdett-Coutts), the philanthropist, a strong advocate of feminist views. She was responsible for establishing sewing schools for girls in the East End as well as forming street arabs into 'shoe blacks brigades'. It was largely through her initiative that domestic subjects expanded in women's training colleges:

> I had gone to London [she wrote in June 1856] to give some things at Whitelands Training Institution for teaching Common Things in Girls Schools . . . however useful a knowledge of the reason of Tides and the height of Mountains and Chemistry agricultural and other precise knowledge may be to Boys in the varied vocations to which they are called, especially in the country, such knowledge would do very little in forming the habits of the future Wives and Mothers of the country. . . .
>   The Things I gave in as quiet a manner as I could; besides being more agreeable to myself I was anxious to produce a feminist and domestic effect on the minds of the female Teachers—but there will be a little notice of it in the papers, for tho' it was desirable to be quiet, I think that the public should be quite in the dark as to the objects and motives of those who seek to impose on Institutions supported by public grant of money their own views and convictions—Do you think I am quite *constitutional* in *this view*? Of course my objects about Needlework cooking etc. are harmless and no one can object to them whether they hold them in the same importance I do or not—but this might not be always the case.
>
> (Angela Burdett to Lord Brougham, 16 June 1856, Brougham MSS., University College, London)

Such pessimism proved to be unjustifiable. Under the Revised Code some six years later, plain needlework, out of all the domestic subjects, was sanctioned for grant purposes and was obligatory for girls in public elementary schools. The reason for this was explained later by a retired inspector:

> Before 1876 the inspection of needlework was very simple. . . . In country schools there was not much fear of neglect, for Mrs Squire and Mrs Rector kept vigilant eyes on this branch of education, and the subscribers to the school funds often got back part of the value of their money by sending their household seaming to be done in schools. It was no unusual thing to find five afternoons a week entirely devoted to sewing.
>
> (E. M. Sneyd-Kynnersley, *Passages in the Life of an H.M. Inspector of Schools*, 1908, p. 314)

With the creation of school boards after 1870, some experimental schemes in cookery were introduced into elementary schools by lady members of the boards, such as Miss F. L. Calder in Liverpool and Miss Buckton in Leeds. There were, however, two difficulties which limited the widespread adoption of this subject. Financially, it was not recognized by the Education Department for grant-earning purposes; in addition it suffered from low status. Eleanor Rathbone, wife of the first Chairman of the Liverpool School Board, wrote to an MP:

5 July 1871

I do not see that extra subjects need be paid by Government *money* . . . I know two large schools where the fees vary from 2d. to 3d.—to 6d. and 9d.—the higher sum being select subjects. . . .

The Masters would find superior instruction very profitable . . . cooking will seldom be managed—Washing and scouring requires great tact or it will cause all the best girls to be withdrawn—a little sink cookery requiring only a saucepan on the school room fire while the children do sewing—may be done if a *Lady* will undertake it—but not else—the mistress lets it drop where the Lady's attention is withdrawn—We teach sulphur fumigation by practice twice a day—and no child has had an inspector's complaint now for eight months.

With regard to the Girls, tho' you cannot afford to pay for sewing, you need not exact so much Arithmetic. Let their year be behind the Boys, or if 3 sums right out of 4 passes a boy—let 2 out of 4 pass a girl.

(E. Rathbone to G. Melly, Melly Papers, Private Correspondence, Vol. XVL, 1871, 920 MEL 22, Liverpool Record Office)

Even after the need for domestic subjects in schools had been acknowledged by the Department, there were those who saw this area of work in terms of domestic economy, with the emphasis on the latter word:

Another result we hope for is, that when girls are rightly instructed in the elements of domestic economy, and understand them, waste will cease. There is shameful waste at present in nearly every house where much management has to be left to domestic servants. . . .

All Waste is Sinful. It is abominable ingratitude to God. It is senseless robbery of the poor. It is worse than downright *picking and stealing* or vulgar thieving because they can be punished by the policeman, the lock-up, and the house of correction; whereas waste cannot.

(Rev. J. P. Faunthorpe (ed.), *Household Science: Readings in Necessary Knowledge for Girls and Young Women*, 1881, p. 4)

The crucial event which led to a thorough rethinking of the role of cookery and needlework in the curriculum was the International Exhibition held in London in 1873 and promoted by the Royal Commissioners of the more famous 1851 Exhibition. Henry Cole, the Secretary of the Science and Art Department, and himself a Commissioner, decided to include aspects of food preparation as part of the Exhibition. Over half a million people attended and the cookery section, which was visited by Queen Victoria, was most popular. As a result, the Commissioners sanctioned the establishment of a National Training School for Cookery in South Kensington in the following year. At first, it was attended by the middle classes, but gradually it became a training school for teachers and its influence spread.

At the same time, in the Code of 1874 domestic economy was recognized by the Education Department. The Code came in for heavy criticism on a variety of grounds.

Sir John Lubbock MP, the scientist and educational reformer, while agreeing with the syllabus prescribed by the Code, argued:

This is all very sensible and appropriate, but it may only be taken up after history, geography and grammar, or two of them; and even then it is restricted to girls. Why should not boys, also, be allowed to learn about food and clothing? Are not cleanliness and ventilation as necessary for men as for women? Are boys never ill? men never

7   *A Manual of Domestic Economy:* suggestions of the Rev. F. C. Cook HMI
1851. The author was Inspector of Female Training Schools.

improvident? Surely there might be advantage, and could be no evil, in allowing boys,
as well as girls, to be instructed in these humble, yet most important subjects.

(Sir J. Lubbock, *Addresses, Political and Educational*, 1879, p. 75)

One of the Education Department's criticisms of school boards wishing to
develop this work was that too much of it was of a theoretical nature; expenditure
on the provision of cooking facilities was not allowed for. A comprehensive petition by ten school boards, which included Birmingham, Sheffield and
Wolverhampton, was sent to the Vice-President of the Council in 1877 urging the
introduction of practical instruction in cookery.

It was in the field of technical education that more progress was to be found.
There were two sources of funding for this work. One was the Science and Art
Department, and the other, the City and Guilds of London Institute, set up in
1879 by the Livery Companies of London. Technical subjects were broadly
interpreted by both authorities to include all forms of theoretical and applied
science, which included domestic economy. Evening classes were held for ex-
elementary pupils who wished to continue with their studies. The superior equipment provided for them, often in elementary school buildings, contrasted sharply

with those available for the day school teachers. Giving evidence before the
Royal Commission on Technical Instruction in November 1882, HMI Mr H. E.
Oakeley was asked for his views on instruction in science in elementary schools.
He replied:

> I am not altogether satisfied with our syllabus. I should like to see physiology struck out
> of the list, and also what is called domestic economy, the so-called scientific subject for
> girls, simply because domestic economy is a subject which eminently requires practice.
> For instance, take cooking; the girls learn by heart recipes, and would not know the
> materials if they saw them. The girls who get the grant come from the better class
> schools, they describe in capital language the way of cleaning a hearth, and when I ask
> I find that they have never done it in their lives.
>
> Do they actually make a pudding?—They do not make a pudding, because there are
> no materials for making it. I have stated in my last report that my colleague who had
> been rather depressed on examining girls who had committed a quantity of facts to
> paper about nitrogenous and other food, seeing in a class room a boiler fitted up and a
> kitchen that was used for some night schools, brightened up at this, and said to the
> mistress 'Of course you have been able here to combine some practical work.' 'Oh,
> dear, no,' she said, in rather a snappish way, 'we have only had time to learn the little
> book.'
>
> If in the instruction in domestic economy practice were combined with theoretical
> instruction you would not have the same objection to make?—I think it would be most
> valuable then.

(2nd Report of Royal Commission on Technical Instruction, Vol. III, 1884, Evidence
Q. 3637–9, p. 403)

8   A Domestic Science lesson 1906

While the Royal Commission was sitting, representations were made to the Education Department by members of Training Schools of Cookery which had been established in various parts of the country in the 1870s for more practical instruction in schools. From 1882, grants for attendance at cookery lessons were given 'in schools where the Inspector reports that special and appropriate provision is made for the practical teaching of cookery', and needlework was similarly recognized.

Apart from financial constraints, the view was expressed that the development of this subject had been hindered because supervision had so far been in the hands of an all-male inspectorate who lacked the required expertise.

Lady Leigh of Stoneleigh Abbey, Warwickshire, had earlier written to the Lord President asking him 'to take into consideration the question of appointing ladies to inspect the School Needlework of the country at large, and to inspect girls in Domestic Economy'.

> A man's inspection really is a mockery—if the work is good his praise is hardly an incentive, as it is so universally felt, and whispered behind his back that 'he knows nothing about it', and if it is bad, ten to one he does not hit the really weak point.
>   The last thing I wish to do is to reflect upon our own particular Inspectors who are capital people but I believe a woman's opinion about hunting or shooting would be as worth having as any man's opinion upon Needlework.

(Lady Leigh to Earl Spencer, 16 Dec. 1880, Spencer MSS., Althorp, Northants)

F. R. Sandford, Secretary of the Education Department, calculated that such a proposal 'would require some 100 ladies to do the work'. As it was, many of the inspectors were helped in schools by ladies of their family. In addition there were the competing claims of other subjects to be considered:

> This addition to the staff—which would save us no *Men* Inspectors—would be costly—and, I fear, rather unmanageable.
>   Special Inspectors all pressing either their own subjects, and not looking at the work, or capacity of the school as a whole, are to be deprecated; and with the claims of Music—Dancing—Science—and other subjects, all asking for 'Special' consideration—I would not like to make Sewing a precedent.

(Sandford to Earl Spencer, 23 Dec. 1880, ibid.)

Shortly afterwards, in 1883, a Directress of Needlework, Miss Emily Jones, was appointed by the Education Department, followed in 1890 by an Inspectress of Cookery and Laundry Work, both on a temporary basis. The broadening concept of domestic economy, to include not only home-making and cooking but also aspects of health and hygiene, was largely due to the influence of the appointment of further inspectors by the Education Department and, at the local level, instructors by school boards. The Code of 1887 recognized 'Domestic Science (The Science of Domestic Economy and Hygiene)' as well as Domestic Economy, adding the rubric 'It is intended that instruction in this subject should be entirely experimental, the experiments, as far as possible, being carried out by the schools themselves and arranged with the object of solving a definite problem'.

As with manual training for boys, domestic subjects were taught in special centres fed by a number of different schools. This naturally had the effect of isolating the work from the rest of the curriculum, a situation which was to continue until after the Second World War.

Some of the bigger school boards provided ample facilities for their schools. For example, by the beginning of the twentieth century, London had 108 centres for its 470 elementary schools. Here is a contemporary account of the work carried on:

> The housewifery centre is practically a four-roomed house, consisting of a bedroom, sitting-room and kitchen, and a lecture-room. Sometimes it has been specially built for the purpose; sometimes it is a dwelling-house or part of one which has been adapted. The rooms are furnished and fitted much as a working man's home might be, and here girls who have already gone through the cookery and laundry classes learn, and as far as may be practise, an astonishing variety of useful household lore. Here the girls practise cooking without the appliances of the cookery school, using only such utensils as might be found in a working man's kitchen.
>
> The principles of lighting, ventilation, drainage and water supply; how to select a house and furnish it; how to lay a table, make a bed, dust a sitting-room; how to make furniture polish and use it; how to apportion the weekly income; the planning of meals at a stated cost, and buying the food (the girls go marketing and drive shrewd bargains with the generally sympathetic tradespeople); suitable clothing for men, women and children; the care of a baby (sometimes a real baby 'assists' at the demonstrations) and the principles of home nursing: these are only some of the subjects studied in the course of a year and a half at the housewifery centre. It is difficult for the mere man to appreciate what all this work means. To him it may seem strange that there can be a right and a wrong way of cleaning a grate or hearthstoning a window sill, though he can more easily conceive of an ill-made bed or a badly cooked chop. It appears, however, that there are pitfalls in all these matters, wherefore is it comforting to know that some thousands of girls annually leave the Board Schools who are expert practitioners in all kinds of useful domestic arts.

(H. B. Philpott, *London at School: The Story of the School Board, 1870–1904*, 1904, pp. 61–63)

The Inter Departmental Committee on Physical Deterioration (1904), set up as a result of 'the alarming proportion of the young men of this country . . . who were unfit for military duty on account of defective physique', recommended in its report that cookery, domestic economy and hygiene should as far as possible be made compulsory for the older girls at school. Further impetus to the development of this subject resulted from the *Special Report on Teaching Cookery to Public Elementary School Children* issued by the Board of Education in 1907.

At first, the new secondary schools provided a largely academic education. By 1909 the regulations had been changed:

> In schools for girls the curriculum must include provision for practical instruction in domestic subjects, such as Needlework, Cookery, Laundry Work, Housekeeping and Household Hygiene; and an approved course in a combination of these subjects may for girls over 15 years of age be substituted partially or wholly for Science and for Mathematics other than Arithmetic.

(Regulations for Secondary Schools, 1909, p. 2)

By the following year, the teaching of housecraft to girls in secondary schools merited a separate section in the Board of Education Report.

Even before the First World War, a number of factors combined to change the nature of women's work. Domestic service as an occupation declined with increasing opportunities in towns for industrial and clerical skills. The suffragette movement questioned some of the basic assumptions of the role of women. The war itself created new opportunities and responsibilities in a large field of occupations. By the 1930s many of the reasons originally adduced for introducing cookery in schools—notably, to combat alcoholism and to teach thrift and economy—were outdated.

Official pronouncements were perhaps more sensitive to the new situation than was actually reflected in the schools. A circular on the teaching of needlework in secondary schools in 1923 is a good example:

> The conditions of modern life and the variety of interests now open to girls have made it necessary to distinguish between those subjects on which much time should be spent and those which must take a secondary place. No pious founder would now be welcome who endowed a school in which girls were to devote most of their time to Needlework, with occasional deviations into reading and writing; and no one denies that Needlework now belongs to the number of those subjects which are a means and not an end in themselves, and which must therefore justify their existence by being of practical use. It is, however, equally impossible to deny that most people have two hands, and that a woman who cannot use her hands has deliberately neglected one side of her development. The best education is that which enables her to do well and quickly the necessary duties that fall to her share, so that she may have leisure to appreciate the wider interests which go to make up the life of a cultivated home.
>
> If, then, Needlework is to be useful from this point of view to the average woman, it must be simplified as much as possible. Much of the time that has been spent on fine stitching and on elaborate mending has been wasted, because most of the stitching can be done as well, if not better, by sewing-machines, while the cost of materials in daily use may make it wiser to find some easier forms of repairing, or even to buy new things. A good housewife, knowing the relative value of time and money in her own circumstances, will use her own discretion.

> (The Teaching of Needlework in Secondary Schools, Board of Education Circular 719, p. 3)

Similarly, the Hadow Report on the Education of the Adolescent (1926) pointed out that 'Attention might, with advantage, be paid to aesthetic as well as to purely practical considerations in regard to household fittings, equipment and furniture' (p. 235). The Report also favoured attempts in senior classes to combine domestic and commercial courses.

Courses were becoming more enlightened, involving more initiative and generating enthusiasm on the part of the pupils, as this account of a Devon school in 1925 shows:

> The syllabus has lately been revised and is now on good lines, the teaching is thorough and effective and the girls are trained to be capable and self-reliant. Proof of this has been given lately on two occasions when the teacher was away, once on account of sickness. The Education Secretary, who takes a great interest in the work, suggested that the girls who were in their third term should plan, cook and serve dinners for six persons entirely on their own in the centre. This they did most successfully, the meals being served up daintily and to time, vegetables and fruit grown in the school garden contributing towards the dinner.
>
> The parents were much interested in the experiment and it has had the desired effect, for the girls are now allowed to plan and cook dinners in their own homes.

> (Copy of Report by HMI Miss A. Bowen, Barnstaple Pupil Teachers' Centre Log Book, 27 May 1925, 1903c/EEL 39 Devon R.O.)

By the following decade, however, it was still generally true that imaginative schemes of work, as outlined by people such as Helen Sillitoe, an experienced inspector (1933), were ahead of practice. More realistic was a recommended syllabus printed two years previously in Helen Atkinson's *The Teaching of Domestic Science*. One term of elementary housewifery for elementary school girls aged between ten and eleven years consisted of sweeping and dusting, washing up and cleaning the kitchen sink, polishing furniture, scrubbing wood and cleaning boots and shoes.

Shortly before the Second World War the Spens Report provided the framework for future developments in this area of the curriculum. It recognized that the low status of the subject was due to the physical separation of its teaching from the schools and the varying qualifications of the teachers. Referring to handicrafts and the domestic arts, the Report continues:

> We regard these subjects as of great importance, and regret that so often in the past they have been relegated to an inferior place in the school programme. Even today in many schools for girls the accommodation and equipment for the domestic arts and home crafts . . . are insufficient to permit of a proper development of these subjects.

(Spens Report, 1938, p. 172)

In advocating specialist rooms, the Report thought it highly important that greater provision of equipment and qualified teachers should be made in grammar and modern schools.

In the post-war years, the rapid changes in technological and scientific knowledge, leading, for example, to greater automation in the home and new methods of food preparation and marketing, have been recognized and built into the home economics syllabus. With the bewildering range of choices available in the shops, consumer education is assuming an important place in courses. Greater equality between husband and wife in running a home is reflected in the teaching of this subject to both boys and girls.

The present-day justification of home economics in the curriculum has been stated in the following terms:

> It gives practice in the organization and planning of work.
> It is concerned with the development of the individual and how to balance individual rights with those of others.
> It links what goes on in school with what goes on outside.
> It is concerned with family life and the making of homes based on the experience of countless generations; it also deals with changing circumstances and changing tools and materials. It can therefore easily demonstrate both the need to understand basic principles and the necessity for continued learning throughout life.
> It can reinforce or complement almost every other subject in the curriculum and can provide a bridging subject linking arts and sciences, drawing on social history, social studies, environmental studies, child development and psychology, and the natural sciences. For some pupils it is the key which unlocks the door to an interest in a wide range of subjects.
> It provides opportunities to think creatively, acquiring and practising linguistic, numerical, and aesthetic skills, and through these to become aware of the pleasures and satisfactions as well as the problems and challenges of present-day family life.

(Schools Council Curriculum Bulletin No. 4, *Home Economics Teaching*, 1971, pp. 11–12)

Social Studies

No area of the curriculum offers a better example of conflicting aims in education than social studies or citizenship. In the nineteenth and twentieth centuries there have been sharply contrasting attitudes to the social purposes of schooling which are reflected in the content of the curriculum. On the one hand we had (and still have) those who saw schools as a means of producing greater conformity; on the other hand we find examples of complaints about that kind of curriculum, and recommendations that schools ought to be concerned with producing an awareness of the injustices and imperfections in society with a view to changing them.

Gilmour (1967) has shown, for example, that the Birkbeck Schools, founded by William Ellis for children of the poor, were expressly designed to equip these children for their economic and social function in an industrial society. The prospectus for the first school included the teaching of Social Economy from the age of seven upwards, 'that they may properly understand their own position in society and their duties towards it'. Similarly Johnson (1970) suggests that the early Victorian obsession with the education of the poor is best understood as a concern about authority and power, and the assertion or reassertion of control. It was not until the end of the nineteenth century that voices were raised against this sort of education where competition rather than cooperation was stressed. The campaigning of H. W. Hobart, a member of the Social Democratic Federation described in the previous chapter, was a typical example.

During the early part of the twentieth century the main vehicle for social studies and civics in elementary schools was moral instruction. The Moral Instruction League produced model syllabuses for schools and the League was sufficiently influential to get some of its recommendations incorporated into the 1906 Code of Regulations for Public Elementary Schools:

> History, which should include, in the lower classes, the lives of great men and women, and the lessons to be learnt therefrom, and in the higher classes a knowledge of the great persons and events of English history and of the growth of the British Empire. The teaching need not be limited to English or British History, and lessons on citizenship may be given with advantage in the higher classes. (Art. 2)

> The lessons to be learned in the playground are, indeed, invaluable. Children who take part in properly organised games will learn, among other things, to 'play the game', to 'give and take', to devote themselves to, and efface themselves for, a common cause, to feel pride in the achievements of others, to accept victory with becoming modesty and defeat with due composure, and, speaking generally, to acquire the spirit of discipline, or corporate life, and of fair play. (Prefatory Memorandum)

The League's work was not entirely free from the tradition of using schools to promote a consensus view of society and to inculcate pupils with a suitably deferential attitude towards their betters. After the First World War it was transformed into the Civics and Moral Education League which was concerned with secondary as well as elementary schools.

The Education Section of the British Association also set up a committee on citizenship and produced a civics syllabus. But the social studies movement at this time met with little success—the accepted view was that the traditional subjects, especially history and geography, were satisfactory for this purpose at secondary level.

In 1926 the Hadow Report's view that the general character of the teaching should take account of the pupil's natural and social environment was generally interpreted as meaning that this should be by means of traditional subjects. The opposite viewpoint was taken by the Association for Education in Citizenship (founded in 1934). This body which was founded by Sir Ernest Simon and Mrs Eva Hubback, and included among its sponsors such well-known 'progressives' as William Beveridge, G. D. H. Cole, Harold Laski and Barbara Wootton, was an influential pressure group with the stated object of advancing:

> the study of and training in citizenship, by which is meant training in the moral qualities necessary for the citizens of a democracy, the encouragement of clear thinking in everyday affairs and the acquisition of that knowledge of the modern world usually given by means of courses in history, geography, economics, citizenship and public affairs.

The Association thus supported the idea of 'direct training' by means of specific curriculum content rather than the indirect training which was the semi-official policy later enshrined in the Spens and Norwood Reports. In 1935 the Association published *Education for Citizenship in Secondary Schools* which consisted of a set of essays covering aims and methods of Education for Citizenship:

> The case we wish to put forward is this: that in the relatively simple society of the nineteenth century when government interfered little with the daily life of the people, indirect education for citizenship was perhaps adequate. Democracy worked fairly well without much specialized training for citizenship, either of the voter or of the states-man. Today things have changed. The political world is so complex and difficult that it is essential to train men just as consciously and deliberately for their duties as citizens as for their vocation or profession. (p. 7)

Another important aspect of the Association's campaign for direct teaching was its criticism of the idea of transfer of training: it refuted the notion that there was no special problem of education for citizenship but only a general problem of training the mind. Sir Ernest Simon tellingly quoted Lord Bryce that, after two generations of general education, the people of this country were no more cap-able of choosing their leaders than they had been before (p. 11).

However, despite very energetic attempts by the pressure group to infiltrate and influence the Board of Education and the Consultative Committee (and especially the Spens and Norwood Committees) their views on the desirability of *direct* training were never accepted. It has recently been suggested that there were political reasons for this opposition. By 1938, the Association had elected a new president, Stanley Baldwin, the recently retired Conservative prime minister. Baldwin saw the post as an opportunity to control developments in education for citizenship. He immediately took objection to a proposed pamphlet by the Association on bias in education which argued for direct education for citizenship through a controversial issues curriculum. As a result, the text had to be amended before publication. (See G. Whitmarsh, 'The Politics of Political Education', *Journal of Curriculum Studies*, Vol. 6, No. 2, pp. 137–8.)

Support for the indirect approach was at this time, the late 1930s, given by some psychological evidence (of a dubious kind). The Spens Report claimed, for example, that modern political and economic history was the best introduction to a study of politics. Similarly, geography, based on a world study, offered scope for the consideration of a number of problems bearing on social, economic and political life (p. 174).

One aspect of the real problem was seen by Michael Stewart in an AEC publication, *Bias and Education for Democracy* (1938):

> The proper handling of controversy is difficult; so is all teaching. This problem is simply the 'subject problem' of the social sciences. The teacher of chemistry must put acids and explosives into his pupils' hands; it is one of the merits of his subject that it gives this opportunity for training in sensible conduct. Similarly, it is a positive advantage of the social sciences that they promote clear and unprejudiced thinking on disputed topics. The advantages to humanity of an increase in the number of people possessed of this power will be enormous; teachers are not likely to refuse their help because the task is difficult. (p. 48)

After the war the point of view of the Association for Education in Citizenship was taken up again by the Council for Curriculum Reform in a report, *The Content of Education*, 1945. This report, edited by J. A. Lauwerys of the University of London Institute of Education, was critical of the 1944 Act for its lack of attention to the question of curriculum. The report recommended a planned curriculum with a common core which would include the social sciences. The whole of Chapter X of the report was devoted to the social sciences, subdivided into three sections: Social Studies, History, Economics and Politics. The following extract is from the third section.

Economics, Politics, and Social Ethics
The principles underlying this book—that education must help young people develop themselves and become responsible members of a democratic society—emphasizes the need to give an important place in the core curriculum to the Social Studies. (p. 170)
   The main advantages of both economics and politics as school subjects, are that:
   They give training in clear, accurate, and objective thinking
Until recently it was thought that training in subjects such as science, languages, and mathematics, would lead to clear thinking in different situations of life. But it is becoming increasingly realized that 'transfer of training' from one subject to another quite different is not the automatic process we had imagined. (p. 171)

However, this idea of a common curriculum was later distorted, partly by the general acceptance of the tripartite (or bipartite) idea of separate schools for different levels of ability. Even those local education authorities which developed comprehensive schools tended to make separate curricular provision for 'able, average and less able' pupils. Social studies tended to become a subject for the secondary modern pupil. A further disadvantage was that the kind of social studies adopted in many schools was vague, and the syllabuses unrealistically broad. By the 1950s there was a drift back to the traditional examination subjects, and there was a tendency for Social Studies to disappear from the curriculum in many schools.

The Crowther Report (1959) represented a return to a consensus-seeking social studies curriculum. It hoped that it would help young workers 'of limited intelligence' to find their way about the modern world and help them form a standard of moral values.

The Newsom Report in 1963 continued the same tradition. A whole section was devoted to 'The proper study of mankind', but no detailed curriculum was suggested. The document was much less specific than the publications of the Council for Education in Citizenship in the 1930s.

During the 1960s social studies moved sharply in the direction of specific teaching of the social sciences rather than a loosely integrated studies approach. One influence was the rapidly increasing number of United States publications describing the 'New Social Studies' approach (e.g. E. Fenton, 1966); another, possibly more important, influence was the growing number of social scientists teaching in secondary schools and further education colleges. The Association for Teaching the Social Sciences (ATSS), founded in 1963, was set up explicitly to foster the social sciences in schools. The ATSS has been an effective 'pressure group' exerting important influences on examinations such as GCE O and A level sociology which were introduced in the 1960s, but has not yet managed to encourage widespread acceptance of social science as part of the core curriculum for all pupils.

To some extent the 1960s also represented a swing back to the social sciences as separate disciplines rather than as an 'integration'. Reference has already been made to sociology as an examination subject, but economics was established much earlier so that by the end of the 1960s A level economics was a very popular choice, especially for boys. In 1967 the Economics Association published *Teaching Economics*, edited by Norman Lee; some of the essays are clearly attempts to stress that rigorous scientific ideas are appropriate for all children: conventional subject-matter was not to be sacrificed for the sake of excessively child-centred education.

One important difference between the ATSS and the Economics Association is that whereas university sociologists (with some notable exceptions) were indifferent or even hostile to sociology in schools, university economists were somewhat more supportive. The same might be said of the Politics Association who had a university spokesman of considerable enthusiasm in Professor Bernard Crick. In 1969 *The Teaching of Politics*, a symposium on the subject, was published. This book focused mainly on politics but covered a wide range of topics. Once again the plea is made on the basis of relevance. Crick wrote:

> As a professor of political studies, I am interested in political education at the secondary level of education because it should be there both in its own right and in the public interest, not as a feeder to the university Moloch. At some stage all young people in all kinds of secondary schools and in industrial day-release courses should gain some awareness of what politics is about. It is more important that all teenagers should learn to read newspapers critically for their political content than that they should have heard of Aristotle or know—may heaven forgive us all—when the Speaker's Mace is or was over or under the table. So the right age for a conscious political education to begin is the age at which children begin to read the newspapers anyway—their political puberty. (pp. 3–4)

What all these approaches have lacked, however, is an effective plan for changing the curriculum of a majority (or even a sizeable minority) of schools. The Schools Council should be able to offer this, but so far they too have failed in this respect. In 1968 a small grant was given to finance a study of social studies for the 8–13 age group. The Report was published in 1971 as Schools Council Working Paper No. 39 but no 'diffusion' was possible. A follow-up project at Liverpool—Social Science, History and Geography 8–13—was launched, but it does not seem likely that the ideas will be taken up by most schools.

In this area of the curriculum schools have shown themselves to be highly resistant to change throughout the century.

Science

There have been three—greatly overlapping—aspects of the argument about science in the curriculum:

1. Should it be there at all?
2. Who should be taught science—i.e. was it for secondary pupils only, or boys only, or able pupils only?
3. What kind of science—including what method?

In the early part of the nineteenth century there was little science in schools and what was taught was often meaningless rote-learning of factual information. One primer, for instance, published in 1821 bore the title *A Catechism of Botany*.

The neglect of science was mainly due to the nature of the Industrial Revolution which occurred during the previous century in England. Many of the industries were founded on non-scientific research industries, such as cotton, wool and metal; many of the inventors and engineers were self-educated men; and traditional universities had not developed a system of scientific education. A divorce had taken place between the practical and theoretical aspects of the subject. Scientific knowledge was applied to industry separated from the main body of liberal studies and may help to account for its inferior status.

Two factors were largely responsible for heightened interest in science from the middle of the nineteenth century; foreign competition and their advanced technology displayed at international exhibitions prompted a call for a reappraisal of the state of the subject in schools. A knowledge of science was also considered to be a necessary antidote to the growing volume of superstitions and fraudulent activities on the continent such as séances which were affecting England by the 1850s.

The work of the Rev. Richard Dawes at King's Somborne School, Hampshire, during the 1840s pointed the way to a successful diffusion of a science curriculum which could be taught by most schoolmasters. Based on a study of common things, Dawes's curriculum widened out to include studies of vegetable and animal physiology, geology and natural philosophy. This work was taken up and encouraged by an HMI, Henry Moseley, and described in the Minutes of the Committee of Council on Education. Further publicity was afforded by Dawes's own writings and, when Moseley drew up a scheme of examination for men teachers in training colleges in 1853, he included physical science as one of the basic subjects of the elementary curriculum. (See Layton (1973) for further details.) By the late 1850s the science movement had achieved some success and the subject was established in many schools. The campaign waged by scientists such as T. H. Huxley, John Tyndall and Michael Faraday in the 1850s, the discussion of Britain's 'scientific backwardness', the work of the Science and Art Department and Herbert Spencer's book *Education* (1861) all served as pressures to change the curriculum.

Another source of encouragement was the setting up of the Department of Science and Art in 1853 (formerly the Department of Practical Art). From 1857, the Department was officially transferred from the Board of Trade to the Education Department but continued to work independently of it. Despite the titular superiority of science it lagged behind the art division for a number of years; a number of science schools had been opened but failed. By 1854 there were only a few hundred pupils studying science, and the aid given by the Department for science classes between 1853 and 1859 totalled only £898. The reason for this failure has a familiar ring:

> The truth has to be faced that science education was caught in a vicious circle. There were few science pupils because there were not enough science teachers; there were insufficient science teachers because there was no one to give them their basic scientific education. To break this circle a means had to be found for providing elementary instruction in science.
>
> (A. S. Bishop, *The Rise of a Central Authority for English Education*, 1971, p. 167)

However, when Henry Cole became Secretary of the Science and Art Department in 1859 he pursued his task more vigorously than his predecessor, Lyon Playfair. Cole and the new inspector for science, Captain Donnelly, developed a system of encouraging science teaching in schools and the training of teachers; the new system was based on examinations and payment of grants according to the results of these examinations. T. C. Buckmaster, a very able scientist, was appointed as 'Organizing Master' to tour the country, explaining the new system of grants and establishing classes. In the eleven years 1861–72 the number of pupils receiving science instruction had risen from 1,330 to 36,783.

In 1859 the subjects for which grant would be paid were geometry, mechanical drawing, building construction, physics, chemistry and natural history; by 1873 there were twenty-three subjects available. The development of science during these years was, however, patchy; only a minority of schools attempted it and science did not become an established basic subject for all pupils, despite the obvious need for this kind of knowledge. There were several reasons for this failure: the problem of teacher supply was never solved; the administrative separation of science from education was a serious handicap, with the Education Department at Whitehall and the Science and Art Department at South Kensington, and there was the nagging fear of the middle classes generally that elementary education should be limited to basic essentials—the three Rs. Science in particular was attacked in the 1850s and early 1860s. The opposition came from two main sources: from some churchmen who feared that science might disturb the religious faith of the lower orders; and from some middle-class ratepayers who felt that this kind of elementary education was too good and too expensive. The story is a complicated one: some of the advocates of science in education were middle-class churchmen, but the general opposition to the kind of elementary education which got too far above basic literacy for bible-reading was clear.

Donnelly's evidence to the Newcastle Commission on the benefits of payment by results led to the adoption of this method in the elementary schools after 1862. Science was not included among the subjects for which a grant was given and was therefore largely ignored by teachers.

Meanwhile secondary schools continued to be criticized for the lack of science in the curriculum. The Taunton Report (1868) recommended the inclusion of science; a few years later a Royal Commission was set up on Scientific Instruction and the Advancement of Science, under the chairmanship of the Duke of Devonshire. The Final Report, published in 1875, commented that

> it appears that, not one half of the 128 Endowed Schools from which returns have been received, have even made an attempt to introduce it; and of these, as we have already stated, only 13 have a Laboratory, and only 10 give as much as four hours a week to these subjects.

(J. S. Maclure, *Educational Documents 1816–1968*, 1968 edn., p. 107)

Partly as a result of these pressures, the endowed schools gradually increased their scientific provision, but even in the more enlightened schools, science was for a long time regarded as a fringe subject. For example, at Uppingham under Thring in 1880 all boys learned classics and mathematics, but had to choose between a modern language or drawing or science, so that out of 320 boys only 25 were doing science (Lawson and Silver, 1973, p. 345).

Meanwhile there had been a revival of science in elementary schools after the 1870 Education Act and the subsequent relaxation of the Codes. Once again the question of Britain's industrial efficiency was in the air: in 1868 a select committee had been appointed, chaired by Bernhard Samuelson, to inquire into 'the provisions for giving instruction in theoretical and applied science to the industrial classes'. The committee found three major defects in the educational system: inadequacies in elementary schools; neglect of science at the secondary stage, and—once again—a shortage of science teachers. The Devonshire Committee (1870–5) confirmed these findings, and by this time some improvement had taken place. The grants given by the Science and Art Department were gradually encouraging more elementary schools to introduce science, and in addition some more inspectors had been appointed to give expert advice.

But even this kind of progress left much to be desired; the majority of elementary pupils received little or no science in their curriculum. This was the view expressed by the Royal Commission on Technical Instruction in 1884 and 1886 and a national policy was called for. No legislation was passed, however, until the Technical Instruction Act of 1889 which provided for the financing of technical education by means of a local penny rate. It should be noted, however, that elementary schools were excluded from receiving benefit under this legislation and that grants were to be given for 'technical or manual instruction'. New 'technical' institutions were built which were chiefly used in the evenings. During the day, these were occupied by pupils receiving full-time instruction which had a strong science bias. These Organized Science Schools came to occupy the position of secondary schools. As the Act was to be administered by the Science and Art Department and not the Education Department, the branching of interests became even more obvious from this time. By the 1890s, the Science and Art Department had become a victim of its own success: it was swamped with examination candidates, some 214,000 science and 123,700 art entries in 1892.

> The National Association for the Promotion of Technical Education criticized very effectively the payment-by-results system, quoting the case of the 16 year old boy at Bradford Technical College, who in May 1888, passed in no fewer than 19 subjects in the Department's science examinations, while at least three had passed in 18 subjects and many in 16 or 17.
>
> (D. S. L. Cardwell, *The Organization of Science in England*, 1972 edn., p. 159)

Many of the difficulties in the development of a science curriculum stemmed from the multiplicity of authorities concerned with the subject. The Bryce Commission reported in 1894:

> The rise of the local authorities has increased, as it were, the centrifugal tendencies in education, and has shown how easily the very vigour of the local life may become creative of conflicting interests and aims. Thus we have at Manchester the Grammar School under its Charity Commission Scheme, the Organized Science Schools under the school board, the Technical Schools under the corporation, and the Owen's College, all at certain points rivalling rather than supplementing each other, while the science grants encourage and increase the confusion rather than repress and reduce it.
>
> (Quoted in E. J. R. Eaglesham, *The Foundations of Twentieth Century Education in England*, 1965, pp. 24–5)

The examinations grant system was a poor substitute for a genuine national curriculum policy for science. It was only with the absorption of the Science and Art Department into the Board of Education in 1899 that a more rational course could be pursued.

By this time science classes were flourishing in some higher elementary schools, even if the situation nationally was unsatisfactory. However, these classes suffered another blow when the Cockerton Judgment made such work illegal in elementary schools. This had the long-term effect of diverting science to the curricula of secondary schools established after the Act of 1902. The Regulations which followed (1904) required science to be taught: $7\frac{1}{2}$ hours were stipulated for the mathematics and science curriculum. Science was now officially established and from this time on the argument turned on what kind of science and for whom.

One opportunity had, however, already been missed, namely the chance of linking science education with technical education. In 1877 T. H. Huxley made a speech (*Collected Essays* (1885), Vol. 3) on 'Technical Education' which advocated a very broad approach to technical education which would include science as part of everyone's preparation of life. In the same year Huxley and others pressed for a committee to investigate how the City Companies could assist technical education. As a result, in 1878 there was established the City and Guilds of

London Institute for the Advancement of Technical Education. Unfortunately as time went on technical education became associated with vocational training of a limited kind and secondary schools concentrated on 'pure' science, mainly chemistry and physics. The Report of the Cross Commission on the Elementary Education Acts 1888 (p. 217) had stated that technical instruction belonged to the factory and had no place in secondary education: a clear example of the élitist curricular tradition—the education of the upper and middle classes should not be 'practical' in any way. Raymond Williams has described ths period in *The Long Revolution:*

> The shadow of class thinking lies over this as over so much other nineteenth-century educational thinking. The continued relegation of trade and industry to lower social classes, and the desire of successful industrialists that their sons should move into the now largely irrelevant class of gentry, were alike extremely damaging to English education and English life. As at the Reformation, a period of major reconstruction of institutions was undertaken largely without reference to the best learning of the age, and without any successful redefinition of the purposes of education or the content of a contemporary liberal culture. The beginnings of technical instruction in the Mechanics' Institutes might have developed into a successful redefinition, whereas in fact the new sciences were radical elements in the society as a whole: a society which had changed its economy, which under pressure was changing its institutions, but which, at the centres of power, was refusing to change its ways of thinking. And then to the new working class, the offered isolation of science and technical instruction was largely unacceptable, for it was precisely in the interaction between techniques and their general living that this class was coming to its new consciousness.

> (R. Williams, *The Long Revolution*, 1965 edn., p. 164)

A different, but related, dispute had been pursued about the *method* of teaching science. H. E. Armstrong (1848–1937) was an advocate of the heuristic method of science teaching, but this system of learning by doing practical experiments rather than rote-learning was opposed by many educationists as an unnecessary waste of time.

Armstrong's views were particularly questioned during the First World War, by which time some of the more extreme advocates of 'heurism' had pressed the 'discovery method' much too far and regarded discovery as the only possible method by which a child could acquire *any* knowledge. In 1916 a committee was appointed by the Prime Minister under the chairmanship of Sir J. J. Thomson to examine the position of natural science in the educational system of Great Britain. They reported (in 1918) that

> The principles are often taught without reference to the phenomena of nature which they explain; the course does not satisfy the natural curiosity of the pupils; it may give them some knowledge of laboratory methods, but little idea of wider generalizations, such as the principle of the conservation of energy, which are quite within their powers of comprehension.

> (Quoted in R. A. R. Tricker, *Contribution of Science to Education*, 1967, p. 4)

The argument was helped but not settled by this report; the question of the right balance between 'discovery' and 'instruction' is still a live issue among science teachers today. One of the benefits of the debate, however, has been a better provision of school laboratories than exists in most other countries. Arm-

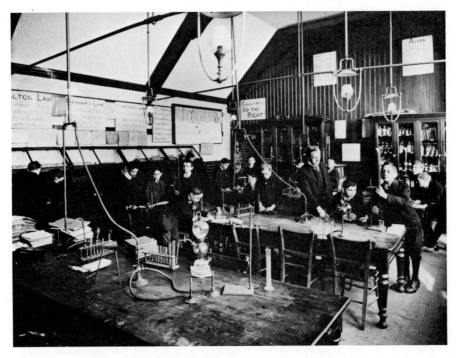

9   A Chemistry lesson 1908
H. E. Armstrong's advocacy of the heuristic method, the teaching of
science on an experimental basis, led to the recasting of the school
curriculum on these lines.

GLC Photograph Library

strong's views, although based on an over-simplified theory of learning, were
influential in the debate for about thirty years and on the whole improved the
teaching of science.

> 'Insistence on the view that experiments by the class must always be preferred to
> demonstration experiments leads to great waste of time,' concluded Thomson. 'Much
> of this waste of time is due to a conscientious desire of the teachers to encourage the
> spirit of inquiry by following the so-called heuristic method; the pupils are supposed to
> discover by their own experiments, with little or no suggestion from the teacher, the
> solutions of problems set to them or of problems which they themselves suggest. The
> spirit of inquiry should run through the whole of the scientific work, and everything
> should be done to encourage it, but it seems clear that the heuristic method can never
> be the main method by which the pupil acquires scientific training and knowledge. He
> cannot expect to rediscover in his school hours all that he may fairly be expected to
> know; to insist that he should try is to waste his time and his opportunities.' Here was a
> caricature of Armstrong's intentions. For him heurism meant 'directed inquiry', with
> the teacher playing a discreet, but positive role.

> (W. H. Brock (ed.), *H. E. Armstrong and the Teaching of Science 1880–1930*, 1973, p. 47)

Another criticism made by the Thomson Committee was that too much time
and energy was spent on the training of future specialists, compared with the
majority who needed a good general understanding of science. In 1918 this

criticism applied to the small percentage of pupils in secondary schools; today it might be applied to the whole population.

Another curious tradition which has remained with us is the sex-linking of science subjects in schools. The Thomson Committee criticized the narrowness of the science curriculum, which tended to be physics and chemistry for boys and biology (mainly botany) for girls. We still have not completely shaken off that strange heritage.

Since the end of the Second World War, curriculum development in science has taken two forms:

1. improved methods, courses and materials
2. general science for all pupils

As early as 1914 the Association of Public School Science Masters (APSSM) had advocated 'Science for All' and, although some credence was given to the idea that if our science education had been better our army in the First World War would have been superior, the postwar years saw little dramatic development in the science curriculum.

After the Second World War, however, there were significant changes resulting from the 1944 Education Act and the idea of secondary education for all. Once again, the story begins in the grammar schools. In 1957 Dr Boulind suggested to the Science Masters Association (SMA) that the aims and content of secondary science syllabuses were in need of rethinking. A sub-committee of the SMA was set up to look into grammar school science teaching and the part that science should play in general education. Eventually the SMA inquiry was widened to include secondary schools in general.

> If it is agreed that no child is sufficiently educated if he does not know something of science, the question arises as to what selection from the science curriculum should be made for the purpose of such basic scientific education, and of how early in the child's school career such teaching should start. It is arguable that much of the detail in a chemistry or physics course designed for pupils specializing in science may be of no use for the ends of a general science education for non-specialists. Equally it is arguable that a very general view of science, too remote from its particular facts, may not be of much interest or educational value.
>
> (R. H. Thouless, *Map of Educational Research*, 1965, p. 184)

In 1961 the Nuffield Foundation financed the Science Teaching Project which undertook the task of devising courses, developing materials and trying them out on a small scale before offering them for general sale. Some of this work was later taken over by the Schools Council.

Another important development of the 1960s was the idea of general science being started in a realistic way in primary schools; the Nuffield Junior Science Project started in January 1964 and was continued after November 1966 by the Schools Council, eventually being renamed *Science 5–13*. *Science 5–13* is also distinguished by the quality of its evaluation by Dr Wynne Harlen. Her book *With Objectives in Mind* (1972) has also become a classic example of stating objectives clearly and outlining a syllabus without undue use of jargon.

Much of the work in science education, however, still tends to be concerned with examinations—especially O and A level GCE. One important development has been the introduction of multiple-choice questions as an additional technique in teaching and testing. The lower level examination—CSE—has also been kept under scrutiny by the Schools Council with a view to improving not only methods of assessment but content of syllabus and methods of teaching. *Examinations Bulletin No. 8* (1965), for example, set out to encourage better teaching for the 'Scientific thinking' paper and to move away from science as rote-learning. This paper was designed to test a candidate's ability to suggest hypotheses in explanation of data and to devise experiments to test hypotheses.

Another promising development is the greater involvement of teachers in assessing their own pupils. This has been encouraged, for instance, by the Nuffield A level biology project. Similar work has been done with teachers of CSE science.

Despite these advances two main general problems remain: too many pupils leave school without achieving any reasonable degree of scientific literacy, and many of those pupils who reach a high standard in science are over-specialized. For many pupils science remains a mystery either because they were allowed to 'drop' science too early or because the syllabus was unsuitable. Although Nuffield Secondary Science, Integrated Science and Combined Science have been a success in many schools, only a tiny minority of schools have adopted them. Similarly, despite the high quality of the course and the materials, *Science 5–13* has been disappointing in terms of numbers of children reached. There are two reasons for this which remain unsolved. The first is the general problem of diffusion of innovation. The Schools Council has not yet been able to spread ideas from projects to teachers in schools—most primary teachers simply have not heard about *Science 5–13*. Secondly, there are not enough science teachers available. This is partly a problem of shortage of scientific manpower (see the Dainton and Swann Reports) and partly the failure of colleges of education to match the needs of the schools with the right balance of specialist and semi-specialist teachers.

Although specific mention has been made of methods of teaching, as well as aims and content, in some of the preceding sections of this chapter, the general question of changes in methods will be dealt with in Chapter 4. The six aspects of curriculum change dealt with above illustrate the extreme danger of making any general statements about change in *the* curriculum. In so far as it is possible to trace general trends, an attempt will be made to link such changes with changes in society as a whole.

4

Effects of Changing Methods on the Curriculum

There has always been an intimate connection between what is taught and how it is taught. At various times in the last two hundred years, differing views on the nature of childhood have been reflected in curricula. For example, if the young were regarded as basically wicked by nature, then schooling had to ensure that the methods of instruction included an element which would assist in disciplining children. On the other hand, a view of childhood which looked towards the revealing of potentialities through self-discovery required a quite different approach. This chapter will be concerned with examining the relationship between method and the curriculum; the division of schools into elementary and secondary in the nineteenth century provides a useful starting point for this exploration.

Elementary

Early nineteenth century

Perhaps the best known of all the early methods of instruction is the monitorial or mutual system, associated with Andrew Bell and Joseph Lancaster early in the last century. Both men had arrived at a similar plan for mass education through different routes. Bell, a Scottish clergyman, in superintending a military orphan asylum in Madras, found difficulty in employing willing teachers and therefore used boys instead of men.

Cheap mass instruction which would teach the rudiments of the three Rs, obedience and godliness, resulted from this system. Bell himself summed it up as

> the perpetual presence and vigilance of *Praepositi*, the incessant occupation and gratification of the scholars, the watchful inspection, superintendence and instruction of the Master—together with the continual exercise and operation of those principles and affections which God has impressed on the mind, and implanted in the breast of the rational Creation, and left us to apply to their proper end.
>
> (Bell to Sir James Langham, 25 June 1821, Langham of Cottesbrooke MSS 310, Northamptonshire R.O.)

Lancaster, born of poor parents in Southwark, based a similar system on his experiences in teaching poor boys in South London. As Lancaster could not

RULES

OF THE

HASLINGFIELD

NATIONAL SCHOOL.

GIRLS.

1. THE Children must be sent to School with their hands and faces well washed, and their hair combed and brushed, clothes clean and neat, and they are not allowed to come to School wearing ornaments, feathers, artificials, or any unnecessary article of dress.

2. The School is opened in the morning with prayers, immediately after the Church clock strikes Nine, by which time all the children must be in School and remain till Twelve o'clock; in the afternoon the Children must be in the School by the time that the Church clock strikes Two, and remain, throughout the year, till Half-past Four o'clock, when the School is closed by prayers.

3. Children of Labourers pay One Penny weekly; Tradespeople's Children, Twopence; and the Children of Farmers and other Parishes, Threepence.

4. Girls are admitted into the School at Seven years of age, and *no Child* is admitted under that age, nor till the Trustees are satisfied that any arrears have been paid which may be due to the Infant Schoolmistress. The admissions from the Infant School take place Quarterly.

5. The Mistress is required to keep a register of the attendance of each Child, and also the amount paid weekly by each Child.

6. Any Child coming to School late, who is inattentive, disorderly, or guilty of using bad language, destroying the Property of the School, or otherwise misconducting herself, will be punished by the Mistress at the discretion of the Trustees, and is liable to be discharged from the School.

7. If any of the Parents or Friends of the Children interfere in the regulations made to maintain discipline, and enforce obedience to the Mistress or others in authority, the Children of such persons cannot be allowed to remain in the School.

8. The Mistress is required, in secular instruction, to teach the Girls Reading, Writing, Spelling, English Grammar, Tables, Arithmetic, General History, and Geography, and such subjects of useful knowledge as may from time to time be directed or authorised by the Trustees; in Religious Instruction, Bible Reading and Bible History, the Catechism, Articles of the Church of England, and general knowledge of the Liturgy.

9. The Mistress is required to teach the Girls every kind of plain Needlework, Marking, Stocking and Plain Knitting, Stocking Darning, &c., &c.

10. The Children are allowed to work one week in four for their Parents, but no Child is allowed to bring to the School, under any pretence, any description of Fancy Work, and during the other three weeks, *all the Children* will do any Work, not Fancy work, which can be procured. The afternoon only of each day is allowed for Needlework.

11. Any sum that may be received for work done at the School will be appropriated for the benefit of the Children.

12. The Children are required to attend the Sunday Schools and also Divine Service at the Parish Church, and the Mistress is required to attend and teach the Children on the Sunday morning from Half-past Nine to a Quarter before Eleven, and in the afternoon from Two till a Quarter before Three, and also to superintend their behaviour during Divine Service at Church.

13. One week's holiday is allowed at Christmas, and five weeks at Harvest, and Saturday in every week.

14. Annual Prizes are given to those Boys and Girls under 14 years of age who show on Examination the greatest proficiency in the repetition and general knowledge of the Church Catechism; and to those Children under 15 years who show the like proficiency in the Articles of the Church of England

15. The Mistress and Teachers are required, so far as is practicable, to set the Children an example in dress; and all the above Rules, where practicable, are to be applied to the Sunday School.

16. The School is subject to the visitation and inspection of Her Majesty's Inspectors of Schools, and of the Diocesan Inspector, and the National Society's Inspector.

17. Any of the above Rules, where practicable, are to be applied to the Sunday School.

C. W. NAYLOR, PRINTER, "CHRONICLE" OFFICE, CAMBRIDGE.

10   Rules of a Church Day School in Cambridgeshire *c.* 1880
      The curriculum is spelled out in some detail.

Cambridgeshire Record Office

afford to employ masters, he used older boys to teach the younger ones. A contemporary account of the method in 1809 stated that its benefits were that a single master could conduct a school of 1,000 children; that one book would serve for the whole school; and that 500 boys could spell and write the same word at the same moment.

The mechanical nature of the process is well illustrated in this report of a master of a Birmingham Lancasterian school in 1815:

> Reading and spelling is taught forwards, backwards, syllabically, &c.; and the lower classes repeat the stops and marks they meet with, so that every time they read they are exercised in punctuation.
>
> I have a monitor-general and two assistants, who take turns in keeping order, exercising the boys, &c. I have eight monitors, whose business it is to keep the class lists and dictate the first hour. Their assistants act as monitors when they are absent, and dictate the second hour; and when these all go out to write in books, or to write sentences upon slates without lines, their places are supplied by substitute dictators.
>
> The boys are exercised by telegraph. When the slates are cleaned, the dictator of the eighth class stands up, and dictates a word with its meaning, or a town, and the name of the county in which it is situated. He then sits upon the desk and writes what he has dictated. When he seats himself, the dictator of the seventh class rises, and dictates words suitable to his class—then seats himself to write: and so on through all the classes.
>
> By this plan only one dictator is heard at a time, and the dictators improve equally with the others. When the slates are full, which is known by the dictators all standing up, the exercising monitor exhibits SS for *show slates*. He then gives a gentle rap, which raises up an inspector at the end of each desk. A second rap sends them forward to inspect the slates, and they remain at the opposite end of the desk till they hear a third rap, when they all return, and write upon the backs of their slates the names of defaulters, adding a mark for each offence. The inspection is over in about two minutes; and being done at the same moment, by a boy seated at the end of each desk for the purpose, gives the school more the appearance of a machine, in which the boys superintend and instruct each other, than when the whole school was inspected by the monitors of classes, who have in that case the appearance and all the consequences of *eight little masters*.

(Report of the British and Foreign School Society to the General Meeting, November 1815, pp. 37–8)

The methods employed by Bell and Lancaster differed only in detail except in one crucial respect. In Lancasterian schools the Bible was the only religious book used, containing, in Lancaster's view, a 'purer morality' than any book in any language. Lancaster's plan did not necessarily assume that the parish priest was to superintend the local school. It was on this point that a bifurcation of elementary schools occurred: the supporters of Lancaster formed a committee which in 1814 became the British and Foreign School Society, representing undenominational religious instruction, while Bell's supporters had formed in 1811 the National Society for Promoting the Education of the Poor in the Principles of the Established Church.

Both men showed that it was possible to meet the demand for large-scale education in an economical manner. But their views represented a mechanistic view of children and education. Neither Bell nor Lancaster took account of the individual child's needs and the stages of development which call for different approaches in method. More serious was the unsuitability of the monitorial system for children under six for whom educators were becoming increasingly concerned.

RULES

FOR A

Sunday and Saints Day

SCHOOL,

On Dr. Bell's system of Instruction, established at CHITTLEHAMPTON, December 25th, One Thousand Eight Hundred & Fifteen.

I. THAT the benefit of this School shall extend to all the Children of the parish of Chittlehampton without distinction, who are required to attend Clean and Neat at the School Room, on the morning of every Sunday and Saints Day, at eight o'Clock during the Summer, and at nine in the Winter.

II. THAT the method of instruction to be adopted in this School, shall be that recommended by Dr. Bell.

III. THAT the Children of this School shall on all Sundays, Saints, and Holy Days, regularly attend Divine Service at the Church of Chittlehampton.

IV. THAT no Books which are not published by the Society for promoting Christian Knowledge, and sanctioned by the Minister of Chittlehampton, shall be admitted into this School.

V. THAT writing and arithmetic shall at no time be taught.

VI. That all annual Subscribers to the amount of five shillings and upwards shall be considered as Directors, and that one Director at least shall be required to attend on each Day the School is open.

VII. THAT two account Books be kept at the School, one as an accurate register of the progress made by the Children in their tasks, and the other of the offences which have been committed.

VIII. THAT the officiating Minister of Chittlehampton be appointed Treasurer of this Institution.

IX. THAT the names of the Scholars shall be called over every morning and afternoon of the Days on which the School is open, and the absentees marked according to the form of the Books.

X. THAT the hours of attendance for the Children shall be as follows, (viz.) on Sundays during the Summer in the morning, from eight o'Clock to eleven, in the afternoon from two to three, and from the end of the Church Service until half past seven. On Saints and Holy Days the same hours shall be observed in the morning, and in the afternoon of those Days the School shall be open from two to six; during the winter months the morning hour of meeting shall be nine o'Clock instead of eight, and the time of dismission in the evening will be regulated by the shortness of the Days, as no candles will be allowed in the School.

XI. THAT the officiating Minister of Chittlehampton be appointed Visitor of the School, to arrange the different classes according to his judgment of the capacities and attainments of the Scholars, and to make such regulations as are necessary for the encouragement and welfare of the Institution.

XII. THAT the Sum of six pounds shall annually be paid as a Salary for the Master, who shall not be appointed to that office without the approbation of the Visitor.

XIII. THAT a number of Common Prayer Books be provided for the use of the Scholars attending the Church, and in order to encourage regularity in their attendance and conduct, ten Prayer Books, together with other presents as may be approved of, shall be annually given to such Scholars as shall best signalize themselves by their improvement and good behaviour.

XIV. THAT the officiating Minister be requested annually to preach a Sermon in the Church of Chittlehampton for the benefit of this Institution.

XV. THAT the religious ends of the Institution be always kept in view: and that the Children be constantly reminded of the design of this School: which is to check and reform vicious habits and all tendencies towards them in the rising generation: to inculcate upon them a becoming regard for the Word and Worship of Almighty God: and the NECESSITY of a FIRM ADHERENCE to the doctrines and practices of our pure and Apostolical Church in this age of Schism and Infidelity, to require their keeping holy the Sabbath Day, to warn them of the evil of sin in general, and of youthful sins in particular, such as pride, pilfering, idleness, swearing, lying, disobedience, &c, and to set before them the excellency and importance of justice, diligence, humility, and a conscientious regard to truth, and a respectful submission to those whom the Providence of God hath set over them: finally to explain to them in a manner suited to their understandings, all the truths and duties recommended in the Holy Scriptures, and promoting a believing and obedient regard to them for their happiness both here and hereafter.

A List of Annual Subscribers.

	£.	s.	d.
The Right Honorable Lord Rolle,	10	0	0
The Miss Rolle's,	3	0	0
Miss Bury,	1	0	0
Miss M. Harding,	1	0	0
Reverend R. Chichester,	1	0	0
Mrs. R. Chichester,	1	0	0
Reverend C. Chichester,	1	0	0
Mr. Nickols,	0	15	0
Mrs. Hacche,	0	10	0
Mr. Graddon,	0	10	0
Mr. J. Huxtable, Leara,	0	10	0
Mr. Tamlin,	0	10	0
Mr. J. Huxtable,	0	6	0
Miss Saltern,	1	0	0
Mrs. Thorne,	0	5	0
Mrs. Graddon,	0	10	0
Mrs. Nickols, Brightly,	0	5	0
Mrs. Nickols, Bidacott,	0	5	0
Mr. William Nickols,	0	5	0
Mr. Thorne,	0	10	0
Mrs. J Huxtable, Leara,	0	5	0
Mr. James Brayley,	0	5	0
Mr. Mildon,	0	5	0

J. HUXTABLE, PRINTER, BOOK-BINDER AND BOOK-SELLER, SOUTHMOLTON.

11 Rules of a Sunday School at Chittlehampton, Devon, 1815
These schools were established to promote religious education.
Devon Record Office

Views on the young

Experimental work in schools, even if it had been considered desirable, would have been difficult in the early 1800s, for there was no supply of trained teachers nor money available to finance it. For this reason, the work of Robert Owen as an innovator stands out. As a self-made man, socialist and cooperative pioneer,

Owen's success in business enabled him to set up at New Lanark in Scotland in 1799 a model self-governing community for spinning-mill workers. Owen quickly realized that the home environment affected the child's performance at school and he was in a position to effect change:

> Thus for instance, in creating the new circumstances for the infant children, they would be provided with superior circumstances, for their day accommodation alone, while the inferior circumstances existing in the houses of their parents, which materially influenced the formation of their character, could not, on account of the great additional expense be removed, but it was beautiful to see how rapidly this partial change from very inferior to superior circumstances effected a beneficial alteration of the most gratifying character upon the children first and upon the parents afterwards through the new influence of the children's superior formed character reacting upon them.

> (Owen to Lord Brougham, *On the Origins of Infant School*, 14 August 1844, Brougham MSS)

Few actual details of his methods are recorded, but the broad outlines of procedure for the first infant classes in Britain are stated in his influential book, *A New View of Society* (1813). In order to be able to form a rational judgment on any subject, children should first be taught the knowledge of facts, starting with those which are most familiar, gradually proceeding, by clear explanation, to more complex knowledge 'as the child acquires strength and capacity of intellect'. Owen was particularly concerned that in many schools for the poor, children were rarely taught to understand what they read and were not encouraged to think or reason correctly.

It is interesting to note that Owen, and those subsequently responsible for infant schools, chose men as teachers, with women in the subsidiary role of nurses.

Owen's assistant master at New Lanark, James Buchanan, was later translated to London at the request of a committee headed by Henry Brougham to organize a school based on New Lanark principles. A second infant school opened at Spitalfields in 1820 was under the direction of a friend of Buchanan, Samuel Wilderspin. As he had no previous experience of teaching, Wilderspin was obliged to evolve his own methods. His first day at the school was both adventurous and illuminating, as his own account shows:

> As soon as the mothers had left the premises I attempted to engage the attention of their offspring. I shall never forget the effort. A few, who had been previously at a dame school, sat quietly; but the rest, missing their parents, crowded about the door. One little fellow, finding he could not open it, set up a loud cry of 'Mammy! Mammy!' and in raising this delightful sound all the rest simultaneously joined. My wife, who, though reluctant at first, had determined, on my accepting the situation, to give me her utmost aid, tried with myself to calm the tumult; but our efforts were utterly in vain. The paroxysm of sorrow increased instead of subsiding, and so intolerable did it become that she could endure it no longer, and left the room; and at length, exhausted by effort, anxiety, and noise, I was compelled to follow her example, leaving my unfortunate pupils in one dense mass, crying, yelling, and kicking against the door!

> I will not attempt to describe my feelings; but, ruminating on what I then considered egregious folly in supposing that any two persons could manage so large a number of infants, I was struck by the sight of a cap of my wife's, adorned with coloured ribbon, lying on the table; and observing from the window a clothes-prop, it occurred that I might put the cap upon it, return to the school, and try the effect. The confusion when I entered was tremendous; but on raising the pole surmounted by the cap all the children, to my great satisfaction, were instantly silent; and when any hapless wight attempted to renew the noise, a few shakes of the prop restored tranquillity, and,

perhaps, produced a laugh. The same thing, however, will not do long. The charms of this *wonderful* instrument therefore soon vanished, and there would have been a sad relapse but for the marchings, gambols, and antics I found it necessary to adopt, and which, at last, brought the hour of twelve, to my greater joy than can easily be conceived.

Revolving these circumstances, I felt that the memorable morning had not passed in vain. I had, in fact, found the clue. It was now evident that the senses of the children must be engaged; that the great secret of training them was to descend to their level and become a child, and that the error had been to expect in infancy what is only the product of after years.

(S. Wilderspin, *Early Discipline Illustrated*, 1832, pp. 3–4)

The organization of the school subsequently centred round this discovery. Wilderspin claimed to be the originator of the playground and equipped his with moving swings, one for the boys and the other for the girls. The only toys provided were wooden bricks, with which the children built squares, pentagons, and hexagons, or houses and castles.

Nevertheless, many of Wilderspin's notions of classroom work were derived from Lancaster. Much of the curriculum for the under sixes consisted of the three Rs, taught in a parrot-like fashion, often in verse form and sometimes even sung. This practice was not confined to England alone. A mistress of an infant school in Morpeth, Northumberland, visiting Scotland in 1836 to examine teaching methods, wrote to the school managers from Edinburgh:

The Teachers tell me, I will never succeed in conducting an Infant School without a great deal of singing; for example, a lesson is given upon arithmetic it is then immediately illustrated by singing something in connection with the questions. I have visited Dr Munro and several other schools and find that most everything is sung. I shall however learn everything and whatever is not according with the Committee can be dispensed with when I return to Morpeth.

(Maria Clarke to Morpeth School Committee, 20 Dec. 1836. Letter Book Records of Morpeth Borough Council 1835–1972. NRO 999/D.16, Northumberland R.O.)

Like Wilderspin, David Stow, a Glasgow philanthropist, was moved by religious motives to improve the character of the poor infants by schooling. Similarly, the two men conceived the idea of the gallery, a succession of steps with the eldest seated on the highest and the youngest at the lowest: this device remained a characteristic of infant schools until the end of the century. Unlike Wilderspin, Stow saw the necessity for training teachers in his method, which was called 'picturing out'. This was the drawing of pictures in words and the use of the oral method rather than books to explain abstract ideas. By this method, pupils were encouraged to be active rather than passive recipients of information. Ellipsis, incomplete sentences for which the pupil provided the missing words, was commonly employed.

It was not until the principles of the Swiss educationist, Pestalozzi, were adopted in England that any systematic training of infant teachers was carried out. Pestalozzi, writing to one of his English disciples in 1819, clearly demonstrated his belief in the need for close teacher–pupil relationships before learning can take place:

There is a most remarkable reciprocal action between the interest which the teacher takes, and that which he communicates to his pupils. If he is not with his whole mind present at the subject; if he does not care whether it is understood or not, whether his manner is liked or not, he will never fail of alienating the affections of his pupils, and of rendering them indifferent to what he says. But real interest taken in the task of instruction—kind words, and kinder feelings—the very expression of the features, and the glance of the eye—are never lost upon children.

(J. H. Pestalozzi, *Letters on Early Education Addressed to J. P. Greaves, Esq.*, 1827, p. 133)

Although he never completely spelled out his new methods, Pestalozzi was concerned to achieve 'child-centred' education, at the same time realizing that the intellectual, moral and practical aspects each needed consideration. Instruction should take into account that the child observes how many and what kind of objects are before him, their appearance, form and outline, and their names. All possible forms have number, appearance or form and names (language) and the teacher should use this division as a starting-point, working from the concrete to the abstract. We shall see in the next section how this method was misused and misinterpreted in English schools.

Kay-Shuttleworth and the Education Office

Kay-Shuttleworth upon his appointment to the new post of Secretary of the Committee of Privy Council in 1839, made an educational tour of the Continent later in the year. He visited the Swiss canton schools for the poor, where Pestalozzi's influence was strong. The curriculum, while stressing manual occupations, was an enlightened one, including music and recognizing the importance of play.

The superiority of Pestalozzian methods over Lancasterian was apparent to Kay-Shuttleworth. Class teaching or simultaneous instruction should replace mutual or monitorial instruction. In an early Minute issued in February 1840, Kay-Shuttleworth set out his recommendations for the information of school committees, inspectors and teachers:

The *simultaneous method* is distinguished from the method of mutual instruction by arrangements which enable the children to receive instruction immediately from the master or one of his assistants, instead of from the most advanced of their fellow-pupils, from which practice the method of mutual instruction derives its name. . . . any number of children under 40 or 50 may be instructed on the simultaneous method in one class, even in the departments of purely technical instruction. A much larger number of the children may thus be brought under the personal care of the superior master, and may be trained by him intellectually and morally. In such classes the instruction is not individual and successive, but is simultaneous, the mind of each child being at all times under the influence of the master. In Holland such classes frequently consist of from 60 to 100 children; but 40 children compose a class, the technical instruction of which can be conducted with ease by an experienced master on the simultaneous method. Moreover, in instruction of a less technical character, and requiring a less careful division of the school according to the attainments of the children in the technical portions of elementary learning, 100 or 120 children may be taught at once, either in a well-arranged school-room, (where their instruction can be conducted without removal from the places they usually occupy in classes), or by means of a central school-hall, in which three or four classes can be assembled for such general instruction in a gallery like that used in infant schools.

In making arrangements for teaching on the simultaneous method, it is therefore necessary to provide for two somewhat conflicting objects:

1. The technical instruction of the children in classes, carefully arranged according to their intellectual proficiency.

2. The general instruction of 100 to 120, or even more children, by the use of suggestion, ellipsis, and interrogation, either in the school-room common to all the classes, or in a gallery provided for that purpose.

(Minutes of Committee of Council on Education 1839–40. Remarks on the mixed method of instruction, 20 Feb. 1840)

While organizationally an advance on previous arrangements, these recommendations were already being misinterpreted. Dr Charles Mayo, the leading English disciple of Pestalozzi, had, with his sister Elizabeth, established a Pestalozzian school at Epsom in 1822 for children of the middle classes. His work at the school resulted in a publication, *Lessons on Objects*, for children between six and eight years of age consisting of a series of model lessons. Mayo was convinced that the best way to lead children to observe the objects around them was by making them describe these objects accurately. Engaging the perceptive faculties in this way would provide a sound basis for education. The 'objects' to be described were graded in difficulty, each one occupying a lesson. A typical model lesson is one on the apple:

LESSON IV

AN APPLE

Parts	*Qualities*
The eye	It is spherical
core	bright
pips	odorous
peel	coloured
pulp	opaque
juice	natural
stalk	vegetable
surface	juicy
inside	hard
outside	nice
	solid
	pleasant
	The eye is dry
	brown
	shrivelled

Remarks on Words

Spher *ical*, is derived from Sphere.
TEACHER.   Give instances of similar terminations.
CHILDREN.   Cylindr *ical*, crit *ical*, con *ical*.
Odor *ous*, is derived from *odor*, scent.
TEACHER.   Give instances of similar terminations.
CHILDREN.   Indigen *ous*, nutriti *ous*.
Vegetable, is derived from veget *are*, to grow as a plant.
TEACHER.   Name other words derived from this.
CHILDREN.   To vegetate, vegetation.
Juicy, is derived from Juice.
TEACHER.   Give some other instances in which the names of qualities are derived from those of substances in a similar manner.
CHILDREN.   Stone, ston *y*; milk, milk *y*; water, water *y*.

(C. Mayo, *Lessons on Objects: As Given to Children between the ages of 6 and 8 in a Pestalozzian School at Cheam, Surrey*, 6th edn., 1837, pp. 47–8)

In later editions, Miss Mayo defended the object lesson against the charge 'that they put fine words into children's mouths, and give them an air of pedantry'. She dismissed the paucity of poor children's language, explaining that 'when no simple and common words can be found to express (for instance) such very important and common qualities as opacity and transparency, the only terms our language affords must be used, and the reproach of pedantry be risked'.

The vogue for object lessons lasted throughout the century, degenerating for the most part in the hands of inexperienced teachers into mere rote learning. A typical scheme of work (approved by HM Inspector) for the year ended 31 May 1900 includes the following:

> *List of Object Lessons (1st stage)*
> Sheep—Elephant—Lion—Camel—Soap—Candles—Flax and Linen—Paper—Coal—Iron—Glass—Leather—Cork—Sugar—Salt—Parts of a River—Day and Night—Seasons.
>
> *Infants*
> Frog—Bee—Mole—Hedgehog—Dog—Cat—Baker—A Basket—Earth—Sun, moon and stars—Rain.
>
> (Charles National School, Log Book, 65 OC/EFL 1, Devon R.O.)

The use of the method on special occasions could be justified as serving an educational purpose. At Dedham in Essex in 1901:

> School opened this morning at 8.30. This was done at the unanimous request of the boys who wished to see the 'Meet' of the Hunt at 11 and the Master acceded to the request feeling that it would serve as an object lesson.
>
> (Dedham Boys' School, Log Book, 1883–1937, 13 Nov. 1901, E/ML 8/1 Essex R.O.)

Simultaneous teaching was attacked by inspectors. The Rev. W. H. Brookfield commented:

> Call upon a class of twenty to repeat the names of the twelve tribes of Israel, and with one clever fugleman to lead, they will catch the first letter of each name, as he utters it, with a quickness almost amounting to intuition, which enables them to accompany him in pronouncing the remainder of the word, and so on through the series, but this without the slightest intellectual effort, the words passed in at the ear—partly, indeed, at the eye, for they watch each other's lips—and out at the lips by a mere mechanical trick, become easy through frequent repetition, and without ever entering into the mind at all; insomuch that, if you were to test the same class narrowly the next minute you might find that no five out of the twenty really knew whether Naphthali was a woman, a mountain, a river or a drug.
>
> (Quoted in B. Boothroyd, *A History of the Inspectorate*, 1923, p. 17)

Underlying the reform of teaching methods urged by Kay-Shuttleworth was an anxiety that a continuation of the existing practices might lead to undesirable changes in society:

> If the mental and moral condition of the rising generation is to be usefully affected through the medium of schools, wider views must be taken of what it is requisite to teach, and of the instrumentality by which it is to be communicated. It is still necessary to repeat that what is commonly called education, namely, the teaching of the mechan-

ical art of reading and writing, with a little arithmetic, and the dogmatical inculcation of scripture formularies, very imperfectly understood, if at all, is not in fact education, or anything more than its unformed, undeveloped germ, possibly containing within it that which may give some additional power to the mind, but very probably in no way reaching and impressing the heart. It is necessary also to repeat, that, if the legitimate educator does no more than this, there are those who will do more—the Chartist and Socialist educator, the publisher of exciting, obscene and irreligious works, he who can boldly assert and readily declaim upon false and pernicious dogmas and principles. . . . To inculcate the leading doctrines of our faith, and to present the main incidents of the holy scriptures in such a manner as shall interest the affections of the young and not alone burden the memory, and to impart some real knowledge applicable to the state of society in which they live and to the world around them, is the work in hand.

(Minutes of the Committee of Council on Education, 1840)

Naturally, church schools looked to their teachers for support in this work. When, for example, one of the first model schools which were attached to training colleges was set up at Chester in 1842, the Diocesan Board stated that the success of the school would depend 'on the personal character of the Master, on his piety, sound Church principles, and aptness to teach'. The daily Scripture lesson, comprising all that a Christian ought to know and believe to his soul's health, was to be taught in an attractive manner. (See Model Schools Scheme of Instruction: with Directions to Masters, 5 Oct. 1841, CR 86/12/3 Chester City R.O.)

In fact much of the teaching continued on the lines of 'dogmatical inculcation of scriptural formularies' which Kay-Shuttleworth had condemned. The report of the weekly examinations in Catechism at a school in Beverley, North Humberside (formerly East Yorkshire), in January 1841 reads as follows:

> 1st Class. Have begun 'Catechism briefly Explained' but have not yet learnt sufficient for examination. Went through 'Church Catechism' with a thorough and minute analysis of it as far as the commencement of the Sacrament which they are well versed in.
> 2nd Class. Have learnt 'Broken Catechism' as far as the end of the Lord's Prayer. Except Widdall, Field, Franks and Simpson, the class knows the answers in the book pretty well. Also answering any other easy Questions that illustrate the text: though in this they are not so ready as they should be.
> 3rd Class. Is learning the Church Catechism the second time.

(Beverley Minster Boys' National School, Syllabus Book 1838–41, 29 Jan. 1841, SLB Beverley, Humberside R.O.)

The wide gulf which existed between the stated aims of Kay-Shuttleworth's curricular reforms and the actual methods employed in schools is graphically illustrated in the case of music. Early reports of inspectors indicated that vocal music was being taught in few elementary schools. In a prefatory memorandum to the 1840–1 Minutes of the Committee of Council on this topic, Kay-Shuttleworth demonstrated the benefits which would accrue to religion and to patriotism by a wider dissemination of music:

> Vocal music, as a means of expression, is by no means an unimportant element in civilization. One of the chief characteristics of public worship ought to be the extent to which *the congregation* unite in those solemn psalms of prayer and praise which, particularly in the Lutheran churches of Germany and Holland, appear the utterance of one harmonious voice. One of the chief means of diffusing through the people national sentiments is afforded by songs, which embody and express the hopes of industry and

the comforts and contentment of household life; and, preserving for the peasant the traditions of his country's triumphs, inspire him with confidence in her greatness and strength.

Every schoolmaster of a rural parish ought to instruct the children in vocal music, and to be capable of conducting a singing class among the young men and women. The instruction thus communicated would enable him, with such encouragement as he might receive from the clergyman, to form a respectable vocal choir for the village church. This, in itself, would tend to increase the attendance on Divine worship among the uneducated, and would spread an interest in the services of religion which might prove the first step to more important benefits. A relish for such pursuits would in itself be an advance in civilization, as it would doubtless prove in time the means of weaning the population from debasing pleasures, and would associate their amusements with their duties.

(Minutes of the Committee of Council, 1840–1, pp. 46–7)

Foreign experience had much to offer, and Kay-Shuttleworth, with John Hullah, an enthusiastic musician, toured Europe in order to obtain ideas for suitable teaching methods. Manuals of vocal music from Switzerland, Holland, the German states, Prussia, Austria and France were collected and carefully examined. They were particularly impressed by the methods developed by M. Wilhem for elementary schools under the Minister of Public Instruction in Paris.

Basically, Wilhem's system was based on monitorial lines, and Kay-Shuttleworth recommended a modified version for use in England. The equipment needed was minimal. About eight pupils gathered round each Tablet on which the notes were printed. A manual for the teacher contained minute detail on methods of organizing lessons as well as exercises and school songs. Much of the spirit was dissipated in the teaching; the art of singing was reduced to a series of exercises.

A third field to which Kay-Shuttleworth turned his attention was that of handwriting. He once again looked to the Continent for his model, and praised the method of Mulhäuser, a Zurich teacher, who in 1829 had been appointed inspector of writing classes by the Geneva Commission of Primary Schools.

The method of Mulhäuser consists in the decomposition of the written characters into their elements, and the classification of these elements, so that they may be presented to the child in the order of their simplicity, and that it may copy each of them separately. The synthesis, or recomposition of these elements into letters and words, is the process by which the child learns to write. He combines the forms which he has learned to imitate. He recognizes each separate simple form in the most difficult combinations, and, if he errs, is immediately able to correct the fault. If the master himself inadvertently commits a blunder, the child will often rectify it, without hesitation. (ibid., p. 43)

Successive editions of English school method manuals for teachers emphasized the advantages of Mulhäuser's system. In the instance of the one quoted below, each section is prefaced with extracts from Kay-Shuttleworth's memorandum, which was itself reproduced in later Minutes of the Committee of Council on Education. The teacher first analysed the script characters into their various elements. Next, the letters were classified in the natural order of their simplicity. Finally came the synthesis, that is, the pupil combined the elements which previous analysis had decomposed.

He made use of various *technical names* for the parts of letters, and after he had taught these parts in separate lessons, he employed *Dictation* very largely, in getting the letters built up from their parts. For example, the word judgment would be dictated thus:

Right line two heights, (down) loop, Half-link   (j)
Right line, Link—Right line, Link   (u)
Double-curve—Right line two heights, Link   (d)
Double-curve, Right line two heights (down), Loop, Half-link   (g)
Hook, Right line, Hook, Right line, Hook, Right line, Link   (m)
Loop, Curve, Link   (e)
Hook, Right line—Hook, Right line, Link   (n)
Right line, one height and a half, Link, Bar   (t)

'The teacher does not dictate a letter which can leave the pupil in doubt as to the precise thing that is required of him, but pronounces in succession each element of the letter, which the writer follows, without thinking of the letter itself. These enigmas both amuse the children and accustom them to reflect. This part of the system calls into action the intelligence of the children by an allurement resembling that of a game.'—*Manual.*

(F. J. Gladman, *School Method. Notes and Hints from Lectures delivered at Borough Road Training College*, n.d., pp. 64–5)

The new approach did not have the initial success which was hoped for. This topic had engaged the attention of Lord Palmerston in 1854, at that time the Home Secretary. He wrote officially to Lingen, Secretary to the Committee of Council on Education, deploring 'the want of proper Teaching in the art of Writing in schools. The great bulk of the lower and middle orders write hands too small and indistinct and do not form their letters.' (*Typed copies of selected letters from Old Letter Books 1847–58*, p. 322, Ed. 9/12, Public Record Office, henceforth referred to as PRO.)

With the increased demands of industry and commerce by the end of the century, the significance of handwriting was pointed out by an author of a manual for school board teachers.

Not only is it thus all pervasive. Throughout civilized society it rises to even greater prominence and significance in the case of hundreds of thousands who act as secretaries, copyists or clerks, follow writing as their profession or business, and derive from it their sole means of subsistence. Such persons are occupied the year round, for from 8 to 16 hours daily, exclusively in clerical work. It is impossible to exaggerate the importance of an art which is pre-eminently the vital principle in the machinery of the Law, the Civil Service, Commerce, Science . . .

(J. Jackson, *The Theory and Practice of Handwriting: A Practical Manual for the Guidance of School Board Teachers*, 1893, pp. 10–11)

In an attempt to eradicate the worst features of the monitorial system, Kay-Shuttleworth introduced pupil–teachers in 1846; apprentice teachers from the age of thirteen or fourteen could be trained in the simultaneous method and take charge of classes. Matthew Arnold later referred to the pupil–teacher system as 'the sinews of English public instruction'. There is however widespread evidence from contemporary records that many pupil–teachers proved to be unsuitable for the work; many others were not attracted by the terms of service.

It is not surprising therefore to find that there was generally a shortage of candidates, leading schools to adopt at best stopgap expedients. At a Derbyshire school in 1895, we read:

The Managers have a difficulty in obtaining another Pupil Teacher. There is one girl in the School likely to do herself credit as a Teacher but she is at present too young being only 12 years of age. Her parents are being approached on the subject and if their consent is forthcoming she will be engaged as temporary monitor.

(Brackenfield National School, Log Book 1863–99, 22 May 1895, 83 C/EF 1 Derbyshire R.O.)

Despite such difficulties, there were innovations in method during this period worthy of note. Perhaps the most remarkable example—that of the Rev. Richard Dawes at King's Somborne, Hampshire—has already been mentioned. Systematic observation and problem-solving techniques were used in all areas of the curriculum. There is evidence too that in other parts of the country a wider curriculum was being offered. In a report of the Children's Employment Commission (1842) one witness gave this account of the Killingworth Colliery Schools in Northumberland:

Frequent exercises are given on the following books, mostly by dictation: Smith's and Guy's *Orthographical Exercises*; Guy's *Astronomy* and *General School Question Book*; Blair's *Universal Preceptor*, and Pinnock's *Outlines of Ancient and Modern History*. Also ornamental writing, the practical uses of mapping, lettering, and the construction of maps and plans are taught, (specimens of which, done by the boys of the colliery, are exhibited in the school-room). Several of the boys use Lennie's *Grammar and Exercises*. Education is not restricted in our schools, and the following is a brief summary of the various branches taught: arithmetic and writing on paper are much practised; book-keeping; mensuration in all its branches; land-surveying and plotting, or laying down plans, also subterraneous surveying; plane and spherical trigonometry, with their application to astronomy, and the use of the globes, if necessary. The master gives to his elder scholars easy and familiar exercises on optics, by the use of the prism, microscope, and telescope, and the nature of the different lenses. One of the greatest losses in schools is the want of simple apparatus to illustrate the many lessons on scientific subjects. Excepting the exercise in reading, the sense is generally lost to the scholars. It may be proper to observe that all the girls learn to write and cipher on paper with the master, and their number may average about 40 each day.

(Notes and Evidence on the Education of Children Northumberland and North of Durham Colliery. Information concerning school, J. R. Leifchild, p. 712, Royal Commission on Children's Employment, 1842. BPP, xvi)

The Codes and School Board era

As already stated, the effect of the immediate results of the Revised Code on payment by results in 1862 was a narrowing of the curriculum to the three Rs and needlework, all of which were examined. We can see from this Leicestershire school what a typical day consisted of two years after the system was introduced:

Gave the first and second classes a blackboard lesson in Numeration. Most of the children can put down as far as millions correctly. Gave out Dictation the fable of the 'Dog and Shadow', to the first class on paper and to the second on slates.

The Reading lesson to the first and second classes as yesterday. Thomas Middleton caned for inattention.

The Arithmetic in the afternoon was an improvement on yesterday, more examples worked by the second class on the blackboard in Subtraction. The sewing from 2.30 as usual. While the first class were writing in Copybooks, and the second class on slates, the third and fourth classes have a simple mental arithmetic lesson.

Thomas Heward and John Osborne working apart from their class. Oliver Pratt caned.

(Hugglescote National School, Log Book 1863–74, 21 June 1864, E/LB/150/1 Leicestershire Museums, Art Galleries and Record Service Leicestershire R.O.)

It followed that, if money grants to schools were dependent on the results of examining the pupils, the Education Department, acting through its inspectors, actively discouraged copying. D. R. Fearon, a former inspector, included a section in his book for teachers, *School Inspection* (1876), entitled 'How to Stop Copying in Arithmetic', as did J. R. Blakiston in *The Teacher: Hints on School Management* (1895).

The importance of achieving good results at annual inspections is illustrated by some of the methods used. At one Exeter school in 1880, the school visitors reported the following case:

Mr Bryan (Master) states that with respect to the punishment of the boy Turner, the Class had been reported by the Teacher to have been very careless in their dictation exercise after considerable practice, and he made an order applicable to the case of his class that in respect to the next lesson, each boy should have as many raps on the hand with the cane, as he made mistakes, provided they extended beyond 4 mistakes in spelling. Turner made 8 mistakes and others more or less, and received the punishment accordingly with no signs of excess.

(School Visitors' Report, Exeter School Board, Vol. 2, 22 May 1879, Devon R.O.)

Additional constraints on the methods used in schools arose from the teaching commitments of individual teachers. One master in Kent, protesting to the managers about a proposal to substitute an assistant mistress for two male teachers, wrote:

At present I manage geography and drawing in this way: 3 afternoons a week I give Stan. I and II a rapid sketch of the lesson, and leave the teacher to fill in the details while I give Stans. IV, V, VI and VII a full geography lesson. Next I give Standard III an outline lesson and leave the teacher to mark it up, while I give St. I and II a drawing lesson, and superintend IV, V and VI. After this I give St. III, IV, V, VI and VII a drawing lesson.

(Charing Parish Records 1886–92, undated letter 1887 P78/25/4, Kent Archives Office)

The powers given to inspectors to approve the timetable virtually meant the power to control it. An Education Department Minute of 7 February 1871 ordered the inspector to report to the Department if he found the work of the school not being carried out according to the approved timetable. A year later this was reinforced in a further circular stating that 'no change may be made without the express sanction of the Inspector. This sanction ought not to be given . . . except upon formal application from the Managers nor unless strong grounds for the change are shown.' The managers were further warned that any neglect of the division of the timetable into its various components would entail a forfeiture of grants. (Circular 51—Time Tables 10 Aug. 1872.) Where the inspector was an open advocate of Church schools, he would be likely to oppose alternative approaches to education. Mr Sewell advised the Department in 1870 not to encourage the growth of Board Schools in Nottingham. 'A check is thus put upon the desire which might otherwise be insatiable to try experiments or gratify the fancies of parties, educational and political, at the expense of the Ratepayers.' (Minute 9 Sept. 1871, Nottingham Ed 16/243 PRO.)

No allowance was made for the location of the school. Rural schools were at a particular disadvantage. What was written after an inspection by a Cambridgeshire teacher in the late 1850s was equally applicable thirty years later:

> ... he made some suggestions which we should be happy to carry out, if the intelligence of our children and limited time they remain at School admitted of it. Inspecting a village School in one part of the country is a very different thing to Inspection of a Town School. The requirements in one case are not necessary in the other. During many months our School is more like an Infant School, than otherwise; and as long as the wages of the labourers are but 8/- a week, it is no wonder that every child who is competent to scare a crow and thereby earn a few pence daily, should be taken from the school and sent into the fields.
>
> (William Challis, *Report to the Cambridge Board of Education*, 23 November 1859, Kirting Parish Records, P101/25/17 Cambridgeshire C.R.O.)

At the elementary stages parental interest in curriculum in the last quarter of the nineteenth century was often low. Occasionally teachers were required to account for the content and methods of their work. At a Devon school in 1880, the log book records:

> Mrs Elliot asked me to excuse her daughter from learning Geography, as it puzzled her. I told her that as the child was not afflicted in any way I could not excuse it, and the puzzling would do her good if it was not carried to excess.
>
> (Aveton Gifford Church School, Notes on the early records by R. R. Sellman, Aveton Gifford Parish Deposit 328A add. 3/PE3, Devon R.O.)

In a Northumberland colliery school for boys at North Seaton in 1868 a parent challenged a master, sending a note informing him that his son was to come home if he was given Weights and Measures again. Three weeks later, the boy's father called at the school:

> Amid many general statements he expressed himself to the effect that a Teacher should not use his own judgment as to whether a boy is fitted to pass from one rule of arithc. to another, but must follow entirely what the parent wishes. I explained to him the folly of a boy going to the higher rules before he was thoroughly grounded in the lower ones— but this, in his opinion amounted to nothing—if the parent wished otherwise and was satisfied in his own mind with the lad's knowledge—and directly referred to the exploded notion that there were some who were anxious to keep education at as low an ebb as possible. He at last asked if I 'would allow the boy to work or learn something else during the arithc. lesson'—I distinctly said 'No! I would allow no such interference'. The result was I told him 'he had better take the boy home'—he did so.
>
> (North Seaton Boys' Colliery School, Log Book, 5 and 25 Feb. 1868, CES 314/1 Northumberland R.O.)

An important innovation following the issue of the New Code of 1880, which itself was aimed at liberalizing the range of the school curriculum, was the setting up of a central body, the Code Committee. This was a forum for discussing the nature and impact of the elementary curriculum. School boards and managers were invited to submit suggestions for improvement; between twenty and thirty inspectors wrote their comments on the leading ideas. From this, a draft report was drawn up and was then considered by the Committee which consisted of senior inspectors, officials of the Education Department and the Vice-President. The amended Code was finally scrutinized by the Committee together with the Lord President and other chief inspectors. (J. Leese, *Personalities and Power in English Education*, 1950, p. 138.)

Among the inspectors on the Committee were Matthew Arnold, H. E. Oakeley, T. W. Sharpe and J. G. Fitch, whose combined views carried considerable weight. Partly as a result of the financial constraints imposed by the Treasury and the political opposition to a widening of the scope of subjects to be allowed in schools, little fundamental reform was possible. The inspectors' philosophies were limited and tentative where boldness could have been decisive, thus rendering the experiment less effective.

Apart from the views expressed by individual inspectors on curriculum matters, account must be taken of the attitudes of politicians holding educational positions. Few Vice-Presidents of the Council expressed their policy as explicitly as Lord George Hamilton, who held office from 1878 to 1880:

> Every sound educationalist knows that the curriculum of the subjects taught to children should be regulated by the age at which their education ceases. Of all forms of education the worst for the children of the industrial class is an ambitious programme truncated by the necessity of the children going to work before they have mastered the extra subjects taught. I got the assent of the Government to the higher-grade schools, and I was preparing for the lower-grade schools a simpler and more compact curriculum. Mundella took my higher-grade schools, and instead of simplifying the curriculum in the lower-grade schools he added an extra standard to those already in existence and additional specific subjects. In my judgment, this was a fatal blunder, and one which in no small degree has contributed to the poor returns achieved by the mongrel but expensive scheme of primary and secondary education into which after this change we subsequently drifted.

> (Lord George Hamilton, *Parliamentary Reminiscences and Reflections—1868 to 1885*, 1917, pp. 185–6)

However, with the widening of the Code, more freedom to experiment was possible. A sub-committee of the London School Board reported on the methods of teaching reading in November 1882. No fewer than four different systems in operation in London schools were fully described—Sonnenschein's, Robinson's Phonic, the American Leigh's and Pitman's Phonetic Methods. Of the last, the report stated:

> An experiment with Pitman's Phonetic System was started at Saunder's-road on June 20th 1878, under the general direction of Miss Parfitt. A class of children, about five years of age, were supplied with Pitman's primer, and the letters on cards; and the same amount of time during the week, viz two hours, was bestowed upon them as upon the other classes in the School. Miss Eyles, afterwards Mrs Boult, learnt the system, and taught these children carefully. She had the advantage of a comparatively small class, because the ordinary vacancies that occurred were not filled up with other children; but, on the other hand, the reading book employed was not so suitable or interesting as our usual readers, and the children, of course, had no chance of any practice outside the class. She taught them first the thirty-eight letters and then came the transition

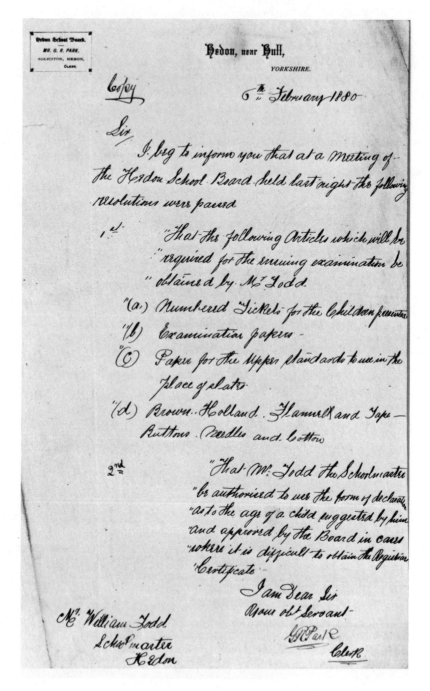

Hedon School Board.
MR. G. R. PARK.
SOLICITOR, HEDON.
CLERK.

Hedon, near Hull,
YORKSHIRE.

Copy

6th February 1880

Sir

I beg to inform you that at a Meeting of the Hedon School Board held last night the following resolutions were passed.

1st   "That the following Articles which will be "required for the ensuing examination be "obtained by Mr Todd.

"(a) Numbered Tickets for the Children presented

"(b) Examination papers

"(c) Paper for the Upper Standards to use in the place of slates.

"(d) Brown Holland, Flannel and Tape — Buttons, Needles and Cotton

2nd   "That Mr Todd the Schoolmaster "be authorised to use the form of declaration "as to the age of a child suggested by him "and approved by the Board in cases "where it is difficult to obtain the Registrars "Certificate

I am Dear Sir
Your obt Servant
G R Park
Clerk

Mr William Todd
Schoolmaster
Hedon

12   Requirements for the Annual Examination in Elementary schools
Letter from a School Board Clerk to a Headmaster.

Humberside Record Office

from vocalizing to reading. This was a difficult process; nevertheless it was 'no drudg-ery to the children, but an evident pleasure from the certainty of the process'; and 'it was delightful to them to read great long words at sight, and make them up from the sounds'. In February 1879 about seven children had to be removed to the First Standard on account of age, but they were brought back to Mrs Boult's class for their reading lessons. No parent was ever known to object to the unusual letters. About November 1879, about three months before the Government Inspection, these children were mixed with another class who had been taught the current system of spelling for about the same period. A few transition lessons were attempted, but the book was too difficult, and the teacher, under whose care they now were, did not understand the Phonetic alphabet, but she gave some additional time to their spelling. At the time of the examination, February 10th 1880, they had become sufficiently well acquainted with the ordinary orthography to be undistinguishable from the other children when they read from a First Standard book, and when they wrote such words as 'small, near, come, &c'., from dictation. The teacher, however, said that those who had been taught phonetically were more ready to pick up new words; and it was perfectly evident that they showed a marked superiority in the clear pronunciation of their words. Her Majesty's Inspector remarked especially upon the distinct enunciation of the final syllable at his examination on the 20th February. Most of these scholars passed into Mrs Dobbs' class (Standard in the Infants' department), and she found them good readers; though they could not spell properly at first, they soon were able to do so, and became generally her best scholars.

Of the children taught in this way, forty-nine at least passed into the Boys' and Girls' Schools, and no distinction was made in their subsequent instruction. In March 1882, an attempt was made to ascertain whether they were in any way distinguishable from the other children of their classes. The teachers did not know which they were; but on inquiry of the children themselves, it was found they were generally amongst the best readers . . .

(School Board for London, Report of the Sub-Committee on the Methods of Teaching Reading, 13 Nov. 1882, SBL 1432 Greater London R.O. (London Section))

Difficulties still abounded. One of the experiments was abandoned after eighteen months 'on account of the difficulty attending the Government Examination. Her Majesty's Inspector, though considerably interested in the experiment, felt obliged to examine Standard I in the ordinary books which had not been used.' But this was a great advance on the situation existing some forty years previously where, at Chester, instructions for reading and spelling in the lower classes read:

No word, the meaning of which is not obvious to every scholar, should be passed over unexplained, and every long or hard word should be spelled. The Master should repeatedly examine whether this is done, by requiring the boys to write on the slates which are suspended from their necks, such words as he may dictate from the lesson, and to give the meaning of them.

(Model Schools: Scheme of Instruction with Directions to Masters, 5 Oct. 1841, CR 86/12/3 Chester R.O.)

The heuristic methods of H. E. Armstrong in science teaching in the 1890s, which required the teacher to proceed on the basis of experiment rather than lecture, was paralleled with advances in other fields. Slöjd, a Scandinavian im-portation of the 1880s, which was a system of manual instruction concerned with hand and eye training in metal, wood and other forms of manual instruction, was widely adopted in elementary schools.

With the ending of the system of annual examinations in the 1890s and the abandonment of the division of the curriculum into obligatory class and specific

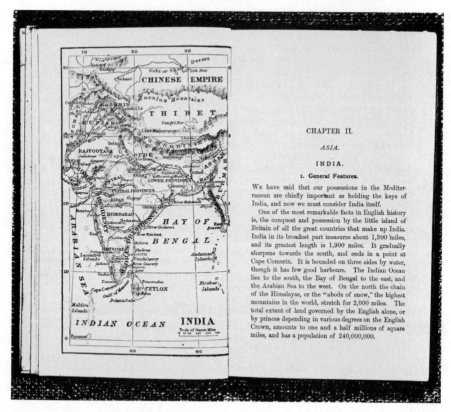

CHAPTER II.

ASIA.

INDIA.

1. General Features.

WE have said that our possessions in the Mediterranean are chiefly important as holding the keys of India, and now we must consider India itself.

One of the most remarkable facts in English history is, the conquest and possession by the little island of Britain of all the great countries that make up India. India in its broadest part measures about 1,500 miles, and its greatest length is 1,900 miles. It gradually sharpens towards the south, and ends in a point at Cape Comorin. It is bounded on three sides by water, though it has few good harbours. The Indian Ocean lies to the south, the Bay of Bengal to the east, and the Arabian Sea to the west. On the north the chain of the Himalayas, or the "abode of snow," the highest mountains in the world, stretch for 2,000 miles. The total extent of land governed by the English alone, or by princes depending in various degrees on the English Crown, amounts to one and a half millions of square miles, and has a population of 240,000,000.

13   A Geography textbook entitled *The British Possessions* 1882

subjects, there were opportunities to experiment with more child-centred approaches.

But the sudden vacuum caused by the relinquishing of central control left the elementary teacher in a difficult position. By long tradition bound down to rigid methods by successive codes, the teacher rejected some of the newer and more enlightened possibilities such as those advocated by Froebelians. Because of this tradition, the system of the German philosopher J. F. Herbart appealed to many during the 1890s and early twentieth century. Herbartianism stressed the importance of the teacher and the role of instruction in planning a curriculum. A Herbartian class lesson would consist of five stages. *Aim and Preparation*, the identification of the topic to be discussed; *Presentation*, the central matter of the lesson; *Association*, the connection between new facts presented and what was already known; *Formulation*, general rules formulated from the whole lesson; and *Application*, how to apply the rules to new situations. A section of such a lesson in natural science, on ocean currents, from a contemporary textbook begins as follows:

Aim. How were the objects, which made Columbus decide there was land to the West, carried to the Eastern Atlantic?

14   Girls drilling 1909
The whole school took part in these lessons.

GLC Photograph Library

Preparation. Why did Columbus sail West? He hoped to find land. Why did he think there was land westward? Various objects had been found in the Eastern Atlantic which he thought had drifted from the West. Mention the objects. (*a*) Pieces of carved wood were found by a Portuguese pilot in the seas west of Portugal. (*b*) Reeds and trees were cast up on the western shores of the Azores. (*c*) The bodies of two men of an unknown race drifted on to the island of Flores.

Require the pupils to quote from their literature Tennyson's 'Columbus', lines indicating the approach of land.

> Still westward, and the weedy seas—at length
> The landbird, and the branch with berries on it,
> The carven staff.

Had Columbus any other reason for thinking there was land westward? He had read accounts of it in old books.
Recapitulation of Preparation.

(C. I. Dodd, Introduction to the *Herbartian Principles of Teaching*, 1898, p. 160)

The rigidity of the method was obvious even to the stoutest supporter. It called for a uniform and unvarying treatment of all branches of instruction: both the originality of the teacher and the spontaneity of the pupil were suppressed. Perhaps the main criticism would be directed towards the artificial way in which the topic was chosen. The following amusing story is quoted of such an example:

A young teacher introducing a lesson on coffee began by asking the children: 'What did you have for breakfast this morning?' To which the obvious but quite irrelevant answers were given: 'Porridge', 'Bread', 'Jam', 'Bacon', etc. 'No,' said the teacher, 'I want to know what you had to drink.' Again the answers (this being England and not France) were quite irrelevant: 'Tea', 'Milk', 'Cocoa', etc. The teacher, at last out of patience, bawled at a child who had said 'Tea', 'No, you didn't—you had *coffee*.'

(M. Sturt and E. C. Oakden, *Matter and Method in Education*, 1937, p. 139)

In almost direct contrast to this rigid approach was the official recognition in 1893 of the Froebelian method in infants' schools. Friedrich Froebel, who had died in 1852, held that 'all the child is ever to be or become lies, however slightly indicated, in the child, and can be attained only through development from within outwards'.

Some private schools in London had been conducted on Froebelian principles in the 1850s; but the main spread of ideas came through the setting up of a training department at Stockwell College and the appointment of an Instructor in Kindergarten Exercises by the London School Board in 1874. At first, the enthusiasts misinterpreted Froebel's message. Canon E. D. Tinling, Chief Inspector for Training Colleges, was asked to comment on a report in the following year from the Oxford School Board that Froebelian methods should be employed. Tinling, in his minute to the Secretary of the Education Department,

15   A school playground 1906
A Departmental Committee on the uses of playgrounds in elementary schools recommended in 1912 that playing fields should be provided for sport.

GLC Photograph Library

recommending that 'the grant should be refused unless the minimum of attainments be reached', expressed doubts about the system:

> Inquiry from E. Weiber's Manual, and the Guide by Rosza, where no 'mechanical grind' (to use the words from the letter of the Oxford Board), even for the formation of the letters of the Alphabet, appears to be sanctioned for a great length of time—ascertaining, from the German Teacher employed at Stockwell, that no reading or writing should be introduced under Froebel's system until after 6 years of age; and ascertaining that this German teacher had herself removed a box of letters given to the institution from her 'gifts', i.e. material for 'occupations', or in other words Infant School apparatus, as such letters are contrary to the principles taught in the Kindergarten System: I should decline to consider such System 'alone' as sufficient.
>
> (Oxford School Board, 13 April 1875, Ed. 16/250 P.R.O.)

Two other points were added marginally: 'the German teacher at Stockwell does not consider that an Infants School Mistress should instruct under this Kindergarten System more than 12 to 14 children' (this at a time when an infants class averaged between 60 and 70), and 'a piano is considered an essential "gift" as far as the games are concerned', an extravagance likely to be disallowed by the district auditor.

Although a number of boards adopted the method, many inspectors regarded such teaching with dislike. At a school in Danbury, Essex, the following report was made in June 1888:

> *Infants Class.* The infants are fairly taught, but they might be brought into far better condition by more skilful management. As the room is resonant, the greatest care is needed to guard against indiscriminateness of speech, the shuffling of feet, and want of stillness in general on the part of the children, and also against any unnecessary noise on the part of the Teacher. The attainments of the infants' classes are fair, except their mental arithmetic which is very backward.
>
> (Danbury National School, Report 11 June 1858. School Portfolio 1858–1930, E/N 2/17, Essex R.O.)

Official change in policy resulted from the Minority Report of the Elementary Education Commission (Cross) 1888, which recommended that no pressure should be put upon teachers in infants' schools 'to give prominence to direct instruction in reading, writing and arithmetic to the younger children' (Final Report, p. 161). On the return of a Liberal Government four years later, a circular to inspectors issued by A. H. D. Acland encouraged kindergarten activities by raising the age of a pass at Standard I to seven years of age and recommended that the lower classes of infants should be 'relieved from premature preparation for these subjects on methods ill-suited to their tender age'. A list of 'suitable occupations' was added to the circular; children between five and seven, it was suggested, could make use of a wide range of material:

> Games with or without music, picture and object and story-lessons, recitations, paper-folding, mosaic with coloured paper and gum, drawing with pencil and with brush, plaiting paper, ruling simple geometrical forms, measuring and estimating lengths and weights, setting a table without spilling water or breaking crockery, modelling in clay, basket-work, cutting out patterns and shapes with scissors, word-building, number pictures with cubes and beads.
>
> (T. Raymont, *A History of the Education of Young Children*, 1937, p. 257)

Progress in adopting these methods was slow; much depended upon the attitude of individual inspectors, managers and teachers in the extent to which these suggestions were translated into activity. The compromise position which had to be adopted by Froebel enthusiasts is seen in the evidence given in 1897 by one headmistress before the London School Board Special Sub-Committee on Infant School Method:

> In play in the Kindergarten we get them to imitate animals, but we often have to suggest the movements to them. It is not spontaneous, but sometimes they will do it on their own account. I would not be angry because of variations, but I would work them up to pattern. I am afraid we do not always get them up to the one pattern, but as a matter of theory we do do so. Only a very few games have been witnessed by the Inspector, but we have in our minds the idea that he would like to keep them uniform. Arms folded in front and behind and hands behind I never allow, not a stiff position; the normal position is hands hanging loosely at the side. In a class all the children are in the same attitude. I make a definite provision for free play. It is on the time-table under the head of 'Toys'. We should like the 'Conversation Lesson' to mean the children talking to the teacher, but my experience is that they do not talk. They have not any means of expressing themselves. We have to give them a vocabulary. We teach them to talk. They are not talked to at home, and that makes a great difference. The word Kindergarten on the time-table means the whole-class are doing something with their fingers, and that what they are doing is taking place with material which I requisition from this office. I think the Kindergarten Requisition List could be improved if it were more varied or were more suggestive. I have asked for things not on the list several times, and in many cases I have had them given, while at other times I have had them refused. I remember a time-table which I drew up in 1885 and 1886 and which Mr Sharp signed, that excluded all teaching of reading till after the child was five years of age. It was a time-table drawn up as far as possible on Kindergarten lines. When I went to Kennington Lane I took that with me, but I was bound to alter my time-table. I had to climb down in a way.

> (Miss Vigor, Evidence. Report of the Special Sub-Committee on Method in Infants School, London School Board, 23 July 1897, p. 3, SBL 1415, Greater London R.O. (London Section))

Later developments

One of the criticisms levelled at the kindergarten method was that it required small group-teaching in order to be effective. Those who enthusiastically hailed the work of Dr Maria Montessori saw in it a solution to this problem. On other grounds too it proved to be an acceptable alternative to Froebelian practice. In her own influential book written in 1912, she compares the two systems:

> The broad contrast between a Montessori school and a kindergarten appears on actual observation to be this: whereas the Montessori children spend almost all their time handling *things*, largely according to their individual inclination and under individual guidance, kindergarten children are generally engaged in group work and games with an imaginative background and appeal.

> (Maria Montessori, *The Montessori Method*, English edition 1912, p. xxvi)

Based on her experiences when working with feeble-minded children in Italy, Montessori conceived the idea of didactic apparatus for training the senses. It differed from the Froebelian 'gifts' in that hers was based on objects most commonly met with in everyday life, such as tables, doors and window-frames.

16   A practical Geography lesson 1911

GLC Photograph Library

Montessori's work with the poor children of Rome, where she organized Houses of Childhood, demonstrated to her the need for schools to take more responsibility for the child than had hitherto been claimed. As a result, the curriculum included training in social habits and activities based on practical life. The role of the teacher was more that of an inspirer than an instructor as the apparatus was programmed for the child. On the other hand,

> the liberty of the child should have as its *limit* the collective interest; as its *form*, what we universally consider good breeding. We must therefore check in the child whatever offends or annoys others, or whatever tends towards rough or ill-bred acts. But all the rest, every manifestation having a useful scope, whatever it be, and under whatever form it expresses itself, must not only be permitted, but must be *observed* by the teacher.

(Montessori, op. cit., p. 87)

The path had been opened for Montessorian ideas with the increasing attention paid by the new Board of Education to nursery and infant education, and the institution of a school medical service in 1907. Perhaps the pioneer nursery classes started by Rachel and Margaret McMillan at Deptford in 1911, where children spent the whole day at school, provided the fertile soil for the spread of the Montessori movement shortly afterwards.

Margaret McMillan, however, like many other educationists, rejected Montessorian methods, mainly on the grounds that they were based on faulty psychological premises and left little to the child's imagination, and that the role of the teacher was diminished. One eloquent critic was Charlotte Mason. She had been responsible for the formation of the Parents' National Education Union (PNEU) in 1887 and five years later established a training college for both governesses and mothers at Ambleside, Westmorland, at which the theory and methods of education suitable for children between the ages of six and sixteen were expounded. Training was 'on the natural methods and principles advanced by the PNEU' and took two years. It was a fairly enlightened training college, compared with contemporary grant-aided ones:

> Psychology, Ethics and the Philosophy of Education, Practical Teaching; the teaching of Modern Languages (French, German and Italian); Nature Lore (including Botany and Natural History), Art, Modelling in Clay and Brushwork on broad artistic lines; Hygiene and Physiology, Arts and Crafts, etc.
>
> (Minute Book, The House of Ambleside 1899–1903, PNEU MSS, University of London)

As an alternative to either class-teaching or the oral lesson, the PNEU system was based on the belief that educability in all social classes was greater than had hitherto been supposed. If psychological factors were correctly considered, then good progress could be made. A balance sheet of Miss Mason's method was drawn up by an LCC inspector in July 1921, when reporting on two elementary schools which had adopted the system:

> *Method.* A syllabus is drawn up by the PNEU for each term. The work proceeds on the theory that vividness of original impression and interest are of the first importance, and that the actual words of an author are superior to any others; it aims at a wealth of ideas, and to banish narrowness. Formal correctness, if unaccompanied by knowledge, enthusiasm, and good taste is, in the eyes of the originators of the scheme, of small value.
>
> The essence of the school practice is that a piece of a text or textbook is read by the teacher to the class, who thereafter, at the time, piece by piece, or as a whole, or after a shorter or longer interval, reproduce orally to the teacher, or in writing, what they have heard read. This practice can be varied in a large number of ways.
>
> *Merits.* It develops self-confidence, power of expression, interest, and ability to remember. The oral powers of these children are much above the average, in precision, in range of vocabulary, and in general qualities of speech. It makes the children much more articulate. It gives scope for individual work (see below). It has a high culture value, because the syllabus is extensive and ambitious, and gives much miscellaneous information. It brings a supply of good books into the class room and creates a literary atmosphere, and it imparts a liking for reading and for ideas. In these ways it accomplishes what it sets out to do.
>
> *Defects.* It is a very good method for governesses with two or three pupils. In large classes it renders sectional teaching difficult and individual teaching impossible—if this is a defect. On the other hand, as it excites interest, it enlarges the possibility of individual private work. Compared with ordinary Elementary School teaching it lays much less stress on the rudiments, which are weaker here than elsewhere. For instance, spelling is not as good, but composition, oral and written, is better. The syllabus is drawn up outside the school and for the teachers. It is an ambitious and idealistic

scheme, but it leads to a very close reproduction of the *form* of the original—as indeed is intended. To use old terms, it develops the memory more quickly (but not necessarily further, in the ultimate) than the reason; it is relatively superficial; there is a tendency to verbalism, for the children often repeat phrases whose meaning is only vaguely known to them. There lurks in it a danger of indefinite thinking.

(Report presented to the Elementary Education Sub-Committee of the LCC Education Committee, 19 July 1921, ED/PS/2/27, Greater London R.O. (London Section))

Much of the subsequent development of PNEU methods was carried on in private schools, although in some areas, such as Gloucestershire and Leicestershire, elementary schools also were able to proceed on these lines. The then Chief Inspector of the London County Council, F. H. Spencer, ended the London experiment in 1924, noting somewhat paradoxically, that 'it would be better to have schools responsible for their own curriculum, even if a loss of liberty were to be accompanied by a gain of efficiency'. A few years previously, in 1920, another attractive alternative to class teaching appeared in England, the Dalton Plan. A disciple of Montessori, Helen Parkhurst, devised schemes of individualized work for pupils in order that she could attend to those with special needs. This 'laboratory' plan draws its name from Dalton, Massachusetts, where Miss Parkhurst carried out her experiments in the local school. By 1926 more than 2,000 English schools had adopted the system.

A basic assumption was that children liked learning. The Dalton Plan therefore would transform the learning process into a cooperative adventure, which would enable community principles and practices to be introduced into the school. Motivation of children for learning was the first essential; this could best be achieved by attending to organizational principles.

Begin your re-organization by breaking up your curriculum into smaller portions, say into as many allotments as there are months in the school year. Each portion in all its parts forms a large unit which we call a 'job' and each job should be a series of related ideas. Call a joint meeting of the staff to examine these jobs. Frank discussion and examination, combined with collective thinking will help to weave them into a single idea or a real unit. If for instance the history of the first centres of civilization is to be studied, let the geography and topography of the earliest primitive peoples be studied with it. When science is the subject, the use of an inclined plan should be studied in connection with the building of the Pyramids. Greek art must be taken with Greek history, and thus in innumerable ways the job can be treated so that the pupil will realize that a single idea dominates the whole. . . .

. . . Next you will do away with class-rooms in the formal sense, and substitute workshops or laboratories wherein the pupil can browse intelligently. Maps, globes and pictures, sand-tables, and everything useful in the study of geography should be collected in one of these laboratories. In another, adjoining if possible, put the books, charts and apparatus necessary to historical research. This arrangement should stimulate pupils of different grades to build up pictorial charts of the various epochs of civilization under the headings of Supply; Conduct; Environment; Events, etc. The whole course of history might thus be simultaneously worked out by the entire school in cooperation, and appear pictured as a glorious and continuous pageant. Though no hard and fast division should be drawn between laboratories, for practical purposes all the apparatus proper to each subject should be housed in one place, the books in the school library being distributed on the same lines, so that they may be easily available. I draw attention to the word 'laboratory', for it is significant of a place where a pupil research-worker experiments with and on his job. This conveys just the reverse of the current idea that a teacher experiments on his pupils.

(Helen Parkhurst, *An Explanation of the Dalton Laboratory Plan*, 1926, pp. 4–5)

17   A typical triple-decker London Board School 1904
Schools were individually designed but their solidity made adaptation to
new purposes difficult.

GLC Photograph Library

Practical difficulties in a less than ideal world were noticeable in carrying out
the Plan. Teachers often lacked the skill in drawing up suitable assignments; in
these cases the work simply became copying and reading from books. Further-
more, the Plan assumed the existence of a good supply of suitably written and
arranged textbooks, which were not, in fact, available.

An additional difficulty in England was the shortage of specialist accommodation in the majority of schools, especially at the elementary level. As a result, the
single classroom tended to house 'corners' with reference material instead of a
suite of rooms. By the mid-1930s, the Dalton Plan had disappeared, to be
replaced by either formal class teaching or a modified form of individual assignments.

Since the beginning of the twentieth century, it may be noticed that innovators
in curriculum and method had been influenced by findings in the new science of
psychology: these related mainly to theories of intelligence and learning. The
implications of the writings of Spearman, Thomson and Burt were taken up by
educational theorists such as J. J. Findlay, John Adams and Percy Nunn. The
latter's influential book *Education: Its Data and First Principles* published in 1920
was typical of many of the period: it had an evangelical ring in its view of
childhood in such passages as this:

On the one hand, joy tends naturally to express itself in the physical movements and the imitations of serious activities which are typical of children's play; on the other hand, any task becomes play to the man who can do it with the ease of mastery which brings joy in the doing.

(T. P. Nunn, *Education: Data and First Principles*, 1920, p. 78)

One fruitful method to arise from the cross-fertilization of philosophy and psychology in education was that of the 'project'. John Dewey in the United States had focused in his book, *The Child and the Curriculum* (1902), on the relationship between the learner and knowledge. The 'inquiry' method as a reflective process could be used as a means of harnessing the child's experience to an understanding of his environment. Before leaving Chicago in 1904, Dewey had set up his own Laboratory School to try out some of the methods he was advocating. He eschewed the notion of worked-out assignments, syllabuses and prepared materials. Instead, he experimented with the project approach, taking themes based on human occupations such as cooking, textiles and handwork. At the Laboratory School, young children were able to examine the historical, geographical and practical aspects of these occupations, which laid a basis for more systematic work later. (M. Skilbeck (ed.), *John Dewey*, 1970, pp. 23–4.)

The project method was taken up and championed by W. H. Kilpatrick in America from 1918 and later in England, and is still popular, under various names, in primary schools.

Besides the psychological influence upon changing methods, the impact of the First World War on educational thinking was profound. The 'New Education' movement which was burgeoning before 1914 received an impetus, resulting in a number of educational experiments being attempted in the postwar years. One writer, commenting on some of these experiments in 1920, voiced in her book the sentiments of many educationists:

One of the great lessons of the war, which we are finding it terribly hard to learn, is that the old things must pass away, and that we must work in the future for such a cooperation between individuals, between peoples and nations as has never yet been known. . . .

To every school plan, to every educational device, we should bring this test: 'Does it make for cooperation, for union between man and man or for disunion?' If we are agreed on the point we must face the consequences, and many of our most cherished plans must go. Prizes, marks, and place-taking must become barbarous devices of the past. For the refusal to allow our pupils to help one another, the privilege of the more advanced to give aid to the backward must be substituted. In this connection it is worth considering how much the growing plan of individual teaching noticed in so much of our experimental work tends to the overthrow of marks and prizes. Cooperation comes in quite naturally in the place of competition, and the danger of an idle child relying entirely on another's work does not seem to be a serious one.

(A. Woods, *Educational Experiments in England*, 1920, pp. 223–4)

One tangible consequence of this was the introduction, on a small scale, of family grouping into infant schools. Organizational changes since the 1918 Education Act have played their part in determining the relationship between matter and method. The raising of the school leaving age to fourteen under this Act led to a separation of junior departments from previous all-age schools. Between 1927 and 1930, the number of pupils in separate junior departments rose

50.

March

March 21st   Mrs Sadgrove paid a visit to the school to
examine the Needlework.

" 22nd   The University Boat Race was explained to
Standards IV to VII in the early part of the week.
I decided to have a Boat Race Examⁿ of these
Standards and this morning was fixed as the day.
The children were allowed to choose their own
colour, light or dark blue: the numbers were
13 for Oxford & 12 for Cambridge. Last night
I put a dark blue mark on the Oxford papers
and a light blue on the Cambridge.
This morning the children were very keen on the
contest as to which side would gain most points.
10 points were allowed for every sum right and 10
for every piece of correct & nicely written
dictation or Composition.
Special sums were given. The Dictation &
Composition all related to the Boat Race and a
good morning's work was done.
The sums set were as follows in Stds IV
V . VI & VII respectively.

18   An early example of a 'project', Winston School, Durham, 1895
Durham Record Office

from 150,000 to 400,000; this resulted in a readily identifiable primary school population.

More recently, there has been a further shift in the modern primary school towards a child-centred curriculum, according to the needs and interests of the individual. Another influence has been the work of research workers such as

51

St IV I If £31,101 - 12 - 10 was allowed to the Oxford + Cambridge Students for 394 days, How much would that be for each day?

II The Oxford Boat is 60 ft long. How many boat lengths will cover the whole distance of 3 miles?

III What would 204 boats cost at £204 - 4 - 10¾ each?

IV There are 18 men in the two boats. If each man drinks 3 pints of milk a day. How much would they all drink in three months? (12 wks).

Standard V

I If the Cambridge crew spent £199 - 14 - 9¾ every year, How much would that amount to in 949 yrs (practice)

II Make out a Bill for building a boat
990 ft of wood at 1/3 per foot: 620 nails @ ¼ each
4 Oars at £1.12.6 each 18½ doz Brass screws at 3ᵈ ea:
2½ dozen men at work for one day at 2/3½ each.

Bruner and Piaget which has shown that children learn more effectively from concrete situations; how children acquire concepts is related to the organization of materials. Much attention has therefore been devoted to providing within the curriculum the necessary experiences and approaches as reflected, for example, in the Schools Council projects materials.

19   Country Dancing at Furzedown Training College 1929
Cecil Sharp had pioneered the introduction of dancing in schools; by
1919, the Board of Education allowed games and dancing to occupy up
to a half of a physical training lesson.

GLC Photograph Library

Up to 1944, the content of the primary school curriculum had remained
virtually unchanged since the beginning of the century. In the postwar period the
widespread introduction of a second language, social studies and science which
has replaced nature study, illustrate the changing attitude towards curriculum
thinking. This has been paralleled by flexibility in grouping pupils, seen most
notably in the rise of middle schools, which span the primary and secondary age
group. School design, as seen, for example, in open-plan classrooms, has followed
changing patterns of primary education. Some of these changes in educational
thought and practice are now being questioned. N. Bennett (in *Teaching Styles and
Pupil Progress*, 1976), in examining the relationship between teaching styles and
primary children's performance in the basic subjects, opened up a debate on the
effectiveness of 'progressive' as compared with 'traditional' methods. Similarly,
throughout the 'great debate' on education (1976–7) there was some criticism of the
over-emphasis on and misinterpretation of child-centred methods in primary

schools. The Green Paper, *Education in Schools: A Consultative Document,* recommended that a core of basic skills should be a 'protected' part of the curriculum.

The history of the development of methods and curriculum in the secondary sector has followed a rather different course, and to this we now turn.

Secondary

A description of the curriculum of, and methods used in, 'secondary schools' from the Middle Ages to the mid-nineteenth century bears two characteristics: the remarkable narrowness in the range of curriculum and methods, and their virtually unchanging nature.

The majority of the ancient grammar schools had been founded and endowed by the Church; Latin, then a universal language in government, religion and law, was therefore the main subject to be mastered. Roger Ascham, a tutor to Princess Elizabeth, published the first English textbook on method, *The Scholemaster,* in 1568. In it, he set out a procedure which was to be slavishly followed:

> MASTER. Let *him* teach the child, cheerfully and plainly, the cause and matter of the letter. Then let him construe it into English, so often as the child may easily carry away the understanding of it. Let him parse it over perfectly.
> LEARNER. Let the child, by and bye, both conspire [i.e. combine] and parse it over again. So that it may appear, that the child doubteth in nothing that his master taught him before.
> So far it is the Mind and Memory comprehending and reproducing the Oral Teaching.
> Then the child must take a paper book, and sitting in some place where no one shall prompt him, by himself, let himself, let him translate into English his former lesson.
> MASTER. Then shewing it to his master: let his master take from him his Latin book.
> LEARNER. Then, pausing an hour at the least: let the child translate his own English into Latin, in another Paper Book.
>
> (R. Ascham, *The Scholemaster,* 1570 edn., E. Arber (ed.), 1870, p. 10)

One of the most potent consequences of the Renaissance in England was the rediscovery of the literature of the ancient civilizations. Such schools as Oakham and Uppingham, both in Rutland, established by Archdeacon Johnson in 1584, indicate this. At the former, over the schoolroom door is an inscription in Hebrew, Greek and Latin, an indication of what was taught there.

Ascham was of the opinion that the grammar school should be 'the house of play', a somewhat different picture from the one usually associated with such schools at this period. We can see that, by the following century, some of Ascham's precepts were being put into practice. In Charles Hoole's comprehensive work, *A New Discovery of the Old Art of Teaching Schoole,* published in 1660, there is an account of a first form's work. The whole year was occupied in preparing pupils for Latin, helping them to obtain a vocabulary of words and showing how to vary them. Hoole recommended the use of Comenius' *Orbis Pictus,* a pictorial Latin primer, in order to encourage the training of observation. (Foster Watson, *The Old Grammar Schools,* 1916, pp. 101–2.)

One of the conditions of entry to a grammar school, often stipulated in its

MISERABLE PLIGHT AT 4·P.M. OF H.M.I WHO HAS UNDERTAKEN TO SHOW THE H.D.MASTER OF A COLLIERY SCHOOL HOW MODERN DISCIPLINARY METHODS SHOULD BE APPLIED

20   Two cartoons by F. O. Mann HMI (b. 1882) drawn possibly about 1930.

statutes, was that candidates should already be competent in reading and writing. For this purpose, there developed reading and writing schools, either privately or Church owned, for children aspiring to grammar schools. In this way began the two traditions in education—the elementary and secondary.

The rigidity of the grammar school curriculum, limited as it was by the original statutes, excluded the teaching of any 'new' subject such as history or modern languages until 1840, when legislation opened up new possibilities. An account by a schoolboy written in 1800 gives a picture of the work carried on:

> Owing to my indifferent State of Health for the two last Years my Progress in Latin was not considerable. Though I had been put for some Years to learn Latin Authors, I was not sufficiently acquainted with the Latin Grammar, and indeed that Part of it, which treats of Quantity, I had not been put to learn. That Part, therefore, I was required to learn immediately, as without a Knowledge of it, I ought not to begin studying the Roman Poets, which, on Account of the Time I had lost, Mr Turner wished me to begin as soon as possible. After, then, learning some Part of Prosodia, I began Ovid's *Epistles*, and as soon as I had made myself acquainted with the Construction of Hexameter and Pentameter Verses, I was put to learn Ovid's *Metamorphoses* with my Brothers. This Author, with Caesar's *Commentaries* and the Greek Grammar, which I lately began, together with the Latin Grammar, are the Books which form my Study at present in the Latin and Greek Languages. Ovid, I not only construe, but commit to Memory; and Caesar, after construing and analizing it, I translate. To these Books I devote myself from ten till twelve o'Clock in the Morning.
>
> My other Studies are Arithmetic and Mathematics, which I learn from seven till nine in the Morning, and French, which I study from twelve till two in the Afternoon.

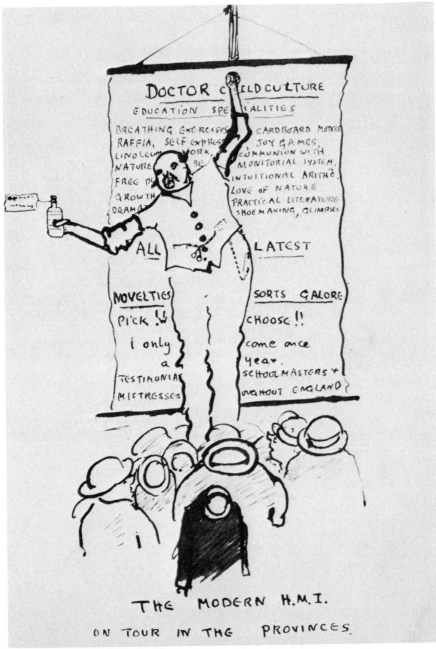

I also learn Elocution, Drawing, Dancing, and the Military Exercise. Sensible of the Advantage of a good Enunciation, it shall be my Endeavour to benefit myself by paying particular Attention to the Instruction I receive from the Elocution Master.

From this Account you will see that my Time is fully employed, and particularly, when I inform you that I, besides, every Night write Latin and French Exercises.

(James Webb to his guardian, Edward Arrowsmith, 11 Dec. 1800, 9467, Dorset R.O.)

21   Roger Ascham's book *The Scholemaster or plaine and perfite way of teaching children to understand, write and speak the Latin tongue* 1570. It established a new method of teaching languages.

Even at sixth-form level, the diet was unvaried. An Eton boy in 1814 described in his diary a typical day:

Sunday, 23 Oct. 1814
Got up at 7 o'clock altered my verses & walked about College with Dickey Watson, after 12 took my verses to Otway he helped me to alter them, after 4 took them to Drury, one copy with the alteration & another with the original. Then in a great hurry set to work at my Aschylus which kept me till ¼ past 7. Went to my tutor with it, he was very witty, but made me construe 60 lines out of the 100 the first time over, as it was a 4 exercised week we had no Juvenal to say. When I came back, had my supper, wrote out my Saturday's speech for Townshend & did derivations.

(Thomas Francis Fremantle, Journal, D/FR/93/31, Buckinghamshire R.O.)

It is not surprising that by the end of the eighteenth century the grammar school, catering for the requirements of Oxford and Cambridge, came under attack. Private and Nonconformist schools, free from statutory interference, flourished, pointing the way to a wider range of curricular activities. A few of the old grammar schools, such as Eton, Winchester and Harrow, evolved into public schools at this time; but many others, with poorly qualified masters and few pupils, attracted much public criticism, and gradually decayed.

Some of the new developments in curricula outside the grammar schools were attacked in an influential book published in 1781, *Liberal Education or a Practical*

22 An old 'Grammar' school
   Oakham School, Rutland, was founded in 1584. This inscription over
   the door is in Hebrew, Greek and Latin.

   Oakham School

Treatise on the methods of acquiring useful and Polite learning, by Vicesimus Knox, the
headmaster of Tonbridge School. While acknowledging the newer developments
in curricula, such as natural sciences and modern languages, Knox pointed out
that there was a lack of teaching expertise as compared with classics. A second
argument, using an economic analogy, emphasized the principles of learning
rather than the content of the curriculum:

> The elements of the Latin grammar and classical learning are a general preparation for
> all employments, occupations, and professions above the lowest. These must be
> acquired, and there is no necessity to ask, on every occasion, *cui bono?* what good will
> learning *propria quae maribus* &c do me? The gaining of learning is to be compared to
> the gaining of money, as Gesner observes. A man does not say or know to what purpose
> every shilling he gains shall be applied. No, he joyfully takes the gain, and adds it to the
> common flock, and thus at last becomes rich: so in acquiring learning, he gains all he
> can and becomes learned.

(V. Knox, *Liberal Education*, 1785 edn., p. 19)

Even Knox acknowledged that a liberal education could not be brought about by such a diet alone. In recommending attention to the teaching of English, he admitted that the little the boys learned would not be of great value to them after leaving school: but a knowledge of English would be a valuable acquisition.

Reforms and social change in the nineteenth century

Changes in society, especially the social structure since the Industrial Revolution, combined with the economic theories and political philosophies of the day, brought about reform in the grammar schools. The emergence of a 'new' middle class gave rise to a demand for an expansion of suitable educational facilities for two reasons. Firstly, new industrial techniques called for an increase in more specialized non-manual operations which demanded a sound education. Secondly, there was the desire on the part of parents to obtain for their sons the education which many lacked themselves; the public school offered a model to emulate. The economic thought of Adam Smith and his followers, later to be supplemented by Herbert Spencer's philosophy of individualism, favoured the competitive market principle in the provision of middle-class schools. However, their operation was investigated by royal commissions set up in the 1850s and 1860s to study the universities and the public and endowed schools, in order to secure greater efficiency in the education system.

The commissions suggested reform based on a careful grading of curriculum in each of the schools to correspond with the appropriate social class for whom it was intended. Endowed schools which so far had educated children of all classes were, by the mid-nineteenth century, considered to be the rightful province of the middle classes.

Official recognition of the need for a hierarchy of schools at post-elementary level was enshrined in the Clarendon Report on Public Schools in 1864 and the Taunton Report four years later. The nine public schools singled out for separate investigation were to remain essentially classical schools.

While not prepared to recommend Modern Departments based on the newer independent schools such as Marlborough and Cheltenham, the Commissioners expressed regret that mathematics and science were hardly taught. For those schools below 'the nine', a more lively set of proposals were put forward. The three 'grades' of schools suggested by the Taunton Commission corresponded to the gradations of society. The first grade, for intending university students, should follow a modified public school curriculum. The second grade included subjects which could be turned to practical use in business, English, arithmetic, in some cases natural science, in some cases a modern language.

Only the third-grade school would not have Latin. Instead natural science, well taught, mathematics, drawing and other useful subjects should predominate.

It would have been difficult for rapid reform in either curriculum or method to occur as a result of the Commissioners' work. Schools reflected the state of subjects taught at the universities. The teaching of history bears out this point. At the universities the subject was a by-product of classics studies, being confined to

REGULATIONS

FOR THE

Admission of Gentlemen Cadets into the Royal Military Academy at Woolwich.

I. NO Cadet to be admitted under *Fourteen* or above *Sixteen* Years of Age, or below the Height of Four Feet Nine Inches ; a Certificate of the Time of every Candidate's Birth to be transmitted to The Master-General's Secretary, at the Office of Ordnance, Westminster, taken from the *Parish Register,* and signed by the *Minister :* as likewise an Address where he may be sent for on a Vacancy. If the Parish Register cannot be resorted to, an *Affidavit* of one of the Parents, or from some other Person who can *attest* the Fact, will be accepted.

II. Every Candidate, previously to his Admission, must be *well grounded in Arithmetic, including Vulgar Fractions,* write a *very* good Hand, and be *perfectly* Master of the *English* and *Latin* Grammars.

III. All Candidates are *Publickly* examined by the proper Masters in the *Royal Military Academy,* and, if found deficient in any of these preparatory Parts of Learning, will be *rejected.*

IV. The *above* Qualifications are *indispensible* at the Time of Examination ; but, the future Studies of each Candidate, will be very materially forwarded, with a view to obtaining a *Commission,* if he has also learnt to draw, and acquired a Knowledge of the French Language before he is appointed a Cadet.

* The Days of Examination are Tuesdays and Wednesdays, precisely at Eleven o'Clock, and the Candidates are to present themselves to the Lieutenant-Governor, or Inspector of the Royal Military Academy at Woolwich.

23   Education for the Army
      Prior to the introduction of competitive examinations for entry into
      Woolwich in the later nineteenth century, candidates were not expected
      to have high attainments.

                                        Devon Record Office

Greece and Rome. Accordingly, masters would tend to teach history in a similar manner.

> Pupils learned Latin grammar and prose and verse passages by heart, so that they could recite them to their master; they learned their translations from a crib, so that they could construe at his demand. Where history was taught in class in set lessons, it was learned in much the same way, so that dates, reigns, genealogical tables, statutes, and battles simply took the place of declensions and conjugations, and pupils committed to memory passages from set books in history. Pupils often stood before the master in the order of their past achievement, and were asked questions in succession, 'taking place' in the order according to their success or failure in answering. Sometimes

history was actually learned in the class, but usually by the pupils' reading aloud from a history book. Where history was read by the pupils as a private exercise, the master's oral examination would often take the same form or would consist of a written examination which placed the same premium upon the memorization of bare facts. In the school time-tables of these days we frequently find the bleak remark 'Say history', or 'Say history to Mr So-and-So', or 'History reading—repeat'.

(J. L. Dobson, 'The Teaching of History in English Grammar Schools and Private Schools 1830–70', *Durham Research Review*, Vol. 2, No. 8, 1957, pp. 132–3)

Giving evidence before the Public School Commissioners, the headmaster of Winchester, Dr Moberly, answering the question 'Is it not the habit to teach modern or ancient history by set lesson?' confessed 'No, I should not know how to do it. All I can do is to say "We will examine in such a period at such an examination".' (Clarendon Commission, Vol. I, p. 17)

New approaches at this level therefore had to be pioneered by individuals, with little but trial and error to guide them in their endeavours. Much of the initiative stemmed from the headmaster, such as the work of Arnold and Temple at Rugby, Butler at Shrewsbury and Thring at Uppingham. All were clerics, and the method was often infused with religious beliefs: Thomas Arnold at Rugby from 1829 to 1842 began the first systematic teaching of history in public schools. He advocated such teaching in the hope that it would lead to an understanding of intellectual and spiritual values.

Frederick Temple had anticipated the criticisms of the Royal Commission concerning science education. Chemistry, geology, botany and physics were the chief scientific subjects introduced by Temple in 1864; he advised that botany should be made the subject first taken throughout the Middle School because, unlike some others, it could be taught without the need for special accommodation.

J. M. Wilson, then science master at the school, an early advocate of the experimental method, warned that the teaching of science could rapidly degenerate into cramming. He condemned this method and recommended that pupils should be encouraged to make generalizations based on facts and accurate observations. Wilson describes a botany lesson to illustrate his beliefs: 'Suppose then your class of thirty or forty boys before you, of ages from thirteen to sixteen, as they sit at their first botanical lesson; some curious to know what is going to happen, some resigned to anything; some convinced that it is all a folly. You hand round to each boy several specimens, say of the Herb Robert; and taking one of the flowers, you ask one of them to describe the parts of it. 'Some pink leaves' is the reply. 'How many?' 'Five.' 'Any other parts?' 'Some little things inside.' 'Anything outside?' 'Some green leaves.' 'How many?' 'Five.' 'Very good. Now pull off the five green leaves outside, and lay them side by side; next pull off the five pink leaves, and lay them side by side: and now examine the little things inside. What do you find?' 'A lot of little stalks or things.' 'Pull them off and count them': they find ten. Then show them the little dust-bags at the top, and finally the curiously constructed central column, and the carefully concealed seeds. By this time all are on the alert. Then we resume: the parts in that flower are, outer green envelope, inner coloured envelope, the little stalks with dust bags, and the central column with the seeds. Then you give them all wall-flowers:

MR. WOODGATES' ACADEMY,

HONITON, DEVON,

FOR THE INSTRUCTION OF A LIMITED NUMBER OF YOUNG GENTLEMEN,

IN COMMERCIAL, NAUTICAL, MATHEMATICAL, AND CLASSICAL

EDUCATION.

The System of Tuition comprises Reading, Writing, Arithmetic, English Grammar, Book-keeping by single and double Entry, Geography, the Use of the Globes, Mapping, and History; Practical Geometry, Mensuration, Trigonometry, Navigation, Astronomy, Stenography, the Elements of Euclid, Algebra, Surveying, &c. &c.

TERMS for Boarders,	£18	18s.	*per Annum.*
Entrance,	1	1	
Washing	2	2	
Tea, &c.	1	1	
Single Beds (if required,)	1	1	
Day Scholars	4	4	
Latin and Greek	4	4	

THE FRENCH LANGUAGE, DRAWING AND DANCING, ON THE USUAL TERMS.

PARSING is particularly attended to;—GEOGRAPHY and ENGLISH COMPOSITION are also distinguished Studies in this Academy.

Corporeal Punishment is avoided as much as possible, while every Encouragement is given to the diligent and deserving Pupils, by appropriate Rewards; they have the use of an excellent School Library, and nothing is omitted which can in the slightest degree contribute to promote their Comfort, Happiness, and Improvement.

Each Young Gentleman must be provided with a Knife and Fork, Spoon, and Towels.

☞ *A QUARTER'S NOTICE is expected on the removal of a Pupil, or the ensuing Quarter must be paid.*

The Number of Day Scholars is limited and select, and they have the same advantages in the School as Boarders.

The HOUSE is situated in a delightful, open, and healthy part of the Town, and a spacious Play-Ground is attached to the Premises.

24   Prospectus of a private school, early nineteenth century
Although it offered a wide range of subjects, languages were charged as
an extra.

Devon Record Office

and they are to write down what they find: and you go round and see what they
write down. Probably some one has found six '*storks*' inside his wall-flower, and
you make him write on the black-board for the benefit of the class the curious
discovery, charging them all to note any such accidental varieties in future; and
you make them very minutely notice all the structure of the central column.
Then you give them all the common pelargonium and treat it similarly; and by

the end of the hour they have learnt one great lesson, the existence of the four floral whorls, though they have yet not heard the name.' (J. M. Wilson, 'On Teaching Natural Science in Schools', in F. W. Farrar (ed.), *Essays on a Liberal Education*, 1868, pp. 272–3)

One of the most serious difficulties which confronted the public schools was discipline. Outbreaks of rebellion by pupils at Eton and Harrow, the result of oppressive living conditions and high spirits, occurred in the early nineteenth century. Games, organized by the boys themselves, were introduced as an escape valve: mainly cricket and football and later rugby. Edward Thring, headmaster at Uppingham for twenty-four years, looked for alternative outlets, especially for the less gifted, within the framework of a revised curriculum:

> If a boy finds his only solid position in games, what wonder that he avenges himself on the work—reproaches his masters by unduly exalting games, and alas, too often by making vicious indulgence his claim to manliness and power, because masters forbid it. At least where masters are on identical terms with convict-gang task-work this adds to the flavour. This state of things must be, as long as a proper standing-point is not found for each boy in the intellectual life of the school. This is what boys are sent to school for, and it ought to be found for them; gross evil will always be the result if it is not. But a choice of subjects gives this. In Music, French, German, Drawing, and various branches of Natural Science, such as Botany, Natural History, etc., the most backward in Classical knowledge can take refuge. There they can find something to interest them; something too which others do not know, something in which they can attain distinction, and by so doing restore the balance of self-respect, or at least make some progress where many are quite ignorant.

(E. Thring, *Education and School*, 1864, pp. 100–1)

Thring was the first to set up handicraft rooms in a public school. Music was a significant feature in the curriculum, the high standard of performance attracting visitors of the stature of Joachim and Stanford.

So far, we have considered two of the influences on changes in curriculum and method in the last century—specialist commissions appointed by reforming governments and innovating headmasters. A third factor was the growth of public examinations, to be discussed in the next chapter; for example, the introduction of English literature into the curriculum was a direct result of external examinations. A fourth factor was the criticism directed at the existing curriculum by contemporary writers.

One of the most influential was the sociologist Herbert Spencer. Spencer republished four essays as a book, *Education, Intellectual, Moral and Physical* (1861), in which he asks, 'What knowledge is of most worth?' and concludes that it is to be found in a study of social and physical sciences.

In Spencer's definition, science included the fine arts. The curriculum would include physiology, mathematics, mechanics, chemistry, astronomy, geology, biology and sociology. The latter subject formed the crown of Spencer's curriculum, replacing history. A Descriptive Sociology, according to Spencer, was the only history of any practical value. It should aim at showing how consensus in beliefs, customs and institutions have evolved in societies. Such information would be useful to the citizen in regulating his conduct: those facts and activities which are considered the most important in regulating the conduct of a society should form its basis.

Spencer's methods have been attacked on the grounds that they were too intellectual for practical use. Nevertheless his scientific approach to curriculum and methods laid the path for others to follow.

Dean Farrar, then an assistant master at Harrow School, and a number of influential reformers expressed dissatisfaction with the conventional curriculum in his essays in education (1867): Farrar quoted the philosopher Henry Sidgwick's views on the necessity for all pupils to have some knowledge of natural science as well as literature, if they are to understand the progress of humanity. Two years after

25   Nature Study in a London school 1904

GLC Photograph Library

Farrar's volume appeared, Dr Butler at Harrow was prepared to create a 'Modern' side. E. E. Bowen, a contributor to the *Essays on Liberal Education* on the teaching of grammar, was chosen as master in charge. To ensure that there was equality with the Classical side, Butler agreed that only intelligent boys should be accepted and that first-class teaching was to be looked for. The curriculum was broad, and included mathematics, modern languages, Latin, English and science.

A reinforcement of the link between science and a liberal curriculum was provided by Thomas Huxley, the distinguished scientist.

'That man, I think, has had a liberal education who has been so trained in youth that his body is the ready servant of his will, and does with ease and pleasure all the work that, as a mechanism, it is capable of; whose intellect is a clear, cold, logic engine, with all its parts of equal strength, and in smooth working order; ready, like a steam engine, to be turned to any kind of work, and spin the gossamers as well as forge the anchors of the mind; whose mind is stored with a knowledge of the great and fundamental truths of Nature and the laws of her operations; one who, no stunted ascetic, is full of life and fire, but whose passions are trained to come to heel by a vigorous will, the servant of a tender conscience; who has learned to love all beauty, whether of Nature or of art, to hate all vileness, and to respect others as himself.' (L. Huxley (ed.), Science and Education', in *Collected Essays*, Vol. 3, 1895, p. 86.)

Yet a further influence on the shaping of the curriculum and methods was contained in the views expressed by leading politicians of the time. Gladstone, a fine classical scholar and shortly to become the Liberal Prime Minister, told the Clarendon Commission that the sciences, modern languages, modern history and other subjects were ancillary to the classics in the curriculum and 'should be limited and restrained without scruples'. (Clarendon Commission, Vol. 2, p. 42.)

From the Conservative side, Lord Salisbury, when Prime Minister, grumbled that the three Rs had been supplemented in recent years by 'French, pianoforte playing and trigonometry; and no doubt German and astronomy will come next'. (Salisbury to Balfour, 20 Nov. 1896, Balfour MSS. BM Add MS 49690, ff. 181–2, British Museum.)

In 1899 when a new form of advisory body, the Consultative Committee, was established by the Board of Education Act, the Chancellor of the Exchequer expressed his doubts to the Lord President: 'I hope', he wrote, 'the Committee will not be given a permanent character. I look with horror on the projects which would be started directly or indirectly by a Committee of educational faddists.' (Hicks Beach to Duke of Devonshire, 28 Feb. 1899, Devonshire MSS, 1340.2792. Chatsworth, Derbyshire.)

One important but often overlooked factor in curriculum development at secondary level was the founding of the provincial university colleges in the last quarter of the nineteenth century—for example, Newcastle, Birmingham, Sheffield and Leeds. Graduates in science left the colleges and entered teaching. Although there were signs of a more liberal curriculum at the end of the last century, significant changes in content and methods awaited upon British involvement in three wars.

Effects of war

During the long-drawn-out war against the Boers in South Africa, Lord Rosebery wrote on 13 January 1900 to Dr Warre, the Headmaster of Eton:

> Our present crisis will necessitate an educational change, that we shall require more science and more modern languages, and to work harder. I have long thought that we cannot face the competition of the world on Latin and Greek; but I am afraid this is heresy to you.
>
> (C. R. L. Fletcher, *Edmund Warre*, 1922, p. 162)

While the higher standards of elementary schools had developed scientifically oriented curricula, the secondary schools before 1903 had remained largely literary. But there were powerful forces at work inside the Education Department and in the secondary schools which were alarmed at 'the encroachment of scientific studies at the expense of traditional subjects'. These views were expressed more openly, especially by inspectors, after the Board of Education had been established in 1899, with special responsibility for secondary as well as elementary education.

> These fears for the future of secondary education were brought very forcibly to the notice of the Board of Education by the Report, in 1902, of an HMI on 'The Teaching of Literary Subjects in Some Secondary Schools'. The author, J. W. Headlam, roundly denounced the state of literary studies in the schools he had visited. 'In the majority of schools', he wrote, 'both those that receive grants from the Board of Education and others, I find that the nature of the literary education . . . requires the most serious attention of those interested in education. . . . In many of the schools visited no attempt is now made to give a classical education . . . Greek has practically disappeared from all these schools. . . . In many schools Latin is also disappearing. In the teaching of French there is at least hope for the future. In English subjects this is not the case. The very first elements of good work are absent.'
>
> This report was given wide publicity and seems to have been received with considerable alarm. It was debated at some length in the House of Commons in July 1903, and the following year saw a radical alteration in the Regulations for Secondary Schools.
>
> (O. Banks, 'Morant and the Secondary School Regulations of 1904', in *British Journal of Educational Studies*, Vol. 3, No. 11, 1954, p. 35)

The Secondary Schools Regulations of 1904, while allowing a generous allocation of time for science and mathematics, included the stipulation that 'where two languages other than English are taken, and Latin is not one of them, the Board will require to be satisfied that the omission of Latin is for the advantage of the school'. Local education authorities, with their new municipal 'grammar' schools, were obliged to follow a largely academic curriculum which did not meet the changing industrial and technological demands of the country.

Some of the defects in both the curriculum and the methods of secondary schools were laid bare by the events of the First World War. An influential diplomat and educationist, Sir Harry Johnston, quoting a retired ambassador that 'Science is not necessary; Geography, beyond elementary notions is not of great value', deplored the readiness of the Civil Service Commission in 1907 to eliminate geography from its examinations:

> It is curious to note the dislike to *Geography* in those who sit at the fountain-head of British rule. One would have thought that if one subject more than another was overdone, and absorbed an excess of our time in education, it would be Geography.
>
> As I review the Empire mentally, calling up pictures I myself have seen or which others have seen and implanted on my mental retina, I *marvel* that our governing class and its school-masters are so indifferent to the lure of Geography; I marvel how any man, however strong in Parliamentary influence and fluent in oratory, can, like Mr Austin Chamberlain, attain to Cabinet rank and to the charge of India's affairs who can say of himself: 'I am not a Fellow of your [the Royal Geographical] Society, and I am afraid if any geographical knowledge is necessary to qualify for that position I shall never attain to it. My recollections of geography are of a painful study which, laboriously acquired, was inevitably quickly forgotten . . . You . . . will feel that these confessions hardly indicate my fitness for my present position.'
>
> (Sir H. Johnston, *On the Urgent Need for Reform in our National and Class Education*, 1918, pp. 29–31)

At a more serious level, Johnston demonstrated the weakness of modern language teaching in public and secondary schools. In 1917 *The New Statesman* had reviewed the backgrounds of Cabinet Ministers:

> Lord Grey was esteemed a masterly writer of despatches and admirable in his dealings with America, but otherwise very faulty. It was held that three times the Foreign Office has lost the chance of winning the War in the Balkans, and that the greatest of all our mistakes in the Balkans have been Foreign Office mistakes. It was held that Lord Grey still stands for the old Foreign Office system, and that no attempt whatever has been made to reform it. The serious City now openly admits that our public school and university education, despite its admirable results in the hunting-field, wants a little altering. In this connection it is worthwhile to note the accomplishment of our highly educated Ministers in the use of the key-language of Europe. Mr Balfour speaks no French. Lord Grey speaks a French disgraceful on the lips of a Foreign Secretary. Mr Asquith's French is excessively bad. Mr Runciman speaks fair French. Mr McKenna speaks excellent, fluent, conversational (though not colloquial) French. But, then, Mr McKenna never went to one of our great public schools.

(ibid., pp. 26–7)

Some of the writer's criticisms, although fair, did not take cognisance of the prewar endeavours of subject associations to effect reform. These associations—such as the Modern Languages 1892, Geographical 1893, Classical 1903, Historical 1906 and English 1907—owed their establishment largely to the enthusiasm of public and grammar school masters. The 'direct method' in language teaching was introduced by Dr W. H. D. Rouse at the Perse School, Cambridge, in 1904, for Latin and Greek. Rouse refused to accept them as 'dead' languages and his method was aimed at enabling the pupil to think in a foreign language.

It was not until after the First World War that the method was widely adopted for modern as well as ancient language teaching. An early enthusiast described it thus:

> The Direct Method assumes that a language is meant to be spoken and we can best learn it by speaking it. Latin and Greek were specially meant for oral delivery. Cicero at a banquet did not take out his tablets, write on them with a stilus 'Da mihi panem' and pass them to his neighbour in silence, but turned to him and spoke up like a man. The method has been called 'Direct' because it seeks to connect, in the pupil's mind, the word or phrase directly with the object it describes, avoiding the intervening obstacles of grammar and translation. Translation is after all only a magnificent treachery, and an exercise for Sixth Formers in the use of their own language. It is not worth all the trouble. As the Frenchman said, 'Les traductions sont comme les femmes. Lorsqu'elles sont belles, elles ne sont pas fidèles, et lorsqu'elles sont fidèles elles ne sont pas belles.'
>
> Grammar too can be an obstacle to the young who try to learn a language. To ask a child to concentrate on pure grammar while speaking this foreign language, is as tiresome for him as to ask him to concentrate on pure mathematics when buying a packet of sweets.

(C. W. E. Peckett, 'Direct Method and the Classics', in *Educational Review*, Vol. 4, No. 1, 1951, p. 10)

Parallel advances in method were made in other curriculum areas. Philip Hartog in *The Writing of English* (1908) stated the need to motivate pupils in essay writing by encouraging an informal approach to their work. English grammar, which has been called 'the best hated subject in the curriculum', was made simpler. In 1909, teachers of all languages united to agree on a standard grammatical terminology applicable to all schools. Grammar was recognized merely as a body of terms used to describe certain phenomena of language and not an explanatory science. (R. L. Archer, *Secondary Education in the Nineteenth Century*, 1921, p. 333.)

Similarly, geography was transformed by the synthesizing of the physical and human aspects of the subject. Mathematics and science reforms proceeded more slowly. Manual and artistic skills were minority subjects, mainly because of their low status in the eyes of examiners.

A defence of the still largely traditional secondary curriculum was made by Cyril Norwood, headmaster of Harrow in 1929:

> It is the business of the schools so to draw their curriculum that no scientific ability runs to waste, but their first business is ever to bear in mind that man cannot live by bread alone, and therefore to teach the children what the true values are. That is the justification of the pursuit at school of what is so often termed 'useless knowledge', by which is usually meant knowledge which has no apparent or immediate value in cash. It is doubtful whether any knowledge is useless, though there is knowledge of which the learners make no use. But in any case, the imparting of knowledge is only a part of the school's business, which is concerned with the whole nature and character of man.

(C. Norwood, *The English Tradition of Education*, 1929, pp. 212–13)

The developments in elementary education at this time, described earlier in this chapter, influenced some of the more progressive secondary headmasters. E. Sharwood Smith, at Newbury Grammar School from 1903 to 1924, was deeply impressed by Edmond Holmes's visionary book, *What Is and What Might Be* (1911), and dedicated his autobiography to Holmes.

Ancient history and languages came to life by using 'the dramatic way', the production of plays. Gilbert Murray's translations of Euripides and scenes or acts from Molière acted by the boys roused an enthusiasm for and appreciation of the works which are described in the autobiography.

Sharwood Smith considers other possible developments in a chapter entitled 'The New School':

> However, there seems little doubt but that in the schools of the future boys will follow more and more the more active side of learning. Less time will be spent on listening and repeating, and far more attention will be devoted to the making and doing of things. But, after all, we need not confine the word craft to the manipulation of wood and stone and metal and so forth. There is the song-smith as well as the black-smith; and after all what is poetry, but making? So, in the more progressive schools the pupils are encouraged to write original verse in their own language instead of devoting long hours to the gradus and the lexicon, as was the custom of old, the better thereby to patch together elegiacs and iambics in imitation of the great exemplars of Greece and Rome. And does that seem a great innovation?

(E. Sharwood Smith, *The Faith of a School Master*, 1935, p. 201)

For the generality of schools, such a statement was well ahead of practice. The traditional secondary curriculum and teaching methods, after a flurry of innovation at the beginning of this century, remained largely unchanged during the following fifty years.

Tripartitism and after

Not all secondary education was carried on in grammar schools. As early as 1913 the junior technical schools had been recognized by the Board of Education. They were to serve a different purpose from the grammar school and were 'definitely not intended to provide courses furnishing a preparation for the professions, the universities, or higher full-time technical work, or even for commercial life: they are intended to prepare their pupils either for artisan or other industrial employment or for domestic employment'. (Board of Education Report 1912–13, p. 124.)

The Report on the Education of the Adolescent (Hadow), published in 1926, added a third type of school called 'Modern', for pupils between eleven and fifteen. A commercial or industrial bias with more practical training in the last two years was recommended. In fact, the Board of Education did not envisage their widespread development. By 1938, the Spens Report was repeating the 'three grades' of the Taunton Commission: grammar schools with a broad curriculum up to eighteen years; technical schools to promote a good intellectual discipline apart from its technical value to sixteen years; and modern schools with a general and practical but not vocational education up to fourteen years.

When the 1944 Education Act was being framed, the tripartite division of secondary education was further reinforced by the Norwood Report of 1943. Different abilities and characteristics of pupils attending the three types of school were identified. The Modern school child was described thus:

> The pupil in this group deals more easily with concrete things than with ideas. He may have much ability, but it will be in the realm of facts. He is interested in things as they are; he finds little attraction in the past or in the slow disentanglement of causes or movements. His mind must turn its knowledge or its curiosity to immediate test; and his test is essentially practical . . .
>
> (Norwood Report, p. 3)

Seventy per cent of the secondary school population attended the Modern school in the postwar years.

Some of the interesting innovations of the interwar years in secondary education, broadly labelled as progressive, were officially encouraged by the new Ministry of Education; but circumstances often militated against change.

> Some [schools] began to experiment with 'modern methods', projects, centres of interest and so on. Soon, however, there arose a concern with the standards of work being achieved in the Modern schools, particularly with standards of attainment in the basic subjects, and with pupils' attitudes towards the school and their work. This concern can be accounted for partly as social protest, generally of middle-class origin, against the social doctrines that seemed to be implied by the idea of free secondary education for all and the expenditure of large sums of money on 'working-class' schools. In this it became associated with the demand for economy, the cutting out of 'frills' and a concentration upon essentials. In addition, there were many teachers and others who were of the opinion that the interwar revolution against formalism had had too much influence on the work of the schools, and that the time was ripe for a restatement of traditional aims. Standards of basic literacy were clearly affected by the war and its aftermath; it was very easy, however, to use progressive methods as the whipping boy

for any defects that might make themselves felt. Thirdly, it became clear that economic developments were making it more than ever necessary that pupils should have a good standard of general education, and qualifications began to be relevant to more and more types of jobs.

(W. Taylor, *The Secondary Modern School*, 1963, p. 97)

While a minority of pupils attempted public examinations in these schools, the vast majority followed a curriculum which was less academic and more practical. One disillusioned secondary modern teacher commented:

> The vast and fruitful harvest of English literature was reduced to desiccated abridgments of classics and war escape stories, collections of indifferent bits and pieces known as 'readers', and school or class libraries consisting all too often of shabby cast-offs from adult libraries mingled with bright new books of the Enid Blyton and Biggles type, which are anti-educational in that they combine an easy-running narrative with a total absence of either human reality or creative fantasy. Even music, a subject of great potential cultural value in the secondary modern school, seems often to have missed the boat, but then it has had a good deal of extraneous noise to contend with.
>
> The reverse of this state of affairs is to be seen in the practical subjects. It seems to be assumed that all secondary modern boys will like and be quite good at woodwork and metalwork, all girls domestic science and needlework, and that both sexes will find release and expression in art. There is even the assumption—unspoken, but certainly implied in the system—that the less intelligent a child is, the better he will be at doing things with his hands, which must be consoling to the teachers of the craft subjects.
>
> The results of this system can be imagined. I have personally known many children who were miserable at being forced to do woodwork, needlework, or art badly, but who would probably have been quite happy doing algebra, French, or chemistry badly—or possibly not so badly.

(C. Hughes, 'Stones Instead of Bread: The Secondary Modern Mistake', in *The Times Educational Supplement*, 16 Oct. 1964, p. 651)

When in 1963 the Newsom Report considered the education of the 'average' child between the ages of thirteen and sixteen a division of the curriculum was made into three broad fields—practical subjects, maths and science, and the humanities. But it is clear from the report that methods were being discussed in relation to existing traditional subject patterns.

> We might have grouped our suggestions round certain methods of teaching instead of round the traditional subjects, and written chapters on projects or assignments. It is not because we think a wise choice of methods unimportant that we did not do this. It is because in our view this might have concealed one of the most important aspects of any discussion of the curriculum—the subject matter that is actually taught. The traditional subject divisions may sometimes seem artificial and restrictive, but at least they have the merit of a certain precision. A boy or a girl can at least come home and say what his lesson was. This has a value which ought not to be sacrificed. Some subjects necessarily stand apart in their own right. Learning a foreign language, for instance, is not really like anything else in the curriculum, and it is almost inevitable that the word French (or German or Spanish as the case may be) should appear on the timetable. Similarly what goes on in the laboratory is almost bound to be labelled 'Science', and the gymnasium is naturally the scene of Physical Education. A good deal of the curriculum is, therefore, almost bound to carry subject names. It seems to us that there are advantages in carrying the practice right through it.

(Ministry of Education: *Half Our Future*, 1963, p. 125)

Two important influences on curriculum and methods which have brought about changes have been the introduction of comprehensive secondary education and the findings of curriculum development researchers.

The London County Council, in the period 1946–9, set up eight large secondary schools of an experimental nature, formed by amalgamating senior and central schools, the first experiment in comprehensive education. Leicestershire in 1957 established high schools with three-year courses (eleven to fourteen) grouped to serve a nearby grammar school. Catering for a wide range of abilities, the organization of teaching and methods had to be re-assessed. By 1966, considerable experience had been gained, as a report on London schools shows:

> In a number of schools a critical look is being taken at traditional subject divisions, possibly as a result of the integration of learning which is developing in the primary schools. Kidbrooke, for example, has introduced social science for years II and III, though it originally entered the curriculum for IV year leavers. In the first three years, social science, history and geography are treated as what is termed 'humanities', an approach based on man's place in society. Hygiene, and Speech and Drama are also subjects in their own right in the first three years at this school. Spoken English has been developed too at Parliament Hill. Here too, syllabuses have included more provision for 'practical' or 'active' work in all subjects, especially in the middle and lower ability ranges. The influence of CSE syllabuses has permeated downwards (or the primary school approach upwards) with a loosening and fertilizing effect. At Elliott a traditional subject—art—has seen a big range of choices added to the field: painting, drawing, modelling, pottery, sculpture, fabric printing, typography and much more has been attempted in special projects for groups.

> (Inner London Education Authority: *London Comprehensive Schools*, 1966, p. 59)

Linked with changes in the structure of secondary schools has been the exploration of curriculum material by development teams using a wide range of teaching techniques. The open-endedness of the teaching process is a feature of many of the projects:

> A decade ago it was common to define curriculum as 'planned learning experience', now the question is being asked, 'Whose plan?' A concept of curriculum which limits the term to a *post hoc* account of teaching is of little value, for curriculum should surely play *some* part in guiding teaching. At the same time a useful concept of curriculum must leave room for creativity and individual style in teaching method, as well of course as for individual differences among pupils. Accordingly, there has emerged a newer definition of curriculum as a structured series of intended learning outcomes, the output of a curriculum development system and the input into a teaching system (Johnson 1967). In other words, a curriculum prescribes (or at least anticipates) the *results* of teaching; but it does not prescribe the *means*, i.e. the activities, materials or teaching content to be used in achieving these results. Where this definition is adopted it should go far towards resolving anxieties often expressed during the past decade lest national schemes of curriculum development constrain teacher freedom in the classroom.

> Apart from national schemes, the past decade has seen the initiation of many local (often within-school) schemes. Such schemes were generally based on convictions that teaching needs to be individualized, that education is a continuing process and that it should aim for 'real understanding' including insights across the disciplines as fields of knowledge. Non-streaming, team teaching, flexible time-tabling, resource centres, independent study using multi-media materials, work experience and social service schemes are examples of innovations stemming from such ideas.

> (W. G. A. Rudd, 'Teachers as Curriculum Developers: A Second-generation Viewpoint' in P. H. Taylor and J. Walton (ed.), *The Curriculum: Research, Innovation and Change*, 1973, pp. 53–4)

One further factor affecting curriculum and method in secondary schools in recent years has been a consideration of the differentiations so far made between boys and girls' studies. The 1926 Hadow Report had confirmed the view held since the last century that separation was especially desirable in schools consisting of pupils who are passing through the early years of adolescence. Even in 1945, the first pamphlet issued by the newly-formed Ministry of Education, *The Nation's Schools*, confirmed this traditional view. While admitting that it was advantageous for boys and girls to learn together in primary schools and further education institutions, the pamphlet advocated the separation of the sexes at the secondary stage (p. 25).

Since then, the Crowther Report has mentioned that it is sometimes implied that few girls are interested in physics or mathematics, and few boys in biology or English literature (Crowther Report, Vol. I, 1959, pp. 212–13). It was in order to test such assumptions that a recent survey was conducted by the Department of Education and Science into curriculum differences between the sexes. Many of the conclusions have implications for a revision of traditional attitudes in secondary education:

> It is clear that curricular differences in secondary schools spring in part from custom. Of the 98 per cent of mixed schools in which the sexes are separated for some aspects of their work only a very small proportion of heads give educational considerations as major reasons for such separation. Some heads have continued long-standing practice; others have declared that the resources of accommodation and of staffing have made the existing pattern inevitable; others again that separation of boys and girls for certain subjects is convenient for purposes of organization. In individual cases any one of these views may be valid in present circumstances. Nevertheless, judged by the 10 per cent sample of schools visited for purposes of this enquiry, the overall consequences for secondary education are inescapable.
>
> First, at the age of 13-plus, when boys and girls choose, under guidance, courses to be pursued in the fourth and fifth forms, the question is too often one of 'Hobson's choice'. Pre-emptive patterns of curriculum in the first three years affect 27 per cent of mixed schools in England, and specialization 28 per cent of all schools; boys are more affected by the latter than are girls.
>
> Second, in the fourth and fifth forms, there are significant differences in subjects studied by girls and by boys, and these differences are too striking to be accepted without question ... The enquiry was not designed to seek answers to the question whether boys and girls should be educated separately or together. Evidence shows that the tendency for girls to choose foreign languages rather than physics and chemistry is less marked in girls' schools than in mixed schools. ... The fact that in matters of subject choice mixed schooling tends to underline rather than to blur the distinction between the sexes should alert parents as well as heads and teachers to the need to examine those areas of the curriculum in which they may well perceive that deep-rooted traditions and assumptions are no longer valid.

(DES *Curricular Differences for Boys and Girls* Education Survey 21, 1975, pp. 21–2)

Recent changes in curriculum and methods at secondary level have been largely the result of an educational philosophy which involves maximizing educational opportunity for all pupils. A further dimension has been the development of the community school which has established links with the neighbourhood.

New groupings of subjects gathered under a faculty structure within schools reflect changes in knowledge as does interdisciplinary inquiry as a mode of working. It does seem, however, that the newer organizational aspects are not being matched by innovative processes in curriculum. The basically traditional approach to secondary school curricula has persisted in the face of new challenges brought about by the introduction of comprehensive education and the raising of the school leaving age. In looking at staffing at secondary schools, the Bullock Report remarked that a third of those teaching English had no discernible qualifications for the role. The DES memorandum for the Prime Minister mentions that teaching methods have been modified in many cases in order to enlist the cooperation of difficult pupils at the cost of setting standards. One of the solutions to these problems which has been put forward is the establishment of a core curriculum for all pupils with special provision for those in the later years of schooling. Such a move would obviously have important consequences for teaching methods.

5

The Influence of Examinations

Examinations present us with some of the most powerful indicators of curriculum change in the nineteenth and twentieth centuries. It is fashionable today to blame examinations for many of the ills of the educational system, but this is far too simple a generalization. Examinations have at times restricted curriculum development, but at other times they have certainly been a progressive influence on the educational system. Sometimes examinations are a mixture of restriction and useful development: it is rarely a simple story of good or evil. At a time when accountability is in the air it may be useful to look back at some of the early examples of accountability such as payment-by-results.

In this chapter we will examine three aspects of the development of examinations in the nineteenth century:

1. Utilitarianism—a philosophy of competition
2. From patronage to competition—a general review of the development of competitive examinations
3. The scholarship ladder—examples of examinations being used as a means of limited social mobility

1. Utilitarianism—a Philosophy of Competition

In Chapter 2 we briefly reviewed the importance of Utilitarian ideas in changing the curriculum. We suggested there that Utilitarianism became the dominant driving force behind educational planning in the nineteenth century; in this chapter we will examine Utilitarianism in more detail with particular reference to examinations and their effect on the curriculum.

Much of the debate concerning the place of examinations and competition in schools stems from the writings of the classical economists in the late eighteenth century. Two aspects of their thinking had direct consequences for the nature of the curriculum: their view of the structure of knowledge, and their view of the structure of society.

The creed of Utilitarianism was accepted as a means for working towards a better society. It was based on the principle of the greatest happiness for the greatest number, which held that actions were right if they promoted happiness and wrong if they produced the opposite. The main problem facing society, therefore, was to devise the means for maximizing happiness by, for example, removing ignorance, and to arrive at a rationality to serve as the foundation of morals. Jeremy Bentham, although generally opposed to state intervention, argued for an exception to be made in the case of education. Part of his Utilitarian argument was that a society needed a code of laws which everyone should be taught. If everyone learnt the laws this would extend their influence over people's moral nature, provided the laws were good ones.

However, it was not intended that such teaching would encourage the challenging of the existing social order. Bentham, for his part, listed some of the virtues which should be fostered, but on a strictly social class basis:

> The divisions in these codes might correspond to the several virtues which are the most looked for in the persons by whom these stations are respectively filled: such as intrepidity, promptitude of obedience, long-suffering, humanity in the soldier; disinterestedness and humanity in the physician and lawyer; disinterestedness, humility, mildness, tolerance, liberality of sentiment in the divine; integrity and frugality in the trader; incorruptibility, public spirit, assiduity, firmness, affability in the statesman . . .

(M. P. Mack, *Jeremy Bentham: An Odyssey of Ideas 1748–92*, 1962, p. 313)

It was not clear from Bentham's writings who would bear the responsibility for translating the scheme into reality. Perhaps the most comprehensive and clearly stated expression of a later Utilitarian is contained in J. S. Mill's essay *On Liberty* (1859). Mill, a sympathetic if critical follower of Bentham, regarded a state system of schooling as an infringement of individual liberty and, worse, that it would make for a deadening uniformity. The use of annual public examinations could, argued Mill, counteract this possibility.

We should also bear in mind that one of the major concerns of society up to the first half of the nineteenth century was the maintenance of the social order, which had been threatened since the French Revolution, and the need to suppress crime. The latter could probably be alleviated by educating the masses. Kay-Shuttleworth pursued a policy of providing elementary education based on the assumption that the ignorant man had no natural desire for education. It was necessary for governments to create this appetite.

Education, then, was to percolate down to the lower classes and at the same time allow for a rising out of the ranks by means of examinations:

> These uncivilized classes are trained by example and discipline: they are, as minors are, the care of the governing classes in some form . . . they are sought by the missionary, by the teacher, by the agent of industrial progress, and they are rescued, not by their own art, but by that of the State and the upper classes, to whom their progress has become a social and political necessity.

(J. P. Kay-Shuttleworth, *Four Periods of Public Education*, 1862, pp. 610–11)

From a Utilitarian point of view, government intervention, if it were necessary at all, should be kept to a minimum. Many reformers therefore assumed that education was to be controlled by the two religious bodies who were the main providers of elementary schools. In February 1839 the Whig Government faced the full opposition of Church authorities in attempting to assert the claims of civil power in education, especially on the question of curriculum control. Lord John Russell proposed to the Queen a committee 'for the consideration of all matters affecting the Education of the People: ... and that it is Her Majesty's wish that the youth of this kingdom should be religiously brought up, and that the rights of conscience should be respected'. A Committee of the Privy Council, Russell suggested, should be formed to superintend funds voted by Parliament for this purpose. The Commons approved the establishment of a Privy Council Committee by a tiny majority. Russell wrote later of the occasion:

> I explained in the simplest terms without any exaggeration, the want of education in the country, the deficiencies of religious instruction, and the injustice of subjecting to the penalties of the criminal law persons who had never been taught their duty to God and man.

(John, Earl Russell, *Recollections and Suggestions 1813–73*, 1875, p. 372)

A compromise was arrived at between Church and State over the issue of control and content of the curriculum in schools. By a concordat of July 1840 it was agreed that the appointment of the first two of Her Majesty's Inspectors should be made by the Committee of Council but that the National Society should suggest persons for appointment, receive duplicate copies of inspectors' reports and issue instructions on religious teaching. The importance of the latter point was made clear in the Instructions to Inspectors of August 1840 issued by the Council, which stated:

> that no plan of education ought to be encouraged in which intellectual instruction is not subordinate to the regulation of thoughts and habits of the children by the doctrines and precepts of revealed religion.

It is interesting to note the influence of Utilitarian philosophy in the correspondence of the Committee of Council and the inspectors' reports, especially in the 1840s and 1850s. The Rev. Dr J. D. Morrell, an early Dissenting member of the inspectorate who had studied philosophy at German universities, wrote in 1848:

> If, for the sake of example, we suppose the case of a school, placed in the centre of a district from which 150 or 200 children require to receive daily instruction; then the true object which such a school should aim at is—*to exert the greatest influence for good upon the largest number possible.* If a few scholars are stimulated and the rest comparatively neglected, the whole amount of benefit done to the neighbourhood is very inconsiderable. On the contrary, though no *striking* results should appear in an examination, yet, if a master be placed in such a locality who is really devoted to his work, who feels teaching and instructing to be his proper destiny, who succeeds in gaining the affection of his pupils, who softens them by kindness, moulds them by friendly sympathy with their wants, instils the knowledge of *things* rather than *words*, and awakens wholesome sentiments in the minds of the entire mass, such a school is assuredly accomplishing a great work in connexion with the mental and moral improvement of the community.

(Committee of Council on Education, General Report for 1848–9, p. 465)

By the time the Newcastle Commission was taking evidence, the economic after-effects of the Crimean War were causing concern. Gladstone, then Chancellor of the Exchequer, reluctantly raised the income tax in 1859 from fivepence to ninepence, a peacetime record. He told Palmerston, the Prime Minister, who protested at some of Gladstone's 'clap trap' reductions, 'that you are feeding not only expenditure, but what is worse, the *spirit* of expenditure'. (J. Morley, *Life of Gladstone*, Vol. 1, 1905, pp. 683–4.)

The Government were alarmed by the rapid increase in schools—from 40,042 in 1850 to 58,975 in 1860—and the consequent expense. The Newcastle Commission's call for cheap and efficient education was therefore readily accepted. Value for the money expended on education was seen in terms of the amount of knowledge learned by pupils. Here is the Rev. W. H. Brookfield, HMI, writing in 1859:

> I should, in ordinary circumstances and places, count that school 'fair' in which three-fourths of the first class (the first class is usually about one-fifth of the whole school) could read such a book as *Robinson Crusoe* with sufficient fluency and distinctness for me to follow them without a book; they should work a plain sum in compound multiplication accurately; they should write a few lines legibly, and with pretty fair spelling, either from memory or of their own composition, about a domestic animal, or a ship, or a railroad; they should know that the world is a globe, with continents and oceans on it, and that Australia is on the other side from us; they should be able to guess, pretty nearly, the height of the table, the width of the school and the distance of the church. Something they should know of the topography of their own county, of its rivers and railroads, with the proximate position of a few other countries, and the names of their capitals as well as those of the more conspicuous European kingdoms. They should be able to distinguish between animal, vegetable, and mineral substance: and to name some of the productions in these kingdoms of their own neighbourhood. They should repeat accurately the table of measure, and be able to show, by illustration, that they realize the different dimensions specified—as, for instance, that there were about so many weeks since such an occurrence; so many yards to such a spot; so much weight in such an object; so much capacity in such a vessel. It would be desirable that they should be able to apply the appropriate name to every object that they ordinarily see, and the adjectives and verbs which express its most obvious qualities and functions. I should be content, at present, with a very scanty knowledge of history, and with one still more scanty of the rules of grammar. The custom of speech, as acquired by the ordinary intercourse of life, is grammar enough for them. I should require an acquaintance, general, though not succinct, with the life, actions and precepts of our Saviour, with a tolerably practical interpretation of the Ten Commandments. More than this I should not exact simply as it would usually be in vain to extract it. With this prescription for a first class, it is easy to imagine, what gradations of attainment might reasonably be expected from the four or five below—ending with the learners of the alphabet. Such is, I hope, an intelligible standard of what, together with cleanliness, good order, and competent mechanical arrangements (and in girls' schools, good needlework) would entitle an elementary school to be classed as 'fair', and where I really and unequivocally find all these qualities combined, I should even pronounce the more indulgent verdict 'good', whilst a marked defect, or scanty and slipshod, or precarious proficiency in most of them would depress the estimate to 'inferior'.

(Committee of Council on Education General Report for 1859, pp. 78–9)

This Benthamite stress upon efficiency characterized the educational work of Robert Lowe, who took office as Vice-President of the Committee of Council on Education in the same year that Brookfield's Report was written. The Revised Code followed logically from a policy of cheap and efficient education. Lowe's famous speech *Primary and Classical Education* delivered some three years after his leaving the Education Department, illustrates his attitude towards the nature of society and the education appropriate to the different social classes:

> I have said that I am most anxious to educate the lower classes of this country, in order to qualify them for the power that has passed, and perhaps will pass in a still greater degree, into their hands. I am also anxious to educate, in a manner very different from the present, the higher classes of this country, and also for a political reason. The time has gone past evidently when the higher classes can hope by any direct influence, either of property or coercion of any kind, to direct the course of public affairs. Power has passed out of their hands, and what they do must be done by the influence of superior education and superior cultivation: by the influence of mind over mind—'the sign and Signet of the Almighty to command', which never fails being recognized wherever it is truly tested. Well, then gentlemen, how is this to be done? Is it by confining the attention of the sons of the wealthier classes of the country to the history of these old languages and these Pagan republics, of which working men never heard, with which they are never brought into contact in any of their affairs, and of which, from the necessity of the case, they know nothing. Is it not better that gentlemen should know the things which the working men know, only know them infinitely better in their principles and in their details, so that they may be able, in their intercourse and their commerce with them, to assert the superiority over them which greater intelligence and leisure is sure to give, and to conquer back by means of a wider and more enlightened cultivation some of the influence? I confess, for myself, that, whenever I talk with an intelligent workman, so far from being able to assert any such superiority, I am always tormented with the conception, 'What a fool the man must think me when he finds me, upon whose education thousands of pounds have been spent, utterly ignorant of the matters which experience teaches him, and which he naturally thinks every educated man ought to know.' I think this ought easily to be managed. The lower classes ought to be educated to discharge the duties cast upon them. They should also be educated that they may appreciate and defer to a higher cultivation when they meet it; and the higher classes ought to be educated in a very different manner, in order that they may exhibit to the lower classes that higher education to which, if it were shown to them, they would bow down and defer.

(R. Lowe, *Primary and Classical Education*, 1867, pp. 31–2)

As the New Code was based on the three Rs, it was relatively simple to examine the pupil's proficiency in these subjects. When, in 1867, a few other subjects were named in the Code which attracted grants, at least one inspector defended the New Code:

> It has been said, however, that the Revised Code by its demands for individual grounding in reading, writing, and sums has lost to us the intelligence-awakening influence of the Old Code's favourite subjects, geography, grammar, and history.
>
> I consider that up to the coming out of the Minute of February 1867, in which extra money grants were connected with the successful teaching of such subjects as the above, the Revised Code quite rightly ignored them. The gross want of lower-class accuracy that obtained under the Old Code was only just being worked off by the end of 1866; and indeed there are still many schools in which the lack of good grounding has not yet been removed, and for which the time for introducing extra and higher subjects has not yet therefore come.
>
> First let a school be thoroughly in working order from top to bottom as regards accuracy of elementary grounding, then extra subjects, such as history, geography, or grammar, can be introduced; and that not only without creating any risk of the children's failing in our individual test of their successful grounding in elementary subjects; but, by stimulating their intelligence, these extra and higher subjects of instruction will make them infinitely more self-confident and easy under an inspector's examination.

(Committee of Council on Education, General Report for 1868, p. 68)

The stark reality of the situation, however, was that teachers, whose income depended on their classes' examination success in the three Rs, could ill afford to offer a wider curriculum. One master entered the following statement in his log book:

> Believing that one-fourth of the school time that was devoted to subjects not recognized by Government, and consequently, not paid for by grants, had the effect of keeping a well-informed school, but of causing the percentage results to be lower than those of the schools that are mechanical in their working and unintelligible in their tone; I have been compelled against my inclination to arrange that less time be devoted to them in future, and more time to those that pay best.

> (North Street Wesleyan School, Log Book 1863–98, 21 April 1871, Bristol R.O.)

Many inspectors protested against the demoralizing effect of the Code. Matthew Arnold, writing at the time when the New Code was being introduced, advocated, like J. S. Mill, the intervention of the State in matters of popular education but arrived at a different set of conclusions:

> The State's proper business in popular education is to help in the creation and maintenance of the schools necessary; to cause fit local bodies to be appointed with the function of watching over these schools; and, finally, itself to exercise over these bodies, and their performance of their functions, a general supervision. When it goes far beyond this, when it makes its aid a system of prizes requiring the most minute and detailed examinations; when it tries to test the acquirements of every individual child to whose instruction it contributes, it goes beyond its province; it invests itself with municipal, not imperial, functions, it creates an administrative expenditure which is excessive. It is as if (to revert to our old comparison of prisons) the State, proposing to support prisons by a capitation grant on reformed criminals, had to ascertain for what criminals the grant was due. The staff of officers to conduct this minute inquisition would absorb funds which might have provided prison-discipline enough to reform scores of criminals.

> (M. Arnold, 'The Twice Revised Code', *Frazer's Magazine*, March 1862)

But the social and political climate of England was in a state of transformation. Political rights were granted through successive Reform Acts which extended the franchise to artisans. It was now vitally necessary, as Lowe remarked, for the preservation of the institutions of the country that the new class of voters was suitably educated. (Lowe, op. cit., p. 8.)

Legal rights, such as the Employers' and Workmen's Compensation Act of 1875, altered the relationship between master and servant. Educational rights were secured in the series of Education Acts from 1870 and, with the advent of the school boards, a breaking of the monopoly of Church-provided elementary education. The higher grade schools established by ambitious boards, such as Leeds and Sheffield, soon vied with the middle-class endowed grammar school in the curriculum which they offered.

The two Royal Commissions of the 1860s on public and endowed grammar schools (Clarendon and Taunton) had left many middle-class parents discontented. The main grievances were the reform of the curriculum by the Endowed Schools Commission and the lack of provision of suitable schools over the country. Proposed curriculum changes within the secondary schools met with

26   Galleries, consisting of raised parallel seats, were constructed for easier
      supervision of pupils. The photograph dates from the late nineteenth
      century.

                                                        GLC Photograph Library

suspicion and conservatism. An interesting sidelight is thrown on the topic in a
diary entry of Lady Knightley of Fawsley, Northamptonshire, wife of one of the
most influential Tory backbenchers in the Commons. It is, perhaps, worth noting
the extent to which Utilitarian ideas were now affecting general discussion of
education—even in Tory circles:

> I see I have not mentioned a book in wh. I have lately been deeply interested, i.e.
> Matthew Arnold on *Continental Schools & Universities.* The comparison between our
> system—or rather no system—of Secondary Instruction—& that pursued in France &
> above all in Germany, is *by no means* satisfactory—& I trust that this subject may be
> taken up in earnest by the new Parlt. tho' I very much fear that public opinion is yet
> by no means prepared for the radical reform wh. is required.—The division of the very
> numerous public schools into classical and so called 'real' studies enable those intended
> for trade or business to get a real good *useful* education—the certificates of fitness
> required from every teacher whether in public or private schools—the leaving examin-
> ation so arranged as to be, as it were, the crowning point of the whole course of study—
> not as they are here a mere cram—the manner in wh. the classics are taught—so as to
> import the real spirit of ancient literature—instead of being a mere question of verbal
> criticism—valuable to the scholar—but forgotten before the end of the year by the
> ordinary pupil—all these things seem to me so infinitely superior to our plans—that
> one cannot help thinking there must be some counterbalancing disadvantage, or we
> shd. have adopted them long ago.

(Knightley of Fawsley Diary, 12 December 1868, K2984, Northamptonshire R.O.)

A rather different view of education was provided by Sir Michael Hicks Beach. Then a member of Disraeli's government and later to be twice Chancellor of the Exchequer, he wrote to the Vice-President of the Committee of Council on Education: 'Some busy people here are keen about the education of women; which (in my private unofficial opinion) is all bosh.' (Harrowby MSS, Vol. LII, pp. 21–2, Sandon Hall, Staffs.)

This letter reflected the general unease caused by the growing demand for suitable provision of secondary and higher education for girls and women from the 1860s. The view expressed by Rousseau in Book V of *Emile* still largely prevailed:

> The whole education of women should be related to that of men. To please them, to be useful to them, to become loved and honoured by them; to bring them up when young, to care for them when grown; to advise, to console them, to make life easy and pleasant for them—these are the duties of women at every age, and this is what they should be taught from childhood. (p. 328)

This can be seen in the debate over admitting women to degrees at London University in 1868. The Chancellor at the time, Lord Granville, had been elected to the post in 1856 and was to remain in office for thirty-five years. He was Lord President when the New Code was formulated. In an address to Senate, Granville outlined his own philosophy on women's education:

> It having been proposed that the charter of the institution should be altered to enable them to examine ladies as well as gentlemen, the matter was put to the vote. He was the unfortunate man who had prevented, by a casting vote, the question being carried. ... But he still retained the opinion that it was not desirable that young women should be mixed up with men at examinations for the same degrees, subjecting themselves to competition with men, and on many occasions to what might be very injurious to their health as well as to their minds. A middle course had been adopted, and the University had obtained power to consider what might be an equivalent to such an examination care having been taken to establish proper conditions with regard to the limitation of age and the formation of a standard examination, and not a competitive one.
>
> (*The Times*, 14 May 1868)

By the 1880s, the growth of the examination system was causing widespread concern. This found expression in a protest, signed by over 400 leading figures in public life, including over 100 Members of Parliament, to the influential magazine *The Nineteenth Century* in November 1888. Part of the manifesto, which was headed 'The Sacrifice of Education to Examination' and which was republished as a book in an expanded form the following year, pointed out that examinations were affecting education at all levels:

> Children ... are treated by a Public Department; by managers and schoolmasters, as suitable instruments for earning Government money; young boys of the middle and richer classes are often trained for scholarships, with as little regards for the future as two-year-old horses are trained for races; and young men of real capability at the Universities are led to believe that the main purpose of education is to enable them to win some great money prize, or take some distinguished place in an examination.
>
> (*The Nineteenth Century*, Vol. 24, November 1888, p. 617)

The supporters of the existing system were fairly specific in their reasons for wishing to retain examinations. For instance, the Rt Hon. Sir William Gregory KCMG, a distinguished member of the Indian Civil Service, laid emphasis on the need to 'obtain a class of men whose high qualities would render them safe governors of that vast possession'. His ideal curriculum was a wide-ranging one:

> I cannot see how examinations can be avoided, but I should have them so fashioned as to obtain young men of thought and wide views, with a thorough knowledge of the great principles of jurisprudence, civil and international; with fairly good instruction in Latin and Greek, something more than in Porson and Elmsley's criticisms, and a facility for composing verses; and a thorough acquaintance with French and German. I should require, were it possible, that the young men selected should have the manners and self-respect of well-bred English gentlemen; a good training in horsemanship; and I should even go so far as to welcome as an adjunct a course of veterinary study.

(A. Herbert (ed.), *The Sacrifice of Education to Examinations*, 1889, p. 29)

Others, such as Sir Lyon Playfair, a distinguished scientist and leading politician, saw both the need for and the disadvantages of competition:

> Examinations are in most cases evils, though they are often necessary evils. Thus in medicine how could you ascertain the qualifications of medical practitioners except by examination? I have known a candidate divide an aorta in an examination—would you let him do it in real practice? But you may admit it in professional qualification, and reject it in professional education. Much as I disliked examinations in the abstract, I could never find how to dispense with them in my classes. . . .
>   Competitive examinations like those in France for every occupation and promotion have been found most damaging. It no doubt stimulates the intellect and produces brilliant results in youth—but after thirty-five the Frenchman's brain, in originality, has become exhausted, and you have few results in later years. Before the days of competitive examinations you had such men as Thiers, Guizot, Chevreuil and others doing splendid work up to the age of eighty. Now how few books of excellence are produced by members of the Institute after forty! (ibid., p. 22)

Educationists and employers, each with very different philosophies, shared views on the relationship between knowledge and education.

Lord Thring, brother of Edward Thring, headmaster of Uppingham School, declared:

> I cannot possibly sign the Protest . . . .
>   With respect to the education of my own class . . . In former days knowledge was flogged into boys—in these days it is introduced by means of prizes and rewards. I do not believe in your inherent love of knowledge. To my mind it is, it must be, put into boys at all events—I do not say anything as to the other sex—by some stimulus applied behind or before. (ibid., p. 123)

In justifying the abolition of competition, one correspondent quoted from John Ruskin's *Fors Clavigera* (1877–8), which illustrates the anti-Utilitarian 'innate capacity' concept of child learning:

> . . . of schools in all places, and for all ages, the healthy working will depend on the total exclusion of the stimulus of competition in any form or disguise. Every child should be measured by its own standard, trained to its own duty, and regarded by its just praise. It is the *effort* that deserves praise, not the success; but partly also out of the radical block-headism of supposing that all men are naturally equal, and can only

make their way by elbowing; the facts being that every child is born with an accurately defined and absolutely limited capacity; that he is naturally (if able at all) able for some things, and unable for others; that no effort and no teaching can add one particle to the granted ounces of his available brains; that by competition he may paralyse or pervert his faculties, but cannot stretch them a line.

The manufacturing view, represented by Lord Armstrong, whose engineering works led to the growth of Tyneside, gave rise to an exchange with Lyon Playfair. In his first article in *The Nineteenth Century* in July 1888 before the Protest was presented, Armstrong, approvingly quoting T. H. Huxley, stated that elementary education was too bookish.

Referring later to this article, Armstrong expands on this theme:

> . . . here I am brought back to the keynote of my former article, which was that 'a man's success in life depends incomparably more upon his capacities for useful action than upon his acquirements in knowledge, and the education of the young should therefore be directed to the development of faculties and valuable qualities rather than to the acquisition of knowledge'. None of my critics have touched upon this cardinal point, and I suspect they fear to do so, being aware, as everybody is, that men of capacity, and possessing qualities for useful action, are at a premium all over the world, while men of mere education are at a deplorable discount. It is melancholy to know, as I do from experience, how eagerly educational attainments are put forward by applicants for employment, and how little weight such claims carry in the selection. I can affirm with confidence that, had I acted upon the principle of choosing men for their knowledge rather than their ability, I should have been surrounded by an incomparably less efficient staff than that which now governs the Elswick Works.

(*The Nineteenth Century*, Vol. 24, November 1888, p. 664)

From the 1870s Utilitarian ideas no longer went unchallenged. It was the idealist philosophers, with their views on the supremacy of the state in deciding, for example, such matters as the purposes and therefore the curriculum of schools, who made a valuable contribution to the educational debate in England, notably through the disciples of T. H. Green. One of their admirers, R. L. Morant, the powerful Permanent Secretary to the Board of Education from 1903, set out the reasons why central control was essential:

> In the midst of the innumerable new steps taken every year in the development of democratic government is not the only hope for the continued existence of a democratic state to be found in an increasing recognition, *by* the democracy, of the increasing need of voluntarily submitting the impulses of the many ignorant to the guidance and control of the few wise, and thus to the willing establishment and maintenance, *by* the democracy, of special expert governors or guides or leaders, deliberately appointed by itself for the purpose, and to the subordination of the individual (and therefore limited) notions to the wider and deeper knowledge of specialized experts in the science of national life and growth, having their outlook over the whole field of national growth?
>
> Surely it is obvious, if we think definitely on this point, that the more we develop our Society on democratic lines, *without* this scrupulous safeguarding of the 'guidance of brains' in each and every sphere of national life, the more surely will the democratic State be beaten in the long run, in the international struggle for existence, 'conquered from without by the force of the concentrated directing brain power of competing nations, shattered from within by the centrifugal forces of her own people's unrestrained individualism and disintegrated utterly by the blind impulses of mere numerical majorities'.

(B. M. Allen, *R. L. Morant*, 1934, pp. 125–6)

Much of the reaction to this view of education, as expressed by educational reformers, is summed up by the philosopher, A. N. Whitehead:

> When you analyse in the light of experience the central task of education, you find that its successful accomplishment depends on a delicate adjustment of many variable factors. The reason is that we are dealing with human minds, and not with dead matter. The evocation of curiosity, of judgment, of the power of mastering a complicated tangle of circumstances, the use of theory in giving foresight in special cases—all these powers are not to be imparted by a set rule embodied in one schedule of examination subjects.

(A. N. Whitehead, *The Aims of Education*, 1932, p. 8)

These views are now generally accepted as the basis for good educational practice by teachers. Learning is tending to become more individualized and Whitehead's notion that the external examiner should not be allowed to ask pupils questions which have not been prepared by their teacher has become accepted practice. This can be seen in the widespread use of internally set examinations, as for instance, in the CSE Mode 3 papers.

In recent years, attention has been increasingly paid to the ways in which this view of knowledge can best be achieved. The architect of the Schools Council, D. H. Morrell, saw the solution in terms of the relationship between the teacher, the child and the parent and the material support needed by the teacher to achieve his objectives. Morrell envisaged the teacher as a trustee both for the child, in respect of a child's natural right to be treated as an individual, and for the parents, in respect of their natural right to do the best they can for their children. Nevertheless the teacher must be free to vary what and how he teaches in order to offer the individual child as nearly as possible the individual educational pattern which he considers right. (D. H. Morrell, 'The Freedom of the Teacher in Relation to Research & Development Work in the Area of the Curriculum and Examinations', *Educational Research*, Vol. 5, 1963, pp. 85–6.)

By the last quarter of the nineteenth century, Utilitarianism was no longer the dominant ideology in education. Nevertheless, Utilitarian ideas are still part of our educational tradition, and notions about the usefulness of competition are accepted by many teachers and parents. There have also been interesting attempts to reinterpret Utilitarian philosophy in a way which would make it a working philosophy for teachers in the twentieth century, for example Moore (1974) and Burston (1973).

2.   From Patronage to Competition:
A General Review of the Development
of Examinations

We move now from a general concern with examinations as one method of ensuring that education produced greater happiness for society as a whole to a more specific example of this utility or efficiency. By the middle of the nineteenth century patronage was beginning to be condemned as both corrupt and inefficient. The philosophy of the Utilitarians advocated efficiency in the conduct of government and especially a system of selection by merit as a test of fitness for posts at many levels.

An early product of this desire for efficiency was the Committee of the Privy Council established in 1839 to superintend grants given to schools, and with powers of inspection to ensure wise and efficient expenditure. Abuses of the administration of educational and non-educational charities, which had previously been the subject of *ad hoc* Commissions of Inquiry, were from 1853 investigated by a permanent board of Charity Commissioners. Newly created departments, such as the Colonial Office in 1855, reformed departments, such as the War Office in 1863, and the growing intervention of government in police, railways, health, merchant shipping and joint-stock companies, led to a need for more bureaucratic and efficient transaction of public business. However, the method of selecting civil servants through a system of patronage made for difficulties in carrying out these new responsibilities efficiently. G. M. Trevelyan has described the situation graphically:

> During the first half of the century, the permanent Civil Service had been jobbed. The offices at Whitehall had been the happy hunting-ground of Taper and Tadpole. Whig and Tory Ministers looked on all such patronage as the recognized means of keeping political supporters in good humour. The public services were filled with the nominees of peers and commoners who had votes in Parliament or weight in the constituencies. Since the privileged families were specially anxious to provide maintenance at the public expense for those of their members who were less likely to make their own way in life, the reputation of Whitehall for laziness and incompetence was proverbial.

(G. M. Trevelyan, *British History in the Nineteenth Century and After*, 1922, p. 356)

Following the lead taken in 1853 by the Indian Civil Service in making entry subject to competitive examination, a committee of inquiry into the organization of the Home Civil Service was set up in the same year. It was headed by Stafford Northcote, then Gladstone's secretary at the Treasury, and C. P. Trevelyan, who had worked in India as a civil servant, and they recommended far-reaching reforms. Shortly before the report was issued in February 1854, Trevelyan wrote to Gladstone:

> Patronage in all its varied forms is the great abuse and scandal of the present age; but we see reason to hope that its days are numbered. . . . It has been proposed that the first appointments made by Her Majesty's Government to the Civil Establishments at home and abroad should, according to the precedent of last session, in regard to the Indian Writerships, be employed in stimulating the Education of our youth, instead of corrupting our constituencies; and considerable progress has been made in working out the practical details. If this could be satisfactorily accomplished, every object would be attained. The Public Establishments would be recruited by the best of the rising generation. The tone of Parliament itself would be raised. Interested parties would have less to do both with obtaining a seat in Parliament, and with the use made of it when obtained. Above all, the Government and the Governing class would cease to be on the side of corruption.

(Gladstone MSS, BM Add MS 14333, 17 Feb. 1854, f. 93)

In their Report on the Organization of the Civil Service, Northcote and Trevelyan recommended that a Central Board of Examiners should be established,

> for conducting the examination of all candidates for the public service whom it may be thought might be subject to such a test. Such board should be composed of men holding an independent position, and capable of commanding general confidence. . . . We are of opinion that this examination should be in all cases a competitive literary examination. . . . This may be so conducted as to test the intelligence, as well as the mere attainments of the candidates. We see no other mode by which (in the case of inferior no less than of superior offices) the double object can be attained of selecting the fittest person, and of avoiding the evils of patronage. For the superior situations endeavours should be made to secure the services of the most promising young men of the day, by a competing examination on a level with the highest description of education in this country.
>
> (Report on the Organization of the Permanent Civil Service, BPP 1854, xxvii, p. 11)

The only immediate result was the setting up of the Civil Service Commission in the following year; the introduction of competitive examination for the Home Civil Service had to wait until 1870.

A parallel movement had been taking place within the Universities. Oxford had introduced examination reform in 1800 with the appointment of examiners, and the award of honours degrees was henceforth based on written examinations. Similar reform followed at Cambridge in the next few years. A Royal Commission which investigated the state of Oxford University in 1852 accepted the inevitability of examinations:

> We are, indeed, well aware that there is some evil mixed with good in all Examinations: they tend to develop docility and accomplishments at the expense of more masculine and efficient qualities. But the system of Examination has grown upon us and we must accept it for the present as the means of stimulating and directing the instruction and the energies of the Students. The question here is not whether we will have Examinations or not; but how many and what sort of Examinations we shall have. The problem to be solved is, how we shall provide Examinations frequent enough to stimulate the flagging energies of the remiss, yet not to diminish the freedom and impede the progress of the real Student.
>
> (Report of the Commissioners appointed to inquire into the State, Disciplines, Studies and Revenues of the University and Colleges of Oxford 1852, BPP 1852, xxii, p. 82)

This view was widely shared by the dons who expressed dissatisfaction at the gaps in the education of their undergraduates on arrival at the universities. One witness, Richard Whately, Archbishop of Dublin and formerly Professor of Political Economy at Oxford, stated:

> As far as regards *University* reform, I have long been convinced that the *very first* step should be a University examination, preliminary to matriculation. . . .
>
> The introduction of a preliminary examination would be an inestimable stimulus to *schools*. They would then become more what a *school* ought to be, and the University would, instead of being a school (and a very poor one), become a real *University*. Schoolmasters now bestow most of their care on a few *bright* lads who are likely to gain *distinction*. And there is no salutary dread of the disgrace of being one of their pupils *refused admission* at the University. But if there were this danger, they would feel ashamed to send forth a lad at 17 or 18 who could not give some account of the New

Testament (about as much as he ought to have previously to being *confirmed*), and of three or four books of Euclid, and of three or four easy Greek and Latin books, which is now all that is required for a degree! (ibid., Evidence, p. 24)

This rather narrow and traditional view of the public school curriculum was challenged by Trevelyan:

The stimulus given to education. . . . This effect will be very great in the Universities and higher education. Hitherto partly in consequence of England being a Commercial Country and the higher education being only the path of the overstacked professions, its diffusion has been less extensive than might have been expected. Where a young man has to go into a Country House at 14 or 15, education of this sort has no chance. Another effect of the change if rightly directed may be to restore Subjects, such as natural Science and general Literature to their proper place in education which our Classical System in Schools and Colleges has tended too much to exclude.

(Gladstone MSS, BM Add MS 14333, 6 Feb. 1854, f. 146)

Even greater benefit would, it was surmised, be the result for the lower classes:

Until now education has both no direct effect in advancing the fortunes of a Labourer or Artisan: it doesn't get him employment as a Shoemaker, Carpenter &c. But the distribution of several hundred places to the best educated persons of this class in each year cannot fail of affording a great stimulus. Adults will begin to thirst for knowledge that bears such fruits. Parents of poor children will struggle to keep them at School for the sake of these prizes. When the system is completely carried out there will be 14,000 well-educated men more than there were before—Nor does this measure the further good that is done by so many persons of education mingling in positions of some trust and importance among their own classes. (ibid., f. 146)

In fact, the effect of examinations on schools at both levels was quite different from those envisaged by Trevelyan. Some of the resultant problems are still reflected in secondary education today.

Secondary schools and examinations

The public and endowed schools, attended mainly by children of the middle class, were being affected by examinations before this period. Besides the highly prized Indian Civil Service examinations, entry to the Army by qualifying test had been introduced in 1849:

Although competitive examinations for Government service did not come into operation rapidly, they flourished strongly once they were established. They had a tremendous influence on the work of the public and endowed schools according to evidence given in the Royal Commission Reports of 1864 and 1868. The former, the Clarendon Report on the Public Schools, showed that although relatively few entered from these majority schools into the Army, nearly all those who went to Woolwich, where there was competitive entry, had to go first to a 'crammer'. These expensive cramming establishments existed to train school leavers to pass examinations to enter their chosen professions, and they were intended to achieve this result and no other. The examinations for the Army and for the Indian Civil Service in particular were affecting the endowed schools also. In some cases the school curriculum was distorted to cater for examination candidates, while in others, boys were leaving school early to attend a 'crammer'.

(R. J. Montgomery, *Examinations*, 1965, p. 28)

It is interesting to note that Manchester Grammar School set up a special Civil Service Form in 1869 when competitive examinations for the Home Civil Service were imminent. These new demands were berated by some schoolmasters who clung to the old order:

> The strangely solemn demeanour of many of the 'cultivated' young men of today is partly, I believe, the result of want of physical vigour and animal spirits. This is what is meant by the 'good student'; and all disproportionate brain-exercise tends to produce this result. And the mischief is exaggerated a hundredfold, is often rendered quite permanent, if it begins in early youth.
>
> For myself, I have not the smallest doubt that almost every boy who is subjected to the long and severe mental strain ordinarily undergone preparatory to the Indian Civil Service Examination, suffers permanently, *to some extent*, from the injurious effects of that strain. It will have left a mark upon him. And it must be remembered that this is applicable both to those who succeed and to those who fail, but usually in a heightened degree to the latter.
>
> (C. C. Cotterill, *Suggested Reforms in Public Schools*, 1885, pp. 64–5)

At the same time, patronage was being replaced by examination as entry into the professions. Modern studies, which had been advocated by both the Public Schools and Endowed Schools Commissions in the 1860s at the expense of classical studies, were given an impetus by these bodies as well as by the Civil Service Commission. This was reflected in the nature of the Oxford and Cambridge 'Locals' which were established in 1858.

A feature of the bureaucratizing process was the association of inspection with examining. The Oxford Locals involved both examination and inspection of schools. There were separate regulations for examination and inspection, but it was not easy to draw a hard-and-fast line between them. No inspection of secondary schools by HMIs was possible until the Board of Education was created at the beginning of the twentieth century but by then competition had been effectively fostered by examinations. Writing in 1911, the Secretary of the Cambridge Board advocated a close link between examining and inspecting:

> The best arrangement seemed to be for the Universities to examine, and for the Board of Education to inspect; but, if that were done, there should be close cooperation between the two. It was essential, for instance, that the inspectors should know exactly what examinations were being taken in the school, and should acquaint themselves with the character and marking of such examinations. They might then do a great deal to ensure that the schools made the best use of examinations.
>
> (Board of Education: Report of the Consultative Committee on Examinations in Secondary Schools, 1911, p. 373)

A shift towards central control over examinations and curriculum from 1900 was reflected in the establishment of the Secondary Schools Examination Council in 1917 and the School Certificate Examination in the same year. This followed consultations between the Board of Education and professional bodies on the question of acceptability of an appropriate examination certificate for the purpose of entry into the professions and which would 'free the secondary schools from the nightmare of a multiplicity of external examinations'. A second or Higher Certificate was also made available for pupils of about eighteen years of age. The cooperation of the universities was secured as the responsible body through whom the examinations in secondary schools should normally be conducted in order to ensure standards. The Spens Report, written some twenty years after this, pointed out that the examinations had been transformed from a school examination into a university entrance examination. Competition had gone too far and was distorting the normal process of evaluating the success of most children in coping with the general curriculum.

In the postwar years, the trend has continued towards a multiplicity of examinations which sort and select students according to a range of different criteria. Michael Young, writing in 1958, coined the word 'meritocracy' to describe a possible future situation where the class structure is based on ability and intelligence, the lower classes being reserved for the less intelligent (*The Rise of the Meritocracy* 1958). Increasingly, as educational and political thinking has changed towards a notion of a more open society, the need for a common examination at 16+ has been mooted; see, for example, the Schools Council Report *Examinations at 16+* (1975). The concept of the new sixth form, unlike the traditional version, caters for a wide variety of ability and needs; it has also raised questions about the relationship between the various parties involved in the examination process. The Schools Council Second Sixth Form Working Party which has been concerned in making recommendations for reform makes the following points in its Report:

> There now appears to be a conflict in the world of examining, a conflict which is sometimes expressed in terms of two opposing examination philosophies. A popular view of the situation puts the opposing sides in their extreme positions, thus:
>
> > (i) those who support traditional external examinations and who therefore believe that examinations should take precedence over the curriculum
> > (ii) those who support Mode III of the CSE and who therefore believe that the curriculum should take precedence over examinations
>
> It would be only too easy to join what would seem to be the side of the angels and go for (ii), but we do not propose to do this because we believe that people who put the situation in these terms have basically misread it, and have missed the point of the conflict. Certainly there is a conflict, but this is not what it is really about.
>
> It is not true that external examinations demand a belief in their precedence over the curriculum. They can be allowed to take precedence, but they need not do so. What happens, or should happen, is that a group of educators meets and decides what it is in each subject which pupils at a given stage might be expected to know or to be able to do, and designs tests to measure the skills involved; the skills may include not merely those derived from knowledge but also powers of understanding, of analysis, synthesis and creativity. The educators define the aims of the subject and the body of knowledge required, and an examination syllabus is published in the interests of the pupils—of any pupils, that is, who think that their preparation has fitted them for the test. But the form this preparation takes is entirely at the discretion of individual pupils and teachers, so long as the examination papers are closely linked to the aims of the syllabus. The extent to which this happens depends on the degree to which there is consultation. Nowhere in this process is there any suggestion that the examination takes precedence over the curriculum.
>
> The essential difference between the two philosophies is to be looked for elsewhere. It concerns, rather, the relationship between the teacher and the examiner. At one extreme the teacher and the examiner are different people; at the other, they are one and the same person.
>
> It was the introduction of the CSE—a new examination designed for a different ability range from that catered for in the GCE, and including pupils who had not had a suitable examination before—which gave impetus to the second philosophy: effective

teacher control of CSE, and in particular Mode III arrangements, have enabled teachers to organize their own syllabuses and make their own assessments of pupils' performances in them, subject only to acceptance of the syllabus by the board at the grades aimed at, and to external moderation to see that standards compare with those at other schools.

(Schools Council Working Paper No. 45, *16–19 Growth and Response*, 1972, pp. 79–80)

3. The Scholarship Ladder

If the Utilitarians wanted efficiency by means of examinations in selecting the ablest candidates for universities and civil service posts, then it was difficult to resist indefinitely the logic of the proposal to start the selection process much earlier—at the stage of entrance to secondary schools. By the first half of the nineteenth century, the local character of public schools had given place to that of a national one. The qualifications for admission had been changed. Initially, the effect was to exclude the poor boy, and local preferences stipulated by the founder were swept away. This was seen in the growing proportion of non-foundationers to foundationers and in the methods by which foundationers were obliged to pay sums of money. Because of the emphasis on classics, it became increasingly difficult for the foundationers, without either coaching or attendance at a private school, to reach the required standard for entry. Patronage was still widely exercised, however. The Public Schools Commissioners discovered, for instance, that at Charterhouse the foundation boys nominated by the Governors in turn were being described as 'persons exceedingly well connected, but really poor' (Clarendon Commission Report, p. 10).

In the same year as the Public Schools Report was issued (1864), the National Association for the Promotion of Social Science sent a deputation to Palmerston asking for a Royal Commission to inquire into the state of the endowed schools of the United Kingdom, 'on behalf of that large portion of Her Majesty's subjects who cannot look for their education either at the great public schools on the one hand or the National Schools on the other'. As a result, the Schools Inquiry Commission (Taunton) was established. Although the Commission eventually recommended three grades of fee-paying schools corresponding to the three assumed social classes of the period, the question of the able poor boy was not overlooked in the reconstitution.

The main problem was the method of selecting for the schools those who would benefit most by such an education. On the question of the selection of free scholars, therefore, the Commissioners favoured competitive examination:

It is uniformly recommended by our Assistant Commissioners as likely to be the most successful remedy for the present state of things, and seems to meet almost all of the objections to any other system of nomination and to indiscriminate admission. It is above partiality, whether personal, social or political, it marks by natural selection those who can profit by an education higher than the rudiments, it puts the free scholar in the place of honour instead of the place of reproach.

(Taunton Commission, Vol. I, p. 158)

The Devon County School, West Buckland.

OBJECT OF THE SCHOOL.

This School was started towards the close of the year 1858, under the immediate patronage of Earl Fortescue, K.G., the Lord Lieutenant, in order to afford at a moderate cost, a thoroughly good education, adapted to the wants of the Middle Classes, and particularly the Farmers.

ITS PROGRESS.

It was commenced in temporary premises with only three pupils; but its numbers have steadily increased, till at present there are 70 pupils belonging to it of whom 50 are boarders.

The increase in its numbers rendered it necessary that new buildings should be erected, and an Association having been formed for the purpose, numbering among its members, His Grace the Duke of Bedford, K.G., Earl Fortescue, K.G.. the Earl of Devon, Viscount Ebrington, Sir T. D. Acland, Bart., J. W. Buller. Esq., M.P., T. J. A. Robartes, Esq., M.P., T. Newman, Esq., J. Sillifant, Esq., &c. &c., the foundation stone of the new school was laid by the late Earl Fortescue, K.G., Lord Lieutenant of the County, on the 4th of October, 1860, in the presence of a large number of its friends and supporters.

The late lamented Lord Lieutenant having died a few days before the time he had fixed for the opening, the School was formally opened by his son, the present Earl Fortescue, in the presence of the Earl of Devon and several hundreds of its friends, on the 8th of October, 1861.

THE SCHOOL BUILDINGS

stand in a very healthy situation on the boundary line of the parishes of East and West Buckland, and are exceedingly well adapted to their purpose. They are surrounded by ten acres of ground belonging to the School, one half of which forms the boys' playground, and the other half is being laid out as a lawn and ornamental grounds. A large and handsome covered playground, for the use of the boys in wet weather, is in course of erection.

COURSE OF INSTRUCTION.

The course of instruction is such as to fit pupils for Agricultural or Mercantile pursuits, for the Civil Service Examinations, for the Oxford and Cambridge Local Examinations (which have already been passed by pupils from this School), and, in general, to prepare them for honourable and independent positions in life.

The chief subjects taught in the ordinary course are:—

The Scriptures.

English, including Reading, Writing. Writing from Dictation, and Spelling, Grammar and Analysis, Composition, Geography, and History.

Mathematics, including Arithmetic, Algebra, Euclid, and Higher Mathematics. Book-keeping and Land Surveying are taught to those who desire them.

Languages : French is taught without extra charge to all pupils whose parents desire it.

Vocal Music.

The following subjects are taught at an extra charge:—

Classics (Latin and Greek).

German.

Drawing.

Agriculture.—This department, with a farm, has been undertaken by Richard Edmonds, Esq.

27   Education for the Middle Classes: the Devon County School, West Buckland, Devon, about 1870. This school was a pioneer in using public examinations on a large scale.

Devon Record Office

There was some evidence to show that this scheme would work. The Commissioners quoted the example from Doncaster where, in 1862, the Corporation subsidized the school with £250 per annum in the form of capitation fees for ten free boys. These Corporation scholars were selected by competitive examination in reading, writing, arithmetic, English grammar, geography, English and Bible history.

When the Endowed Schools Act was being debated in the Commons in 1869, W. E. Forster, the Liberal Vice-President of the Education Department, following the advice of his Commissioners, asked:

> How then can we make this Bill a working man's Bill? The way to really get him in is to substitute for admission by favour, admission by merit, and let the free boys come in by open competition. These schools, therefore, might be made to provide good masters and good education for the middle classes and also to meet those comparatively excep-tional cases, in which children of working men are both specially fitted for high educa-tion and can be allowed by their parents to remain at school.
>
> (Hansard 3 cxciv, col. 1366, 15 March 1869)

The Endowed Schools Commissioners who were to administer the working of the Act differed in their interpretation of the standard procedure to be adopted in choosing exhibitioners. Lord Lyttelton, the Chief Commissioner, when asked by a Select Committee 'With respect to the reward of merit, at what age do you think competitive examination should begin?' replied:

> That is a question for practical educationists; but it is a very fair point to consider. I think that competitive examination, on paper chiefly, a strictly intellectual competitive examination, ought not to take place before eleven years old at the earliest. But that is a matter of opinion. We never say anything about that in our schemes.
>
> (Select Committee on the Endowed Schools Act (1869), 1873, BPP 1873, viii, Q.1421)

The schemes of the Commissioners setting out the conditions which governed the award of scholarships and exhibitions reflected this difference of outlook. One of the recommendations—testing by HMI—was sometimes followed; reports of headmasters with 'selection' based on academic subjects were often demanded by the endowed schools: most frequently of all the pupil was required to sit an examination set by the endowed school. This latter form often proved to be the most difficult one.

A form of streaming was adopted in many elementary schools when the time approached for the competition for exhibitions; those who seemed likely to do well were chosen by the headmaster for this purpose.

The scholarship awards often lapsed because of the rivalry existing between the elementary and grammar schools or a lack of funds to finance them. By the last quarter of the century, there is evidence to show that the number of poor able pupils attending the reformed endowed schools had declined as more middle-class children took advantage of the awards.

The proud claim of Lord Lyttelton that there was a 'ladder of ability' was therefore somewhat premature:

> Just as we open the way from the 2nd Grade Schools through exhibitions and scholar-
> ships and so on, to the higher schools above them, so we open the advantages of 2nd
> Grade Schools to 3rd Grade Schools below them, and in the same way the 3rd Grade
> Schools to the Public Elementary Schools of the district, which we believe to be far the
> best way of benefiting the labouring classes in those districts.

(Select Committee on the Endowed Schools Act (1869) 1873, Q.1280)

Two important political events occurred in 1892 which changed the picture dramatically. Nationally, a Liberal government was returned with A. H. D. Acland, a reforming Vice-President of the Education Department, in the Cabinet: locally, in London, Sidney Webb, leading the Progressives at the LCC elections, had scored a resounding victory and commissioned a survey of London's educational needs. With Liberal support and Acland's encouragement, the London Technical Education Board was established; one of its main concerns was to provide, on a massive scale, a series of scholarships and exhibitions at all levels from the elementary school to the university. This was now possible since the newly created county councils had been made responsible for administering technical instruction funds (three Acts were passed in the three years 1889–91); and the councils were expressly permitted to found scholarships at schools approved by them.

Webb was concerned to equate 'technical education' with 'secondary education' in its widest sense. In an interview with Acland, Webb persuaded the Minister to allow every subject which the Art and Science Department had sanctioned for other schools. Beatrice Webb noted in her diary that this resulted in 'a long list of subjects . . . including all the sciences, arts and foreign languages, together with modern history, economics, geography, commercial education and what not. "We can now lawfully teach anything under the sun except ancient Greek and theology" observed Sidney complacently.' (B. Drake and M. I. Cole (eds.), B. Webb, *Our Partnership*, 1948, p. 80.)

One link was still missing: effective liaison between the elementary and secondary schools. This problem was examined by a committee of the London School Board under Huxley's chairmanship as early as 1871. A historian of the Board has written:

> The chief recommendation of the Committee was that the Board should enter into
> communication with the Endowed Schools Commissioners and seek to establish a
> system of scholarships providing maintenance grants equivalent to the earnings of
> children between the ages of 13 and 16, tenable for the periods during which they
> might remain in the secondary schools. Little came of this proposal. The School Board,
> of course, had no money to spend on schools and the Endowed Schools Commissioners
> did not display any great eagerness to devote to this object any of the funds they
> controlled.

(H. B. Philpott, *London at School—The Story of the School Board 1870–1904*, 1904, p. 54)

Negotiations between the Technical Education Board and the Headmasters' Association, a body formed in 1890 and composed of headmasters of public and endowed schools, resulted in the Association receiving grants on condition that schools should be open to inspection by representatives of the Board and that there should be a joint examinations board for the award of scholarships.

The success of the Association's scheme for administering the scholarship examinations can be judged by the fact that by 1894 all the schools under the jurisdiction of the Technical Education Board and two-thirds of all the secondary schools in London used their examinations, and in the following year eleven county councils adopted them also. By 1896, there were 6,679 candidates for the examinations. In 1895, the successful venture was handed over to a Joint Scholarship Board, which was officially independent of the Association.

Although the 1895 Royal Commission on Secondary Education (the Bryce Report) conceived of secondary schools as catering for the needs of the middle classes and the elementary schools for the working classes with a slender ladder between the two for the able poor, this view was now being increasingly contested. A number of interested parties, such as the National Union of Teachers, advocated entry to secondary schools to be based on a qualifying rather than a competitive basis:

> *As to the passing of Scholars from Primary to Secondary Schools*
> (b) In the opinion of the Union, public aid of any kind should not be given to any Secondary School in future unless a substantial portion of the school places shall be open to free scholars.
> (c) The practical acquaintance of members of the Union with the evils of existing systems of awarding Scholarships and Exhibitions according to the result of competitive Examinations causes the Union to strongly favour the plan of attaching to each school a system of Leaving Exhibitions, assignable as the managers and teachers may in each case decide. There appears to be no reason why under District Boards of Education, there may not be allotted each primary school in a District, a certain number of leaving Exhibitions; and a similar system could be applied to Secondary Schools as circumstances warrant.
> (d) With regard to the age at which scholars may be thus transferred from Primary to Secondary Schools, the Union recommends that a minimum age, but no maximum age, should be fixed.
> (f) It is the opinion of the Union that in all cases Scholarships should be bestowed preferentially upon the children of parents whose circumstances would not otherwise warrant the continuance of their children at school.
>
> (Bryce Report, Vol. V, BPP, 1895, xlvii, p. 326)

It was, however, the Bryce Commission's view which prevailed when the municipal grammar schools, aided out of rates, were set up after the 1902 Education Act. The courses laid down by the Board of Education were heavily academic, with a great emphasis on English, geography, history, possibly two languages and science and mathematics.

The deliberate raising of standards taken with the almost exclusively academic nature of the secondary school curriculum had obvious implications for elementary school pupils. One of the earliest actions of the Liberal Government which came into office in 1906 was to establish Regulations which made it possible for local education authorities to offer 'free places' at secondary schools exclusively for elementary school pupils. In the following year, the Regulations required that the number of free-place pupils normally admitted should be 25 per cent of the total admissions of the previous year. Some authorities supplemented the number of free places with scholarships, but the overall picture was varied:

BROMSGROVE SCHOOL. 4621

February, 1901.

OXFORD AND CAMBRIDGE SCHOOL EXAMINATIONS.

To the Chairman of the Governing Body of Bromsgrove School.

SIR,

We are instructed to send you the following Report on the Examination for an Entrance Scholarship recently held at Bromsgrove School, under the authority of the Oxford and Cambridge Schools Examination Board.

The substance of the following remarks is taken from the Report of the Examiner.

Examiner—F. E. KITCHENER, M A., Trinity College, Cambridge.

Mr. Kitchener says,—I have examined the candidate from Bromsgrove School, with a view to seeing whether his attainments are adequate for his receiving a Scholarship in that School.

The Subjects of Examination were :—

1. ARITHMETIC.
2. ENGLISH HISTORY AND GEOGRAPHY.
3. LATIN.

In ARITHMETIC, questions were set on simple, and compound rules, vulgar and decimal fractions, proportion, practice and simple interest.

The work sent up attempted every question except one, but was poor and inaccurate throughout. The Candidate knew more or less how to do the sums, but not a single sum was completely answered. The simple and compound multiplication sums were wrong ; and only parts of the sums on fractions were right. *Mark : 14 out of 100.*

In HISTORY, the Candidate got 17 out of a maximum of 50, this was the best paper done ; some knowledge of the English Kings and their dates was shewn, but the answers were incomplete.

In GEOGRAPHY the paper was very poor ; attempts at the drawing of a sketch map of parts of England were bad, and very little was known of the Industrial products of English towns.—I could only award *7 marks out of 50* for this paper.

In LATIN some knowledge of the declension of nouns and conjugation of verbs was shewn. The translation of English sentences into Latin was worthless, but a few marks were obtained in the attempt to translate the easy continuous piece into prose, with the aid of a dictionary. The piece of translation of Latin into English (with the aid of a dictionary) was not attempted. The Latin mark was *21 out of 100.*

The result is thus : *Arithmetic* ... ... 14 out of 100.
History and Geography 24 „ „ 100.
Latin ... ... 21 „ „ 100.

Total ... ... 59 out of 300.

I may further add that the spelling and grammar of the English used in the answers (for which no deduction has been made) were illiterate; such words as 'Sout' for 'South,' ' the ' for 'they,' 'gret' for 'great,' 'barrons' for 'barons,' may be taken as examples.

On the result of this Examination I do not think the Candidate entitled to a Scholarship. In coming to this conclusion I have considered the papers set and standards required for similar Scholarships in other Schools, and I have considered also the papers set, and the marks obtained in the Competition for Minor County Scholarships by boys from Elementary Schools in my own County, with which I am familiar. Had the Candidate obtained half marks on the Arithmetic and the History and Geography papers, I should not have recommended withholding the award because of the failure in Latin ; but in not one of the three papers does the candidate get a quarter of full marks.

I regret therefore that I cannt recommend the Candidate for the award of a Scholarship under clause 15 of their scheme.

We have the honour to remain,

Your obedient Servants,

E. J. GROSS, } Secretaries to the Board.
P. E. MATHESON, }

12th February, 1901.

28   Report on an Examination for an Entrance Scholarship 1901
Candidates from elementary schools eagerly sought such scholarships.
Public Record Office

Taking the country as a whole, children from public elementary schools constituted, even in 1907, rather more than half the pupils in the schools, those of them who paid fees and those who did not being about equal in number. But, while some schools consisted almost entirely of such children, others had few or none of them, and their incursion on a large scale was dreaded.

(Board of Education: Educational Pamphlet No. 50, *Recent Development of Secondary Schools in England and Wales*, 1927, p. 10)

A Committee of Enquiry presided over by Lord Haldane in 1927 clearly showed that the original intention of requiring children only to pass a qualifying examination had not been fulfilled:

This aspect of the free-place examination, as a qualifying test, is still uppermost in the public mind; but obviously, under present conditions, with the lack of secondary school places, so far from being a merely qualifying examination, it has become a competitive test of great severity, and, with the considerable variation in the number of school places available in different parts of the country, the standard needed for success varies from district to district in a most distracting way.

(*The Next Step in National Education*, 1927, p. 192, quoted in Association of Education Committees and the National Union of Teachers, *Examinations in Public Elementary Schools*, 1931, p. 23)

The use of the new instrument of selection, intelligence testing, was taken up by county and borough authorities in the 1920s, but neither the form of test used nor the additional 'subjects' required was uniform. A report published in 1931 gave some examples of this:

Ten of the county authorities which use intelligence tests conduct only a single written examination for selective purposes, and appear to regard the intelligence test as a useful adjunct to what otherwise might prove an imperfect method of selection. In Huntingdonshire, for example, intelligence questions are included in all the subject papers taken at the selective examination, and are considered to be of great importance. Lindsey (Lincolnshire) has an intelligence paper which counts equally with either the papers in English or arithmetic, and to which the same maximum mark is attached. Essex includes intelligence questions in the general knowledge paper, while in Surrey a special paper is devoted to them. In Rutland, where the examination is for central school admission, a general intelligence paper is included in addition to an oral test, while in Gloucestershire a good intelligence quotient qualifies for admission to the oral examination irrespective of the results in the written work. In Buckinghamshire thirty marks may be awarded for intelligence out of a total of two hundred and thirty in the whole examination, and in borderline instances special inquiry is made into the intelligence result.

(Association of Education Committees and the National Union of Teachers *Examinations in Public Elementary Schools*, 1931, p. 191)

In this fiercely competitive situation the original aim of the framers of the 1907 Regulations was blurred. Olive Banks summed up the situation in 1955 as follows:

In fact the number of areas offering free places to children of 'quite average ability' has remained very small. The popular demand for secondary education, slow and uncertain in 1907, increased enormously during and after the First World War at a rate beyond the capacity of the local education authorities to supply. The resulting competition for free places destroyed all hope of a secondary education for the 'average' elementary schoolchild, except as a fee-payer. 'The increase in the demand for secondary education', said the President of the Board in 1923, 'has been quite remarkable, spontaneous and universal in all parts of the country in England and Wales, industrial and agricultural, and, in spite of bad times, it persists. Parents who a few years ago would not have thought of a secondary education for their children, are now making great sacrifices to obtain it. I doubt whether, even in normal times, with money easy, we could have been able adequately to cope with the demand.'

The secondary schools, consequently, continued in practice to select only the ablest working-class children, while providing the sons and daughters of the lower middle classes with a secondary education at much below cost price. It is unlikely, however, that such a development was foreseen by the Board in 1907.

(O. Banks, *Parity and Prestige in English Secondary Education*, 1955, p. 69)

With the questioning by Professor P. E. Vernon and others of the validity of intelligence testing in the 1950s, authorities such as Hertfordshire dropped these tests from their selection examinations. A study carried out in that county between 1952 and 1954 by Jean Floud, A. H. Halsey and F. M. Martin demonstrated that the vaunted equality of opportunity made available by the 1944 Education Act was in fact a myth. Both in terms of the social distribution of opportunity before and after the change in selective procedure and in equality of opportunity for children of equal ability irrespective of social origins, the selection of pupils for grammar schools in south-west Hertfordshire reflected an over-representation of middle-class children. The authors of this study concluded:

This is social waste no less serious than that resulting from the social discrimination in selection which has been so successfully tackled since 1945. It must be admitted that it is difficult to avoid so long as grammar school provision takes the relatively inflexible form of places in separately organized and housed schools, entrants to which are selected by competitive examination.

(Jean Floud and A. H. Halsey, 'Intelligence Test, Social Class and Selection for Secondary Schools', *British Journal of Sociology*, VII, 1957, p. 39)

For many, the answer was to be found in a system of comprehensive education where selection and competition as a basis for entry was non-existent. So far, tentative studies, such as that of Julienne Ford in *Social Class and the Comprehensive School* (1969), have shown that, where children are taught in ability groups or streams, the middle-class child is likely to find himself in the grammar stream even though of similar ability to the working-class child.

These differences are exacerbated, as Marten Shipman points out, by an extension of the old 'grammar' and secondary modern traditions within the comprehensive school. One has its roots in the academic curriculum based on traditional subjects, the other is experimental, focusing on contemporary problems and grouped subjects. These differences are reflected in the types of examinations for which pupils are entered at the end of their courses. These developments may divide education into two systems as effectively as selection has done in the past. (M. Shipman, 'Curriculum for Inequality', in R. Hooper (ed.), *The Curriculum: Context, Design and Development*, 1971, pp. 106–7.)

One possible solution to this problem which has been put forward is the common-culture curriculum. The content of such a curriculum cannot be easily spelt out, but proponents of this approach emphasize that it does not involve holding pupils down to a minimum level of achievement or content.

Examinations, which in the nineteenth and early twentieth centuries were part of a reform movement to enable poorer children to gain access to secondary and higher education, have gradually come to be regarded as a barrier for some children. In this respect examinations provide us with a good example of the need for reappraisal and change in curriculum and evaluation: a system which may be an advantage at one time can become a mixed blessing or even an anachronistic barrier at other times.

This chapter has attempted to describe the part played by examinations in influencing the curriculum throughout the nineteenth and twentieth centuries. It is not a simple, straightforward account and it will undoubtedly be interpreted in a variety of ways. One difficulty about the word 'examinations' is that in the second half of the nineteenth century it began to have a variety of emotional effects on readers, and it still has today. For some, examinations meant an efficient means of judging standards of attainment by pupils and hard work by teachers; for others, examinations conjured up ideas of learning by rote, trivial syllabuses, harsh teaching methods and unreliable results.

We suggest that neither of these two views is necessarily correct. What has to be clarified is the distinction between an examination as a method of evaluating learning and a method of selecting. Today most educationists would accept the need for evaluation, but the selective function of education has become suspect.

29 A school staff portrait 1906
The information on the board in the background is of interest.
GLC Photograph Library

Where examinations are used to select it is likely that the curriculum will be in danger of distortion or trivialization. Similarly if examinations are used as a basis for teachers' promotion or payment then similar distortion is likely. The general lesson to be learnt from this chapter is that since the middle of the nineteenth century competition has become more acceptable than patronage, but care must be taken not to allow instruments of evaluation to become instruments of selection and to distort the curriculum.

6

Pressure Groups

One of the basic reasons for the existence of pressure groups is to affect or modify the behaviour or actions of a body holding power. Much of the literature on this subject is concerned with analysing the relationship between government, the legitimate holder of power, and pressure groups, in a democratic society. Many decisions which have to be taken at national level cannot be carried out by mass participation. It is for this reason that people with common interests band together to make information available to governments which may be taken into account in deciding on policy issues. J. Blondel (in *Voters, Parties and Leaders*, 1963, pp. 160–1) has suggested that they may be divided into two types: *protective* groups, which defend a section in society, such as trade unions and motoring organizations, and *promotional* groups which want to promote a cause, such as the Council for the Preservation of Rural England.

Of course, strategies of pressure groups vary according to the outcome which it is hoped will be achieved. *Local* pressure groups usually try to achieve a *national* platform so that their case receives wider dissemination. How to achieve a satisfactory balance between the two levels is not always easy, especially when we consider the superior resources available to government departments.

When we look below at the various pressure groups which have influenced, to a greater or lesser extent, the school curriculum, we can add to the types already mentioned. The groups may be small, consisting of a few people, or they may be on an international scale. Some have long-term aims, while others arise in response to an immediate issue and then cease to exist. There are pressure groups to promote change and others to prevent it. What follows is only a selection of some of these types, chosen to illustrate the different forms the activity may take and their various outcomes. It will be seen that the operations and ultimate effects of pressure groups on policy are complex; they are not a simple account of 'progress'.

Religious and Secular Instruction

As we have already seen, in the section concerned with moral instruction, the debate on the merits and demerits of a purely secular curriculum is a long-standing one. In a bid to make universal free education available to children by local authorities, the Birmingham radical Nonconformists established the National Education League early in 1869. The Committee included Joseph Chamberlain, George Dixon and Jesse Collings; it set out to establish a national network of committees to contest concessions to the Church of England contained in Forster's Elementary Education Bill:

> Such concessions to the Anglicans as 'the year's grace', 'permissive compulsion', the 'conscience clause' and 'the election of boards by vestries', inflamed the League, which reacted swiftly by demanding universal School Boards, elected immediately on passage of the act by ballot of the ratepayers, providing free schools at which attendance was to be compulsory and in which 'no creed, catechism or tenet peculiar to any sect was to be taught'. These points they made in a deputation of 46 MPs and 400 members representing 96 branches, described by its secretary and historian as 'probably the most numerous and representative which had ever visited Downing Street', to the Prime Minister on 9 March 1870.
> The battle for alterations continued. The League's chairman during the second reading of the bill threatened that, unless concessions were made, a movement for exclusively secular education would arise. After a three-night debate, he secured a promise from the Prime Minister that alterations would be made. Here the Central Nonconformist Committee went critical, and secured the signatures of two-thirds of all the nonconformist ministers in England and Wales to a petition to the House of Commons against allowing local boards to determine religious teaching in schools. The petition was followed by a deputation to the Prime Minister. Even Forster's advisers changed their minds, and against such pressure the government withdrew, conceding ballot elections for the School Boards, with a time-table conscience clause for their schools. Elections were to be based on a cumulative vote, and the 'year of grace' was reduced to five months.
>
> (W. H. G. Armytage, 'The 1870 Education Act', in *British Journal of Educational Studies*, Vol. 18, No. 2, 1970, p. 125)

The compromise solutions of the 'conscience clause' and the undenominational nature of Bible reading in schools was not strictly followed. At Birmingham, for example, the first school board, which had an Anglican majority, insisted that the Bible was to be read and taught along with periods of worship.

A historian of the League noted a worsening on the succession of the Conservative Administration in 1874:

> Under Mr Forster's administration there had been grievous complaints of the partiality shown to the Church. On Lord Sandon's succession the evil was aggravated. Whitehall was crowded by clerical wire-pullers and friars of all colours, and the Department was interviewed and memorialized without cessation. A clerical minority unable to carry its policy on a School Board had nothing to do in order to frustrate the majority but to hold a private meeting, and pass resolutions and forward them to the Department. The wishes of the representatives of the ratepayers were coolly ignored.
>
> (F. Adams, *History of the Elementary School Contest in England*, 1882, reprinted 1970, p. 312)

As the Church had no equivalent to school boards who were responsible for the superintendence of curriculum as well as the organization of their schools, Church Day School Associations were set up in the 1870s. At Manchester, a Day Schools Association was formed, virtually co-terminous with the school board districts of Manchester and Salford: it collected statistical information in the area, and gave grants to schools. Two conditions were that a member of the committee became manager of the schools and that an organizing inspector was admitted to supervise the work. A so-called Church School Board later took over the secular management of schools 'that were either so weak or so self-distrustful that they would be handed over to the School Boards'. (Report of the Manchester and Salford Day Schools Association, 1886, p. 9, 372/942/M6, Manchester Central Library, Archives Dept.)

By the 1897 Voluntary Schools Act, a much more ambitious scheme was attempted. The Associations were entrusted by the Education Department with the allocation of aid grant and to ensure the general efficiency of schools in their area.

The Conservative Government under Lord Salisbury saw the Associations as potential bulwarks against the rising tide of secularism:

> The Education Department issued Circular 394 to all managers of voluntary schools, suggesting that if they had not yet taken any step toward association they should, as soon as possible, 'communicate with the managers of those voluntary schools in your neighbourhood with which the association of your school would seem most natural and desirable, or with any bodies or persons who may appear to you authorized to confer and arrange with you on behalf of such schools'. In order to expedite the first allocation of aid grant to such Associations, the details of the proposed Association were to be sent to the Department within three months of the Circular.
>
> The area of the Association was taken to be the diocese or arch-deaconry in the case of Church of England, the diocese only for Roman Catholic schools. The Wesleyan and British schools divided their areas into geographical regions of England, and the Jewish schools had a national Association. By 1898, there were 75 Associations—46 Church of England, 11 Roman Catholic, 11 British and other schools, 6 Wesleyan and 1 Jewish.

(P. Gordon, *The Victorian School Manager*, 1974, p. 215)

The main target of attack was the 'de-christianized' nature of instruction given in board schools. Despite the efforts made, the Church was unable to compete either in staffing or instruction.

A compromise arrangement between Church and State was achieved by the 1902 Act. Local education authorities would maintain and keep efficient all public elementary schools in their area and allow for the 'dual system' to continue. In return, teachers could not be dismissed for refusing to give religious instruction; and in denominational schools, the control of religious instruction was taken out of the hands of the local clergy and vested in the managers, who now consisted of lay as well as clerical elements.

Pressure groups were founded by all the parties concerned. Some Nonconformists, fearing that the Church of England and Catholics would be strengthened in educational affairs, attempted to affect the course of events by withholding payment of rates for the maintenance of denominational schools. The Church of England, on the other hand, formed a group with more positive aims: to preserve the voluntary school system and provide resistance to any further encroachments on their rights. The Church Schools Emergency League, founded in 1903, consisted of school managers, members of education committees and others anxious to support the aims of the League. It carried out a large-scale programme of activities, including the lobbying of MPs, publishing leaflets, seeking views of candidates in county council elections and providing legal advice on the interpretation of the 1902 Act. (B. Sacks, *The Religious Issue in the State Schools in England and Wales 1902–14*, 1961, pp. 55–6.)

Fundamental changes in the position of the teaching of religious education were made by the 1944 Education Act. The course pursued by the various pressure groups was complex. A reconsideration of the dual system which had existed since 1902 was long overdue. R. A. Butler, in introducing the Bill, had to take into consideration the views of the parties concerned. As the Anglicans owned 85 per cent of non-provided schools, their views were important. There was a large body of agreement on the need to ensure sound Christian teaching for all children in all schools, by means of an agreed syllabus.

A start had already been made as early as 1924 when Cambridgeshire issued an Agreed Syllabus for the schools in the county; many other authorities soon adopted it. In 1941, it seemed that a combination of religious bodies could bring about religious instruction in all schools:

> Already in February 1941, Anglican and Free Church leaders had united in launching a public appeal for the firmer recognition of religion in the schools. Their joint recommendations, published in the form of the 'Archbishops' Five Points', had included the universal provision of religious observance and instruction, and the inspection of that instruction by His Majesty's Inspectors. Obviously the Archbishops' recommendations were part of the larger problem of dual control, and the Green Book now integrated them into the general scheme of reform. Firstly, religious observance and instruction were to be enjoined by statute in all provided primary and secondary schools, such instruction to be given in the form of agreed syllabus instruction and to be inspected; secondly, in the non-provided schools, the agreed syllabus was to be available where parents required it; lastly, regulations for all types of secondary schools were to become uniform by the abolition of the Cowper–Temple Clause in provided modern schools. It was expected that the suggested interference with the Cowper–Temple Clause would provoke attack; nevertheless, it was deliberately included as part of the general balance and was intended to compensate the churches for the measure of public control over their schools.

(M. Cruickshank, *Church and State in English Education*, 1963, p. 146)

Although there was opposition from Roman Catholics, teachers' unions and trades unionists to these proposals, the main principle of universal religious teaching was written into the Act. The ultimate acquiescence of the parties concerned was achieved with some significant consequences:

> Scarcely any managers of such schools were at this time availing themselves of the freedom allowed since 1870 to dispense with religious instruction, and the new declaration of principle gave rise to surprisingly little comment except from some teachers' representatives who considered it unnecessary. Yet it clearly indicated a desire for closer cooperation between church and state, and seemed to signal the end of the long struggle to confine state-supported education to secular subjects. But its influence was more than symbolic: henceforward religious instruction in council schools would be, generally speaking, greater in extent and more systematic; moreover, since the daily act of worship would in practice normally be conducted by the head teacher, this lent support, as we shall see, to the contention of those who felt that, whatever the 1944 Act might elsewhere prescribe, head teachers should be chosen from among committed Christians. The implications could hardly be inconsiderable.

(J. Murphy, *Church, State and Schools in Britain, 1800–1970*, 1971, p. 115)

This section on pressure groups in religious education has indicated the close links between the changing attitudes of the state on the one hand and denominational interests in education on the other; and the formation as a matter of expediency of new alliances among these interests.

Central and Local Interests

The existence of a national system of education in England which is locally administered gives rise to an overlap of responsibilities. The balance between the two parties is delicate and local pressures have for the last hundred years been applied to obtain the most favourable terms from central government. A study of the school board system from 1870 to 1903 shows that, as a body, it formed a powerful pressure group, often able to challenge the Education Department and, where necessary, Church interests.

School Board influences

In the urban areas, the boards were large and could recruit influential figures. In rural areas, religious issues often predominated. The interests of the users of elementary schools in establishing a school board were not, however, necessarily an indication of hostility to the Church.

A student of Norfolk village life concluded that

> the desire to control the village school was not due to dissatisfaction with the instruction given there; most labouring people had little desire for a really liberal education, and were quite content if their children learnt to read, write, and do simple arithmetic. There were no real difficulties about religious instruction in the school. Labouring politicians simply thought that control of public education should not be in the hands of one sect or one individual. Where there were School Boards they had their remedy . . .

(L. M. Springall, *Labouring Life in Norfolk Villages 1834–1914*, 1936, p. 113)

Although, to a certain extent, these features were also characteristic of the larger school boards, the latter were able to devote themselves to a number of curriculum issues and were able to weld themselves together into an effective pressure group. The restrictive nature of the annual Code was the boards' main target. Broadly, two methods were available to them 1. exchange of information to ascertain like-mindedness, 2. national representation.

1. *Exchange of information.* Views on various topics affecting their operations were circularized by like-minded boards. We have already noted in Chapter 4 the joint petition by ten school boards on the need for domestic subjects to be allowed in the Code.

Visits to board schools in other areas assisted in disseminating information. The Bradford Board authorized its two superintendents of schools to visit London, and their subsequent report was discussed by the Board. As a result, better methods of teaching and a more advanced curriculum for older scholars were introduced.

The School Board for London was instrumental in producing a memorial for the consideration of the Committee of Council on spelling reform:

My Lords,
    On the 22nd November last the School Board for London adopted the following resolutions:
        1. That this Board is of opinion that a great difficulty is placed in the way of education by our present method of Spelling, and that it is highly desirable that the Government should be moved to issue a Royal Commission for considering the best manner of reforming and simplifying it.
        2. That a copy of the above resolution be forwarded to the Society of Arts and the various country School Boards, inviting them to unite in a joint representation to be addressed to the Education Department on the subject.
    The Society of Arts, and upwards of 100 Provincial School Boards, have expressed their concurrence in the purpose of these resolutions, and the principle of them has been affirmed by large majorities in the London Board which has since been elected. Your Memorialists, therefore, respectfully appeal to your Committee to take steps for obtaining a Royal Commission to inquire into English Spelling with a view to such reform as is required in the interest of Elementary Education.

(*Memorial on Spelling Reform adopted by the School Board for London on Wednesday 25 July 1877*, p. 1)

In the first instance, a board would send a copy of their resolution direct to either the Education Department or the House of Commons and simultaneously to other boards, asking for support. For example, in 1880 the Oldham Board asked Parliament to enforce Article 28 (Arithmetic) of the 1874 Code which stated that 'In all Schools the Children in Standards V and VI should know the principles of the METRIC SYSTEM, and be able to explain the advantages to be gained from uniformity in the method of forming multiples and sub-multiples of the unit'. It also sent a circular to other school boards to enlist support for a New Code which would reinstate the Article and thus help to prepare the nation 'for the introduction of an international system of coinage, weights and measures'. (Oldham School Board, 21 June 1880—Circular to School Boards.)

2. *National representation.* A more effective and speedier way of exchanging information and gaining status was by establishing a national body. In October 1893, the first meeting of the Association of School Boards took place. Its terms of reference were to establish 'an Association to watch over the interests of School Boards and to be powerful to take steps to protect such interests'. The boards quickly saw the value of such a forum. The opening address by the President of the Sixth Annual Meeting in June 1899 contains a useful summary of the strength of the body.

    Our Association now comprises no fewer than 289 school boards, embracing within their several authorities a population of 14,600,000 out of 20,000,000 under the administration of school boards throughout the country. About 700 representatives are in attendance today, embodying a force of public opinion to which no inconsiderable weight, I feel sure, must be attached. . . . The Executive Committee has met at least once a month during the year last past, and has held an extraordinary meeting for the special purpose of dealing with the question of local authorities for secondary education. The Executive have given tangible proof of their devotion to your interests by establishing *The School Board Gazette* as an accurate record of their own proceedings and of the proceedings of the Association and as a means of keeping the Association in close touch with all matters affecting the educational system of the country, so far as it is entrusted to the care of the school boards.

(*The School Board Gazette*, Vol. 1, No. 6, June 1899, pp. 422–3)

The Association had been formed in response to mounting pressure by the Church for greater aid to their schools; and to the possibility of school boards losing their advanced work to a new authority which would be responsible for secondary education. Also discussed at the meeting were items concerning the education of pupil-teachers, vagrant and boat children and those of 'weak intellect'.

Direct pressure could be brought to bear by teachers at both local and national levels. Asher Tropp has shown how this could be accomplished locally, even though teachers could not be members of the board under which they were serving:

> In every large town (where alone was it possible for the teachers to exercise influence) every candidate for election to the school board would be waited on by deputations of teachers, and his attitude on salaries, liberty of classification, religious teaching and corporal punishment would be probed. By canvassing for votes and by their own use of the cumulative vote the teachers wielded a great deal of influence.

(A. Tropp, *The School Teachers*, 1957, pp. 143–4)

A second approach was to operate at national level:

> Until the elementary teachers secured direct representation in Parliament their chief methods of work were deputations and memorials to the Education Department and to members of Parliament. Not unimportant were the efforts made to keep the teachers accurately informed of educational matters by means of *The Schoolmaster* and the general press, and by visits to local organizations by the leaders of the Union. Obviously, an organized body of workers, controlled as the teachers were by the central government, would find its most effective weapon in the political field. This has been true of the National Union of Teachers and they were not slow in realizing the possibilities of political influence.

(D. F. Thompson, *Professional Solidarity Among the Teachers of England*, 1927, p. 85)

The School Board Clerk. Each school board appointed a clerk as a permanent secretary. Their continuity in office put them in a strong position to influence the officers of the board. For instance, the first and only clerk to the Sheffield School Board (1870–1903) was J. F. Moss who operated in a number of fields. With W. E. Forster's support, one of the earliest Central Higher Grade Schools was established there. Moss played a substantial part in a committee for the promotion of Firth College, later Sheffield University, and gave evidence before royal commissions and parliamentary committees. (*Sheffield Weekly News*, 13 January 1900.)

The larger boards were able to recruit clerks with impressive qualifications. G. H. Croad of the London Board (1871–1902) had obtained a double honours degree at Trinity College, Cambridge, later becoming head of the modern department at Rossall School and secretary of the Bishop of London's Fund. Edward Hance, of the Liverpool School Board (1871–1903), one of the ablest of the clerks, was a barrister-at-law. He was widely consulted by other clerks on the interpretation to be placed on ambiguously worded legislation affecting schools.

Hance's salary was raised in 1892 from £700 to £800, a princely sum. (*Liverpool Mercury*, 2 November 1892.)

Well might a former Vice-President of the Committee of Council and a Churchman write to Lord Salisbury, concerned at the clerk's position:

> As to the School Board District, people forget when talking of the Ratepayers' check, the great and growing power of that most able set of men—the Clerks of the large Town School Boards, banded together I believe in an Association, acting in concert with their army of School Board Teachers who largely affect the Board Elections: working for the most part steadily against the Voluntary Schools (or at any rate for the multiplication of Board Schools), and, as the members of the Board constantly change, and *they* remain, mostly masters of the position.
>
> (Lord Harrowby to Lord Salisbury, 16 July 1891, Salisbury MSS, Hatfield House, Herts)

In 1871, a School Board Clerks' Conference was formed. Their meetings were not held in public, but members of school boards were invited to attend. The conferences lasted four days; the time was divided between discussing issues and visiting board schools.

At the eighth annual conference, the chairman, A. H. Burgess, Clerk for the Leicester School Board, in his opening address, was anxious to point out that the conference was not intended to represent a pressure group:

> Mr Burgess took occasion to remark that the kind manner in which the Conference had been received at Leeds, at Newcastle, at Liverpool, Sheffield and Manchester on their respective visits to those towns was due no doubt, in a great measure to the fact that it had soon become known that the members did not meet in this manner to consider questions affecting their interests as clerks, but to exchange the results of their experience in the administration of the Education Acts under the varying circumstances of their respective districts, and to take counsel together as to the best manner of overcoming the difficulties which they had to encounter from time to time in their work.
>
> (*The School Board Chronicle*, 1 October 1881, p. 312)

Nevertheless, the conference provided a vehicle for an expression of views which were noted by the Education Department.

Matters dealt with during the Hull Conference included the operation of the Summary Jurisdiction Act in relation to cases under the Education Acts, pre-payment and remission of fees, science teaching and school organization. The last topic occupied eight columns of the report of the Conference and was a condemnation of the New Code which had recently been issued by A. J. Mundella.

The network of interests in school board policy was strengthened later in the century. Membership of the Association of School Boards and of the School Clerks' Conference overlapped. Hance of Liverpool was Vice-President of the Conference in 1881 and President of the Association eighteen years later. Attempts were made by Sir F. R. Sandford, Secretary of the Education Department and an enemy of the boards, to disallow expenses incurred in such meetings. But final recognition of the important part those meetings played in formulating policy was granted by the passing of the School Board Conference Act in 1897; it provided for expenses incurred by delegates in relation to conferences and thus took the matter out of the auditors' hands.

The Public School Interest

We have seen in previous chapters the influence of the great headmasters of public schools in moulding the character of their institutions. One outstanding feature of this group was the community of interests and outlook in matters affecting the organization and curriculum of the schools. This may be partly accounted for by the similarity in background, milieux and family inter-connectedness to which Noel Annan has given the label of 'the intellectual aristocracy'. By the beginning of the nineteenth century, a particular type of middle-class family started to intermarry, producing children who became scholars and teachers. They led the movement for academic reform within universities and were involved in the founding of the new civic universities. They also provided headmasters at the leading public schools. (N. G. Annan, 'The Intellectual Aristocracy', in J. H. Plumb (ed.), *Studies in Social History*, 1955, p. 243.)

The Vaughan family demonstrate this linkage. Starting with Henry Halford Vaughan, 1811–85, Fellow of Oriel and Regius Professor of Modern History at Oxford, we can trace the lineage through a network of educational interests. His son was W. W. Vaughan, headmaster of Wellington and Rugby; his daughter became Principal of Somerville College, Oxford. H. H. Vaughan's brother, the Rev. E. T. Vaughan, by his second marriage started a line which included C. E. Vaughan, Master at Clifton and Professor of English at Cardiff, Newcastle and

30   The School Board for London in session, late nineteenth century
GLC Photograph Library

Leeds; C. J. Vaughan, Headmaster of Harrow who married the sister of A. P. Stanley, Dean of Westminster; and his grandson, T. H. Green, the Oxford philosopher and educationist.

Another example is the Butler family:

> Occasionally a family develops that seems to possess a special interest in education. The best example of this is the family that stemmed from George Butler, who became headmaster of Harrow in 1805. Four headmasters are to be found here, besides heads of Oxford or Cambridge colleges, dons, a diplomatist, major social reformers, besides another outstanding descendant, R. A. Butler (now Lord Butler). In addition, there are linkages with at least three other families also distinguished in scholasticism and research—the Darwins, Galtons and Edgeworths. Again, from these starting-points, it is possible to construct extremely elaborate links not only across the families of one era but also in historical depth.
>
> (T. W. Bamford, *The Rise of the Public Schools*, 1967, pp. 146–8)

The headmasters of the public schools in the nineteenth century were aware of what was expected of them in the training of the youths entrusted to them:

> As a group they believed themselves destined to rule, whatever their exact position in the status system of the public school may have been. They felt that it was only natural that those who ruled the country and administered its empire should be selected from their midst. Seen in the life-cycle of the individual, the school, as a body, took the place of a harsh father who was the product of a similar upbringing, and it educated to loyalty towards the Church, the Monarchy, the Empire or whatever symbols the educational and political system might choose to express the accepted order of things. In the eyes of its members the public school thus assumes a place much above an ordinary place of education. It embodies the traditions accepted by the class which sends its children there and hands down the social values which they cherish. 'When the call came to me to form a government', Lord Baldwin declared, 'one of my first thoughts was that it should be a government of which Harrow should not be ashamed. I remembered how in previous governments there had been four or perhaps five Harrovians—and I determined to have six.'
>
> (W. L. Guttsman, *The British Political Elite*, 1965, pp. 154–5)

Links at yet another level existed in the schooling of future headmasters. In the instance quoted below, the school laid great store on compulsory games:

> Between 1860 and 1880, games became compulsory, organized and eulogized at all the leading public schools. It is interesting to observe that six of the most prominent headmasters of this period had all been boys together at Edward Wickham's private school at Hammersmith—Eagle House. They were George Ridding (Winchester), Montagu Butler (Harrow), A. G. Butler (Haileybury), G. J. Blore (King's School, Canterbury), E. C. Wickham (Wellington) and Edmond Warre (Eton). Of these, Ridding had something of Charles Wordsworth's enthusiasm for athletics, being a keen player of cricket and fives and setting a great value upon games 'as a means of instilling *esprit de corps* and discipline, and as a training of character'.
>
> (D. Newsome, *Godliness and Good Learning*, 1961, p. 222)

The gathering together of these headmasters in the face of the tabling of the Endowed Schools Bill in 1869 and their method of combating the forces arraigned against them illustrate the theme of this section. Apart from the nine public schools which the Clarendon Commission had earlier scrutinized, all other endowed schools came within the scope of the new Bill. The most vociferous elements of the heads were those who had been aggrieved at being omitted from the provisions of the Public Schools Act of 1868.

The main causes for alarm were contained in Part 2 of the Bill. It was suggested that provincial authorities should be set up with direct control over the schools. Governing bodies were to be liberalized; they would have power to dismiss the headmaster and determine the subjects of instruction. Clause 53 of the Bill provided for examination in any subject the Council wished to choose, and textbooks were to be prescribed by the Council. Provision was made for a register of suitably qualified teachers, based on inspection and examination:

> In effect these clauses were designed, not to set up a professional register similar to the Medical Register, which gave the body of practitioners effective control of their profession, but for the very different purpose of bringing the secondary schoolteacher under the control of the State and of instituting a certificate which would be parallel to that already prescribed for elementary schoolteachers.
>
> (G. Baron, 'The Teachers' Registration Movement', in *British Journal of Educational Studies*, Vol. 2, No. 2, May 1954, p. 134)

Not only were schools to be unrepresented on the Council, but the powers of the headmaster would be limited to his selection of staff and choice of examinations.

The leading figures in opposing Part 2 of the Bill were Edward Thring of Uppingham and Hugo Daniel Harper of Sherborne. Harper had been headmaster since 1850 and had gained an impressive reputation for the school in a number of ways. He applied for the headship of Rugby in 1857 because it had been represented to him that 'where so many others were standing, the Head Master of Sherborne ought, for the sake of his own school, to put in an appearance on the field': his biographer states that

> it was his invariable habit, whenever a question of great practical importance had to be solved, to write to the head masters of the public schools, and other acknowledged authorities on the subject of education, and to tabulate the information he received, and afterwards digest it into what proved to be a lengthy document.
>
> (H. V. Lester, *Memoir of Hugo Daniel Harper DD*, 1896, p. 36)

Edward Thring, whose pioneering work in liberating the curriculum of public schools has already been noted, believed that the headmaster's role should be that of an autocrat. He had earlier complained before the Schools Inquiry Commissioners of the intrusion of one of the Assistant Commissioners into the sixth form classics lessons during his visit to the school. Thring asked for a special note to be inserted in the Report on his school: 'we believe such examinations to be full of danger, and, if constant, sure to introduce strong disturbing influences into good steady school work'. (Taunton Commission, Vol. XVI, 2 May 1866, p. 133, BPP 1867–8, xii.)

The Bill itself ran into difficulties on its Second Reading in March 1869 and in August the Government admitted defeat by abandoning the controversial Part 2 of the Bill, reserving it 'for consideration'.

To ensure that the movement against direct control of the endowed schools could be halted, Thring enlisted Harper's help in establishing a conference of leading schools. A circular was sent out by Thring proposing that an annual meeting of headmasters should be held at which matters of common interest could be discussed.

The first meeting of what was to become the Headmasters' Conference took place in London at the end of that year:

> In December 1869, out of the sixty schools invited, twelve gathered with Thring for the first Headmasters' Conference. The second took place the following year at Sherborne and thirty-four schools attended. From the make-up of the Committee on the admission of new members—Winchester, Eton, Harrow, Repton, Cheltenham, Clifton, Uppingham, City of London School, and Sherborne—it is evident that, under the stimulus of attack, most of the old and the new Public Schools joined together to defend themselves.
>
> (P. Stansky, 'Lyttelton and Thring: A Study in Nineteenth-Century Education', *Victorian Studies*, Vol. 5, No. 3, March 1962, pp. 219–20)

Ridding of Winchester at the 1877 Conference asked for a settlement of the question of eligibility for membership. The matter was settled by the Committee after considering the general character of each school and of the status of its headmaster. Ridding stated that it 'had nothing to do with "first grade" '. It was intended to be a conference of public schools, an indefinite name—a sort of club of schoolmasters, who are at liberty to elect their own members' (Quoted by G. Baron in 'The Origins and Early History of the Headmasters' Conference 1869–1914', *Educational Review*, Vol. 7, No. 3, June 1955, p. 224).

The safeguarding of the interests of the members of the 'club'—some two hundred headmasters—received little challenge until the Board of Education Bill was being enacted in 1899. In the course of the reorganization of the Department which was likely to take place, it seemed at one point that secondary education might become a branch of the Science and Art Department, inferior to the elementary and technical branches.

After a committee of the Headmasters' Conference had called for 'the three main factors of national education to be placed on a separate, equal and independent footing', Michael Sadler, a former Rugby and Oxford man, composed a minute for the Department supporting this view. Even when a Secondary Department was established, Sadler envisaged that its relationships with the schools would be tentative:

> The most urgent function of the Secondary Education Department will be in the direction not of administrative coercion but of diplomatic negotiation, in order that reforms may come from within by consent and not too roughly imposed by departmental order from without. It is unquestionable that the social forces which lie behind English secondary education of the best types are too strong to be dealt with in a summary, bureaucratic manner.
>
> (Minute, M. Sadler, 7 July 1899, Ed. 24/64 P.R.O.)

The success of the Conference during the first thirty years of its existence confirmed Thring's original intention of bringing together 'thoughtful educated men', the headmasters of leading public schools, to be able to act in concert on matters affecting them.

Other Pressure Groups

The range of pressure groups active in education is enormous. In this final section, it is intended to point out a few of the more interesting categories which have not so far been mentioned. In many cases, influential groups do not necessarily reveal their identity in public, but prefer to operate at a more informal level. This is particularly so in the field of British science, starting with the Birmingham Lunar Society in the eighteenth century.

Perhaps the best-known example was the X-Club, a group of nine men who promoted laboratory teaching from the 1840s: The aim of the group was to bring the issue of science education before scientific societies, the British Association for the Advancement of Science and the universities. Monthly meetings were held near the Royal Institution and the Club was able to propagate its views in influential quarters through friends who were connected with scientific institutions overseas and in England. Among its members were Thomas Huxley, Herbert Spencer, Sir John Lubbock, the group's parliamentary spokesman, Thomas Archer Hurst, Professor at University College, London, and Assistant Secretary of the British Association, and Edward Frankland, Professor at Owen's College and an examiner for the Department of Science and Art. (W. H. Brock, 'Prologue to Heurism', in *The Changing Curriculum*, 1971, pp. 78–9)

At a more public but informal level, subject associations were often formed on a single issue, later to become permanent bodies. The Mathematical Association, for example, originated from an Association for the Improvement of Geometrical Teaching.

The introduction of the 'new geography' early in this century was the result of the teachers' acceptance of a more scientific approach even in the face of 'established' opinion. When H. J. Herbertson presented a paper at the Royal Geographical Society in 1904 on 'The Major Natural Regions: an Essay in Systematic Geography', it was coolly received.

> Unlike Fellows of the Royal Geographical Society, members of the Geographical Association, most of whom were teachers, were quick to welcome Herbertson's essay in systematic geography because it provided them for the first time with a simple and pre-eminently teachable classification of geographical facts. Though pre-eminently the subject specialist, Herbertson was well aware of this virtue in his proposals. 'Knowing each of the [fourteen] chief types [of major natural regions],' he said, 'it was a simple matter to learn the peculiarities of each variety' and by this means to effect 'a great saving of time' in teaching the geography of the world to children at school. Practical teachers quickly appreciated this virtue of the scheme and within a year of the publication of Herbertson's 'The Natural Regions of the World' in *The Geographical Teacher* of 1904, that organ of the Geographical Association carried two commendatory articles— Cooper's 'Regional Teaching of Geography' and Sweeting's 'The Teaching of Regional Geography'.

> (R. D. Bramwell, *Elementary School Work 1900–25*, 1961, pp. 30–1)

Curriculum innovation has from time to time come about on the initiative of individuals; in order to be effective, he or she requires access to a wide audience and the ability to express clearly the changes advocated. Franz Cizek (later Professor) in Austria began, in the closing years of the nineteenth century, the

'Child Art' movement; this was a movement, now an established practice, aimed
at encouraging the creative side of young children—a reaction from the imitative
nature of previous teaching.

Cizek's initial opportunity to promote his ideas came about as a result of
outside support.

> So Cizek opened his Juvenile Art Class (at that time a private school) in 1897, having
> at last received permission to do so. Naturally such a school as soon as it became known
> was received with considerable opposition. About the same time, in 1896, Cizek was
> appointed art teacher in the Realschule of the 7th district of Vienna. He likes to
> describe what he was forced to do with these eleven to eighteen year-old pupils,
> according to the official curriculum, such as copying ornamental designs, drawing
> plaster models, but secretly he allowed his pupils to work independently. Fortunately
> visitors from abroad, among others Goetze from the Hamburg Society for Art
> Education, interested themselves in this new type of art teaching. (In Austria much has
> been left for foreigners to discover.) Goetze brought this young art teacher to the notice
> of Hartl, then Minister of Education. Another fortunate circumstance was that
> Myrbach, the director of the State School of Applied Art, came to hear of Cizek.
> Myrbach boldly incorporated Cizek's Juvenile Art Class in his *Kunstgewerbeschule*. This
> happened in 1904. The children, regular schoolchildren, attended the art class there on
> Saturday afternoons and Sunday mornings.

(W. Viola, *Child Art and Franz Cizek*, 1936, pp. 13–14)

31   Children as artists 1907
     Compared with many other aspects of the curriculum, art was taught in
     an enlightened way.

GLC Photograph Library

As a practitioner himself, Cizek was able to promote child art on an international scale through exhibitions of children's work and by appearances at art
education conferences. The influence which Cizek's work exerted on English
teachers was reinforced by the activities of Marion Richardson at Dudley High
School. She had studied Cizek's method and consequently directed her teaching
towards releasing the creative power in children. Like Cizek, her work was taken
up by practising artists, such as Roger Fry, who staged a special exhibition of
paintings and drawings by her pupils in 1917. Later, as an art lecturer at the
London Institute of Education and then as an inspector, Marion Richardson
achieved a wide audience for the revolutionary views of teaching children art
rather than drawing.

Where the causes promoted received lukewarm support from the public, pressure groups have traditionally adopted an aggressive role in the first instance.
The move for women's education in the nineteenth century was of this order.
When the official inquiry into middle-class education, the Taunton Commission,
was announced in October 1864, Emily Davies, later the first mistress of Girton,
wrote to Lord Lyttelton, one of the Commissioners, who was persuaded to
include girls' education in their remit. This followed the presentation to the
Commissioners of a Memorial, devised by Emily Davies and a colleague, signed
by representatives of Queen's and Bedford Colleges, a number of headmistresses
and many influential people. While the Commission was still deliberating, Miss
Davies read a paper on 'The Application of Funds to the Education of Girls', to a
meeting of the Social Science Association. A successful outcome to the campaign,
leading to better provision for girls' education, was also achieved by manipulat-
ing the course of the Schools Inquiry Commission. Emily Davies obtained as
witnesses J. S. Mill, Dr Mark Pattison, Rector of Lincoln College, Oxford and
Thomas Huxley, knowing that their opinions would carry much more weight
than those of schoolmistresses. (J. Kamm, *Hope Deferred: Girls' Education in English
History*, 1965, p. 202.)

Occasionally, a pressure group was able to influence government policy in a
more direct manner. Bernhard Samuelson, a firm believer in the promotion of
technical education, was able to achieve the setting-up of a Royal Commission on
Technical Instruction (RCTI) in 1881 and became its Chairman.

> On the evidence it is difficult to avoid the conclusion that the RCTI was an ad hoc
> committee engineered by Samuelson and his friends in the House, with Magnus as a
> minor éminence grise and Mundella as an (outwardly) doubting accomplice (probably
> fighting against Cabinet apathy). Consider the facts: the members of the Commission
> were, without exception, as we shall see, already converted to the cause; they were in
> fact in the position of 'experts', who should always be in a minority on a fact-finding
> body; they should have been witnesses before the Commission, not members of it.

> (M. Argles, 'The Royal Commission on Technical Instruction 1881-4' in *Vocational
> Aspects of Secondary and Further Education*, Vol. 9, No. 23, Autumn 1959, p. 98)

Teachers' unions represent one of the more important pressure groups in curriculum matters. In an earlier section, attention was drawn to the attempts by
teachers' professional bodies in the last century to influence educational policy.
At first, most of the issues were concerned with such matters as terms of service,

superannuation and official recognition by the education authorities. This is not surprising if we consider, for example, the view of Robert Lowe who stated in the 1860s that 'teachers desiring to criticize the Code were as impertinent as chickens wishing to decide the kind of sauce in which they would be served'. (D. Thompson, op. cit., p. 76.) It was not until the second decade of the present century that the Department's officials recognized the National Union of Teachers as a body to be consulted in the formulation of educational policy. On the other hand, the second largest union, the National Association of Schoolmasters (NAS), which now includes the National Union of Women Teachers, was virtually denied access to the Department's officials until it achieved membership of the Burnham Committee in 1961, where teachers' salaries are determined.

The different interests in teaching are represented by a range of unions. For those secondary heads who were not included in the Headmasters' Conference, a Headmasters' Association (HMA) was formed in 1890. Within the NUT there is the National Association of Head Teachers (NAHT). Coalitions of and disagreements with established bodies have resulted in a changing pattern of representation over time. The interests of secondary school teachers who largely taught in selective schools and were graduates are reflected in the 'Joint Four'; this is made up of the Assistant Masters' Association (AMA), the Association of Assistant Mistresses (AAM), the Association of Headmistresses (AHM) and the Headmasters' Association (HMA).

Obviously, these different groups have different ways of bringing pressure to bear on official policy. Members serve on the Department's permanent advisory committees concerned with legislation and administrative regulations. Michael Locke has indicated that in 1971, teachers' unions were asked for comments on a circular concerning the education of autistic children, work experience, the raising of the school leaving age and children with learning difficulties. The last proposal met with much criticism and the circular was not issued. (M. Locke, *Power and Politics in the School System, A Guidebook*, 1974, p. 31.) They are also the means of maintaining pressure on the Department when informal contacts fail. For example where the Joint Four consider that a regulation or circular raises matters of importance which they cannot accept, a memorandum on the topic is followed by a deputation to the Department. As many as twelve deputations may be organized in any one year. (R. D. Coates, *Teachers' Unions and Interest Group Politics*, 1972, pp. 11–12.)

Encroachment by central government on teachers' powers over the control of the curriculum has met with resistance from unions in recent years. In March 1960, when Sir David Eccles, then Minister of Education, announced in the House of Commons that the Ministry intended to establish a Curriculum Study Group, consisting of experts, without consulting outside interests, there was strong reaction from teachers' unions. As a result a different body was set up, four years later—the Schools Council for Curriculum and Examinations, on which teachers form the majority on its various committees.

Unions also engage in activities directed at winning public support for their policies. After the issues of the Plowden Report, the NUT mounted a major national campaign, backed by press conferences, mass meetings and the issue of leaflets to draw attention to their views. The NUT is represented on over one hundred outside bodies which provide a ready platform for this purpose. Lobbying of MPs has long been a popular device of teachers' unions: as early as 1871, meetings took place between union members and MPs on teacher reaction to the Code. Many MPs are or were themselves teachers and a number of them are sponsored by unions. As a result, teacher representations are likely to receive, given the constraints of party loyalties, a sympathetic hearing.

Where necessary the machinery of a union can be swiftly brought to bear on curriculum issues. The rising demand for external school examinations outside the GCE framework, as revealed by the Crowther Report (1959), was a matter of growing concern to teachers. In the following year, the Beloe Committee recommended an examination below the level of the GCE for pupils of average ability. The response of the NUT has been described as follows:

> This leisurely process would no doubt have continued without a definite conclusion if the findings of the Beloe Committee had not placed the whole issue in a new context. The report of the Beloe Committee showed the 'movement up' virtually out of control, to such an extent that by strengthening the private Examining Bodies it was threatening the professional freedom of teachers. With a vital interest of the teachers suddenly at stake, the movement, too far gone to be reversed, had to be pressed to a conclusion which was educationally sound but which guaranteed the traditional freedom of the profession. The result was the Certificate of Secondary Education.
>
> (R. A. Manzer, *Teachers and Politics: The Role of the National Union of Teachers in the making of National Educational Policy in England and Wales since 1944*, 1970, p. 90)

Though teachers' unions' primary task is to safeguard the welfare of their members and to negotiate conditions of service, the autonomy of the teacher in curriculum matters is jealously guarded: recent suggestions, therefore, by politicians and industrialists for the introduction of more definite guidelines in the school curriculum have been cautiously received by unions.

Over the past few years a large number of pressure and interest groups have come into being which impinge on both governmental action and teacher's attitudes. These groups can either be on an *ad hoc* local basis or a national body comprising regional branches. An example of the former is the campaign fought by those who were opposed to the introduction of comprehensive education into their areas:

> Thus around the individual grammar schools sprang up the defence societies, the 'save our schools' committees, the preservation societies, the grammar-school action groups. The fighting funds and the fighting associations of the prestige grammar schools were fully operational whenever local authority planning of reorganization looked like taking place. In towns like Leicester, Flint, Liverpool, Enfield, Ealing, Bexley, Dudley, and dozens more, they organized. A national grammar group was born through the Old Boys' Association of Hampton Grammar School—calling itself the National Education Association—but it was almost superfluous. Local groups could take care of themselves. The grammar schools themselves were the actual centres of campaigns. Headmasters provided facilities for meetings and urged parents to sign or circulate petitions, sometimes sending pupils home with anti-comprehensive leaflets. Old Boys' and Old Girls' Associations campaigned against the reforms. The more prestigious the school, the bigger and better its support—both financially and otherwise.
>
> (C. Benn and B. Simon, *Half Way There: A Report on British Comprehensive School Reform*, 1970, p. 89)

The national bodies represent a wide spectrum of interests. For instance, CASE (Confederation for the Advancement of State Education) operates at both local and national levels. It informs parents of issues in their area, lobbies education authorities and formulates policies on various aspects of curriculum. It has, for instance, given evidence to the Schools Council and other educational commissions and had a member on the Plowden Committee.

Specific aspects of education give rise to other types of pressure groups. The National Campaign for Nursery Education, founded in 1965, is comprised of representatives of teachers' unions, health visitors and many other interests. The White Paper of 1972 on nursery education was one successful outcome of the campaign. Parents are less involved in another group, the Campaign for Comprehensive Education, also founded in 1965: teachers, politicians and educationists constitute the main elements. Much of its activity is directed towards the gathering and dissemination of information on comprehensive education which can be used when local education authorities are drawing up new schemes. At a different level, the National Association of Governors and Managers, founded in 1970, is a smaller body confined to looking at reforms in the present system of representation on governing and managing bodies, such as the inclusion of parents.

Questions concerning the curriculum offered in schools are often central to their deliberations. The growing involvement of the community in matters affecting education is finding increasing expression in the activities of these groups. In turn, the consumers' considered views are taken into account by government departments and committees concerned in formulating and recommending appropriate policies in education.

In this chapter we have looked at various types of pressure groups which have influenced the curriculum. The wide variation in the origins, membership and tactics employed by various groups over the past hundred years is remarkable. A feature which is common to all, as Duverger (1972) noted, is that they seek to influence the people who wield power rather than to place their own men in power. There has been, as the final section has shown, a great increase in the number of pressure groups representing many shades of opinion which are in some way concerned with aspects of the curriculum. This reflects the growing concern, as expressed in the recent national education debate, on the nature, purpose and direction of curriculum change in present-day society.

Conclusion

The account we have given of curriculum change is clearly incomplete in the sense that each of the aspects of curriculum analysed in the book is still being discussed today in a way which suggests that the debate will continue for some time. Indeed the curriculum is increasingly seen as a key question in many kinds of decision-making.

One of the areas of controversy relating to legislation is whether there should be greater control of the curriculum, and what part the Schools Council and other bodies such as the Assessment of Performance Unit (set up by the DES) should play in a changing situation of greater 'accountability'.

There is also no sign of any shortage of social and educational theories which affect the curriculum: it might even be said that curriculum has now become a central feature of arguments about the kind of society we want and the kind of educational system necessary for that society. It has become increasingly apparent that whether politicians and educationists are talking about social justice or economic efficiency the real question is one of the curriculum, not merely school organization and teaching methods.

Similarly, the curriculum is still changing rapidly in terms of subjects and subject-matter. New subjects are being suggested, new groupings are being tried out, such as integrated humanities in place of history, geography, religious education and possibly English. Often it is as difficult today as it was in earlier years to be able to detect the real reasons, or even a rational justification for many innovations, and there is a danger in that without some kind of theoretical plan behind the changes little or no improvement will take place.

Teaching methods, too, continue to evolve: individualized learning, team-teaching and various kinds of grouping have been tried out in recent years. Perhaps the greatest stimulus and challenge for this kind of change is the increasing tendency for schools to be organized in a variety of ways, for example, mixed ability groups rather than sets or streams. But, once again, unless teachers are prepared for these changes—both in terms of attitudes and of skills—then we are likely to be faced with 'innovation without change'. The *raison d'être* for various kinds of grouping needs to be justified, and the recent Lancaster University report on primary schools methods (Bennett, 1976) reopened—but did not settle—the arguments about progressive and traditional teaching styles.

The influence of examinations has also continued to be a powerful control on curricula. Just as arguments about economic efficiency and social justice have tended to lead in the direction of comprehensive schools and new methods of organization and teaching, there has also been considerable pressure to reform the examination systems. Separate examinations for GCE and CSE have been criticized and a common examination at 16+ advocated. At sixth-form level most educationists blame the examination structure for the extent of over-specialization in the sixth form. The control of examinations is also in dispute. How much power should teachers have? To what extent should examinations be school-based rather than public? Should examinations be replaced by a more general system of standards and accountability?

There are also signs that pressure groups continue to be influential in changing curricular policies as well as other aspects of education. Such national groups as CASE, the Committee for Comprehensive Education and PRISE (Programme for Reform in Secondary Education) as well as local groups increasingly discuss curriculum rather than matters of organization. Decisions made by schools are called into question and have to be justified in public terms—another aspect of the difficult issue of accountability.

We hope to have illustrated in this book three related points: first that the topics discussed in Chapters 1 to 6 are of relevance today as well as being of historical interest; secondly, that questions about curriculum are nearly always close to the central issues of educational debate, although they often appear to be neglected at the time; and finally that the six topics chosen for analysis are not isolated but are all closely interrelated. In order to make sense of curricular problems it is necessary to seek multi-causal explanations.

Appendix 1

Biographical Notes

ACLAND, Sir Arthur Herbert Dyke, 13th baronet (1847–1926). Liberal politician; educated Rugby and Christ Church, Oxford: BA 1870, MA 1873. Son of T. D. Acland; Lecturer 1871 and Tutor 1872–5, Keble College, Oxford. Ordained Deacon 1872; resigned 1879 under Clerical Disabilities Act, 1870; Principal, Oxford Military Schools, Cowley, 1875–7; Steward of Christ Church, Oxford, 1880; Senior Bursar, Balliol College, Oxford, 1884; MP Rotherham, W. Riding, 1885. Played considerable part in promoting Welsh Intermediate Act (1885–9), anticipating the Education Act 1902 in making Welsh County Councils an educational authority (see account of this in *Studies `in Secondary Education*, edited by Acland and H. Llewellyn Smith, 1902). In Gladstone's 4th Ministry: Vice-President with seat in Cabinet 1892. Achievements included the appointment of inspectors from elementary schools and raising the age of compulsory attendance from 10 to 11; reorganized the Science and Art Department, and abolished payment by results. Resigned from politics in 1899 through ill-health but actively opposed the 1902 Education Act. Chairman of the Consultative Committee of the Board of Education

BALFOUR, Arthur James (1848–1930), created 1st Earl of Balfour 1922. Conservative politician; nephew of 3rd Marquess of Salisbury; educated Eton and Trinity College, Cambridge (Moral Science Tripos); lifelong interest in philosophy.

MP Hertford, 1874–85, Manchester E., 1885–1906, City of London, 1906–22; President of Local Government Board 1885–6; Chief Secretary for Ireland, 1887–91; Member of Senate, London University, 1887; FRS 1888. Leader House of Commons, 1891–2 and 1895–1906; Prime Minister, 1902–5 on Salisbury's retirement; with Morant (*q.v.*) responsible for the passing of the 1902 Education Act. First Lord of Admiralty, 1915–16; Foreign Secretary, 1916–19; President of the Council, 1919–22.

PUBLICATIONS: *A Defence of Philosophic Doubt*, 1879; *Essays and Addresses*, 1905; *The Foundations of Belief*, 1895; *Theism and Humanism*, 1915; *Essays, Speculative and Political*, 1920.

BUTLER, Richard Austen (born 1902), Baron Butler of Saffron Walden (life peer) 1965, KG, PC, CH, MA. Conservative politician; educated Marlborough and Pembroke College, Cambridge (double first class, Modern Languages Tripos, 1925–9); Fellow, Corpus Christi College, Cambridge. MP Saffron Walden, 1929–65; Secretary of State, India Office, 1932–7; Parliamentary Secretary, Ministry of Labour, 1937–8; Under Secretary of State, Foreign Affairs; Minister of Education and responsible for the passing of the 1944 Education Act, 1941–5; Minister of Labour, 1945; Chancellor of the Exchequer, 1951–5; Lord Privy Seal, 1955–9; Leader of the House of Commons, 1955–61; Home Secretary, 1957–62; Deputy Prime Minister, 1962–3; Foreign Secretary, 1963–4; Master of

Trinity College, Cambridge, 1965; President Modern Language Association, 1972.
PUBLICATIONS: *The Art of the Possible*, 1971.

CAVENDISH, William, 7th Duke of Devonshire (1808–91). Educated Eton and Trinity College, Cambridge; BA 1829 (first class, Classical Tripos). MP Cambridge University, 1829–31; Malton, Yorks, 1831; Derbyshire, 1832–4. From 1858, when Cavendish succeeded to the Dukedom, he gave up politics and devoted his time to science and industry. He was responsible for the development of Barrow-in-Furness, especially the iron-mining and steel industry and the harbours facilities; also presented the Cavendish Laboratory to Cambridge University. One of the founders of the Royal Agricultural Society, 1838, President, 1870; First President, Iron and Steel Institute, 1868; Trustee, British Museum, 1871. Wide interest in education; Chancellor, University of London, 1836–56; Chancellor, University of Cambridge, 1861–81; Chancellor, Victoria University, Manchester, 1881. Chairman, Royal Commission on Scientific Instruction and the Advancement of Science 1870–5, known as the *Devonshire Commission*.

COLE, Sir Henry (1808–82), CB 1851, KCB 1875. Administrator; educated Christ's Hospital, 1817–23; appointed to the Record Commission 1823, became one of senior assistant keepers 1838–51; responsible for erection of Public Record Office in Chancery Lane. Versatile in many fields, Cole designed some of the earliest stamps; exhibited at the Royal Academy; illustrated children's books; and designed a best selling tea-service for Minton's. Chairman of Royal Society of Arts, 1851; Member of the Executive Committee of the Great Exhibition, 1851; appointed Secretary of the School of Design, 1851, and built up the nucleus of items which later became the Victoria and Albert Museum. Joint Secretary of the Department of Science and Art with Lyon Playfair (*q.v.*) 1853, and sole Secretary 1858–73. Launched scheme which resulted in the building of the Albert Hall (opened 1871) and a National Training School for Music (1876) which later became the Royal College of Music. After his retirement, Cole was active in organizing the National Training School of Cookery, 1873–6.

CROWTHER, Geoffrey (1907–72) knight 1957; Baron Crowther of Headingley (life peer) 1968. Educated Leeds Grammar School, Oundle, and Clare College, Cambridge (first class in Modern Languages and Economics). Further studied at Yale and Columbia Universities, USA. Joined the staff of *The Economist* in 1932, becoming Assistant Editor in 1935 and Editor 1938–56. Ministry of Production: Deputy Head of Joint War Production Staff, 1942–5. Chairman, Central Advisory Council for Education (England) 1956–60; produced Report on the education of 15–18 year olds known as the *Crowther Report*. Chairman, Commission on the Constitution. Chancellor, The Open University, 1969.
PUBLICATIONS: *An Introduction to the Study of Prices* (with W. T. Layton), 1935; *Ways and Means*, 1936; *Economics for Democrats*, 1939; *An Outline of Money*, 1941.

DONNELLY, Sir John Fretchville Dykes (1834–1902), CB 1886, KCB 1893. Administrator; educated Highgate School 1843–8, and Royal Military Academy, Woolwich. Joined Royal Engineers, second lieutenant 1853; commanded detachment of men in preparing for the Museum and Science Art Department in South Kensington; appointed Inspector for Science in the Science and Art Department 1859. Although not returning to the Army, he achieved the rank of Major-General by 1887. Responsible for introducing 'payment by results' in science and arts 1859–74. He obtained recognition for drawing and manual training as class subjects. Became Director of Science in 1874 with additional responsibility for important institutions, including the School of Mines and the Royal College of Chemistry. Appointed Assistant Secretary (1881) and Secretary (1884) of the Science and Art Department.

Encouraged development of City and Guilds Institute for technical education in 1871.

FORSTER, William Edward (1818–86). Liberal politician; educated Fishponds House, Bristol, and Grove House, Tottenham, 1831–5. Member of a Quaker family; entered woollen business at Bradford and became partner in a firm from 1842 to the end of his life; married Dr Arnold's daughter 1850; MP Bradford, 1861–86. Vice-President of Committee of Council under Gladstone 1868–74; responsible for successfully piloting the Endowed Schools Bill, which implemented many of the recommendations of the Taunton Commission, through the Commons, 1869; best remembered for the Elementary Education Act 1870, afterwards called 'Forster's Act', which extended popular education through the creation of School Boards. Chief Secretary for Ireland, 1880–2.

HADOW, Sir William Henry (1859–1937), Knight 1918; CBE 1920; MA Hon. DMus Oxford, Durham and Wales; FRCM. Educated Worcester College, Oxford (first class Classical Moderations and Literae Humaniores); Delegate of Oxford Locals 1894–1909; Examiner in Literae Humaniores, 1900–2; Modern Languages, 1905; English, 1907–9. Fellow and Tutor, Worcester College, Oxford; Principal, Armstrong College, Newcastle, 1909–19; Vice-Chancellor, Sheffield University, 1919–30; Director of Education (for YMCA) on lines of communication in France, 1918; Assistant Director of Staff Studies (Education), War Office, 1918–19; Member of Council, Royal College of Music; Member, Royal Commission on University Education in Wales; Chairman of the Archbishops' Commission on Religious education; and Departmental Committee on Local Government Officers. Editor, Oxford History of Music; Chairman Consultative Committee, Board of Education during the period when the Reports on The Education of the Adolescent (1926), The Primary School (1931) and Infant and Nursery Schools (1933) were issued.

PUBLICATIONS: Piano Sonata, 1884; Sonata Form, 1896; Oxford Treasury of English Literature (with G. E. Hadow), 3 vols, 1906–8; Citizenship, 1923; Music, 1926; Church Music, 1926; Collected Essays, 1928; English Music, 1931.

HOLMES, Edmond Gore Alexander (1850–1936). Educated Merchant Taylors' School and St John's College, Oxford (first class Moderations, first class Final Classical School). HM Inspector of Schools, 1875–1905; Chief Inspector of Elementary Schools, England, 1905–11. PUBLICATIONS: What Is Philosophy?, 1905; The Creed of Buddha, 1908; What Is and What Might Be, 1911; The Tragedy of Education, 1913; In Defence of What Might Be, 1914; In Quest of an Ideal (an Autobiography), 1920; Give Me the Young, 1921.

HUXLEY, Thomas Henry (1825–95). Son of a schoolmaster, but received irregular education. MB London University, 1845; joined Royal Navy as assistant surgeon 1846; FRS 1851; Lecturer, Royal School of Mines, 1854; elected to School Board of London, 1870; while serving, became Chairman of Scheme of Education Committee, which laid down an enlightened curriculum for its schools, 1871; retired through ill-health, 1872. Secretary, Royal Society, 1871, President, 1880; Member of the Royal Commission on Scientific Instruction and the Advancement of Science (the Devonshire Committee), 1870–5. PUBLICATIONS: Man's Place in Nature, 1863; Science, Culture and Other Essays, 1881; Social Diseases and Worse Remedies, 1891; Collected Essays, 9 vols, 1893–4.

JAMES, Eric John Francis (born 1909), Knight 1956; Baron James of Rusholme (life peer) 1959. Vice-Chancellor, University of York, 1962–73. Educated Taunton's School, Southampton, and Queen's College, Oxford: BA, BSc, MA, DPhil. Assistant master, Winchester College, 1933–45; High Master of Manchester Grammar School, 1945–62; Member, University Grants Committee, 1949–59; Chairman, Headmasters'

Conference, 1953–4; Member, Central Advisory Council on Education, 1957–61. Chairman, Committee of Inquiry into Teacher Training (James Report) 1970–1; Member, Press Council, 1963–7; Social Science Research Council, 1965–8; Fellow, Winchester College, 1963–9.

PUBLICATIONS: *Elements of Physical Chemistry* (part author), 1938; *Science and Education* (part author), 1942; *An Essay on the Content of Education*, 1949; *Education and Leadership*, 1951.

KAY-SHUTTLEWORTH, Sir James Phillips (1804–77), born Rochdale, Lancs; MD University of Edinburgh, 1827; studied condition of poor in Edinburgh and Dublin; after working in Manchester, appointed Assistant Poor Law Commissioner in East Anglia and later in London, 1836, and became convinced of need for national educational reform. Appointed first Secretary of Committee of Privy Council for Education in England and Wales, 1839; responsible with E. C. Tufnell of the Poor Law Board for establishing Battersea Training College for teachers of the poor in 1840 (the curriculum was based on ideas gained from a visit to Holland, Prussia, France and Switzerland where they were influenced by the work of Pestalozzi and Fellenberg). Kay-Shuttleworth's notable administrative innovation was the introduction of inspection of schools receiving government grants by Her Majesty's Inspectors. One of his most interesting appointments was that of John Hullah, who introduced new enlightened methods of singing into elementary schools. Kay-Shuttleworth was responsible for introducing Pestalozzian methods in the teaching of geography and arithmetic, as well as insisting that drawing should be included as part of the curriculum. His main achievement, however, was the concordat which he engineered with the religious authorities which made possible a combination of secular instruction with religious teaching. Kay-Shuttleworth resigned from the Privy Council post in 1849 because of ill health and was created baronet in the same year. He was a mem-

ber of the Royal Commission on Scientific Instruction (Devonshire), 1870–5.

LABOUCHERE, Henry, Baron Taunton (1798–1869), created Baron 1859. Liberal politician; educated Winchester and Christ Church, Oxford (first class in Classics BA, 1821, MA 1828); Barrister, Lincoln's Inn, 1817, but never practised. MP Michael Borough, Somerset, 1826; Taunton, 1830–59. Master of the Mint and also in the same year appointed Vice-President of the Board of Trade, 1835–9, President, 1839–41 and joined Melbourne's Cabinet; Chief Secretary for Ireland, 1846, and President of the Board of Trade 1847–52; Secretary of State for the Colonies, 1855–9. Entered House of Lords, 1860; held no further ministerial posts but was a good administrator. He served as commissioner for the Great Exhibition, 1851; Chairman of Commission to inquire into the state of the Corporation of London, 1853. He was also Chairman of the Schools Inquiry Commission which investigated the endowed schools of England (known as the *Taunton Commission*), 1864–8.

LINGEN, Ralph Robert Wheeler (1819–1905), created Baron 1885; KCB 1878; DCL. Educational administrator; educated Bridgnorth Grammar School and Trinity College, Oxford (took first class in Literae Humaniores 1840); Fellow of Balliol, 1841; Commissioner, inquiry into the state of Welsh education, 1846. Student at Lincoln's Inn; called to the Bar, 1847. Entered Committee of Council under Kay-Shuttleworth (*q.v.*) as one of the two Chief Examiners, the other being Frederick Temple 1847. On Kay-Shuttleworth's resignation in 1849 became Secretary, remaining there until 1870. Gave evidence before the Newcastle Commission on Popular Education favouring a change in the grant-awarding system. With the approval of the Vice-President Robert Lowe (*q.v.*) Lingen was responsible for administering the Revised Code from 1862. Permanent Secretary of the Treasury, 1870–85; Alderman, London County Council, 1889–1902.

LOWE, Robert (1811–92), created

Viscount Sherbrooke 1880, GCB 1888. Liberal politician; educated Winchester and University College, Oxford (first class in Classics and second class in Mathematics), BA 1833; MA 1836. Barrister, Lincoln's Inn, 1842; went to Australia, returning in 1850 as leader writer for *The Times*. MP Kidderminster, 1852–9; Calne, 1859–68; University of London, 1868–80; Joint Secretary, Board of Control, 1852–5; appointed Vice-President of Board of Trade, 1855–7; became Vice-President of the Committee of Council on Education, 1859, introducing the Revised Code regulations in 1862. Forced to resign 1864 after altering an inspector's report. Chancellor of the Exchequer, 1868–73; Home Secretary, 1873–4.

McNAIR, Alistair Duncan (1885–1975), created first Baron McNair of Gleniffer 1955; Knight 1943, CBE 1918, FBA, LLD. Fellow of Gonville and Caius College, Cambridge; educated Aldenham, and Gonville and Caius College, Cambridge; Solicitor, 1906; Law Tripos, 1908. Secretary, Coal Industry (Sankey) Commission, 1919; Chairman, Departmental Committee on Teachers and Youth Leaders, 1942–4; Burnham Committee, 1956–8; Whewell Professor of International Law, University of Cambridge, 1935–7; Vice-Chancellor, Liverpool University, 1937–45; KC 1945; President of the International Court of Justice, 1952–5, and Judge, 1946–55; President of the Court of Human Rights, 1959–65.
PUBLICATIONS: *Legal Effects of War*, 1920 (4th ed. 1966); *Law of the Air*, 1932 (3rd ed. 1964); *Roman Law and Common Law*, 1931 (2nd ed. 1952); *Dr Johnson and the Law*, 1949; *Expansion of International Law*, 1962.

MORANT, Sir Robert Laurie (1863–1920), CB 1902, KCB 1907. Civil servant; educated Winchester and New College, Oxford (first class in Theology, 1885); to Siam as tutor to King's nephew in 1886 and laid foundation for public education system in that country. Assistant Director of Special Inquiries and Reports with Sir Michael Sadler from 1895; wrote reports

on the French system of higher primary schools and the national organization of education in Switzerland. In 1899 became Private Secretary to Sir John Gorst, then Vice-President of Committee of Council on Education. From 1902 Acting Secretary and in the next year Permanent Secretary of the Board of Education.

The Act of 1902 afforded a broad foundation for subsequent administrative and legislative development; and the organization of English education, in the schemes both of the central and local authorities, was transformed by Morant's administrative genius and indomitable energy. He showed himself a great constructive organizer. . . . The Board of Education he entirely remodelled, adjusting it to the new division of responsibility between the central and local authorities, and making it capable of giving and receiving stimulus for a great expansion of the service of public education. *Dictionary of National Biography* (1927), pp. 386–7.

MORRELL, Derek (1921–68). Civil servant; educated Harrow County School and Keble College, Oxford. Entered Ministry of Education in 1947; one of the prime movers in the Architects' Development Group in the Architects and Buildings Branch. Later, became joint Head of the Branch. Thereafter, involved in fostering the Curriculum Study Group, which led to the creation of the Schools Council, 1964. First Joint Secretary Schools Council 1964–6, and encouraged public discussion of curriculum matters. Assistant, Under Secretary of State in charge of children's Department, Home Office 1966. Played key part in the Children and Young Persons Act, 1969.

MUNDELLA, Anthony John (1825–97). Liberal politician; educated St Nicholas National School, Leicester (left school at the age of nine). He was apprenticed to a hosiery manufacturer and became manager 1844. Partner in Nottingham hosiery firm, 1848, and made sufficient money to enable him to devote the rest of his life to politics. His two main interests were factory legislation and popular education: Mundella studied the German system of instruction and thereafter advanced the cause of technical education in England. MP Sheffield, 1868–85, and Sheffield Brightside, 1885–91. Vice-President, Committee of Council for Education, 1880–5; responsible for introducing universal compulsory education in English elementary schools in 1881. The 1882 Education Code, called the 'Mundella' Code, allowed Froebelian methods to be introduced into schools and for a wider variety of specific and optional subjects in the curriculum. President of the Board of Trade, 1886 and 1892–4.

NEWSOM, Sir John (1910–71), Knight 1964. Educated Imperial Service College and Queen's College, Oxford. Various posts in social and community service. Lecturer in Philosophy, King's College, London, and LCC; part-time social worker and first director of Community Service Association, 1931–8. Joined staff of Board of Education, National Fitness Council, 1938; Deputy Chief Education Officer, Hertfordshire County Council, 1939, and later Chief Education Officer. Newsom together with C. H. Aslin, then County Architect, pioneered in Britain the systematic study of school needs and their translation into good modern design, 1940–57. Chairman, Central Advisory Committee on the education of average and below average children which presented the report *Half Our Future*, 1961–3. Deputy Chairman, Plowden Committee on Primary Education (reported 1961); Chairman, Public Schools Commission, 1965–8.

PUBLICATIONS: *Willingly to School*, 1944; *Education for Girls*, 1948; *Child at School*, 1950; *The Intelligent Teacher's Guide to Preferment*, 1954.

NORTHCOTE, Sir Stafford (1818–87), 8th baronet; created 1st Earl of Iddesleigh 1885. Conservative politician; educated Eton and Balliol College, Oxford; BA 1839 Classics and Maths; MA 1840; Barrister, Inner Temple, 1840. With Sir Charles Trevelyan (*q.v.*) drew up Report on the Civil Service, recommending a system of competitive examination

instead of patronage, 1853 (known as the *Northcote–Trevelyan Report*). MP Dudley, 1855; Stamford, 1858; North Devon, 1866; responsible for Reformatory and Industrial Schools Act, 1856; Member, Public Schools Commission, 1862; Member, Endowed Schools Commission, 1865; President, Board of Trade, 1866; Secretary of State, India, 1867; Chancellor of the Exchequer, 1874; succeeded Disraeli as Leader of the House of Commons, 1876–81; joint leader of Conservative Party (with Lord Salisbury), 1881–5; Foreign Secretary, 1886.

NORWOOD, Sir Cyril (1875–1956), Knight 1938. Educationist; son of a grammar school headmaster in Lancashire; educated Merchant Taylors' School and St John's College, Oxford (first class in Classical Moderations 1896 and Literae Humaniores 1898). Entered Civil Service, but left to join staff of Leeds Grammar School, 1901; Headmaster, Bristol Grammar School, 1906–16; Master of Marlborough College, 1916–26; Headmaster of Harrow School, 1926–34; President, St John's College, Oxford, 1934–46. Chairman, Secondary Schools Examination Council, 1921–46; Chairman of a special committee of the Council on Curriculum and Examinations in Secondary Schools 1943 (*Norwood Report*).

PUBLICATIONS: *The Higher Education of Boys in England* (with A. H. Hope), 1909; *The English Tradition of Education*, 1929; *Religion and Education*, 1932; *The Curriculum in Secondary Schools*, 1936.

PLAYFAIR, Sir Lyon (1818–98), created 1st Baron Playfair of St Andrews 1892, KCB 1883, GCB 1895. Liberal politician; educated at St Andrews Parish School and St Andrews, Edinburgh and Giessen (Germany) Universities. Worked as office clerk, medical student and chemist before graduating PhD at Giessen 1840. Inspired by Liebig's work there, carried on important investigations in Britain, such as the action of gases of the blast furnace in conjunction with Bunsen. Chemical manager at Clitheroe, Lancs, 1841; Professor, School of Mines, 1845; FRS 1848;

President, Chemical Society, 1857, and of the British Association, 1855; Member Royal Commission on Public Health, 1844; 'from that date there was never a single year in which he was not appointed to act and generally to preside over Royal Commissions or Select Committees of the House of Commons' (*Who was Who 1897–1915* (1935) p. 566); this included the Great Exhibition, the Cattle Plague, the health of towns and old age pensions. Secretary for Science, Department of Science and Art, 1853; Secretary for the Department, 1855. Professor of Chemistry, Edinburgh, 1858–69; Liberal MP for Edinburgh and St Andrews University, 1868–85; Leeds S., 1885–92; Postmaster-General, 1873; Chairman and Deputy Speaker, House of Commons, 1880–3; Vice-President of the Council, 1886; responsible for setting up the Select Committee on Scientific Instruction, 1868.

PUBLICATION: *Subjects of Social Welfare*, 1889.

PLOWDEN, Lady (Bridget Horatia), DBE 1972. Governor and Vice-Chairman of BBC since 1970; Chairman of the Advisory Committee for Education of Romany and other Travellers; President, Pre-School Playgroups Association; co-opted member ILEA Education Committee, 1967–73; Chairman Central Advisory Council for Education (England), 1963–6. The Report on *Children and Their Primary Schools*, 1967, is known as the *Plowden Report*.

ROBBINS, Lionel Charles (born 1898), Baron Robbins of Clare Market (life peer) 1959, MA, BSc(Econ), CH, CB, FBA. Educated Southall County School, University College, London, and London School of Economics; Lecturer, New College, Oxford, 1924; Fellow, 1927; Professor of Economics, London School of Economics, 1929–61; Director of Economic Section of Offices of the War Cabinet, 1941–5; President Royal Economic Society, 1954–5; Chairman, Committee on Higher Education (outcome known as the *Robbins Report*), 1961–4. Chairman, *Financial Times*, 1961–70.

PUBLICATIONS: *The Economic Problems of Peace and War*, 1947; *Politics and Economics*, 1963; *The University in the Modern World*, 1966; *The Evolution of Modern Economic Theory*, 1970; *Autobiography of an Economist*, 1970.

SAMUELSON, Sir Bernhard (1820–95), Baronet 1884. Ironmaster and promoter of technical education. Liberal politician. Born Hamburg, educated at private school in East Yorkshire. From the age of fourteen, he had wide experience in industrial fields, especially locomotive and iron production. Travelled widely on the Continent, establishing railway works at Tours, in France. His main achievement was the building of an ironworks at Middlesbrough, Yorks in 1870; this was the largest and most up-to-date plant in operation at that time. MP Banbury, 1859 and 1865–85; N. Oxfordshire, 1885–95; FRS 1881. One of the founders of Iron and Steel Institute: President, 1883–5. A firm advocate of technical instruction, Samuelson presented a report to Parliament on scientific instruction in main European centres 1867. Shortly afterwards he was appointed Chairman of the Select Committee to inquire into provision for instruction in theoretical and applied science to the industrial classes, 1868; Member, Royal Commission on Scientific Instruction, 1870–5; Chairman, Royal Commission on Technical Instruction, 1881–4, whose report bears his name; Member, Royal Commission on Elementary Education, 1887.

SELBY-BIGGE, Sir Lewis Amherst (1860–1951), CB 1905, KCB 1919, created Baronet 1919. Civil servant; educated Winchester and Christ Church, Oxford; Fellow and Lecturer in Philosophy, University College, Oxford, 1883; Barrister, Inner Temple, 1891; Assistant Charity Commissioner, 1894. Principal Assistant Secretary, Board of Education, 1908–11; Permanent Secretary (succeeding R. L. Morant), 1911–25; Member of Departmental Committee and Statutory Commission for London University, 1927–8; Member,

Committee on Growth of Education in India, 1928.

PUBLICATIONS: *Hume's Treatise*, 1888; *British Moralists*, 1897; *Hume's Enquiries*, 1907; *The Board of Education*, 1927.

SPENS, Sir Will (1882–1962), Knight 1939, CBE 1918, MA. His mother was the daughter of J. R. Selwyn, Master of Selwyn College, Cambridge. Educated Rugby, and King's College, Cambridge; Fellow 1907, Tutor 1912, Master 1927–52, Corpus Christi College, Cambridge. Secretary of Foreign Trade Department, Foreign Office, 1917; Statutory Commission of Cambridge University, 1923; Vice-Chancellor, Cambridge University, 1931–3; Chairman Governing Body of Rugby School, 1944–58; Chairman of the Consultative Committee on Secondary Education with special reference to grammar and technical high schools, known as the *Spens Report*, 1938.

PUBLICATIONS: *Belief and Practice*, 1915; *The Relationship between the work of Secondary Schools and Universities*, 1939.

TAWNEY, Richard Henry (1880–1962), FBA 1935. Educated Rugby and Balliol College, Oxford, graduating in Moderations and Greats 1903. Assistant lecturer, Glasgow University, 1906–8; teacher, Tutorial Classes Committee, Oxford University, 1908–14; Director, Ratan Tata Foundation for study of poverty, London School of Economics, 1913–15; Fellow, Balliol College, 1918–21; Member, Executive of Worker's Educational Association, 1905–47; President, 1928–44. Reader in Economic History at London School of Economics, 1919–31; Professor 1931–49. Drafted important sections of the Hadow Report on the Adolescent, 1926 (*q.v.*). Served on a number of national committees: Coal Industry Commission, 1919, Chain Trade Board, 1919–22, and Cotton Trade Conciliation Commission, 1936–9.

PUBLICATIONS: *English Economic History, Select Documents* (part author), 1914; *Studies of Minimum Wages Rates*, 1914 and 1915; *The Acquisitive Society*, 1921; *Secondary Education for all: A Policy for Labour*, 1922; *The British Labour Movement*, 1925; *Religion and the Rise of Capitalism*, 1926; *Equality*, 1931; *The Radical Tradition* (posthumous), 1964.

TREVELYAN, Sir Charles Edward (1807–86), KCB 1858. Civil servant; educated Taunton Grammar School, Charterhouse and Haileybury; entered East India Company's Bengal civil service, 1826; married Hannah More, Lord Macaulay's sister, 1834; became enthusiastic promulgator of European literature and science among Indian population. Assistant Secretary to the Treasury, London, 1840–59. With Northcote (*q.v.*) prepared Report on system of admission into the Civil Service, 1853, known as the *Northcote–Trevelyan Report*. Governor of Madras, 1859–60; Finance Minister, 1862–5.

PUBLICATIONS: *On the Education of the People of India*, 1838; *The Purchase System in the British Army*, 1867; *Three letters on the Devonshire Labourer*, 1869.

VILLIERS, George William Frederick, 4th Earl of Clarendon (1800–70). Liberal politician; diplomat, whose career began as attaché to British Embassy in St Petersburg at the age of 20, followed by other missions on the continent. Lord Privy Seal, 1839; President, Board of Trade, 1846; Lord-Lieutenant of Ireland, 1847–52; Foreign Secretary, 1853–8, taking leading part in the events leading up to the outbreak of the Crimean War and subsequent peace negotiations. Chairman, Royal Commission on the Revenues of Management of Public Schools, 1861–4, known as the *Clarendon Commission*. 'He was a familiar master of most European languages, deeply learned in all European affairs, a man of the finest and most dignified manners, an acute judge of character.' (*Dictionary of National Biography* (1921 ed), p. 350)

Appendix 2

Glossary of Terms

Board of Education   One of the consequences of the Board of Education Act of 1899 was the transfer of functions of the Committee of Council and the Science and Art Department to the new Board. The work was organized in three branches—elementary, secondary and technical. Its head held the title of President of the Board.

Central Advisory Councils   These Councils which replaced the Consultative Committee (*q.v.*) under Section 4 of the 1944 Education Act differed from the former in that they included persons of experience from outside the education field.

The Councils' functions were to advise the Secretary of State in matters of educational theory and practice referred to them and to offer advice on their own initiative. Three important Reports emanating from the councils were *Crowther* on the early grammar school leaver (1959), *Newsom* on secondary modern school leavers (1963) and *Plowden* on the state of primary education (1966). The Councils have not been reconstituted since the Plowden Report was issued.

Certificate of Secondary Education(CSE)   A national examination established in 1965, controlled by fourteen boards. Unlike the General Certificate of Education (*q.v.*), the examinations are regionally operated. Teachers form a majority on the committees of the boards. There are three modes of examining. Mode 1 is an externally set and marked examination. With Mode 2, a school's or group of schools' own syllabus can be externally examined. An interesting feature of Mode 3 is that schools set and mark their own examinations, based on their own syllabuses, with some external moderation. A grade I result is equivalent to a General Certificate of Education pass.

Circular   Issued by the Department of Education and Science (DES) and signed by the Secretary of State or the Permanent Secretary for the guidance of local authorities and others on matters concerning governmental educational policy. A well-known example is *Circular 10/65*, which gave guidance to local education authorities (LEAs) on the form comprehensive school reorganization might take.

Circular Letter   Sets out, under the signature of an officer of the Department, the substance of a Circular (*q.v.*) for those bodies or persons who are likely to be affected by its operation.

City and Guilds of London Institute   The largest examining body concerned with technical education, it was set up in 1878 to advance this work. The Institute prepares syllabuses and sets examinations for craftsmen and technicians of post-school age.

Codes   Until 1860, the regulations of the Committee of the Privy Council on Education (*q.v.*) for schools wishing to receive a Parliamentary grant, were in the form of Minutes.

These dealt with the syllabuses of elementary schools, conditions of grants, instruction and advice on the training of pupil-teachers and students in training colleges. Robert Lowe, as Vice-President, consolidated the Minutes into a Code in 1860 which was thenceforward issued annually. From 1904, the Codes dealt only with matters of minor detail.

Committee of the Privy Council on Education   A recognition of the need for governmental supervision of elementary education led to the Committee's formation in April 1839. It consisted at first of four Ministers, the Lord President of the Council who was the nominal head, the Lord Privy Seal, the Chancellor of the Exchequer and the Home Secretary; a Secretary, Dr J. P. Kay, was also appointed. Conditions for making grants available to schools and instructions to inspectors were devised by the Committee.

In order to establish a link with the House of Commons, the Committee was reorganized in 1856. A Vice-President was appointed from the House who was responsible for the day-to-day running of educational affairs. An Education Department was also set up with responsibility for the Committee and the Science and Art Department's (*q.v.*) affairs.

Consultative Committee   Set up by the Board of Education Act 1899 to advise the Board on any matters referred to it. The first Committee consisted of eighteen members, the majority of whom were from universities. After its reconstruction in 1920, and under the chairmanship of distinguished academics, influential reports, such as the *Hadow* (1926 and 1931) and *Spens* (1938) covering the whole field of elementary and secondary education, were issued.

After the 1944 Education Act, the Committee was replaced by two Central Advisory Councils (*q.v.*) for England and for Wales.

Department of Education and Science (*DES*)   The merging of the functions of the Minister of Education with the Minister of Science, together with those relating to the parliamentary grant to universities, into the Department of Education and Science took place in April 1964. The DES is now also responsible for matters concerning sport and the development of the arts. There are up to three Secretaries of State for Education with ministerial rank.

Direct Grant School   A type of secondary school, first established in 1926, which was not maintained by the Board of Education. In return, a proportion of places was reserved for children from primary schools to be paid by L E A s or the school's governors in accordance with the Direct Grant Regulations 1959. After September 1976 the schools will continue to receive grants on condition that they join the maintained system.

Dual System   From 1870, when school boards were established, the elementary school accommodation was provided by either church bodies or school boards. From 1902, local education authorities replaced school boards but responsibility for recurrent expenditure in both types of school was largely undertaken by successive governments. The 1944 Act reiterated the principle of co-existence of county and voluntary primary and secondary schools.

Endowed Schools   So called because the origins of this class of schools were the result of a donor's gift of an endowment for educational purposes. Many schools, such as Eton, Harrow and St Paul's, originated in this way. For the most part, these schools were limited to teaching the ancient languages and became known as 'grammar schools'.

Because of the abuses of endowments and the decaying of many schools, reforms were instigated following the investigations of the Clarendon Commission in 1864 and the Taunton Commission four years later.

General Certificate of Education (GCE)   Replaced the School and Higher School Certificates in 1951. The GCE is administered by eight examining boards. There are two levels: the Ordinary (O), the Advanced (A) with Scholarship papers (S). The examination is recognized by higher education and professional bodies for entrance requirements. Since 1964 the Schools Council has coordinated the activities of examining boards.

Grants   From 1833, parliamentary grants were awarded to voluntary bodies for the purpose of erecting school buildings. These increased from £30,000 a year in 1839 to more than £800,000 by 1861. From the latter date, the Code stated that grants would be related to attendance and attainment of pupils with proven efficiency in stipulated areas of the curriculum.

There were eventually three types of grants:

  1   *General*   From 1862, two-thirds of grants paid to schools were based on examinations in the three Rs. The money was paid to the managers and not, as formerly, to teachers, thus affecting the latter's status.

  2   *Specific*   Introduced in 1867 to relieve the narrowness of the curriculum caused by 'Payment by Results'. They were defined as 'sufficiently distinct from the ordinary Reading Book lessons to justify the description as a "Specific Subject of Instruction" '. Extra payments were made if such work was undertaken. At first, only upper forms were allowed to take these subjects and were limited to two in number.

  3   *Class*   Dating from 1875, a grant was given for certain subjects which were examined on a class, as distinct from individual, basis. Grammar and history were two examples.

Headmasters' Association   Originally founded in 1890, for heads of secondary schools to safeguard their interests. The Association was active in promoting the Joint Scholarship Board for the award of scholarships to promising boys from elementary schools. It also has links with the Headmasters' Conference (*q.v.*). The Association became incorporated in 1894 and it holds an annual meeting each January.

Headmasters' Conference   Started in 1869 by Edward Thring of Uppingham, a public school headmaster, to oppose the encroachment of the Government on the independence of headmasters. It consists of heads of boys' secondary schools, including most of the public schools. The Conference has a membership of approximately two hundred.

Her Majesty's Inspectors (HMIs)   First appointed by the Crown in 1839 to supervise the £30,000 parliamentary grant for school buildings. From 1840, a regular system of examining and reporting on schools was begun. Early inspectors were approved by religious denominations and included a large proportion of clerics. Later, inspectors such as Matthew Arnold were drawn from either Oxford or Cambridge. Their functions were mainly confined to supervising the provision of the Codes (*q.v.*) and acting as a liaison between the schools and the Education Department. Nowadays a much wider range of functions are undertaken. HMIs are not to be confused with advisers and inspectors appointed by local authorities, who are responsible to their education officers.

Higher Grade Schools   There were two types of higher grade elementary schools following the 1870 Elementary Education Act. One was for pupils of parents willing to pay higher fees for a more advanced education. The other was a collection of pupils from the upper standards of small elementary schools which specialized mainly in technical and scientific subjects. Sheffield and Leeds provide early examples of higher grade schools. After the 1902 Education Act, these schools were absorbed into the secondary system.

Local Education Authority (LEA)   Responsibility for the provision and administration of education in England and Wales since 1902 has been given by central government to local education authorities (LEAS). Each LEA has a permanent officer, usually a Chief Education Officer or Director of Education with an elected education committee as the policy-making body. Financing is partly from government sources and partly from locally raised rates.

Ministry of Education   From 1945, the Board was superseded by a Ministry of Education, with a Minister at its head. The powers of the Minister were considerably increased by the 1944 Education Act (Part I, Section I) which gave him responsibility: 'to promote the education of the people of England and Wales and the progressive development of institutions devoted to that purpose, and to secure the effective execution by local authorities, under his control and direction, of the national policy for providing a varied and comprehensive educational service in every area.'

National Education League   A Nonconformist pressure group founded in 1869. Its aim was to ensure that state education should be secular, free and compulsory. One of the governing principles was that local authorities should provide school accommodation; all schools aided by the rates were to be unsectarian. The League originated in Birmingham: George Dixon was Chairman, Joseph Chamberlain was Vice-Chairman and Jesse Collings Secretary. Some of the aims of the League were achieved in the 1870 and 1876 Education Acts and it therefore disbanded in 1877.

National Education Union   The Union was formed in the same month as the National Education League (*q.v.*) (1869) by supporters of the voluntary schools in order to counteract the league's activities. The first President was the 2nd Earl of Harrowby and the Union was based at Manchester. It promoted denominational teaching in schools. The endeavours of the Union were rewarded in the 1870 Act which admitted for the first time the principle of a dual system (*q.v.*).

Office of Special Inquiries and Reports   A section of the Education Department established in 1895 by the Liberal Vice-President, A. H. D. Acland. Its main function was to prepare reports on the state of subject teaching in Europe and the United States for the guidance of the Minister. Between 1895 and 1914, twenty-eight volumes were produced. The first director of the office was Michael Sadler with Robert Morant, later the first Secretary of the Board of Education, as his assistant.

Royal Commissions   These Commissions are given the duty of inquiring into and reporting on specific issues for which terms of reference have been stated. They are the most prestigious of the various inquiring bodies. Members are appointed by the Queen in Council and can consist of Members of either or both Houses of Parliament and other persons representing a range of interests. Where the issue concerns education, persons with special knowledge in the field are included.

Much of the work is done by hearing evidence from witnesses and calling for the production of documents. When complete, the Commission's findings are presented in the form of a Blue Book. Important examples are the *Clarendon* (1864) and *Taunton* Commissions (1868) on public and endowed schools and the *Cross* Commission (1888) on elementary education.

Secondary School Examinations Council (SSEC)   The Council was set up in 1917 to act as a coordinating body between schools and university examining bodies in matters concerning the School and Higher School Certificate Examinations. Membership consisted of teachers, local education authorities and university representatives. Decisions arrived at were subject to the Board's approval.

In 1946, the Council was restructured. Subject panels attempted, by scrutinizing examination questions and marked scripts from the different boards, to achieve some parity of standards. When the Schools Council was set up in 1964, this function was transferred to it and the SSEC ceased to exist.

Scholarship System   More correctly, under the 1907 Education Act a 'free place' system. To encourage better educated teachers, the Liberal government stipulated that not less than a quarter of the annual entry into fee-paying secondary schools' places were to be reserved for ex-elementary school pupils. From 1932 the name was changed to 'special place' with a requirement for parents to pay part of the fees according to income. These places were awarded as a result of an examination which became competitive and was the origin of the 11 + examination. Since the 1944 Education Act all maintained secondary school places are free.

School Boards   These were brought into being by Forster's Education Act of 1870. Their purpose was to provide and maintain public elementary schools where insufficient provision had been made by voluntary bodies. Town councils in boroughs and ratepayers in parishes could request a school board to be elected. Every three years, ratepayers elected representatives by means of the cumulative system of voting. The relationship between the town council and the school board varied from place to place depending often on the religious and political complexions of the two bodies. The Boards were eventually replaced by the local education authorities created under the Education Act of 1902.

School Certificate Examination   This Examination was introduced in 1917 by the newly formed Secondary School Examinations Council to replace the great number of external examinations taken in schools. There were two levels—the School Certificate to be taken at sixteen, and the Higher School Certificate at eighteen. Passing five subjects with at least one taken from each group of English, foreign languages, science and mathematics at credit level in the School Certificate examinations granted matriculation exemption from universities.

Schools Council for the Curriculum and Examinations   A body instituted in 1964 to promote research and development in curriculum innovation, new teaching methods and forms of examinations. It is a partnership between the DES, LEAs and teachers with all three parties represented on the Council's committees. The Schools Council took over the functions of the Secondary School Examinations Council (*q.v.*).

Science and Art Department   The Department was created as a result of the Great Exhibition of 1851, in order to encourage industrial skills. In 1852 a Department of Practical Art was established and in the following year a Science Division was added. The Department, situated at South Kensington, administered parliamentary grants in the fields of science and art. By the 1890s it had assumed the role of a central authority for technical education. The Department was eventually absorbed into the new Board of Education at the end of the century.

Tripartite System   Refers to the threefold classification of secondary schools postulated by the Spens Report in 1938 (*q.v.*), i.e. grammar, technical and modern schools. Later, in 1943, the Norwood Report (*q.v.*), basing its finding on psychological evidence, claimed that there were three types of minds corresponding to the schools—the academic, the applied scientific and technical, and those with the ability to handle concrete things rather than ideas. No mention of *types* of schools was made in the 1944 Education Act; but local education authorities were allowed to establish various kinds of secondary schools with selection tests determining pupil allocation.

White Paper   The name given to government discussion documents, from the colour of the publication. A White Paper describes official policy towards an issue and is often a prelude to legislation: for example the White Paper on Educational Reconstruction in 1943 was followed by the Butler Education Act shortly afterwards.

Bibliography

A. Archive Sources
B. Official Reports
C. Books and Pamphlets
D. Articles
E. Magazines and Newspapers

A. Archive Sources

Althorp—Spencer MSS
Birmingham University Library—Chamberlain MSS
Bristol (R.O.)
Buckinghamshire R.O.
Cambridgeshire R.O.
Chatsworth, Derbyshire—Devonshire MSS
Cheshire R.O.
Chester City R.O.
Derbyshire R.O.
Devon R.O.
Dorset R.O.
Essex R.O.
Hatfield House, Hertfordshire—Salisbury MSS
Hereford and Worcester R.O.
Humberside R.O.
Kent Archives Office
Leicestershire R.O.
Liverpool R.O.—Melly MSS
London: British Museum—Gladstone MSS
                Balfour MSS
   Greater London R.O.
   Public Record Office—Granville MSS
   Senate House, University of London—Parents' National Education Union MSS
   W. H. Smith & Company—Hambleden MSS
   University College, London—Brougham MSS
Manchester Central Library, Archives Department
Northamptonshire R.O.
Northumberland R.O.
Oxford—Bodleian
Sandon, Staffordshire—Harrowby MSS
Somerset R.O.—Carlingford MSS
East Suffolk R.O.—Cranbrook MSS

B. Official Reports

Minutes and Reports of the Committee of Council on Education 1839–99
Reports of the Select Committee on the Education of the Lower Orders (Brougham Commission) 1816–18 P.P. 1816 iv; 1818 iv

Report of the Royal Commission on Children's Employment 1842 P.P. xvi
Report on the Organization of the Permanent Civil Service 1854 P.P. xxvii
Report of the Commissioners appointed to inquire into the . . . University and Colleges of
    Oxford 1852 P.P. xxii
Report of the Commissioners appointed to inquire into the State of Popular Education in
    England (Newcastle Commission) 1861 P.P. xxi
Report of the Commissioners appointed to inquire into the revenues and management of
    certain schools and the studies pursued and instruction given therein (Clarendon
    Commission) 1864 P.P. xx, xxi
Report of the Schools Inquiry Commission (Taunton Commission) 1867-8 P.P. xxviii
Report of the Select Committee on the Endowed Schools Act (1869) 1873 P.P. viii
Reports of the Royal Commission on Scientific Instruction and the Advancement of
    Science (Devonshire Commission) 1872-5 P.P. 1872 xxv—1875 P.P. xxviii
Reports of the Royal Commission on Technical Instruction (Samuelson Commission)
    1882-4 P.P. 1882 xxvii; 1884 xxix-xxxi
Report of Select Committee on Education, Science and Art Administration 1884 P.P. xiii
Reports of the Royal Commission on the Elementary Education Acts (Cross Commission)
    1886-8. 1886 P.P. xxv; 1887 P.P. xxix, xxx; 1888 xxxv-xxxvii
Copies of Memorials to the Education Department on Subjects of Instruction in Cookery
    1887 P.P. lxvii
Report of the Royal Commission on Secondary Education (Bryce Commission) 1895 P.P.
    xliii-xlix

Board of Education:
    Code of Regulations for Day Schools 1902
    Regulations for Secondary Schools 1904-9
    Reports on Children Under Five Years of Age in Public Elementary Schools 1905
    Handbook of Suggestions 1905, 1927
    Circular 753. The Teaching of English in Secondary Schools 1910
    Report 1910-11: 1912-13
    Report of Consultative Committee on Examinations in Secondary Schools 1911
    Special Reports on Educational Subjects. (The Sadler Report) The Teaching of
        Mathematics in the United Kingdom 1912
    Circular 826: Curriculum of Secondary Schools 1913
    Circular 996: Examination of Secondary Schools 1917
    The Teaching of English in England (The Newbolt Report) 1921
    Circular 1294. The Curricula of Secondary Schools in England 1922
    Report of the Consultative Committee on the Differentiation of the Curriculum for Boys
        and Girls respectively in Secondary Schools 1923
    Circular 719. The Teaching of Needlework in Secondary Schools 1923
    Some suggestions for the Teaching of English in Secondary Schools in England 1924
    Report of the Consultative Committee on The Education of the Adolescent (Hadow
        Report) 1926
    Education Pamphlet No. 50. Recent Development of Secondary Schools in England
        and Wales 1927
    Report of the Consultative Committee on the Primary School (Hadow Report) 1931
    Report of the Consultative Committee on Infant and Nursery Schools 1933
    Regulations for Secondary Schools 1935
    Report of the Consultative Committee on Secondary Education with special reference
        to Grammar Schools and Technical High Schools (Spens Report) 1938
    White Paper on Educational Reconstruction 1943
    Report of SSEC on Curriculum and Examinations in Secondary Schools (Norwood
        Report) 1943

Ministry of Education:

Pamphlet No. 1. *The Nation's Schools: Their Plan and Purpose* 1945

The Report of the Central Advisory Council for Education (England): *Early Leaving* 1954

White Paper on *Technical Education* 1956

Primary Education: Suggestions for the consideration of teachers and others concerned with the work of Primary Schools 1959

Report of the Central Advisory Council for Education (England): *15 to 18* (Crowther Report) 1959

3rd Report of the SSEC: *GCE and Sixth Form Studies* 1960

Report of Central Advisory Council for Education (England): *Half Our Future* (Newsom Report) 1963

Department of Education and Science:

Teaching Mathematics in Secondary Schools. Education Pamphlet No. 36 1958 reprinted 1968

Report of Working Party on Schools' Curricula and Examinations (Lockwood Report) 1964

Report of the Central Advisory Council for Education (England): *Children and Their Primary Schools* (Plowden Report) 1967

White Paper: *Education: A Framework for Expansion* 1972

Curricular Differences for Boys and Girls (Education Survey No. 21) 1975

Report of the Committee of Inquiry: *A Language for Life* (Bullock Report) 1975

Other Official Reports:

Secondary School Examinations Council, Report of the Committee appointed by the SSEC: *Secondary School Examinations other than GCE* (Beloe Report) 1960

Committee Appointed by the Prime Minister: *Report on Higher Education* (Robbins Report) 1963

Committee on Manpower Resources for Science and Technology, Report of the Work Group on Manpower for Scientific Growth: *The Flow into Employment of Scientists, Engineers and Technologists* (Swann Report) 1968

Council for Scientific Policy. *Enquiry into the Flow of Candidates in Science and Technology into Higher Education* (Dainton Report) 1968

Schools Council:

Working Paper No. 2, *Raising the School Leaving Age* 1965

Working Paper No. 45, *16–19 Growth and Response, 1. Curricular bases* 1972

Working Paper No. 46, *2. Examination Structure* 1973

Working Paper No. 47, *Preparation for Degree Courses* 1973

Working Paper No. 53, *The Whole Curriculum 13–16* 1975

Bulletins

No. 1 *Mathematics in the Primary School* 1965

No. 4 *Home Economics Teaching* 1971

Examination Bulletin No. 8: *The Certificate of Secondary Education: Experimental Examinations: Science* 1965

Examinations at 16+: Proposal for the Future 1975

C. Books and Pamphlets

Adams, F. *History of the Elementary School Contest* (Chapman and Hall) 1882 (new edn. Frederic Chivers, Bath 1970)

Adams, J. *Herbartian Psychology Applied to Education* (D. C. Heath) 1897

Adamson, J. H. *English Education 1789 to 1902* (Cambridge University Press) 1930

Allen, B. M. *Sir Robert Morant* (Macmillan) 1934

Anon. *Essays on Duty and Discipline: A series of Papers in the Training of Children in Relation to Social and National Welfare* (Cassell) 1910

Anon. *An Account of the Progress of Joseph Lancaster's Plan for the Education of Poor Children and the Training of Masters for Country Schools* London 1809

Arber, E. (ed.) *English Reprints: R. Ascham's The Scholemaster* London 1870

Archer, R. L. *Secondary Education in the Nineteenth Century* (Cambridge University Press) 1921

Armytage, W. H. G. *A. J. Mundella* (Benn) 1951

Armytage, W. H. G. *Four Hundred Years of English Education* (Cambridge University Press) 2nd edn. 1970

Arnold, M. *Reports on Elementary Schools 1852–82* (Macmillan) 1889

Association for Education in Citizenship *Education for Citizenship in Secondary Schools* 1935

Association of Education Committees and the NUT *Examinations in Public Elementary Schools* 1931

Atkinson, E. *The Teaching of Domestic Science* (Methuen) 1931

Ball, N. *Her Majesty's Inspectorate 1839–49* (Oliver and Boyd for University of Birmingham Institute of Education) 1963

Bamford, T. W. *The Rise of the Public Schools* (Nelson) 1967

Banks, O. *Parity and Prestige in English Secondary Education* (Routledge and Kegan Paul) 1955

Barker, R. *Education and Politics 1900–51. A Study of the Labour Party* (Oxford University Press) 1972

Barnard, H. C. *A History of English Education from 1760* (University of London Press) 2nd edn. 1961

Bernard, Sir T. *On the Education of the Poor: A Digest of the Reports of the Society for Bettering the Poor* London 1809

Barnett, P. A. (ed.) *Teaching and Organization with special reference to secondary schools: A manual of Practice* (Longmans, Green) 1897

Benn, C. and Simon, B. *Half Way There: Report on the British Comprehensive School Reform* (McGraw-Hill) 1970

Bennett, N. *Teaching Styles and Pupil Progress* (Open Books) 1976

Bentham, J. *Chrestomathia: being a collection of papers explanatory of the design of the Crestomathic Day School* 1815

Bernbaum, G. *Social Change and the Schools* (Routledge and Kegan Paul) 1967

Bishop, A. S. *The Rise of a Central Authority for English Education* (Cambridge University Press) 1971

Blakiston, J. R. *The Teacher: Hints on School Management* (Macmillan) 1895 edn.

Blondel, J. *Voters, Parties and Leaders* (Penguin) 1963

Bloom, B. S. *Taxonomy of Educational Objectives Handbook 1. Cognitive Domain* (Longmans) 1956

Bloom, B. S., Hastings, J. T. and Madaus, G. F. *Handbook of Formative and Summative Evaluation of Student Learning* (McGraw-Hill) 1971

Boothroyd, H. E. *A History of the Inspectorate* (Board of Education Inspectors' Association) 1923

Brabazon, Lord (ed.) *Some National and Board School Reforms* (Longmans, Green) 1887

Bramwell, R. D. *Elementary School Work 1900–25* (University of Durham Institute of Education) 1961

Brock, W. H. (ed.) *H. E. Armstrong and the Teaching of Science 1880–1930* (Cambridge University Press) 1973

Bruner, J. *The Process of Education* (Harvard University Press) 1960

Bruner, J. *Towards A Theory of Instruction* (Harvard University Press) 1966

Burchnall, C. R. *The Story of Education and the Schools of Deeping St James*, Peterborough Central Printers Ltd 1957

Burn, W. L. *The Age of Equipoise* (Unwin) 1968

Burston, W. H. *James Mill on Education* (Cambridge University Press) 1969

Burston, W. H. *James Mill on Philosophy and Education* (Athlone Press) 1973

Buxton, S. *Overpressure and Elementary Education* (Swann, Sonnenschein) 1885

Cardwell, D. S. L. *The Organization of Science in England* (Heinemann) 2nd edn. 1972

Castle, E. B. *Moral Education in Christian Times* (Allen & Unwin) 1958

Christian, G. A. *English Education from Within* (Wallace Gandy) 1922

Coates, R. D. *Teachers' Unions and Interest Group Politics* (Cambridge University Press) 1972

Cole, G. D. H. *Socialism In Evolution* (Penguin) 1938

Cole, G. D. H. and Postgate, R. *The Common People 1746–1946* (Methuen) 2nd edn. 1961

Cole, Sir H. *Fifty Years of Public Work of Sir Henry Cole KCB, accounted for in his deeds, speeches and writings* 2 vols. (G. Bell) 1884

Compayré, G. *Jean Frederic Herbart* (George Harrap) 1908

Cotterill, C. C. *Suggested Reforms in Public Schools* (Wm. Blackwood) 1885

Cox, C. B. and Dyson, A. E. (eds.) *Black Paper I: Fight for Education* (Critical Quarterly Society) 1969

Cox, C. B. and Dyson, A. E. (eds.) *Black Paper II: The Crisis in Education* (Critical Quarterly Society) 1969

Cox, C. B. and Dyson, A. E. (eds.) *Black Paper III: Goodbye Mr Short* (Critical Quarterly Society) 1970

Cox, E. *Changing Aims in Religious Education* (Routledge and Kegan Paul) 1966

Crewe, Lord *Lord Rosebery* Vol. 2 (Murray) 1931

Cruickshank, M. *Church and State in English Education* (Macmillan) 1963

Curtis, S. J. and Boultwood, M. E. A. *A Short History of Educational Ideas.* (University Tutorial Press) 1965

Curtis, S. J. *History of Education in Great Britain* (University Tutorial Press) 7th edn. 1967

De Cecco, J. P. *Human Learning in the School* (Holt, Rinehart & Winston, N.Y.) 1963

Dewey, J. *The Child and the Curriculum 1902 — The School and Society* 1899 (University of Chicago Press) reprinted 1956

Dictionary of National Biography 1885–1960 (Oxford University Press)

Dixon, J. *Growth Through English* (National Association for Teaching of English) 1967

Dodd, C. I. *Introduction to the Herbartian Principles of Teaching* (Swann, Sonnenschein) 1898

Drake, B. and Cole, M. I. (eds.) *Our Partnership by Beatrice Webb* (Longmans, Green) 1948

Duverger, M. *Party Politics and Pressure Groups* (Nelson) 1972

Eaglesham, E. J. R. *The Foundations of Twentieth Century Education in England* (Routledge and Kegan Paul) 1967

Eisner, E. W. (ed.) *Confronting Curriculum Reform* (Little, Brown, Boston) 1971

Engels, F. *The Condition of the Working Class in England 1844*, transl. W. O. Henderson and W. H. Chaloner (Blackwell) 1971

Farrar, F. W. *Essays On a Liberal Education* (Macmillan) 1868

Faunthorpe, Rev. J. P. (ed.) *Household Science: Readings in Necessary Knowledge for Girls and Young Women* (E. Stanford, London) 1881

Fearon, D. *School Inspection* (Macmillan) 1876

Fitch, Sir J. *Educational Aims and Methods: Lectures and Addresses* (Cambridge University Press) 1900

Fletcher, C. R. L. *Edmund Warre* (Murray) 1922

Ford, J. *Social Class and the Comprehensive School* (Routledge and Kegan Paul) 1969

Fry, G. K. *Statesmen in Disguise: The Changing Role of the Administrative Clerks of the British Home Civil Service 1853–1966* (Macmillan) 1969

Gautrey, T. *'Lux Mihi Laus': School Board Memories* (Link House Publications) 1937

Gladman, F. J. *School Method: Notes and Hints from Lectures delivered at Borough Road Training College* (Jarrold) n.d.

Glenday, N. and Price, M. *Reluctant Revolutionaries: A Centenary of Headmistresses 1874–1974* (Pitman) 1974

Goldstrom, J. M. *The Social Content of Education 1808–70. A Study of the Working-Class School Reader in England and Ireland* (Irish University Press) 1972

Goodwin, M. *Nineteenth-Century Opinion* (Penguin) 1951

Gordon, P. *The Victorian School Manager* (Woburn) 1974

Gosden, P. H. J. H. *The Development of Educational Administration in England and Wales* (Blackwell) 1966

Gosden, P. H. J. H. *How They Were Taught* (Blackwell) 1969

Gosden, P. H. J. H. *The Evolution of a Profession: A Study of the Contribution of Teachers' Associations to the Development of School Teaching as a Professional Occupation* (Blackwell) 1972

Gould F. J. *Moral Education: Chapter from Story of Schools in England and Wales 1895–1925* (Lindsey Press) 1929

Graham, E. *The Harrow Life of Henry Montagu Butler DD* (Longmans, Green) 1920

Graves, A. P. *To Return to All That: An Autobiography* (Cape) 1930

Greenough, J. C. *The Evolution of the Elementary Schools of Great Britain* (D. Appleton, N.Y.) 1903

Griffiths, H. B. and Howson, A. G. *Mathematics, Society and Curricula* (Cambridge University Press) 1974

Guttsman, W. L. *The British Political Elite* (MacGibbon and Kee) 1963

Hamilton, Lord George *Parliamentary Reminiscences and Reflections 1868 to 1885* (John Murray) 1917

Harlen, W. *With Objectives in Mind* (Macdonald Educational) 1972

Hayward, F. H. *The Psychology of Educational Administration* (Ralph Holland) 1912

Hayward, F. H. and White, E. M. *The Last Years of a Great Educationist* (Richard Clay, Bungay, Suffolk) 1939

Heafford, M. R. *Pestalozzi* (Methuen) 1967

Heater, D. (ed.) *The Teaching of Politics* (Methuen) 1969

Herbert, A. (ed.) *The Sacrifice of Education to Examinations* (Williams and Norgate) 1889

Hill, D. M. *Participating in Local Affairs* (Penguin) 1970

Hinder, E. F. *The Schoolmaster in the Gutter* (E. Stark) 1883

Hirst, P. H. and Peters, R. S. *The Logic of Education* (Routledge and Kegan Paul) 1970

Hirst, P. H. *Knowledge and the Curriculum* (Routledge and Kegan Paul) 1974

History of Education Society *The Changing Curriculum* (Methuen) 1971

Hodgson, W. B. *Exaggerated Estimates of Reading and Writing as a Means of Education* London 1868

Hogben, L. *Political Arithmetic* (Allen and Unwin) 1938

Holmes, E. G. A. *What Is and What Might Be* (Constable) 1911

Hooper, R. *The Curriculum: Context, Design and Development* (Oliver and Boyd) 1971

Hopper, E. (ed.) *Readings in the Theory of Educational Systems* (Hutchinson) 1971

Hullah, J. *Wilhem's Method of Teaching Singing* (J. W. Parker) 1841

Hurt, J. S. *Education in Evolution* (Hart-Davis) 1971

Huxley, L. (ed.) *Collected Essays of T. H. Huxley* Vol. 3 (Macmillan) 1885

Jackson, J. *The Teaching and Practice of Handwriting: a Practical Manual for the Guidance of School Board Teachers* (Sampson Low, Marston) 1893

Jephson, A. W. *My Work in London* (Pitman) 1910

Johnson, H. *Report of Moral Instruction in Elementary Schools in England and Wales* (David Nutt) 1908

Johnston, Sir H. *On the Urgent Need for Reform in Our National and Class Education* (Watts) 1918

Joint Mathematical Council of the U.K. *A Statement on the Present State of Change in Mathematics at Secondary Level* 1970

Judges, A. V. (ed.) *Pioneers of English Education* (Faber and Faber) 1952

Kamm, J. *Hope Deferred: Girls' Education in English History* (Methuen) 1965

Kay-Shuttleworth, J. P. *Four Periods of Public Education* (Longman, Green, Longman and Roberts) 1862

Kekewich, G. *The Education Department and After* (Constable) 1920

Kenny, C. S. *Endowed Charities* (Reeves and Turner) 1880

Knox, V. *Liberal Education: or a Practical Treatise on the method of Acquiring useful and Polite Learning* 4th edn. 1795

Koerner, J. D. *Reform in Education: England and the United States* (Weidenfeld and Nicolson) 1968

Kogan, M. *The Politics of Education* (Penguin) 1971

Kogan, M. and Packwood, T. *Advisory Councils and Committees in Education* (Routledge and Kegan Paul) 1974

Lamb, G. F. *The English at School* (Allen and Unwin) 1950

Lancaster, J. *Improvements in Education. As it respects the Industrial Classes of the Community, containing among other important particulars an account of the institutions for the education of 1,000 poor children, Borough Road, Southwark* (Darton, Harvey, London) 3rd edn. 1805

Latham, H. *On the Action of Examinations Considered as a means of Selection* (Bell) 1877

Lauwerys, J. A. (ed.) *The Content of Education* (The Council for Curriculum Reform/University of London Press) 1945

Lawrence, E. (ed.) *Friedrich Froebel and English Education* (University of London Press) 1952

Lawson, J. and Silver, H. *A Social History of Education in England* (Methuen) 1973

Lawton, D. *Class, Culture and the Curriculum* (Routledge and Kegan Paul) 1975

Layton, D. *Science for the People* (Allen and Unwin) 1973

Lee, J. M. *Social Leaders and Public Persons. A Study of County Government in Cheshire since 1888* (Cambridge University Press) 1963

Lee, N. (ed.) *Teaching Economics* (Economics Association) 1965

Leese, J. *Personalities and Power in English Education* (Arnold) 1950

Lester, H. V. *Memoir of Hugo Daniel Harper DD* (Longmans, Green) 1896

Lidgett Scott, J. *Reminiscences* (Epworth Press) 1928

Lindsay, K. *Social Progress and Educational Waste* (Routledge and Kegan Paul) 1926

Lloyd, R. *The Church of England 1900–65* (SCM Press) 1966

Lloyd, W. Arnold *An International Dictionary of Educational Terminology* (in collaboration with the DES) 1969

Locke, M. *Power and Politics in the School System: A Guidebook* (Routledge and Kegan Paul) 1974

London County Council *Report of a Conference on the Teaching of Arithmetic in London Elementary Schools 1914* reprinted 1923

Lovett, W. and Collins, J. *Chartism: A New Organization of the People* (J. Watson London, 1840) new edn. Leicester University Press 1969

Lowe, R. *Primary and Classical Education* (Edmonston and Douglas, Edinburgh) 1867

Lubbock, Sir J. *Addresses, Political and Educational* (Macmillan) 1879

McBriar, A. M. *Fabian Socialism and English Politics, 1884–1918* (Cambridge University Press) 1962

McClelland, V .A. *Cardinal Manning. His life and Influence 1865–92* (Oxford University Press) 1962

McDougall, W. *An Introduction to Social Psychology* (Methuen) 1908

Mack, M. P. *Jeremy Bentham: An Odyssey of Ideas 1748–82* (Heinemann) 1962

Maclure, J. S. *Educational Documents, 1816–1968* (Methuen) 2nd edn. 1968

Magnus, L. (ed.) *Church Schools and Religious Education—Essays towards a Conservative Policy* (John Murray) 1901

Magnus, Sir P. *Educational Aims and Efforts 1880–1910* (Longmans) 1910

Manzer, R. A. *Teachers and Politics: the Role of the NUT in making of national individual educational policy in England and Wales since 1944* (Manchester University Press) 1970

Marsden, D. *Politicians, Equality and Comprehensives:* Fabian Tract 411 (Fabian Society) 1971

Marshall, M. P. *What I Remember* (Cambridge University Press) 1947

May, P. R. *Moral Education in Schools* (Methuen) 1971

Mayo, C. *Lessons on Objects. As given to children between the ages of 6 to 8 in a Pestalozzian School at Cheam, Surrey* (R. B. Seeley and W. Burnside) 6th edn. 1837

Michaelis, E. and Keatley Moore, H. *Froebel's letters on the Kindergarten* (Swann, Sonnenschein) trans. 1891 1904 edn.

Mill, James 'Essay on Education' *Encyclopaedia Britannica* 1821

Mill, J. S. *Utilitarianism, Liberty and Representative Government* (Everyman edn.) 1910

Mill, J. S. *Autobiography* (Longmans, Green, Reader and Dyer) 1873

Montgomery, R. J. *Examinations* (Longmans) 1965

Montessori, M. *The Montessori Method* (Heinemann) 1912

Moore, T. W. *Educational Theory: An Introduction* (Routledge and Kegan Paul) 1974

More, Hannah *Mendip Annals: narrative of charitable labours of H. and M. More, Being the journal of Martha More* (ed. A. Roberts) 3rd edn. 1859

Morley, J. *Life of Gladstone* (Macmillan) 2nd edn. 1905

Murphy, J. *Church, State and Schools in Britain, 1800–1970* (Routledge and Kegan Paul) 1971

National Association of Labour Teachers *Education: a Policy* (Socialist Educational Association) 1930

National Union of Teachers *Open Planning: A Report with special reference to Primary Schools* 1973

New, C. F. *The Life of Henry Brougham to 1830* (Oxford University Press) 1961

Newsome, D. *Godliness and Good Learning—Four Studies on a Victorian Ideal* (Murray) 1961

Norwood, C. *The English Tradition of Education* (Murray) 1929

Nunn, T. P. *Education: Its Data and First Principles* (Arnold) 1920

Open University *Educational Studies. The Curriculum, Patterns of Curriculum:* E283 1972

Owen, R. *A New View of Society* (Everyman edn.) 1927

Parkhurst, H. *An Explanation of the Dalton Laboratory Plan* (Dalton Association) 1926

Parkin, G. R. *Life of Edward Thring* (Macmillan) 1891

Parkinson, M. *The Labour Party and the Organization of Secondary Education 1918–65* (Routledge and Kegan Paul) 1970

Pedley, R. *The Comprehensive School* (Penguin) 1969

Pelling, H. *Origins of the Labour Party 1880–1900* (Oxford University Press) 2nd edn. 1965

Pestalozzi, J. H. *Letters on Early Education. Addresses to J. P. Greaves Esq* (Sherwood, Gilbert and Piper) 1827

Peters, R. S. *Ethics and Education* (Allen and Unwin) 1966

Peters, R. S. *Perspectives on Plowden* (Routledge and Kegan Paul) 1968

Philpott, H. B. *London At School. The Story of the School Board 1870–1904* (T. Fisher Unwin) 1904

Plumb, J. H. (ed.) *Studies in Social History. A Tribute to G. M. Trevelyan* (Longmans, Green) 1955

Pym, B. *Pressure Groups and the Permissive Society* (David and Charles) 1974

Raymont, T. *A History of the Education of Young Children* (Longmans, Green) 1937

Reed, C. E. B. *Memoir of Sir Charles Reed by his son* (Macmillan) 1883

Rhodes, G. *Committees of Inquiry* (Allen & Unwin) 1975

Roach, J. *Public Examinations in England 1850–1900* (Cambridge University Press) 1971

Roberts, B. C. *The Trades Union Congress 1868–1921* (Allen and Unwin) 1958

Roberts, R. D. (ed.) *Education in the Nineteenth Century* (Cambridge University Press) 1901

Rousseau, J. J. *Emile* (Everyman edn.) 1911

Runciman, J. *Schools and Scholars* (Chatto and Windus) 1887

Rusk, R. R. *The Doctrines of the Great Educators* (Macmillan) 4th edn. 1969

Russell, Earl *Recollections and Suggestions 1813–73* (Longmans, Green) 1875

Sacks, B. *The Religious Issue in the State Schools in England and Wales 1902–14* (University of New Mexico) 1961

Sandford, E. G. (ed.) *Life of William Temple* Vol. 1 (Macmillan) 1906

Sangster, P. *Pity my Simplicity: The Evangelical Revival and the Religious Education of Children 1738–1800* (Epworth Press) 1963

Scott, R. P. (ed.) *What is Secondary Education?* (Rivingtons) 1899

Selleck, R. J. W. *The New Education: The English Background 1870–1914* (Pitman) 1968

Selleck, R. J. W. *English Primary Education and the Progressives 1914–39* (Routledge and Kegan Paul) 1972

Sharpless, I. *English Education in the Elementary and Secondary Schools* (P. Appleton, N.Y.) 1892

Sharwood Smith, E. *The Faith of a School Master* (Methuen) 1935

Sillitoe, H. *A History of the Teaching of Domestic Subjects* (Methuen) 1933

Silver, H. *Equal Opportunity in Education* (Methuen) 1973

Simon, B. *Intelligence Testing and the Comprehensive School* (Lawrence and Wishart) 1953

Simon, B. *Studies in the History of Education 1780–1870* (Lawrence and Wishart) 1960

Simon, B. *Education and the Labour Movement 1870–1920* (Lawrence and Wishart) 1965

Simon, B. *The Politics of Educational Reform 1920–40* (Lawrence and Wishart) 1974

Skilbeck, M. (ed.) *John Dewey* (Collier-Macmillan) 1970

Smart, N. (ed.) *Crisis in the Classroom* (International Publishing Company/Hamlyn) 1968

Smith, A. *Wealth of Nations* (Everyman edn.) 1910

Smith, F. *The Life and Work of Sir James Kay-Shuttleworth* (Murray) 1920

Smith, F. *A History of English Elementary Education 1760–1902* (University of London Press) 1931

Smith, W. O. Lester *Government of Education* (Penguin) 1965

Sneyd-Kynnersley, E. M. *Passages in the Life of an H. M. Inspector of Schools* (Macmillan) 1908

Soloway, R. A. *Prelates and People: Ecclesiastical Thought in England 1783–1852* (Routledge and Kegan Paul) 1969

Sonnenschein's Encyclopaedia of Education A. E. Fletcher (ed.) (Swann, Sonnenschein) 1906

Spalding, T. A. *The Work of the London School Board* (P. S. King) 1900

Spencer, F. H. *An Inspector's Testament* (English Universities Press) 1938

Spencer, H. *Essays on Education and other Subjects* (Williams and Norgate) 1861 reprinted 1911

Spiller, G. *Moral Education in Eighteen Countries* (Watts) 1909

Spiller, G. *The Ethical Movement in Great Britain* (printed for the author by The Farleigh Press, London) 1934

Springall, L. M. *Labouring Life in Norfolk Villages 1834–1914* (Allen and Unwin) 1936

Stephen, B. *Emily Davies and Girton College* (Constable) 1927

Stewart, M. *Bias and Education for Democracy* (Association for Education in Citizenship) 1938

Stewart, W. A. C. and McCann, W. P. *The Educational Innovators* Vol. 1 1750–1880 (Macmillan) 1967

Stewart, W. A. C. *The Educational Innovators* Vol. 2 Progressive Schools 1881–1967 (Macmillan) 1968

Stewart, W. A. C. *Progressives and Radicals in English Education 1790–1970* (Macmillan) 1972

Stone, D. *The National: the story of a Pioneer College, The National Training College of Domestic Science* (Brighton Polytechnic Press) 1973

Sturt, M. and Oakden, E. C. *Matter and Method in Education* (Kegan, Paul, Trench, Trubner) 3rd edn. 1937

Sturt, M. *The Education of the People* (Routledge and Kegan Paul) 1967

Sutherland, G. (ed.) *Studies in the Growth of Nineteenth-Century Government* (Routledge and Kegan Paul) 1972

Sutherland, G. (ed.) *Matthew Arnold on Education* (Penguin) 1973

Sutherland, G. *Policy-Making in Elementary Education 1870–95* (Oxford University Press) 1973

Sylvester, D. W. *Robert Lowe and Education* (Cambridge University Press) 1974

Tarver, J. C. *Essays on Secondary Education* (Constable) 1898

Tawney, R. H. *The Radical Tradition: Twelve Essays on Politics, Education and Literature* Rita Hinder (ed.) (Penguin) 1964

Taylor, P. H. and Walton, J. *The Curriculum: Research Innovation and Change* (Ward Lock) 1973

Taylor, W. *The Secondary Modern School* (Faber and Faber) 1963

Thirteen Essays on Education (Percival) 1881

Thompson, D. F. *Professional Solidarity Among the Teachers of England* (P. S. King) 1927

Thouless, R. H. *Map of Educational Research* (National Foundation for Educational Research) 1965
Thring, E. *Education and School* (Macmillan) 1864
Trevelyan, G. M. *British History in the Nineteenth Century and After* (Longmans, Green) 1922
Trevor-Roper, H. A. *Official Guidebook to Christ Church, Oxford* 1956
Tricker, R. A. R. *Contribution of Science to Education* (Mills and Boon) 1967
Tropp, A. *The School Teachers. The Growth of the Teaching Profession in England and Wales from 1800 to the Present Day* (Heinemann) 1957
Tuke, M. J. *A History of Bedford College for Women 1849–1937* (Oxford University Press) 1939
Urry, J. and Wakeford, J. (eds.) *Power in Britain* (Heinemann) 1973
Viola, W. *Child Art and Franz Cizek* (Austrian Junior Red Cross, Vienna) 1936
Watson, F. *The Old Grammar Schools* (Cambridge University Press) 1916
Webb, S. *The Educational Muddle and The Way Out* Fabian Tract 108 (Fabian Society) 1901
Webb, S. *London Education* (Longman's) 1904
Wells, H. G. *Experiment in Autobiography* (Gollancz) 1934
White, J. P. 'The End of the Compulsory Curriculum' in *Studies in Education (New Series)* 2 *The Curriculum The Doris Lee Lectures* (University of London Institute of Education) 1975
Whitehead, A. N. *The Aims of Education* (Williams and Norgate) 1932
Who Was Who 1897–1915 (A. and C. Black) 1935
Wilderspin, S. *Early Discipline Illustrated* (James S. Hodson) 3rd edn. 1840
Williams, R. *Culture and Society 1780–1950* (Chatto and Windus) 1958 (Penguin) 1961
Williams, R. *The Long Revolution* (Chatto and Windus) 1961 (Penguin) 1965
Wilson, J., Williams, N. and Sugarman, B. *Introduction to Moral Education* (Penguin) 1957
Wollheim, R. *Socialism and Culture* (Fabian Society) 1961
Woods, A. *Educational Experiments in England* (Methuen) 1920
Young, M. *The Rise of the Meritocracy* (Thames and Hudson) 1958
Young, M. F. D. (ed.) *Knowledge and Control* (Collier–Macmillan) 1971

D. Articles

BJES	British Journal of Educational Studies
BJS	British Journal of Sociology
DRR	Durham Research Review
ER	Educational Research
Ed Rev	Educational Review
H of E	History of Education
IR	Independent Review
JCS	Journal of Curriculum Studies
JEAH	Journal of Educational Administration and History
NC	Nineteenth Century
PP	Past and Present
VASFE	Vocational Aspects of Secondary and Further Education
VS	Victorian Studies

Alsobrook, D. 'The Reform of the Endowed Schools: the Work of the Northamptonshire Educational Society 1854–74' *H of E* 2 no. 1 January 1973
Argles, M. 'The Royal Commission on Technical Instruction 1881–4' *VASFE* 9 no. 23 1959
Armytage, W. H. G. 'J. F. Donnelly: Pioneer in Vocational Education' *VASFE* 2 no. 4 1950
Armytage, W. H. G. 'The 1870 Education Act' *BJES* 18 no. 2 1970
Banks, O. 'Morant and the Secondary School Regulations of 1904' *BJES* 3 no. 11 1954
Baron, G. 'The Origins and Early History of the Headmasters' Conference 1869–1914' *ER* 7 no. 3 1955

Bibby, C. 'The First Year of the London School Board: The Dominant Role of T. H. Huxley' *DRR* **2** no. 8 1957

Brennan, E. J. T. 'Sidney Webb and the London Technical Education Board' II The Board at Work *VASFE* **12** no. 24 1960

Cannon, C. 'Social Studies in Secondary Schools' *ER* **17** no. 1 1964

Dobson, J. L. 'The Teaching of History in English Grammar Schools and Private Schools 1830–70' *DRR* **2** no. 8 1957

Doherty, B. 'The Hadow Report 1926' *DRR* **4** no. 15 1964

Fitch, J. G. 'Possible Amendments to the Education Act' *NC* **51** June 1902

Flemming, W. 'The Teaching of Arithmetic' *ER* **11** no. 1 1959

Floud, J. and Halsey, A. H. 'Intelligence Test, Social Class, and Selection for Secondary Schools' *BJS* **8** no. 1 1957

Fowler, W. S. 'The Origin of the General Certificate' *BJES* **7** no. 1 1959

Gilmour, R. 'The Gradgrind School: Political Economy in the Classroom' *VS* **11** no. 2 1967

Hilliard, F. 'The Moral Instruction League 1897–1919' *DRR* **3** no. 12 1961

Johnson, R. 'Educational Policy and Social Control in Early Victorian England' *PP* no. 49 1970

McCann, W. P. 'Trade Unionists, Artisans and the 1870 Education Act' *BJES* **18** no. 2 1970

Macnamara, T. J. 'The State and Secondary Education' *IR* May 1909

Mann, T. 'The Development of the Labour Movement' *NC* **27** May 1890

Morrell, D. H. 'The Freedom of the Teacher in Relation to Research and Development Work in the Area of Curriculum and Examinations' *ER* **5** 1963

Peckett, W. E. 'Direct Method and the Classics' *Ed Rev* **4** no. 1 1951

Roach, J. 'Middle Class Education and Examinations: Some Early Victorian Problems' *BJES* **10** no. 2 1962

Robertson, H. 'J. G. Fitch and the Origins of the Liberal Movement in Education 1863–70' *JEAH* **3** no. 2 1971

Rogers, A. 'Churches and Children—A Study in the Controversy over the 1902 Education Act' *BJES* **8** no. 2 1959

Shewell, M. E. J. 'Religious Education in Birmingham Board Schools' *Ed Rev* **13** no. 1 1961

Stansky, P. 'Lyttelton and Thring: A Study in Nineteenth-Century Education' *VS* **5** no. 3 1962

Tompson, R. S. 'The Leeds Grammar School Case of 1805' *JEAH* **3** no. 1 1970

Whitmarsh, G. 'The Politics of Political Education: An Episode' *JCS* **6** no. 2 1974

E.   Magazines and Newspapers

Birmingham Morning News
Frazer's Magazine
The Guardian
Journal of the National Association for the Promotion of Social Science
Liverpool Mercury
New Society
School Board Chronicle
School Board Gazette
Sheffield Weekly News
Times Educational Supplement
The Times

Index